EMOTIONS
AND
MEMORY

THE MENNINGER CLINIC MONOGRAPH SERIES NO. 2

EMOTIONS
AND
MEMORY

By DAVID RAPAPORT, Ph.D.
Research Associate, Austen Riggs Foundation

Fifth Edition

New York
INTERNATIONAL UNIVERSITIES PRESS, Inc.
1971

CONTENTS

CHAPTER IX

INTRODUCTION TO THE FIFTH EDITION

By Lester Luborsky, Ph.D

An old memory, always evoked with strong positive affect, comes to mind when I think of this book—it was presented to me by David Rapaport at a Menninger Foundation Christmas party shortly after I began working in his research department in 1947. Therefore—and I believe it *is* "therefore"—I have pleasurable affect in re-evoking and preserving the memory. Increasing the readership of this book is one way to re-excite the affect. It has remained "seminal" in my work, to use a favorite word of Rapaport, and I believe it will prove so for others working in the field of emotions and memory. His wish to do the pioneering job of uniting the two areas fueled him during the grueling time it took to sieve through the vast, scattered literature from both the experimental and clinical traditions. He did not merely write a précis of what he had extracted—he organized, criticized, and reinterpreted the vast literature, and in a final brief chapter offered bold generalizations from both literatures. That chapter is especially worth rereading.

Rapaport's work, of which his *Emotions and Memory* is one of the earliest contributions, has influenced a generation of researchers and clinicians working on this topic. It is good to list some of these, since this is one way of documenting the breadth of his impact: George S. Klein, Robert R. Holt, Erik Erikson, Merton M. Gill, Margaret Brenman, Herbert J. Schlesinger, Philip S. Holzman, Roy Schafer, Lester Luborsky, Jean Schimek, Fred Schwartz, Peter Schiller, Richard Rouse, Phebe Cramer, Howard Shevrin, Martin Mayman, Donald Spence, Peter Wolff, Richard Siegal, Hartvig Dahl, David Wolitzky, Leo Goldberger, Sydney J. Segal, and many others. Most of these people meet annually at the Austen Riggs Center in Stockbridge, Massachusetts for the Rapaport Study Group, which began in 1963, a few years after Rapaport's premature death.

If David Rapaport were looking over the field of emotions and memory now, how would he revise or maintain the conclusions in his summary chapter? How would he sum up what has happened in this area in the 30 years since his review. (This review is not aimed at completeness, but at exemplification of trends.)

Perhaps he would observe the notable decline in the kinds of memory experiments based upon a misimpression of the psychoanalytic theory of forgetting and repression—"the forgetting of the unpleasant." The few experiments now done in this area are more often based upon greater understanding of the real theory—"the avoidance of arousal of pain through memory." This formulation allows for the variety of other ways of achieving the avoidance, besides forgetting.

Rapaport had expressed the opinion in one of his conclusions that viewing emotions in physiological terms had prevented many investigators from seeing relationships between emotions and memory. He felt that such "physiologizing" was premature, but he expected that at some later stage it might be amalgamated with corresponding physiological theory of memory, and both of these related on a psychological level. Some inroads have already been made in this direction by the work of Karl Pribram (16) and Howard Shevrin (20).

Finally, Rapaport's aim was to unite the clinical and experimental literature in a single frame of reference and emerge with a unified theory of memory. He, in fact, felt at that time in 1942 that such a revolution in memory theory was nascent. Looking around 30 years later, Rapaport would find that the clinical and experimental literatures still tend to stay segregated, although there are many exceptions—mainly by researcher-clinicians who were influenced by him. Combining experimental work with that of the clinician (by which I am referring to psychoanalytic theory, mainly) is still difficult. The work of the late George Klein (9) and his theory building have been especially instrumental in presenting a theory which would fit with "the new revolution in the theory of memory," in that it places "emotional organization" of memories as central in the theory, as Rapaport had anticipated. One of the big reasons for persistence in the segregation of the two types of literature is the difficulty, in the laboratory setting, of discerning emotional factors that might be relevant to memory organization. An attempt has been made (10, 11, 12, 13) to use recordings of the data of the psychoanalytic situation from which the concepts of the clinical psychoanalytic theory had originally been derived, but to process the psychoanalytic data with proper controls. Through this method emotional organizing factors could be shown to influence one form of spontaneous forgetting—momentary forgetting of what the patient was about to say.

In the main, however, the particular revolution Rapaport envisioned did not occur—even in the topic and aim of his subsequent research. He focused mainly on autonomous ego functions rather than on the organizing role of drive derivatives in memory, as in *Emotions and Memory*. His theory of attention cathexis and his outline of a theory of consciousness (17) are not dynamic, but rather structural-economic theories. The work of Rapaport's associates (18, 19) followed these same lines. They were concerned with questions of coding, capacity, and delay—concepts characterizing present-day academic psychological research on memory. Such work deals with the rules governing memory organization, from simple S-R rules to complex cognitive rules, to questions of information load and capacity. In essence, Rapaport had decided that what was needed first was a theory of memory and learning which could fit within the psychoanalytic framework—at that point the relationship between emotions and memory could be re-examined. The work of Rapaport's associate, Phebe Cramer, reflected this program by its intention to demonstrate that a model of mental functioning based on the assumption of deterministic association processes is successful in predicting the phenomenon of memory and errors in memory (1, 2, 3, 4, 5). Also, since *Emotions and Memory*, and mainly through George Klein's impetus to the research on "cognitive styles" (6), experiments have focused on "style of memory organization." This is different from the *effects* of emotions on memory as a disrupter, facilitator, or organizer. Rather, motives are regarded as quasi-stable dispositions, determining the way memories themselves are organized in storage (7, 8, 14, 15).

In general, the era of broad theories of memory—such as association theory or Gestalt theory—has given way to studies of the specifics of the memory process in terms of such concepts as intake, storage (long-term and short-term), retrieval, and reproduction, and recent work tends to be more empiric and eclectic. Emotions and motivation are still underemphasized in theories of memory processes, especially in academic psychology. The nascent revolution is still to come, so that Rapaport's book remains a modern work. For anyone who is working in this terrain and interested in bridging the clinical and experimental kinds of literature that have grown up around emotions and memory, going back to inspect the original bridge that Rapaport built is an essential beginning point.

REFERENCES

(1) CRAMER, P. Mediated clustering and importation with implicit verbal chains. *Psychonom. Sci.* 2:165-166, 1965.
(2) CRAMER, P. The recovery of a discrete memory. *J. Personal. & Soc. Psychol.* 1:326-332, 1965.
(3) CRAMER, P. Semantic generalization: IAR locus and instructions. *J. Experiment. Psychol.* 84:164-172, 1970.
(4) CRAMER, P. A study of homographs. In: L. J. Postman & G. Keppel (Eds.), *Norms of Word Association*. New York: Academic Press, 1970.
(5) CRAMER, P. Associative strength as a determinant of mediated priming. *J. Verb. Learning & Verb. Behav.* 9:658-664, 1970.
(6) GARDNER, R. W., HOLZMAN, P. F., KLEIN, G. S., LINTON, H., and SPENCE, D. P. *Cognitive Control: A Study of Individual Consistencies in Cognitive Behavior*

[*Psychological Issues*, Monogr. 4] New York: International Universities Press, 1959.

(7) HOLZMAN, P. F., & GARDNER, R. W. Leveling and repression. *J. Abnormal Soc. Psychol.* 59:151-155, 1956.

(8) HOLZMAN, P. F., & GARDNER, R. W. Leveling-sharpening and memory organization. *J. Abnorm. Soc. Psychol.* 61:176-180, 1960.

(9) KLEIN, G. *Perception, Motives, and Personality.* New York: Knopf, 1970.

(10) LUBORSKY, L. Momentary forgetting during psychotherapy and psychoanalysis: a theory and research method. In: R. R. Holt (Ed.), *Motives and Thought: Psychoanalytic Essays in Honor of David Rapaport* [*Psychological Issues*, Monogr. 18/19]. New York: International Universities Press, 1967, pp. 177-217.

(11) LUBORSKY, L. New directions in research on neurotic and psychosomatic symptoms. *Amer. Sci.* 58:661-668, 1970.

(12) LUBORSKY, L. Forgetting and remembering (momentary forgetting) during psychotherapy: a new sample. In: M. Mayman (Ed.), *Psychoanalytic Research: Three Types of Experiments in Subliminal Processes* [*Psychological Issues*], in press, 1971.

(13) LUBORSKY, L., & MINTZ, J. Onset conditions for momentary forgetting in a psychoanalysis: explorations of controlled methods of observation. In: *Psychoanalysis and Contemporary Science.* New York: Macmillan, in press, 1971.

(14) PAUL I. *Studies in Remembering: The Reproduction of Connected and Extended Verbal Material* [*Psychological Issues*, Monogr. 2]. New York: International Universities Press, 1959.

(15) PAUL, I. The concept of schema in memory theory. In: R. R. Holt (Ed.), *Motives and Thought: Psychoanalytic Essays in Honor of David Rapaport* [*Psychological Issues*, Monogr. 18/19]. New York: International Universities Press, 1967, pp. 219-259.

(16) PRIBRAM, K. Freud's project: an open biologically based model for psychoanalysis. In: N. S. Greenfield & W. C. Lewis (Eds.), *Psychoanalysis and Current Biological Thought.* Madison, Wisc.: University of Wisconsin Press, 1965, pp. 81-92.

(17) RAPAPORT, D. On the Psychoanalytic Theory of Motivation. In: M. M. Gill (Ed.), *The Collected Papers of David Rapaport.* New York: Basic Books, 1967, pp. 853-915.

(18) SCHWARTZ, F., & ROUSE, R. *The Activation and Recovery of Associations* [*Psychological Issues*, Monogr. 9]. New York: International Universities Press, 1961.

(19) SCHWARTZ, F., & SCHILLER, P. *The Psychoanalytic Model of Attention and Learning* [*Psychological Issues*, Monogr. 23]. New York: International Universities Press, 1970.

(20) SHEVRIN, H. *Brain Wave Correlates of Subliminal Stimulation, Unconscious Attention, and Repressiveness.* To be published in *Psychological Issues*.

PREFACE TO THE SECOND UNALTERED EDITION

During the nine years that have passed since the first publication of this volume, considerable material has been published concerning the influence of selective factors in various aspects of thought-organization. This new material might have been summarized as a complement to this re-edition of *Emotions and Memory*, particularly since this volume has endeavored to show that what is usually termed "emotion" shades imperceptibly into "selective factor," and that what is usually termed "memory" is but one aspect of, and shades into other aspects of, "thought-organization."

Yet I chose to republish this volume unaltered. The main reasons are:

(1) In recent literature the memory aspect of thought-organization is no longer the center of interest. Instead, learning (e. g., Tolman), sensory-motor effects (e. g., Werner), and particularly perception (e. g., Bruner, Klein) play an increasingly important role. A summary of these contributions can, therefore, no longer be treated as a side issue in a monograph on memory.

(2) In the material I reviewed in the first edition of this volume, *misunderstandings* of the "pleasure-principle" of psychoanalytic theory played a paramount role in stimulating investigation; consequently it was the aim of this volume to clarify psychoanalytic id-psychology and to point up the irrelevance or cogency, or novelty of published experimental, clinical, and theoretical studies. Though my review strongly suggested that we are dealing with an extensive array of selective and organizing factors and a wide variety of forms through which they exert their effect, and that these factors and their effects have a hierarchical organization, the relation of all this to psychoanalytic ego-psychology was at the time obscure to me. I believe that what I have since learned in this respect does not invalidate the factual data collated, nor even those of my views which appeared in the organization of the material, between the lines, and in a few summarizing formulations. What is new and important does, however, make those views appear insufficient. No addition of new material could have made up for this deficiency without breaking the framework of the monograph and making it unwieldy.

What then is the justification for reprinting this monograph?

(1) Today the interest in the relationships between psychoanalytic and experimental findings, as well as in the experimental validation of psychoanalytic propositions, is greater than ever before. This monograph is a summary of the successes and failures of such endeavors. It provides both warnings and hints. That these are still needed becomes quite clear, for instance, from the discussion of emotions that arose in the wake of Leeper's article "A Motivational Theory of Emotion" (*The Psychological Review*, 1948) and from Mowrer and Kluckhohn's treatment of learning (in Hunt's *Personality and the Behavior Disorders*).

(2) The sections of this volume on the theory of emotions, the psychoanalytic theory of memory, and the psychopathology of memory are, in spite of many limitations, still the sole systematic treatment of these fields.

Further pursuit of the conception of *the hierarchy of organizing factors* developed in this monograph led to what I hope to be a contribution to an understanding of the relation between the id- and the ego-psychology of thought-processes, in the volume *Organization and Pathology of Thought* (in press). The sections on *the rationale of tests,* in Rapaport, Schafer and Gill: *Diagnostic Psychological Testing* (1945), are also attempts to continue the work initiated in *Emotions and Memory*. They too endeavor to clarify the nature of memory and thought-organization.

David Rapaport

Stockbridge, August, 1950.

FOREWORD

In the practice of medicine an accurate account of the sequence of events leading up to the onset of symptoms has always been the corner stone upon which diagnosis, prognosis and treatment are built. Any interference with the patient's memory for these events will give the physician a false impression and may lead to erroneous diagnosis.

In the large group of illnesses in which emotional factors are now known to play an important role, an adequate history can rarely be obtained by the usual question-answer technique because the crucial information is nearly always excluded from the patient's memory. Moreover the physician, too often unaware that the emotionally charged memories will have been repressed and that it is this very repression, distortion or displacement which gives them potency to precipitate, prolong or intensify the somatic disturbance, is over-ready to dismiss the possible role of affective factors at the patient's first denial of their existence.

Signs and symptoms of bodily dysfunction are prone to evoke apprehension in the afflicted individual. Anticipation of the physician's examination accentuates this feeling. It is from such anxious individuals—so aptly termed "frightened people" by Elton Mayo*—that the physician must seek to elicit data which, because of their disturbing nature, have been excluded from the patient's memory.

The inevitable failure of the direct question-answer technique of history-taking, when the physician is seeking evidence which has been forgotten, points to the need for new methods of medical teaching which will reveal to the student the role of emotion in disease and for new methods of history-taking which, by providing a setting of reassurance and encouragement, will relieve anxiety and thus facilitate the recall of disturbing memories.

It was with these thoughts in mind that the plan for a review of the literature dealing with the relationship between emotions and memory was first discussed with Dr. Rapaport. He at once appreciated that to limit the study to the medical aspects alone would be to fail to do justice to the broader implications of the problem, which demand a reinterpretation of the processes of feeling and of remembering, and of their dynamic relationship to each other and to other aspects of mental functioning.

With prodigious energy and rare discernment of fundamental issues, Dr. Rapaport has interpreted and correlated the literature from the fields of psychology, psychopathology and psychoanalysis. He has not only made a contribution to the understanding of the role of emotions in remembering

* Mayo, Elton: Frightened People. Harvard Medical Alumni Bulletin, January 1939, Vol. 13, # 2, pp. 36–41.

and forgetting but has also laid the ground work for the development of a
new and challenging theory of memory function.

The Josiah Macy, Jr. Foundation welcomes this monograph of the
Menninger Clinic series as a contribution to the concept of psychosomatic
unity and is happy to have had the opportunity of joining the Menninger
Clinic in furthering this study.

FRANK FREMONT-SMITH, M.D.
Medical Director,
Josiah Macy, Jr. Foundation

New York, N. Y.
October, 1942

PREFACE

Language, common sense, and the great tradition in Western philosophy, have agreed that *thoughts* and *feelings* are two independent entities, or indeed two entities starkly opposed. The evolutionary theory, bringing in its turbulent wake the philosophy of James and Dewey, has offered us, in rebellion against the tradition, another period of effort to find in thought and feeling two intimately related, perhaps only relatively distinguishable aspects of one continuous struggle to adapt to the environment. Psychoanalysis, talking a different language but saying the same thing, has made many doubt whether "pure" or "cold" intellectual process exists; memory, judgment, logical analysis express the same ultimate dynamics that appear in our cravings, our aggressions, our acts of self-defense.

Through the half century of experimental psychology and of psychoanalysis a vast research literature on the interrelationships of the intellectual life and the feeling life has been accumulated—a literature founded in a wide diversity of theoretical systems, and urgently in need of overhauling and interpretation. Such a survey might both focus what we know about the relation of cognitive to affective processes, and show where better, fuller research is needed.

Dr. Rapaport has undertaken one large and important sector of this attack. While confining himself for the most part to the relation of emotion to memory, he has touched upon many related dynamic problems. It is earnestly to be hoped that he will give us a companion volume on the relation of emotion (and of all affectivity) to perception in all its aspects; and another on affectivity in relation to creative thinking. But the present volume, with its immense bibliography, its careful and sympathetic comparison of huge quantities of experimental and clinical material, is the big beginning for a really big achievement, and he has put psychologists and psychoanalysts everywhere in his debt. He has taken the trouble to understand those who speak not only in different languages but from different cultural frames of reference; and he has modestly but cogently put his own frame of reference forward when needed in the assay. This is the kind of book that the serious student of human psychology will not only read, but keep nearby for repeated and grateful reference.

GARDNER MURPHY,
Head of the Psychology Department,
College of the City of New York

ACKNOWLEDGEMENTS

Historically, expression of my gratitude is due first to my teacher, Dr. Paul von Schiller, who encouraged my interest in the vicissitudes of memory functioning; it was under his guidance that my previous two historical studies (1, 2) in memory theory were undertaken. To Dr. Samu Rapaport and Dr. Tibor Rajka I owe much for their stimulation in forming my point of view.

This country provided a new home and security, and generous possibilities for work; I cannot express adequately my gratitude for this. Dr. L. S. Kubie, Dr. F. Fremont-Smith, Dr. David Levy, Dr. R. M. Fellows, and Dr. K. A. Menninger, by guidance, help, and encouragement, made it possible for me to combine three years of adjustment with concentrated work.

The preparation of this monograph was made possible by a generous grant of the Josiah Macy, Jr., Foundation. I am indebted to Dr. F. Fremont-Smith, Director of the Medical Division of the Foundation, whose special interest in the problem and appreciation of the need for its clarification made this study possible, and whose personal assistance by suggestion and discussion helped greatly in clarifying the issues and determining the sphere of this monograph.

The publication of this monograph was made possible by grants of the Josiah Macy, Jr., Foundation and the Menninger Foundation. I am indebted to Dr. K. A. Menninger, the Chief of Staff of the Menninger Clinic, for his encouragement and liberal allowances in time, help, and expense to complete this study. My thanks are due also to the Clinic as such, to the officers of the Menninger Foundation, and especially to its Secretary and the editor of this Monograph series, Dr. W. C. Menninger.

It is with warm gratitude that I acknowledge my indebtedness to Doctors G. Murphy, K. Lewin, B. Mittelmann, J. B. Massermann, R. P. Knight, G. Katona, M. H. Erickson, J. F. Brown, and P. T. Young for reading the manuscript and contributing helpful advice. The present form of this monograph is due in part to the efforts of my friends Dr. Margaret Brenman, Will Gibson, and Dr. Merton Gill, who worked on it in detail. Dr. Brenman advised on its continuity and clarity; Will Gibson reworked its expression throughout; and Dr. Gill contributed many additions, formulations, and corrections of weaknesses. I owe them more than an acknowledgement.

To the secretaries Mrs. Helen Henderson and Mrs. Katherine Laughlin my thanks are due for their careful work on the preparation of the manuscript and the indexing.

Finally, thanks are due to my wife, whose participation in every phase of the three years' work of this study makes her a tacit co-author.

INTRODUCTION

1

A monograph may be expected to open by defining the topic stated in its title. We are, however, in no position to define either emotions or memory, and even less the influence of emotions on memory. Yet the literature gives ample evidence that an interrelation is generally assumed. The psychiatric literature explains the greater part of amnesias as a result of emotional disturbances. The psychoanalytic literature considers forgetting and false remembering to be caused by emotionally charged complexes of ideas. General psychological theory suggests that memories are assimilated to, and integrated with, the personality and its strivings. The literature of hypnosis adds data of similar implication. Our aim here is to survey the most important contributions to this topic, in order that we may clarify what has been meant by "the influence of emotions on memory," and prepare the ground for further investigations to establish a better understanding of that influence.

In the first chapter we will outline the general psychological background of our problem. The second chapter will survey the literature of emotions in an attempt to clarify what is meant by the term when "emotions and memory" are under discussion. In the third chapter pertinent experiments reported in the literature of general psychology will be surveyed. The fourth chapter will deal with the theoretical contributions of general psychology to the relation of emotions and memory. In the fifth chapter we shall attempt to infer the pertinence of psychoanalytic theory and observations to our problem. The sixth chapter will survey the relevant literature of hypnotic memory phenomena. In the seventh chapter the literature of amnesias will be discussed. The eighth chapter will describe a number of experiments, tests, and techniques which to us appear to be exceptionally clear demonstrations of the effect of emotions on memory, and which, when applied appropriately, seem to promise further elucidation of the issue. Finally, in the ninth chapter we shall endeavor to summarize our findings, giving a tentative interpretation of our problem insofar as its present status will allow.

2

Several factors have prompted the undertaking of an analysis of emotional influences evidenced in the functioning of memory. Scientific attention has become focused on emotional factors in the course of the past few decades. Prescott's survey, "Emotion and the Educative Process" (3), tried to sum up the implications this new development held for the educational field. Dunbar's survey, "Emotions and Bodily Changes" (4), collected the pertinent medical psychosomatic material. In general psychology, however, the systematizing interest has still dwelt on the problems of the expression of emotions, the physiology of emotions in general, and the localization of the nervous action of emotions in particular. This is regrettable, because it was not in the scope of either of the surveys mentioned above to clarify the concepts used and the hypotheses implied in dealing with this new field. This task awaited the psychologist. It is regrettable also in that the psychological literature has carried many accounts of pertinent experiments and discussions using concepts whose content remains an unknown entity.

The psychoanalytic literature, with its emphasis on the significance of slips of the tongue, forgetting, and repression, has had much repercussion in the general psychological literature in the form of attempts to prove or disprove Freudian theory. Many experiments were conducted; but neither the experimental reports nor the surveys systemizing them clarified the concept of emotion as used in the experiments, or even the problem of whether the experiments were relevant to the psychoanalytic theory they undertook to prove or disprove. (Meltzer, 5; Beebe-Center, 6; Cason, 7; Gilbert, 8, etc.) There were few and only vague attempts at integrating findings in the field of memory pathology—so frequently related to emotional interference—with the general psychological theory of memory. (Ray, 9; Lundholm, 10; Sears, 11; Gillespie, 12.)

Moreover, in the past two or three decades the concept "memory" has undergone the greatest change since Plato and Aristotle. This revolution of the concept is still in the making; and it appears that to rebuild the concept, clarification of the role of emotional influences will be indispensable. We hope that this survey of the literature will help clarify the concepts ininvolved, encourage experimentation, and contribute to the crystallization of a new theory of memory.

REFERENCES

(1) RAPAPORT, D. *The history of the association concept* (in the Hungarian language). 92 pp. Budapest, Publ. Psychol. Lab. Univ. of Budapest, 1937.

(2) RAPAPORT, D. The modern concept of association, pp. 159–180 (in the Hungarian language; with an English summary, pp. 194–195). In: *Lelektani Tanulmanyok*, vol. II, 195 pp., Budapest, Univ. Press, 1938.

(3) PRESCOTT, D. A. *Emotion and the educative process.* 323 pp. Washingon, D. C., Amer. Council Educ., 1938.

(4) DUNBAR, H. F. *Emotions and bodily changes.* 595 pp. New York, Columbia Univ. Press, 1935.

(5) MELTZER, H. The present status of experimental studies of the relationship of feeling to memory. *Psychol. Rev.* 37: 124–139, 1930.

(6) BEEBE-CENTER, J. G. *The psychology of pleasantness and unpleasantness.* 427 pp. New York, Nostrand, 1932.

(7) CASON, H. The learning and retention of pleasant and unpleasant activities. *Arch. Psychol.* 134: 96, 1932.

(8) GILBERT, G. M. The new status of experimental studies on the relationship of feeling and memory. *Psychol. Bull.* 35: 26–35, 1938.

(9) RAY, W. S. The relationship of retroactive inhibition, retrograde amnesia, and the loss of recent memory. *Psychol. Rev.* 44: 339–345, 1937.

(10) LUNDHOLM, H. The riddle of functional amnesia. *J. Abn. Soc. Psychol.* 26: 355–360, 1932.

(11) SEARS, R. R. Functional abnormalities of memory with special reference to amnesia. *Psychol. Bull.* 33: 229–274, 1936.

(12) GILLESPIE, R. D. Amnesia. *Arch. Neurol. Psychiat.* 37: 748–764, 1937.

CHAPTER I

THE HISTORICAL BACKGROUND OF THE PROBLEM

The past of our knowledge of the "influence of emotions on memory" is long; but its history is brief and foggy. The investigator venturing into this past must frequently exchange the concept "memory" for "association of ideas," and "emotions" for vague "irrational determiners" and "passions."

Elsewhere (1), analyzing the history of the association concept, this author found abundant evidence that the philosopher-psychologists in the early modern centuries were aware of the role of "affective factors" in memory. Here we shall indicate only the manner in which some of these philosophers expressed this knowledge.

Bacon, in describing the four famous "idols" which disturb the association-process underlying human thinking, indicated that these idols were personal factors (2, ⚹ 41–66). He pointed out that facts connected with strong feelings—shame, fear, admiration—were easier remembered than indifferent facts (2, II, ⚹ 26).

Descartes attributed the association-mechanism to the motion of the "animal spirits" (3, ⚹ 21), which were for him also the essence of the passions (3, ⚹ 51). He refers frequently to the emergence of memories as brought about by passions (3, ⚹ 36).

Hobbes divided the association (memory) function into two realms (4, III, ⚹ 1). In the first, the mechanical laws of association prevail; in the other, "order" is lacking and the antagonistic poles of attraction-avoidance prevail—or in modern language, driving forces and not mechanical laws of association determine the emergence of ideas.

Spinoza put a special emphasis on the fact that feelings are frequently the link between *associated ideas* (5, Part III, Prop. 45–46). He advised also that man avoid hatred, because hatred will determine the course of his associations and hinder objective observation and understanding (6, p. 60).

Locke, who coined the concept "association of ideas" (7, II, ⚹ 74), was aware of the fact that pain and pleasure—passions, uneasiness—have a significant role in determining associations (7, II, pp. 542–543, I, pp. 329–335). He discussed the role of such factors in the pathology of associations —i.e., of mental functioning.

Leibniz went so far as to declare that "appetition" leads us from one perception to another (8, ✳15, 9, XX, ✳6), and used Locke's concept of "uneasiness" to express the driving tension (10, ✳289) moving our memory and thought functions.

Hume, in spite of his otherwise mechanistic psychology, considered the passions to be the driving forces of our associations, and even the basis of our rational causes (11, IV, ✳7, V, ✳6).

Kant maintained that pleasure and pain were the basis of the power of judgment, that the ability of knowing was the basis of cognition, and that the appetition ability was the determiner of the reason; thus he attributed an all-significant role to appetition in the functions of the mind, one of which is the memory function (12, pp. 556–57; 13).

Even these few, and necessarily sketchy, historical references may demonstrate that throughout the epoch of Enlightenment, which so energetically strove to "discover" the mechanical laws of the human mind, there existed an insight into the role of "affective" factors in memory functioning. We must admit, however, that such a demonstration has an outstanding weakness: instead of simply making its point, it clearly shows the critical reader that the concepts "memory" and "affective factors" are still so vague that the problem of their interrelation becomes quite parenthetical. This fact should make us aware that here we are entering a field in which the knowledge has outgrown the conceptual framework. It is evidence that we can no longer approach our topic with artless common sense, attributing ill-defined but commonly accepted meanings to the words "memory" and "emotion."

It would be comfortable to fall back on early simple definitions, such as that "memory is our ability to retain and reproduce impressions once perceived," or "emotions are reverberations on the cortex of peripheral bodily changes following the perception of the exciting fact." But these definitions are useless. Memory has long ceased to be definable as the ability of the cortex to fixate stimulations and to revive their traces. It has been differentiated into its three aspects, learning, retention, and recall; the investigation of each has proved to be a specific problem. Learning was found to be a complex process in which material, method, personal motivation, individual psychic make-up, and momentary state all interact. Retention can no longer be thought of as a wax-plate, loyal and reliable. We have learned that "autonomous" changes occur in retention; we have learned too that the retained material is organized, or brought into relation with other retained material, without our conscious contribution. Recall, we know, depends on the actual state of the subject as well as on the context in which reproduction is called for; we have seen also that reproduction does not necessarily occur when called for and that its non-occurrence does not mean it cannot occur. It has recently been emphasized that recall is not simply a revival of traces imprinted in us somewhere, nor is forgetting simply a fading of that imprint. Reproduction is rather an active production, and forgetting also fundamentally implies an active principle. Finally and most essentially, learning, retention, and recall are inextricably interrelated, operating simultaneously in every moment of our lives. The classical memory experiments, trying to isolate and measure these functions, demonstrate only how memory *can* function under given laboratory conditions and not how it does function in everyday life.

A similar situation obtains in the study of emotions. These no longer are considered phylogenetic vestiges of instinctual activities (Darwin), mental elements (Wundt), or reverberations of bodily changes (James). Instead, we have a variegated list of concepts dealt with at times under the term "emotions." A sampling of these would include instinct, drive, affect, feeling, hedonic tone, mood, passion, temperament, sentiment, attitude, complex, motive, determining tendency, wish, tension, need, quasi-need, interest, intention, preference. There has been an indiscriminate application of the words "emotion" and "affect," and their adjectival forms, to almost everything that is not apparently rational or lawful, to any phenomenon that seems determined in a generalized way by the whole-organism, and even to pathological bodily and behavioral manifestations of psychogenic origin. Such loose usage has rendered the terms broad common-sense expressions, and divested them of the unequivocality prerequisite to any scientific concept.

There is another difficulty in attempting to define memory and emotion. In the endeavor to cope with the newly-perceived problems of memory and the increasing fluidity of the concept emotion, the new concepts evolved may be so broad as to lack specific meaning. As long as memory had been solely the faculty investigated in classical memory experiments, the term had a simple meaning. But when it was seen that these experiments demonstrated only how memory *can function under given conditions*, it became necessary to investigate its role in the *organization* of our thought processes. The concept "memory" as an isolated entity, useful though it was, is a mere abstraction; "memory" is but *one* aspect of the organization of thought processes. Actual memory phenomena are encountered only in the context of thought processes; at best the classical memory experiments with nonsense syllables could ignore this fact and make us ignore it, but they could not produce memory phenomena outside this context. In the following pages we shall frequently be compelled to adduce evidence which at first glance will appear—especially to the psychologist of classical training—to be out of place in dealing with memory. Memory will be discussed as an aspect of thought processes. In judging the validity of the evidence this viewpoint should be kept in mind, although no attempt will be made to advance an adequate definition of memory or of its role as such an aspect.

Similar difficulty is encountered in the field of emotions when the multiplicity and the portent of the factors implicit in the term are comprehended. Such is the variety of these factors that no human function can be considered undetermined, unmotivated, uncharged with energy or uncolored by "emotions," or not embedded in them. To attempt to unify related concepts under one major concept is useful only if the interrelation of the specific concepts is clear. In our problem, however, neither the propriety of unifying the factors under one concept nor their interrelation is self-evident; in such a case, a conceptual unification is misleading. It appears that every human function implies "emotional factors"; this finding will be conceptually valuable only after the interrelation of these factors has been clarified. This statement is applicable to the role of emotional factors in memory functioning. We will not attempt to create a new terminology; inasmuch as different authors have used interchangeably such expressions as "emotion," "affect," and "hedonic tone," we shall discuss each contribution in its original terminology. It is hoped that in the course of this discussion the concept emotion will undergo an *autonomous structurization*.

These general formulations of the concepts "memory" and "emotion" have a certain justification. It is doubtful, however, whether in their all-inclusive generality they are more useful than the first definitions in their inadequate simplicity; what we do consider useful is to contrast the two kinds of definitions. They constitute the historical setting of our problem, and should be viewed as the background to this survey. The present status of the problems in our field is complicated; the concepts used are undefined or at best ill-defined. It is not our purpose to construct a theory which will reconcile all the experiments, suggestions, and opinions. It is our view that an attempt at such a definitive theory satisfactory to every investigator would not be justified by the present state of research in the field. The confused state of the problem is not to be attributed simply to haphazard investigations, but in part to the manner of development of modern psychology and in part to different approaches rooted in the personalities of the investigators. The reader will notice, in following the historical sequence of the contributions to our problem, that in the course of the last decades it has been increasingly accepted that memory function is determined by deep strata of personality organization, and that this was given different interpretation by different investigators. Those with a more intellectualist orientation, in a search for the nature of "meaning," found determinants of memory-functioning expressible in logical terms; investigators with a more sociological or utilitarian orientation expressed the same

phenomenon in terms of "interests"; early general psychology was inclined
to express it in terms of "pleasantness" and "unpleasantness," inheriting
these from sensory psychology; more recent experimental psychologists
have expressed it in terms of "context" and "set," which are more amenable
to experimental investigation. Psychologists engaged in studying action
and motivation tend to express it in terms of needs; physiological psychologists, in terms of measurable physiological concomitants of emotion;
clinical psychologists and psychiatrists, in terms of affects; and psychoanalysts, in terms of instincts and drives. These varied individual and
group orientations have resulted in varied theories and methodologies
which, in turn, have fostered varied experimental approaches. Our intention is to survey these differing approaches, and to indicate the relation
of one to another. We shall attempt to demonstrate the continuity in
which they shade into or grow out of each other. Accordingly, our essential purpose is to present an exhaustive and factual survey of the pertinent
publications, indicating both their inadequacies and those features which
will prove to be of further interest and stimulation. The careful reader
will find the author's viewpoint implicit in the organization of the material;
this viewpoint will be indicated in the conclusions of the monograph.
We feel that our task is to show the continuity and interrelations of the
material, leaving the reader free to draw his own conclusions and offering
as a basis for this as much factual material as space and the organization
of our data allow. It must be admitted, however, that an author's viewpoint influences the organization of his material; further, we have summarized the material and commented upon it.

At this point it may be helpful to formulate our problem again: the
motivation of human behavior having become a focal problem in psychological investigation, the question arises whether memory is a *photographic*
or a *motivated* process. The answer has been anticipated above; it is perhaps safe to say that among psychologists there would be little difference
of opinion on the point. It is implied that memory is a *motivated behavior
phenomenon* and that emotions are *motivating factors*. We have attempted
to collect the material demonstrating the mode of operation of the motivating factors called "emotions," insofar as they may be perceived in that
aspect of the organization of our thought processes called "memory."

REFERENCES

(1) RAPAPORT, D. *The history of the association concept* (in the Hungarian language). 92 pp. Budapest, Publ. Psychol. Lab. Univ. of Budapest, 1937.
(2) BACON, F. *Novum organon.* 214 pp. Berlin, Kirchman's Phil. Bibl., 1870.
(3) DESCARTES, R. *Ueber die Leidenschaften der Seele.* 180 pp. Berlin, Kirchman's Phil. Bibl., 1870.

(4) HOBBES, TH. *Leviathan sive de materia, forma, etc.* 362 pp. Amsterdolami, 1670.

(5) SPINOZA, B. *Ethics.* pp. 39–278. In: *Improvement of the understanding. Ethics, and Correspondence.* Trans. Elwes, R. H. M., New York, Wiley, 1901.

(6) SPINOZA, B. *Kurzer Tractat von Gott, dem Menschen und dessen Glueckseligkeit.* 87 pp. Leipzig, Meiner's Phil. Bibl., 1907.

(7) LOCKE, J. *Untersuchungen ueber den menschlichen Verstand.* Vol. I, 326 pp.; vol. II, 367 pp. Leipzig, Reklam's Univ. Bibl., 1902.

(8) LEIBNIZ, G. W. *Kleinere philosophische Schriften.* 334 pp. Leipzig, Reklam's Univ. Bibl., 1907.

(9) LEIBNIZ, G. W. *Nouveaux essais sur l'entendement humain.* 450 pp. Raspe, 1765.

(10) LEIBNIZ, G. W. *Theodicee.* Vol. I, 005 pp.; vol II, 422 pp. Leipzig, Meiner's Phil. Bibl., 1921.

(11) HUME, D. *On passions, essays moral and political.* 315 pp. London, 1748.

(12) KANT, I. *Kritik der reinen Vernunft.* 685 pp. Riga, 1781.

(13) KANT, I. Ueber Philosophie ueberhaupt. In: *Kleine logisch-metaphysische Schriften,* 421 pp., Leipzig, 1794.

Chapter II

THE PROBLEM OF EMOTIONS[1]

What are emotions? This is the first question the reader will expect to have answered. It is important for our problem to clarify what emotions are; it is difficult to see how, without such a clarification, the search for the relation of memory and emotion can become meaningful. Although we attempted to show in Chapter I that the concept and theory of both memory and emotions are in a process of reformation, there seems to be a difference between the status of the two. The concept "memory" will be more generally taken for granted than that of "emotions": "memory" is used at present in an all too narrow sense, a sense which prevents the mutual elucidation and unitary organization of such fields as perception memory, dream, phantasy, and thinking, but which at least makes for clarity of meaning. The concept "emotion," however, is used so broadly that it is difficult to ascertain its precise meaning. It will be our aim to clarify this meaning. First, we shall enumerate and discuss a few recent attempts at defining emotions; secondly, we shall survey the literature of the physiology of emotions; thirdly, we shall summarize the literature of the psychology of emotions; fourthly, we shall discuss the implications of a number of recent investigations which deal with the role of emotions in other processes of the human organism, such as learning, education, and bodily changes.

Before commencing the course of discussion as outlined, a short appraisal of the complexity of the problem will be appropriate. What do we imply if we designate as "emotional disturbances" such a variety of phenomena as psychoses, neuroses, certain somatic maladies—hypertension, gastric ulcer —and behavior and educational difficulties? Is the implication of the term here identical with its implication in the phrase "emotional influence on memory"? Why is it that we speak without hesitation of the "emotional" character and origin of these problems, but investigations and discussions rarely make clear the sense in which they are "emotional"? Why is it that the systematic treatment of the problem of emotions deals in the main with the expressive movements, physiology, and localization of nervous action in emotions? It is not within our present scope to advance an

[1] I am greatly indebted to Dr. Frank Fremont-Smith, director of the medical section of the Josiah Macy Jr. Foundation; it was upon his advice that I include this chapter discussing the problem of emotions. Through many suggestive discussions he helped in the formulation of the chapter.

exhaustive answer.   A careful historical investigation of these problems is urgently needed, if additional complication of them is to be avoided.   Our present discussion must be brief, and indicative of the trend which our survey of the literature of emotions will follow.

The main difficulty in the literature of emotions appears to be that the word "emotion" is sometimes used to designate a *phenomenon*, and sometimes to designate the *dynamics* underlying a phenomenon or group of phenomena.   For instance, in the description of any single "emotion" such as fear or rage, the expression "emotion" refers to a phenomenon; but in a psychosomatic disease the expression "emotion" refers to the dynamics and etiology of the disorder.[2]   Furthermore, when used to denote phenomena the expression "emotion" denotes sometimes physiological and motor phenomena, such as facial expressions, and sometimes phenomena of conscious experiencing, such as "feelings."   Similarly, when used to denote the dynamics underlying phenomena the expression "emotion" sometimes denotes physiological dynamics, as in the case of the Cannon theory, and sometimes psychological dynamics, as in the case of the psychoanalytic theory.

One way to deal with these difficulties would be to say that the expressions "emotion" and "emotional," and such equivalents as "affect" and "affective," have been unjustifiably used for processes and phenomena which have little in common; acceptance of this view would imply an attempt to purify the unjustified old terminology and to establish a new unequivocal terminology.   Another way to cope with these difficulties would be to assume that "emotion" is a process which may have a great variety of phenomenal manifestations.   One would then have to deal with the process "emotion" in psychosomatic terms, maintaining that sometimes its physiological and sometimes its psychological manifestations may become the more obvious, to such an extent that the other may seem altogether absent.   This emotion-process would be conceived also as one which may find direct and momentary manifestations on the physiological level, as seen in emotional expression, or on the psychological level, as seen in "feeling," or on both levels; but which may be denied such immediate discharge and thus issue in a chronic alteration of the physiological processes, as seen in psychosomatic disorders, or of the psychological processes, as

[2] A good example of the latter is provided by the following quotation from an unpublished paper of M. Gill (1):

"The individual with hypertension on the basis of chronically repressed rage—the formula which at present seems best to cover the psychologic mechanisms of the cases of essential hypertension which have received intensive psychologic study—does not go about exhibiting chronic massive autonomic discharge such as we have seen in the animal with stimulated hypothalamus.   On the contrary, his overt behavior is characterized by excessive amiability and apparent calm."

seen in neuroses, psychoses, and character disorders. This attempt at clarifying the problem of "emotions" would also necessitate terminological changes to make palpable the difference between the phenomenon and the underlying process. This second approach seems to us the more promising, and our survey will undertake to show the extent to which this approach has a basis in the observations on, and the theories of, emotions; though it seems that the situation is not yet ripe to yield an easy transition to a new terminology. The influence of emotions on memory could easily be integrated with the theory of emotions built around this second approach. It could be established on the same level as the other emotional manifestations. Here again one would have to distinguish momentary from chronic effects of emotions. Such effects as slips of the tongue and temporary forgettings would be considered momentary; functional amnesias, obsessive ideas, and delusions would be considered chronic effects.

Another consideration requires attention. Where does the dynamic process, of which the chronic and momentary manifestations are the "emotional phenomena," originate? Does it exist in its own right as an isolated factor in the psychic life, in personality organization? or is it merely a specific constellation of the general dynamics underlying the psychic life? In the latter case, the assumption of a continuity of psychic occurrence implies that no psychic process may be considered devoid of emotional participation. The material to be surveyed will have to answer these questions; but it may be presumed that the contemporary taste of scientific psychology will find the latter possibility more acceptable.

1. DEFINITIONS OF EMOTIONS

A full historical and factual account of the development of the concept of emotions cannot be given here; there are thorough-going texts which may be consulted in this respect. The history of the concept is summarized in Gardiner, Metcalf, and Beebe-Center's "Feeling and Emotion; A History of Theories" (2). The problem of "feeling," especially its experimental aspect, is systematically treated in Beebe-Center's "The Psychology of Pleasantness and Unpleasantness" (3). Equally exhaustive and factual is the account given by Lund in his "Emotions" (4). A systematic textbook treatment of the entire field is given in Ruckmick's "Psychology of Feeling and Emotion" (5).[3]

The question of what a theory of emotions must account for has been given different answers. A few recent ones distinguished by their comprehensiveness will be quoted here. Harlow and Stagner (6) write:

"Any projected theory of the emotional response must include, and satisfy the requirements imposed by the following sets of data: (1) behavioristic: facts on emo-

---

[3] See also "Feelings and Emotions; The Wittenberg Symposium" (7), and Washburn, M. (8).

tional behavior, expression, smooth muscle activity, etc.; (2) introspective: the conscious attributes of emotion, its *quale* and concomitants; (3) psychopathological: cases of abnormal behavior and emotional experience; and (4) physiological: the data on physiological and neurological functions involved in the emotional response." (p. 570)

"Unconditioned affective responses form a basis for the emotions (these affective patterns being describable in terms of conscious feelings, induced by activation of sensory thalamic projection centers, and by reaction patterns controlled by diencephalic motor nuclei); and the emotions themselves are conditioned responses subsequently formed. The conditioning process by which all emotions are acquired, modify the unconditioned affective pattern by enormously extending the range of stimuli that will elicit it, and usually by 'damping' the violence of the unconditioned affective response." (pp. 189–190)

"(1) The fundamental conscious emotional states are feelings . . .
(2) Feelings are localized in the thalamus, while sensations . . . are localized in the cortex.
(3) . . . concerning innate emotions . . . our theory . . . *suggests a group of unconditioned responses as a basis from which emotions may develop.*" (p. 190)

Lund (4) discusses emotions as follows:

"It must be clear that we cannot single out some segment of internal or external behavior and regard this as *the* emotion. Emotions are not simple, entitative affairs. They are forms of activity characterized by a given amount of feeling tone, of affective quality. This activity, as we have seen, involves mental and abbreviated adjustments as well as somatic and visceral. A complete description of an emotion— or better, of *emotional behavior*—would have to take account of all these variables, the *mental, somatic and visceral,* as well as of the *stimulus situation.* To be content with anything less would not do, since some of these factors may be identical in different types of emotional behavior, and all may occur under non-emotional as well as emotional conditions." (p. 13)

"With this in mind emotion might be defined as a *strongly affective state involving diffuse somatic reactions and rather widespread, centrally aroused, visceral changes.* In this definition the expression, 'centrally aroused,' calls attention to the fact that visceral changes, when occurring under emotional conditions, are of central origin, whereas under other conditions they are usually of local origin." (p. 14)

P. T. Young (9)[4] summarized his view in these words:

"(1) An emotion has been defined *as a pattern of organic response.* This formula is useful in the laboratory despite the fact that no one has shown how an emotional pattern can be *distinguished from one which is non-emotional.*
"(2) A second definition has affirmed *that emotion is a disturbance* (disruption, upset) *revealed by diffuse, excessive, aimless behavior.* This type of definition is adequate if qualified by two criteria. (1) Emotional disturbances contain *marked bodily changes in the smooth muscles and glands.* These bodily changes distinguish emotional upset from non-emotional disturbances such as being lost, startled, disoriented. (2) Emotional disturbances have *an external*

---

[4] Young, P. T., "By What Criteria Can Emotion be Defined?" paper delivered at the 1941 meetings of the Midwestern Psychological Association. The text quoted above is that of an abstract obtained by courtesy of the author.

origin. This criterion distinguishes emotional disturbances from the appetitive drives and from various aches and pains which have an internal or bodily origin."

These statements are quoted here not as the last word of research on the problem but rather as reflective attempts to do justice to divergent claims.

Harlow and Stagner, as well as Lund, include in their descriptions the behavioral, the introspective, and the physiological aspects of emotions. Lund refers in addition to the central origin of visceral changes present in emotions. Harlow and Stagner refer to the emotional problems of psychopathology, and emphasize the fundamentally *conscious* character of feelings. Young is concerned with the distinction between emotional and nonemotional physiological patterns.

On the basis of these descriptions we shall divide into two groups the facts and problems for which a theory of emotions must account: a physiological group, and a psychological group. Such a grouping will of necessity be arbitrary, for no sharp line divides these two realms of phenomena. For every psychological process there *must* exist a corresponding physiological process, and *probably* every physiological process is part of a complex pattern of similar processes which plays a role in the preparation of the so-called psychological processes. The division between "psychological" and "physiological" is an artifact. Yet the scientific, methodological usefulness of the distinction should not be minimized; the terms designate the frame of reference in which a phenomenon is viewed. If a tissue process is being studied in reference to tissue processes, or memory in reference to the experimental destruction of a portion of the brain, the frame of reference is physiological; yet the latter example approaches what has been recently called the "psychosomatic" frame of reference. If the delusions of a schizophrenic are studied in reference to the structure of his associations, or if a case of hypertension is studied psychoanalytically, the frame of reference is psychological; yet the latter case is a typical psychosomatic problem. It is with these reservations that the dichotomy between "physiological" and "psychological" is made in the following discussion.

2. THE PHYSIOLOGY OF EMOTIONS

The presence of physiological changes in "emotional states" was early recognized; the first systematic attempt to explain their role was the James-Lange (43) theory.[5] One of the main implications of the interrelation of

---

[5] The long line of predecessors of James and Lange is extensively discussed by Ruckmick (5, pp. 149–156).

emotions and physiological changes was clarified considerably later by Sherrington (10). He enumerated three theoretical possibilities:

"(1) that the psychic part of emotion arises first and its neural correlate then excites the viscera, (2) that the same stimulus concurrently excites the mind and the nervous centers controlling the viscera, (3) that the emotional stimulus acts first on the nervous centers controlling the viscera whose reaction, as we apprehend it, is the emotion." (p. 255)

The James-Lange theory had expounded the third view. The historical importance of this view lay in the fact that, in a purely mentalistic period of psychology, it emphasized the physiological influence on psychic processes.[6] James' (11) definition of emotions was that " . . . *the bodily changes follow directly the perception of the exciting fact, and . . . our feeling of the same changes as they occur is the emotion*" (vol. 2, p. 449); this definition implied that the "emotion felt" is the "reverberation" of these bodily changes on the cortex. The physiological mechanisms which could account for the desiderata of this theory were shown by Sherrington (10), Cannon (12), and others to be questionable.[7] The similarity of physiological patterns of different emotions to each other and to those of non-emotional states made it difficult to explain how the reverberation of similar physiological patterns on the cortex would result in different emotions.[8] This non-specificity of organic reaction patterns prompted Young to add further criteria by which emotions might be defined.[9] The failure to produce unequivocal emotional reactions in human beings by adrenalin injections[10] disappointed expectations based on the finding that the adrenalin-content of the blood is increased in emotional states; and Massermann's recent experiments (16) showed that stimulation of the hypothalamus of cats produces almost all of the bodily changes characteristic of emotion in cats, without—judging by behavioral criteria—the cat's experiencing any

---

[6] See Weber, A. O., and Rapaport, D. (13).

[7] Cannon's arguments against the James-Lange theory were summarized by Ruckmick (5) as follows:
"(1) Total separation of the viscera from the central nervous system does not alter emotional behavior; (2) the same visceral changes occur in very different emotional states and in non-emotional states; (3) the viscera are relatively insensitive structures; (4) visceral changes are too slow to be a source of emotional feelings, and (5) artificial induction of the visceral changes typical of strong emotions does not produce them." (p. 185)

[8] Angell, (14, p. 200) maintained that minor differences between these physiological patterns may still be discovered.

[9] See pp. 13–14.

[10] See Cantril and Hunt (15).

emotional state. Thus the James-Lange theory failed to find experimental support.

At present the generally accepted theory of emotions is that formulated by Cannon (12).[11] With his collaborators he experimented primarily on animals and thus restricted his realm of observation to behavioral patterns and physiological changes. He and his collaborators found that expressions of certain emotions are displayed, and corresponding physiological changes occur, as long as the hypothalamus is intact, but do not occur after it has been surgically removed. Thus it was established that the hypothalamus plays a significant role in the mediation of expressive movements of, and physiological changes concomitant with, certain emotions. Cannon (12, pp. 361–368) and Bard (17) proceeded to amend their experimental data with the clinical observations of Head (18), Head and Holmes (19), Wilson (20), and others. On the basis of inferences drawn from his experimental data, and from clinical introspective and observational data on patients with thalamic or hypothalamic lesions, Cannon replaced the James-Lange theory by his "hypothalamic theory." He summarized the James-Lange theory as follows:

"Object—sense organ—cortical excitation—perception—reflexes to muscle, skin and viscus—disturbance in them—cortical excitation by these disturbances—perceptions of them added to the original perceptions; such are the occurrences which result in the 'object-emotionally-felt'." (p. 360)

He formulated his own theory in these words:

"Within and near the thalamus the neurones concerned in an emotional expression lie close to the relay in the sensory path from periphery to cortex. We may assume that when these neurones discharge in a particular combination, they not only innervate muscles and viscera but also excite afferent paths to the cortex by direct connection or by irradiation. The theory which naturally presents itself is that *the peculiar quality of the emotion is added to simple sensation when the thalamic processes are roused.*" (p. 369)

These conclusions gained widespread acceptance. The probable reason for this may be glimpsed in Hunt's (24) review of the recent developments in the field of emotions:

"Psychology seems willing to accept and discuss the subjective aspects of emotion, but unwilling to attempt a scientific treatment of them.

"The amusing result is that psychologist, physiologist, and neurologist alike show preference for the objective approach through a study of behavior, neurohumor, or thalamic lesion; yet no sooner do they find some unique aspect of their material than they proudly offer it as the possible basis for the experience of emotion, an experi-

---

[11] Dana (21) had advocated a similar theory earlier. Recently Papez (22, 23) elaborated it.

ence whose existence, uniqueness, and characteristics are still largely a matter of supposition." (p. 264)

This acceptance was uncritical, inasmuch as the idea of one center for such a complicated function as emotion is alien to the present conception of the human organism; it contradicts accepted views that functions are represented on different neural levels and depend on an axis of centers rather than on one center. The hypothalamic theory contrasts strikingly with the accepted view that functions cannot be understood as processes isolated from the total organism.[12]

This acceptance reached an extreme; it became the basis of widespread speculation concerning the role of the hypothalamus in emotional disturbances of human beings. Speculation linking the hypothalamic theory with the Freudian theory of drive and emotions[13] was dealing with two sets of assumptions, a shaky procedure. The following selection from Grinker (27) is a sample of such speculation:

"As a cephalic representative of the autonomic nervous system, the hypothalamus has to do with energies of visceral origin which are the forces of the instincts. It controls activities of the periphery in metabolism, balancing the constructive and destructive tendencies, and it forces activities of the cerebral cortex. It represents tensions or 'cravings' within the autonomic system (instinctual) which are precipitated and coordinated in the hypothalamus rather than expressed individually and incoordinately. . . . Evolutionary development took away from the hypothalamus its dominant role in emotional expression during the process of encephalization. Instinctual cravings become synthesized and formulated in a slower acting more adaptive structure in which the processes of conditioning, or learning by experience, dominate rapid reflex action. To achieve these slower adaptive responses the hypothalamus became subordinated to higher newer cortical centers by inhibitory processes emanating therefrom. The hippocampal-cinguli formation, subserving the conscious sensation of emotion revalued in relation to other cortical functions, also damps down hypothalamic excessive responses and allows only mild peripheral activities to be carried on in economically graded form, avoiding excessiveness.

"However, in turn the hypothalamus influences activity within the cortex or ego. Its drives are synonymous with its demands or necessities of the instincts. This is represented clearly in the hypothalamic influences on the cortex in sleep, wakefulness and consciousness, which represent modulations of drives called emotional." (pp. 44–45)

In disregard of speculations of this sort, careful surveys of the available clinico-pathological data show that the clinical evidence invoked by Cannon and Bard is by no means conclusive. Thus Alpers (28) concludes:

"It would seem from the assemblage of facts . . . that the hypothalamus is now urged as the seat of the emotions, intellect, and personality. No such conclusions

[12] See to this effect: E. B. Newman, F. T. Perkins, and R. H. Wheeler (25).
[13] See Ratliff (26, pp. 700–701).

are possible. The hypothalamus may be regarded as an area concerned with the expression of emotional reactions which are ordinarily sifted and weighed by the cerebral cortex. . . . If one were inclined to drift into fancy, one might even assert that expressions of rage and temper and coarseness of behavior are hypothalamic in origin. The facts, however, do not warrant such an assumption, true though such an assertion may be." (p. 748)[14]

Hunt (24) in his survey writes:

"There can be little doubt that the hypothalamus is one, and an important one, of a series of stations connected with emotional expression. That it is *the center*, however, is still in doubt, and the complexity of the problem of emotional behavior casts serious doubts upon any hopes of an explanation in terms of the functioning of a single center." (p. 267)

An argument similar to Hunt's is advanced by M. Gill (1):

"Since it has been well established that in the 'functional' psychoses and in the psychosomatic diseases there exist rational relationships between the premorbid personality and the disease picture, it seems that hypothalamic lesions cannot be looked upon as the seat of origin of such disturbances."[15]

He also advances the following consideration:

". . . Let us compare the visceral and somatic nervous systems from the point of view under consideration. When the hypothalamus is electrically stimulated certain visceral and somatic manifestations in a seemingly integrated pattern appear. When the motor cortex is electrically stimulated I move my hand. To say that the hypothalamus is the origin of the patterned response in the normal animal would be equivalent to saying that the motor cortex is the central origin of the action of picking up something by hand in a meaningful situation. Obviously such is not the case. The motor cortex is the point at which the effector mechanism may be stimulated. There occur in the intact animal much higher and more complex central processes, the resultant of which is an impulse passing down from the motor cortex. In the same way the hypothalamus is a point at which the effector mechanisms may be stimulated and the response of rage or fear involves much more complex and higher central processes with the resultant as an impulse passing down through the hypothalamus. We shall see . . . that in other respects the hypothalamus can be considered analagous to motor cortex in the sense that both are effector mechanisms."

Experimental results also have been advanced in opposition to the theory of a hypothalamic seat of emotions. Massermann (16) summed up the results of his experiments thus:

"Work in this laboratory has furnished evidence that a direct somatopsychic relationship between hypothalamic function and affective experience probably does not exist, inasmuch as (a) the reactions induced by stimulation of the hypothalamus do not, within limits, greatly modify spontaneous emotional behavior, (b) animals

[14] To the same effect, see Alpers (29).
[15] From an unpublished paper by M. Gill (1).

with extensive hypothalamic lesions react to emotional stresses and can apparently experience genuine affective states, (c) animals subjected to prolonged conditioning procedures in which sensory signals precede direct hypothalamic stimuli do not learn to respond to either the sensory or hypothalamic stimuli in ways analogous to their spontaneous or experimental adaptations to situations of adequate emotional significance." (p. 20)

In addition to these well-known physiological theories of emotion, many others were proposed: the frontal lobe,[16] endocrine,[17] and brain-wave theories[18] are but a few examples.

Another point of historical interest should be discussed. Even prior to the bold but unsuccessful attempt of Cannon to localize "emotion felt" and "emotional expression," the physiological mechanism of "feeling" had aroused much interest and speculation. The problem was frequently formulated as one of ascertaining the nervous correlates of "pleasantness—unpleasantness." M. Meyer's theory (33) was one of the first:

"The nervous correlate of pleasantness and unpleasantness must be *some form of activity in the higher nerve centers.*" It is ". . . *the increase or decrease of the intensity of a previously constant current if the increase or decrease is caused by a force acting at a point other than the point of stimulation.*" (vol. III, p. 54)

F. Allport's (35) theory was that:

"The craniosacral division of the autonomic, supplemented under certain conditions by the cerebrospinal system, innervates those responses whose return afferent impulses are associated with the conscious quality of pleasantness. The sympathetic division produces visceral responses which are represented in consciousness as unpleasantness. . . . We propose that the differentiating factor arises from the stimulation of the proprioceptors in the muscles, tendons, and joints of the somatic part of the organism; and that afferent impulses from these characteristic sensory complexes by which one emotion is distinguished from another of the same affective class." (pp. 90–92)

Troland (34), attributing affective intensity to a change of the conductance at the synapses, wrote:

"This hypothesis can be expressed very concisely by means of the equation,

$$a = kdC/dt$$

which states that the affective intensity, a, at any instant, is proportional (by a constant, k) to the rate of change of the conductance, C, at the same instant. The equation obviously implies that positive values of dC/dt will yield positive values of a, or a pleasantness which is intense in proportion to the magnitude of the time derivative, whereas negative values of the latter will be accompanied by a similarly regulated unpleasantness. In case dC/dt is equal to zero, the affectivity will be

---

[16] See Calkins (30).
[17] See Gray (31).
[18] See Hoagland et al. (32).

indifferent.   The equation therefore automatically covers all of the logical possibilities of the psychophysical situation." (vol. III, p. 257)

These theories were not supported by direct experimental evidence. Nafe's (36) theory, however, was based on experiments.   He obtained introspective reports of pressure sensations and feelings of pleasantness and unpleasantness.   On the basis of the statistical correlation of the scores of these, Nafe did not hesitate to draw a far-reaching *psychological* conclusion:

"Pleasantness is a bright pressure and unpleasantness is a dull pressure."

In other words, both are merely sensory phenomena.   Young's (37) results flatly contradicted those of Nafe, and Young stated that Nafe's results were due to the training of his subjects to make a certain type of report. Hunt (38) considered that he had substantiated Nafe's findings; his conclusions were, however, more cautious in interpreting the correlation he obtained.   He did not assume an identity of pleasantness and unpleasantness with bright and dull pressure, but considered the latter to be an accompaniment of the former.

Our synopsis may have elucidated the state of the physiological portion of the research; now we shall attempt to give a perspective for evaluating the surveyed theories from the psychological point of view.   This perspective may be approached by calling to mind the first of Harlow and Stagner's definitions: "Feelings are fundamental conscious emotional states." Except for the behaviorists who considered consciousness an epiphenomenon, no investigator undertook to ascertain the neural correlates of consciousness or of the contents of consciousness, except of that called "feeling" or "emotion."[19]   The neural correlates or physiological mechanisms of thinking are beyond the scope of our present knowledge.   Only the Gestalt theories of "isomorphism" and of the dynamics of the "trace-field" promise to shed light on the physiological mechanisms of thinking.   This theory, however, does not approach the issue from the physiological viewpoint: it assumes that the psychological and the underlying physiological (electrochemical) processes are isomorphic; and attempts to infer from the characteristics of the psychological events, the nature of the underlying

[19] This statement should be qualified, inasmuch as the neural correlates of memory have been the subject of many speculations; but only recently in Gestalt-psychological experimentation has investigation reached a stage beyond speculation.   The animal experimentation showing the relation of retention and learning to the amount of excised brain tissue cannot be considered an inquiry into the neural mechanisms of learning and memory.

physiological processes, taking cognizance of the known properties of electrochemical processes in general.[20]

Thus the significance of the physiological processes present in emotional states is obscured by the fog which conceals all psychosomatic interrelations. The experimental accumulation of physiological facts, valuable though it is, has not explained how "emotional experience" occurs. For the understanding of "emotion felt" we must look to the literature on the psychology of emotions.

Summary

a. On the basis of the material surveyed, nothing can be definitely stated as to the relation to "emotion felt" of physiological processes concomitant with emotions. Proof has not been offered to show that the usually-described physiological processes are *always* present when emotion is felt.

b. Nothing is known about the physiological processes *underlying* emotional experience. However, sufficient proof has been adduced that neither the James-Lange theory nor the hypothalamic theory explains the origin of "emotion felt."

c. The investigations into the physiology and the neural correlates of emotional expression are of importance; their relation to the psychic process designated as "emotion felt" is the crucial point of every theory of emotions. However, the knowledge concerning this relation is so scant that investigations into the influence of emotions on other psychological processes will have to be based rather on what is known about the psychology of emotions.

3. THE PSYCHOLOGY OF EMOTIONS

The psychological aspect of "emotions" implies the recognition that the concept originally designated a conscious experience. The reluctance of psychology to accept this view is clearly demonstrated in Dunlap's (41) contribution to the "Wittenberg Symposium:"

"I have spoken of objects and occurrences as demonstrable. By that I mean that they are capable of observation in various ways, and in particular by those methods, indirect though they may be, called physical and chemical. We would not be satisfied as to the reality of an apple which could only be seen, not touched, unless the light wave from it could be registered photographically. We would not be satisfied with the reality of a smell, unless chemical tests showed the presence of a stimulus. We would not be satisfied with the reality of movement of an object, an occurrence, unless that movement could be registered. In the same way, we should not be satisfied with any object of experience unless it is capable of physical or chem-

---

[20] See Koehler (39) and Koffka (40).

ical registration. The 'emotions' of which too many psychologists and most physiologists talk are not facts of this kind. Hence, I have no interest whatever in them. The *visceral occurrences* are demonstrable. Hence, when I use the term emotion, I mean these things. This is the final *demonstration*." (p. 153)

Implied here is a reluctance to acknowledge the existence of psychic facts, of the material of introspection as an independent reality. Dunlap took here an extreme stand, but the essence of his attitude is inherent in the way of thinking of a good many psychologists. It is our belief that the solution of the problem of emotions will be found only by psychologists who acknowledge the reality of subjective experience, and who will be resolute enough to explore the dynamics of psychic processes without falling back on physiology at the outset. Are there any such psychologists? Is there such a theory of emotions? To answer these questions we shall attempt to offer a synopsis of the psychological theories of emotions.

A. EARLY THEORIES

The first question should be, What are "feelings"? Some early psychologists assumed that they are elementary, irreducible "mental" processes; some assumed that they are sensations; some assumed that they are attributes of other mental processes. That these assumptions miss the point can be seen in that none explains the genesis of the "feelings," nor takes cognizance of the fact that feelings are conscious experiences differing from all other conscious experiences, and may accompany other mental functions and contents or may appear independently.[21] When the contradictions of these theories proved irreconcilable and none could advance sufficient experimental evidence to rule out the others, the attention of psychologists turned to the genetic theories which had already been developed. The outdated theories were not, however, completely abandoned; they are still upheld in certain textbooks.

The genetic theories received their main impetus from Darwin's (42) theory of emotional expression, which postulated three principles: the principle of "serviceable associated habits"; the principle of "antithesis"; and the principle of the "direct action of the nervous system." The first advances the hypothesis that emotional expressions are phylogenetic rudiments; the other two are but explanatory amendments. These hypotheses were developed into the theory that emotions are inborn patterns, related to the instincts. James (43) was the first to recognize the need to explain the "feeling" aspect of emotions, although he still designated its behavioral aspect as "instinctive." In defending his views against attacks (44)—

---

[21] We avoid for the present taking unconscious factors into consideration; their role will be discussed on p. 30 ff.

particularly against that of Worchester—he abandoned by implication the theory of the instinctive character of emotional behavior. Answering Worchester's question of why the bear in the forest arouses fear while the bear in the cage does not necessarily, James had to admit that not the single stimulus but the *whole situation* determines the arousal of emotional behavior. Thus he recognized this arousal to be an adaptive response, and indirectly dispensed with the theory of the instinctual—non-adaptive—character of emotional reaction. The recognition of the adaptive features of emotions—suggested by James, and later supported by Cannon's contention that the character of the physiological processes present in emotional states is that of preparation for action—led to an emphasis on the teleological aspect of emotions.[22] Nevertheless, the tacit assumption that emotions and instincts are in some way interrelated has remained influential, and finds expression in McDougall's (46) theory:

"There is every reason to believe that even the most purely instinctive action is the outcome of a distinctly mental process, one which is incapable of being described in purely mechanical terms, because it is a psycho-physical process . . . and one which, like every other mental process, has, and can only be fully described in terms of, the three aspects of all mental process—the cognitive, the affective, and the conative aspects; that is to say, every instance of instinctive behavior involves a knowing of something or object, a feeling in regard to it, and a striving towards or away from that object." (p. 27)

"Each of the principal instincts conditions, then, some one kind of emotional excitement whose quality is specific or peculiar to it; and the emotional excitement of specific quality that is the affective aspect of the operation of any one of the principal instincts may be called a primary emotion." (p. 49)

This theory revived also the old theory that emotions are attributes of other psychic processes. Its advantage over the older theories was that it conceived of emotions as attributes of instincts, rather than of intellectual or sensory processes; its drawback was that it offered no theory of instincts or of the mechanism of the instinct-emotion relationship. We need not discuss here the other difficulties and contradictions of McDougall's theory; but we wish to point out that McDougall was able to describe only the so-called "primary emotions" as aspects of instincts, and explained the complex emotions as expressions of conflicting instincts. Here we encounter for the first time in our discussion another element in the recent psychological theories of emotions, that of the "conflict"; but before entering upon a discussion of it, we must consider another important aspect of McDougall's theory.

[22] See Nahm's (45) paper advocating a teleological theory, and the critical discussion of it by Weber and Rapaport (13) which advances an anti-teleological point of view.

B. THE ENERGY THEORY

McDougall originated the view connecting emotions and "conation," which led to the intimate connecting of emotions and motivation in present day psychology. Similar, but more extreme and explicit, were M. Prince's (47) views; he identified emotion with mental energy, the driving force of mental life:

"If, for instance, it is energy . . . then plainly it needs no argument to show that it does not play the role of 'passive sensory receptions' of visceral functions . . . as the James-Lange theory holds, but its discharge must of itself determine behavior of *some* kind.

"Likewise, again, in the interpretation of behavior as response to a stimulus, emotion, if energy, cannot be regarded as an epiphenomenon correlated with neural reflexes, as behaviorists would have us believe, but must be a factor in the neural discharges affecting motor and other responses, whether it be only by exploding or releasing those discharges or providing the energy for them.

"Nor, in the responses of those innate inherited mechanisms characterized by emotion—call them instincts or not, as you please—can emotion, if energy, play the passive part of an epiphenomenon; it must *do* something; and it is logical to infer that, as a discharge of energy, it provides the drive for the response of the mechanism to the stimulus." (pp. 161–162)

"It is not necessary for me to point out how this conception is in line with McDougall's theory of instincts so far as they are 'prime movers of human activity.' Unless emotion and feeling are energy his theory would, it seems to me, have little weight." (p. 168)

The influence of this type of theory on the laity is exemplified by Carroll's (48) popularizations:

"The emotions are the most powerful, most far-reaching of all the driving forces of human conduct. We like to think that we are governed by pure, cold logic, but there is little that we do that is not tinged with some emotion or feeling." (Preface)

The tenor of Lund's (49) popularly-written book is similar. This attempt to identify emotion with psychic energy found no followers; but, as we shall see later, it had some influence on the further development of theories of emotion.

C. THE CONFLICT THEORY

McDougall derived what he called "secondary emotions" from conflicts of instincts. The first clear-cut conflict-theory of emotions in general psychological literature was advanced by Dewey (50), and advocated by Angier (51). Dewey wrote:

"Confronted by a situation to which it is wholly pertinent the attitude goes over at once into adaptive activity; confronted by a situation to which it is not completely pertinent it is held in suspense and stands out qua attitude.

". . . while some features of the situation evoke appropriate reactions, others do not; the total attitude cannot, therefore, go over without remainder into acts that are useful but is at least partially aborted. There is, consequently, tension, or conflict, within the attitude or, if one will, conflict among the diverse reactions incipiently or overtly issuing from it.

". . . If this be so, then uninhibited activity, however vigorous, is unemotional. . . . The animal or our ancestor so far as it was given up without restraint to the full activity undoubtedly had a feeling of activity; but just because the activity was undivided, it was not 'emotion.' " (II. pp. 26 ff.)

Theories similar to Dewey's were developed by J. R. Kantor (52) and Drever (53); under their influence Bernard (54) wrote:

"Emotions are not the fixed or inherited conscious correlates of the instincts, as McDougall has supposed. They are, in part, conscious correlates of the modified processes which arise . . . resulting from *interruption or inhibition of dominant neural and activity processes*. . . . Thus emotion is seen to belong rather to the field of acquired than of inherited neuropsychic organization . . . Emotions . . . indicate *inhibition or delay or modification of action* instead of being the correlates of uninterrupted activity. Emotion is not the cause of activity, as is so frequently assumed, but one method of evaluating the suspended or inhibited activity for the organism or society." (pp. 505 ff.)

The influence of the conflict-theory is apparent in many recent descriptions of emotions in their strong emphasis on the disruptive character of emotional states. We quote examples of such descriptions. In Boring's (55) handbook we read:

"Thus it seems that emotion can best be characterized as a *relationship existing between many diverse elements of experience and reaction*. This relationship is not well specified, but, generally speaking, it is marked by pleasantness or unpleasantness and by disorganization of usually integrated behavior patterns. An emotion is the total of the experiences of an individual during any period of time when marked bodily changes of feeling, surprise or upset occur." (p. 184)

Murphy (56) writes:

"Emotions, in so far as they can be distinguished from motives at all, can probably be differentiated in terms of upheaval . . ." (p. 65)

Darrow (57) suggests:

". . . Such threats to basic patterns of thought and behavior whether for good or ill are guaranteed attention and demand action because they are to the individual the most important events in the world. They must, we believe, be the occasions of an active or *dynamic* intra-cortical conflict . . . In other words, excited emotion may arise from a partial or relative *functional decortication* occasioned by dynamic cortical conflict." (p. 571 ff.)

Whitehorn (58) defines emotions thus:

"The primary focus of attention in this discussion of emotion is 'the acute emotional experience,' by which I mean to designate a biological condition, characterized subjectively as an excited, tense feeling with considerable tendency to act, but with some uncertainty as to what to do, and characterized objectively by motor restlessness or activity, not smoothly patterned, with indications of excess effort, as shown in the facial and respiratory musculature, tremor of voice and of skeletomuscular action, together with sudden changes in visceral activity. This definition will not satisfy all, I am sure. But it does describe a phenomenon which we may all recognize in ourselves and in others, and it is this phenomenon which is here designated the acute emotional experience.

"This experience is found, in general, to be unpleasant, and those who experience it in intense degree, may well wonder what is the use of such a thing. It is confusing, disorienting, disruptive of the smooth, habitual, integrative modes of behavior—apparently most unphysiological. Yet, when viewed in a longer time span, we may note, not infrequently, that such experiences have been followed by significant improvement in the adjustment to life.

"I would postulate, for these and other reasons, that the acute emotional experience has, as its biological function, the precipitation of an internal crisis, in which habit is interrupted and the more raw or primitive facilities for biological adjustment are summoned up—not merely sugar for energy production and hastened circulation for increased oxygen use, but also the neural capacities of the organism for forming new associations between reaction and situation and for reorganizing behavior. These latter are the resources which we recognize as intelligence—the capacity for modifying reaction by experience—a capacity which might lie latent and unused if not activated by an emotional experience." (p. 260)

But Whitehorn does not fail to emphasize the teleological adaptive features of emotions:

"The medical profession has a tendency to look upon emotion as morbid . . . Emotion does have a tremendous physiological power—but it is a power for good, as well as for evil." (p. 256)

A definition which implies the conflict theory and an energy theory somewhat more cautious than Prince's, is that formulated by another psychiatrist, McKinney (59). This definition follows Spinoza's approach:

" 'By emotion (affectus) I understand the modification of energy (difference of potential) of the body by which the power in action of the body is aided or restrained, increased or diminished, and that this difference of potential may be expressed both psychically and physiologically and that this energy so expressed is the same in kind though differing in organization from that found elsewhere in the universe.' " (p. 64)

Among the three definitions quoted in Section (1) of this chapter, only Harlow and Stagner's took cognizance of the conflict-theory.

D. CRITICAL SYNOPSIS

Most of the theories surveyed here were the result of speculations aimed at fulfilling the systemic needs of certain trends of psychological thinking, or at incorporating certain impressions into a preconceived theoretical framework. Here we sum up the general ideas, the theoretical crystallization of which was attempted in these theories:

a. That an adequate theory of emotions should be able to account for the physiological phenomena concomitant with emotions.

b. That emotions are intimately related to instincts, inasmuch as they have the character of an inherited pattern; even "emotion felt" was considered to be the conscious affective aspect of an instinct.

c. That emotions are "preparations for an emergency"; the concomitant physiological changes appear to prepare the organism for a greater energy exertion, and "emotion felt" as well as "emotional behavior" are adaptive rather than rigid.

d. That emotions are equivalent to psychic energy or to the forces underlying motivation.

e. That the disorganizing character of emotional states is related to, and may be an expression of, conflict.

This sequence of hypotheses shows a tendency toward more dynamic theories; this tendency becomes especially clear when one considers the early static theories, such as the sensory, the mental element, and the attributive theories preceding those summarized here. The basic scheme of all dynamics was, with increasing consistency, applied to the explanation of the function of emotions. This scheme may be described as follows: an energy-distribution finds its expression in the form of forces which either are in equilibrium or result in changes characteristic of the energy-distribution in question; restraint of these forces results in effects other than these characteristic changes, and these may be called "modifications."

Yet in spite of this development, a dynamic solution of the problem of emotions has not been reached. One reason may be that the psychic forces are still obscure entities: such factors as motivating forces and desires are often still conceived teleologically, instead of being analyzed causally. The nature of the difficulty in developing a theory of emotions related to the dynamics underlying psychic life may become clearer if we consider another approach to the problem, one which utterly disregards the underlying dynamics. This approach is exemplified by Young's definition of emotions[23] according to which emotional states are of external origin, as distinguished from appetitive drives, aches, and pains, which are of internal origin. Similar is Woodworth's (60) argument, which like Young's disregards "emotion felt":

"Now that physiology has revealed a peculiar organic state in fear and anger, why do we continue to call them emotions and deny that name to fatigue or drowsiness? It is hard to find a valid distinction, unless it be that the typical emotion is aroused by external stimuli and is directed toward the environment, whereas a state of the organism, such as hunger or fatigue, originates in intraorganic processes and has no direct relation to the environment." (p. 234)

But is it true that "emotions" are of external origin, and "directed toward the environment"? Are sudden unexplained anxieties, to which so-called "normals" and psychiatric patients are equally subject, of external origin, and directed outward? Are not the emotions and their central phenomenon, "emotion felt," internal rather than external in origin? Actually, the terms "internal" and "external" are, in this context, ambiguous. If "external" means that the emotions are invariably evoked by an external stimulus, then they are justifiably called "external"; but then so is hunger, for the lack of food is as much an external stimulus as the stimuli which evoke emotion. Conversely, both hunger and emotions are equally internal in origin in that both are conscious manifestations of psychic dynamics. The assumption in formulations like Woodworth's—that the specific difference between organic states and emotions lies in the evocation of emotions by external stimuli—probably resulted from the fact that while the dynamics underlying hunger appear obvious in the lack of food-intake, the dynamics underlying emotions are unconscious. This fact of unconscious dynamics has been, in the main, disregarded by experimental psychologists; this is probably a paramount reason that the dynamic theory of emotion has remained inconsistent.

E. THE PSYCHOANALYTIC THEORY OF EMOTIONS

This unconscious determination of affects was explored by psychoanalysis. The Freudian concept of affects is not an unequivocal one. In Freud's early writings,[24] and in the early psychoanalytical literature in general,[25] the concept of affect is similar to that advanced by Prince: affects are considered as *a* form or *the* form of psychic energy. Yet it would be erroneous to consider this the definitive Freudian concept of affects. A lack of conceptual crystallization in early psychoanalytic writings resulted in frequent mention of "affective tone,"[26] as though affect were assumed to be a mere attribute of other psychic contents. A tendency to adopt a conflict theory also appears to be indicated in Freud's early statement that "affects are inherited hysterical attacks,"[27] inasmuch as these attacks are

---

[24] See: 61, p. 30, and 62, p. 64.
[25] See K. Landauer (63).
[26] See 61, vol. I, p. 31.
[27] In "The Problem of Anxiety" (64):
"I believe I was not wrong in regarding these [affective] states as the equivalents of hysterical attacks developed later and individually, and in considering the former as the normal prototypes of the latter." (p. 23)

results of conflicts and their expression of an unconscious idea through the body shows a striking similarity to emotional expression. The new element implied here is that the conflict underlying both hysterical attacks and emotions is *unconscious*. This idea was further elaborated in "The Interpretation of Dreams" (65):

"We here take as our basis a quite definite assumption as to the nature of the development of affect. This is regarded as a motor or secretory function, the key to the innervation of which is to be found in the ideas of the Ucs." (p. 521)

In the later essay on "The Unconscious" (66) we read:

"The whole difference arises from the fact that ideas are cathexes—ultimately of memory traces—whilst affects and emotions correspond with processes of discharge, the final expression of which is perceived as feeling. In the present state of our knowledge of affects and emotions we cannot express this difference more clearly." (p. 111)

Thus, affects regulated from the unconscious are defined as discharge processes of energies of instinctual origin.

It will be worthwhile to consider at this point the differences between the view that affects are energies and the view that affects are discharge processes of energies. Let us take a physical example. The kinetic energy of a gas manifests itself in a pressure which may result in the expansion of an elastic container or in the discharge of part of the gas through a vent, or which may be only indicated in a reading on a manometer. Physicists do not regard these manifestations or discharge-processes as being kinetic energy any more than they regard a falling stone as being gravitation. Apparently this stage of conceptual development has not yet been reached in psychology. Sherrington and many later investigators saw the problem of emotions as one of sequence: that is, whether the *feeling* or the *expression*[28] of emotions was prior in time, or whether they were simultaneous. The answer, it was considered, settled the problem of causation. If the physiological processes precede the psychological, then "emotion felt" is only their "cortical reverberation"; if "emotion felt" precedes, then the feeling "elicits" the bodily changes. This theoretical approach has not sufficiently explored the possibility that both "emotion felt" and physiological changes concomitant with emotions may be manifestations of a common variable. This shortcoming also may probably be attributed to the fact that in the final analysis the dynamics of psychic manifestations are *unconscious*, and cannot be found by investigating interrelations of the data of physiology and the data of consciousness.

The Freudian theory of emotions states explicitly that the "key to the

---

[28] "Expression" implies here motor as well as physiological changes.

innervation ... of the emotions ... is to be found in the ideas of the unconscious." Whether emotions are psychic energies or discharge processes of such energies has not been stated with like unequivocalness. In the course of the development of Freudian theory, it became clear that the psychic energies called "libido" or "interest" are of instinctual origin:

". . . an instinct-presentation, and by that we understood an idea or group of ideas which is cathected with a definite amount of the mental energy (libido, interest) pertaining to an instinct." (67, p. 91)

It also became clear that affects are *one* representation of these energies, and that the (unconscious) ideas are another:

"We have adopted the term *charge of affect* for this other element in the mental presentation; it represents that part of the instinct which has become detached from the idea, and finds proportionate expression, according to its quantity, in processes which become observable to perception as affects." (67, p. 91)

The role of the unconscious in the emotional process was emphasized by the psychoanalyst Kulovesi (68) in his discussion of the James-Lange theory:

"James states that between perception and emotion there lies the bodily expression; we must object to this, since between the perception and the bodily expression unconscious psychic complexes become active. These psychic complexes are mobilized when the perception touches upon an object that is in associative connection with the complex." (p. 393)

The psychoanalytic theory of emotions need not assume that the sequence of events in the development of an emotion is: perception—unconscious process—bodily process—"emotion felt." In a psychoanalytic theory of emotions, the unconscious process elicited by the percept may be followed in any sequence by the bodily process or by the "emotion felt," or by only one of these, or by neither; for both are conceived of as manifestations of the same psychic process.[29]

The lack of agreement as to whether emotions are discharge-processes or energies is exemplified in Brierly's (69) recent paper. This author came to conclusions contrary to Freud's; she maintains that her findings "contradict the idea that affect is itself a discharge and support the view that it is a tension-phenomenon impelling to discharge either in the outer or the inner world" (p. 259). The question of what are the discharge processes of the tension phenomena with which she identifies the affects is not an-

[29] The relation between "emotional behavior" and "emotion felt" becomes clearer if we keep in mind a theory stated by Freud in the "Two Principles of Mental Functioning" (72). Here he maintained that thinking is experimenting at action with small amounts of energy; so are conscious processes in general, and so is "emotion felt."

swered; in the same article, however, we read a definition of "affects" which is in harmony with Freud's point of view as represented on these pages, and which characterizes affects as an "index to the fate of the impulse":

"Affect, as inferred from its expression and behavior, can be aroused by internal conditions or by external happenings. It is influenced both by internal need and by the nature of the response from the outer world with which this need is met. The affect manifested is, in fact, the index to the fate of the impulse and to the nature of the beginning psychic object-formation." (p. 262)

This view of Brierly coincides with Freud's view of the nature of pleasantness and unpleasantness. Pleasantness is described by Freud (70) and by G. Jelgersma (71) as the experience of decreasing tension, and unpleasantness as the experience of increasing tension. Both Freud and Jelgersma resisted the temptation to enter into physiological speculations as to the nature of this tension—a temptation to which the general psychologist has often succumbed. Thus, pleasantness-unpleasantness, is described by them as the conscious manifestation—discharge into consciousness—of decreasing or increasing tension.[30]

In the recent development of the psychoanalytic theory of emotions the conflict theory has remained a mere implication; only in Federn's (73, 74) theory of affects did it become explicit. Concerning the origin of these, Federn states:

"Affects, like object-interests, issue from the relation of the ego to something that stimulates it; in the object-interests the ego enters into relationship with a libido-cathexed[31] object, in the affects with a libido cathexed process within the ego itself. . . . Affects come about between two interacting ego boundaries[32] and differ according to the kind of drive-cathexis of the ego on these boundaries . . . e.g. the affect of shame comes about when an anxiety-charged ego boundary interacts with a sexually, especially exhibitionistically, cathexed ego boundary. Sorrow comes about when an object-libido cathexed ego boundary interacts with one cathexed by destructive drives." (74, pp. 13–15)

Thus, according to Federn, when two different drive-cathexes confront each other, in other words conflict, affects result.

[30] It is important to stress this because general psychological theory as well as psychoanalytic theory disregards "pleasant emotions" and deals usually only with the unpleasant.

[31] The term "cathexis" in psychoanalytic theory refers to an amount of psychic energy attached to the ideas of a person.

[32] "Ego boundaries" is a term coined by Federn (73) to designate a division of psychic contents into those representing the "ego" and those representing the rest of the world. This concept of the ego is not the usual one, but we cannot discuss it here in further detail.

We have seen thus far that, according to the psychoanalytic theory, the psychic processes underlying emotions are unconscious; that affects were at one time considered as psychic energies by this theory, but were later viewed as discharge processes of psychic energies; and finally, that affects were viewed as expressions of instinctual conflict.

One may ask why the conflict-origin and the discharge-character of affects are not accepted more widely, for they would seem to agree with the general dynamic conceptions of our science and with the majority of observations. One reason that they are not so accepted—namely, the unconscious character of the conflict—has been already discussed; another reason may lie in the social-patterning, or conventionalization, of emotions. Concerning this Whitehorn (58) wrote:

"For a good many years I have been interested in listening to patients' accounts of their emotions. At one time I naïvely supposed that I might learn thereby just how the patient was feeling, perhaps even be able to label 'the emotions' which he was experiencing. I still listen with great interest to patient's statements along these lines, but not with the expectation of discovering what 'emotions' he or she is really experiencing—rather with the hope of understanding in some measure the conventionalized scheme of symbols by which the patient tries to represent himself to himself and to others. Not only are the words conventional symbols; the motor patterns of behavior are also conventionalized. Sometimes such conventionalized patterns of behavior and the corresponding verbalizations are used with the deliberate intention of deceiving others, but this is not the phenomenon of which I now speak. I refer to the degree of conventionality in the patterning of behavior by which one reacts overtly in an emotional experience. My own observations would lead me to believe that in ordinary living these modes of behavior commonly called 'the emotions' are the modes of reaction by which one *resolves*, and in effect, *escapes from* the essential emotionality of the experience. That is to say, 'the emotions' as we know of them empirically in the clinic and in ordinary life, are the expression of sentiments in whose development there has been a large measure of cultural or conventional training." (p. 263)

According to Whitehorn's observations, emotional manifestations apparently become controlled and patterned under the pressure of conventions. Brierley's (69) view that emotions are "tension phenomena" rather than "discharge phenomena" becomes more understandable here, for conventionalization of emotions tends not to allow discharge of them but rather to dam them up. Landauer's conclusion (75), based on psychoanalytic observations, may contribute to the understanding of this mechanism. According to him, affects which are originally time-restricted and attack-like become continuous, because their release is effected by the constant stimulation of the super-ego.[33] He derived this conclusion from

[33] He writes:
"Are the affects really reactions? In children we still see them as such. But in later life anxiety is apparently continuous in the anxious-minded, the pessimist is

studies on anxiety,[34] and maintained that this conventional "patterning" or "secondary release by the super-ego" of the affect, creates a hierarchy of affects ranging from the free and untamed to the intellectualized and "patterned." It appears that all psychic activity is accompanied by an emotional discharge of a varying degree of conventionalization.

F. MACCURDY'S THEORY

The main tenets of the early psychoanalytic theory of emotions were independently extended by the psychiatrist MacCurdy (77), who wrote:

"A given stimulus, if it be productive of emotion, does not merely arouse conscious perceptions and overt behaviour but activates unconscious mental processes as well." (p. 86)

MacCurdy recognized the close relationship of instincts and emotions, and the presence of both physiological changes and feeling-tone in emotions; he designated the latter as *affect*. He emphasized the inevitably conscious character of the affects and their availability solely to introspection. His theory embracing these tenets is summarized in the following statement:

"If the organism responds to a stimulus immediately and adequately with instinctive behaviour no emotion whatever is engendered. If the instinctive reaction be held up, emotional expression and, if the subject be self-conscious, some affect as well, will appear. The latter represents the activity which is not expressed overtly in any way. Therefore, if the inner tendency to activity be regarded as a constant, the urgency of the affect will be reduced not merely by instinctive behaviour but also by emotional expression. The third stage is, then, one in which affect alone appears, which is as poignant as the emotion is purely subjective." (pp. 87–88)

This advanced conflict theory of emotions, built on a rich collection of psychiatric observations, was overlooked in the pertinent literature. Its terminology, which uses "affect" for conscious experience and "emotion" for the "objective" manifestations, may well serve as a basis for a new terminology.

---

permanently melancholy and the cheerful man consistently buoyant. How does an isolated reaction become a continuous state? Freud has solved this problem in the theory of the affects by demonstrating the function of the super-ego in their release. He illustrated his remarks chiefly from the example of anxiety." (p. 389)
"In his more recent writings he [Freud] has only added two further basic notions to this general theory of the affects. In the first place he states that moods and feelings are constantly repeated reactions to the stimuli constantly applied by the super-ego. Hence the affective process, originally restricted in time, becomes more or less continuous. His second important thesis is that an affective attack is an inherited hysterical attack . . ." (p. 407)
[34] See also Freud, S. (64) and (76).

G. THE WORK OF DEMBO

Dembo (78), a pupil of Lewin, followed the path of experimentation. She was not interested in establishing the nature of the genesis of emotions, or of their relation to instincts, or of the relation of emotion felt to emotional expression. Her purpose was to investigate the "field-conditions" under which emotions occur, and the changes in the "field-conditions" brought about by the occurrence of emotions. In the experimental situation the subject was confronted with an insolvable problem; the resulting frustration and conflict issued in emotions observed and introspectively reported. According to Dembo, the experimentally created emotion of "anger" resulted in a disorganization of the life-space, culminating in the subject's escape from the situation, or in random activities, or in a phenomenal regression to a lower level of activity.[35]   These experiments appear to corroborate the conflict-theory of emotions, and may be interpreted as indicating that conflict which arouses emotions results in a disorganization of the life space and of the behavior.

H. SUMMARY

a. The material surveyed here suggests that the *phenomenon* "emotion" is primarily a conscious experience, and that its understanding can be achieved only by developing an autonomous theory of psychic dynamics rather than by investigating its physiology.

b. It has been found that neither the mechanistic theories nor the energy, instinct, or conflict theories established the *dynamics underlying emotions,* because they failed to assume that these dynamics are unconscious.

c. On the basis of the psychoanalytic theory, which takes into consideration the unconscious dynamics underlying emotions, James's theory has been modified in three respects.   (a) It is assumed that an unconscious process occurs between the perception of the stimulus evoking emotion and the peripheral physiological process.   (b) The peripheral physiological process and the "emotion felt" are assumed to be discharge-processes of the same instinctual source of energy; thus either may succeed the other, or they may be simultaneous, or either may be absent.   (c) The emotions are assumed to be expressions of instinctual conflict.

d. A new terminology may be based on MacCurdy's suggestion that the subjective experience of emotions be called "affect" and the objective manifestations "emotions."

4. THE ROLE OF EMOTIONS

The background to our investigation of the role of emotions in memory-functioning may be sketched by surveying three recent investigations into

[35] See also Dembo, Barker, and Lewin (79).

the role of emotions in other processes. The three investigations were those of Dunbar (80) on "Emotions and Bodily Changes," of Prescott (81) on "Emotions and the Educative Process," and of Zachry (82) on "Emotion and Conduct in Adolescence." Of these, only Prescott attempted to bring his conception of emotions into relation to the general psychological theory of emotions. Prescott came to the same conclusion as our survey of the literature of emotions, that in the present state of knowledge the problem of emotional influence cannot be solved by investigating the concomitant physiological processes. He presented the classical theories of emotions, and commented:

"So little is known definitely that little needs to be said about the physiological relationships between learning and emotion. Lashley indicates something strikingly similar to the production of critical physiological gradients in brain areas as the basis for modifications in behavior. Chapter III of this report sets up the hypothesis that when such gradients pass certain critical slopes, emotional behavior ensues. The implication is that the relationship between emotion and learning may be very direct, because both may be phenomena involving the altering of gradients or of 'ratios of intensity,' as Lashley puts it. However, when all the research studies have been digested, we still know extremely little about the actual role of affective factors in various types of learning." (p. 161)

Also important is the conclusion Prescott drew from the survey of material on the psychology of emotions:

"The important point, perhaps, is that *a continuum of affective experience exists, varying from vague feelings of pleasantness or unpleasantness up to profound experiences which greatly disturb both mental and physical functions.* At various critical points in this continuum adaptive modifications of the body economy occur, varying according to the functional demands of the situation. It is essential to distinguish the level of affective experience involved when discussing the reactive phenomena characteristic of the state or when considering the influence of the affect upon learning, upon the higher mental processes, or upon behavior." (p. 30)

The importance of this conclusion for our survey lies in the fact that at every step we shall encounter in our material the different "levels" of the "continuum of affective experiences" of which Prescott speaks, and memory phenomena characteristic of each of these levels.

Yet Prescott fails to clarify what he means by emotions, and allows the concept to shade imperceptibly into that of "personality needs" and "motivation"; and his survey becomes a survey of the influence of these factors in education. This view is shared by Zachry, who states it explicitly:

". . . emotion as understood in the writing of this book is intrinsic to every experience, is a factor in all conduct. Emotion thus broadly conceived is fused with thinking—for the most part harmoniously—in the healthy, competent individual." (p. 5)
"Nevertheless it has been taken for granted in the past, and to a large extent

still is assumed, that the mind both could and should be trained as a thing in itself, with little reference to the *motives* or *purposes*[36] of the student. It has been thought that, properly trained, the mind not only would serve to equip the individual for intellectual activity but would steer him through life as a useful citizen. . . . This part of the school's task (plus some attention to training of the body) has received its chief attention. It has been assumed that by such means almost alone it was carrying out its duty, to foster social development, and attention to emotional adjustments has been held to be secondary in importance." (p. 4)

These concepts of emotion are extremely broad, and equally so is Dunbar's. Although she does not state explicitly any theory of emotion, a careful reading of the work makes it clear that she classifies all the psychogenic, or functional, bodily disturbances as of emotional origin.

In our survey we shall not adhere to any specific theory of emotions, but the dynamic theory whose gradual development has been outlined in this chapter will underlie the survey. We shall investigate all memory phenomena which it has been or may be claimed are of emotional origin. We believe that such a systematization may clarify not only the relation of emotion to memory, but some of the problems of emotions also.

5. CONCLUSIONS

a. The concept emotion is currently used to designate—in addition to "emotion proper"—bodily changes of psychogenic origin, disturbances of behavior, problems of education of a non-intellective nature, and so on. It has been suggested that instead of lumping many diverse phenomena under the heading "emotions," emotional *phenomena* and their underlying dynamics should be carefully kept apart and momentary manifestations of emotions differentiated from chronic.

b. The physiological changes occurring in emotional states have been extensively dealt with in the literature, but the problem of "emotion felt" has been somewhat neglected. It has been suggested that in the present state of knowledge the problems of emotion cannot be solved by a physiological approach only, and that the interrelation between emotion felt and concomitant physiological changes has by no means been clarified. The relevance of the hypothalamic theory to this problem has been prematurely assumed and over-estimated.

c. We have surveyed the theories maintaining that "emotion felt" is variously an attribute of other psychic processes, a sensory experience, psychic energy, the conscious aspect of instincts, or the result of an instinctual conflict. It was suggested that a synthesis of these views is possible, provided that the conflict which gives rise to emotions is assumed to be instinctual and unconscious.

[36] Italics mine.—D. R.

d. Of the various theories, the following theory of the mechanism of emotions emerges as not conflicting with known facts: an incoming percept initiates an unconscious process which mobilizes unconscious instinctual energies; if no free pathway of activity is open for these energies—and this is the case when instinctual demands conflict—they find discharge through channels other than voluntary motility; these discharge-processes—"emotional expression," and "emotion felt"—may occur simultaneously or may succeed one another, or either may occur alone; as in our culture open pathways for instincts are rare, emotional discharges of varying intensity constantly occur; thus in our psychic life, besides the "genuine" emotions described in textbooks—rage, fear, and so on—an entire hierarchy of emotions exists, ranging from the most intense to mild, conventionalized, intellectualized emotions.

REFERENCES

(1) GILL, M. Psychosomatic medicine and the hypothalamus. Unpublished paper. 16 pp., 1941.

(2) GARDINER, H. M., METCALF, R. C., AND BEEBE-CENTER, J. G. *Feeling and emotion. A history of theories.* 445 pp. New York, Amer. Book, 1937.

(3) BEEBE-CENTER, J. G. *The psychology of pleasantness and unpleasantness.* 427 pp. New York, Nostrand, 1932.

(4) LUND, F. H. *Emotions: their psychological, physiological, and educative implications.* 305 pp. New York, Ronald, 1939.

(5) RUCKMICK, C. A. *The psychology of feeling and emotion.* 529 pp. New York, McGraw-Hill, 1936.

(6) HARLOW, H. F., AND STAGNER, R. Psychology of feelings and emotions. I. Theory of feelings. *Psychol. Rev.* 39: 570–589, 1932. II. Theory of emotions. *Psychol. Rev.* 40: 184–195, 1933.

(7) REYMERT, M. L. (ed.). *Feelings and emotions; The Wittenberg symposium.* 454 pp. Worcester, Mass., Clark Univ. P., 1928.

(8) WASHBURN, M. F. Feeling and emotion. *Psychol. Bull.* 24: 573–595, 1927.

(9) YOUNG, P. T. By what criteria can emotion be defined? Abstract of paper delivered at the 1941 Meetings of the Midwestern Psychological Assn. *Psychol. Bull.* 38: 713, 1941.

(10) SHERRINGTON, C. S. *The integrative action of the nervous system.* 411 pp. New York, Scribner, 1906.

(11) JAMES, W. *The principles of psychology.* Vol. I, 689 pp.; vol. II, 704 pp. New York, Holt, 1890.

(12) CANNON, W. B. *Bodily changes in pain, hunger, fear, and rage.* 404 pp. New York, Appleton, 2nd ed., 1929.

(13) WEBER, A. O., AND RAPAPORT, D. Teleology and the emotions. *Phil. Sci.* 8: 69–82, 1941.

(14) ANGELL, J. R. A reconsideration of James's theory of emotion in the light of recent criticisms. *Psychol. Rev.* 23: 251–261, 1916.

(15) CANTRIL, H., AND HUNT, W. A. Emotional effects produced by the injection of adrenalin. *Amer. J. Psychol.* 44: 300–307, 1932.

(16) MASSERMANN, J. H. Is the hypothalamus a center of emotion? *Psychosom. Med.* 3: 3–25, 1941.

(17) BARD, P. The neuro-humoral basis of emotional reactions. Pp. 264–311. In: *Handbook of general experimental psychology.* Worcester, Clark Univ. P., 1934.

(18) HEAD, H. *Studies in neurology.* Vol. I, 329 pp.; vol. II, 862 pp. London, Frowde, 1920.

(19) HEAD, H., AND HOLMES, G. Sensory disturbances from cerebral lesions. Pp. 102–254. A case of lesion of the optic thalamus with autopsy. Pp. 255–271. *Brain,* v, 34, 1894.

(20) WILSON, C. A. K. Pathological laughing and crying. *J. Neurol. Psychopath.* 4: 299–333, 1924.

(21) DANA, C. L. The anatomic seat of the emotions: a discussion of the James-Lange theory. *Arch. Neurol. Psychiat.* 6: 634–639, 1921.

(22) PAPEZ, J. W. A proposed mechanism of emotion. *Arch. Neurol. Psychiat.* 38: 725–743, 1937.

(23) PAPEZ, J. W. Cerebral mechanisms. *J. Nerv. Ment. Dis.* 89: 145–159, 1939.

(24) HUNT, W. A. Recent developments in the field of emotion. *Psychol. Bull.* 38: 249–276, 1941.

(25) NEWMAN, E. B., PERKINS, F. T., AND WHEELER, R. H. Cannon's theory of emotions: a critique. *Psychol. Rev.* 37: 305–326, 1930.

(26) RATLIFF, M. M. The varying function of affectively toned olfactory, visual, and auditory cues in recall. *Amer. J. Psychol.* 51: 695–701, 1938.

(27) GRINKER, R. R. Hypothalamic functions in psychosomatic interrelations. *Psychosom. Med.* 1: 19–47, 1939.

(28) ALPERS, B. J. Personality and emotional disorders associated with hypothalamic lesions. Pp. 725–752. In: *The hypothalamus.* Ed. Fulton, J. F., Ranson, S. W., and Frantz, A. M. Baltimore, Williams & Wilkins, 20, 1940.

(29) ALPERS, B. J. Personality and emotional disorders with hypothalamic lesions—A review. *Psychosom. Med.* 2: 286–303, 1940.

(30) CALKINS, M. W. *A first book in psychology.* 428 pp. New York, Macmillan, 4th ed., 1914.

(31) GRAY, S. J. An objective theory of emotion. *Psychol. Rev.* 42: 108–116, 1935.

(32) HOAGLAND, H., CAMERON, D. E., RUBIN, M. A., AND TEGELBERG, J. J. Emotion in man as tested by the delta index of the encephalogram: I. *J. Genet. Psychol.* 19: 227–245, 1938. II. Simultaneous records from cortex and from a region near the hypothalamus. *J. Genet. Psychol.* 19: 247–261, 1938.

(33) MEYER, M. The nervous correlate of pleasantness and unpleasantness. *Psychol. Rev.* 15: 201–216, 1908.

(34) TROLAND, L. T. *The principles of psychophysiology.* I: 429 pp. II: 397 pp. III: 446 pp. New York, Nostrand, 1929.

(35) ALLPORT, F. A physiological-genetic theory of feeling and emotion. *Psychol. Rev.* 29: 132–139, 1922.

(36) NAFE, J. P. The psychology of felt experience. *Amer. J. Psychol.* 39: 367–389, 1927.

(37) YOUNG, P. T. Studies in affective psychology. *Amer. J. Psychol.* 38: 157–193, 1927.

(38) HUNT, A. W. The relation of bright and dull pressure to affectivity. *Amer. J. Psychol.* 43: 87–92, 1931.

(39) KOEHLER, W. Zur Theorie des Suksessivvergleichs und der Zeitfehler. *Psychol. Forsch.* 4: 115–175, 1923.

THE PROBLEM OF EMOTIONS

(40) KOFFKA, K. *Principles of Gestalt psychology.* 720 pp. New York, Harcourt, 1935.

(41) DUNLAP, K. Emotion as a dynamic background. Pp. 150–160. In: *Feelings and emotions: The Wittenberg Symposium.* 454 pp. Ed. Reymert, M. L., Worcester, Mass., Clark Univ. P., 1928.

(42) DARWIN, C. *Expression of the emotions.* 397 pp. London, Murray, 1904.

(43) JAMES, W., AND LANGE, F. *The emotions.* 135 pp. Baltimore, Williams & Wilkins, 1922.

(44) JAMES, W. The physical basis of emotions. *Psychol. Rev.* 1: 516–609, 1911.

(45) NAHM, M. C. The philosophical implications of some theories of emotion. *Phil. Sci.* 6: 458–486, 1939.

(46) McDOUGALL, W. *An introduction to social psychology.* 418 pp. Boston, Luce, 1921.

(47) PRINCE, M. Can emotion be regarded as energy? Pp. 161–169. In: *Feelings and emotions, The Wittenberg Symposium.* 454 pp. Ed. Reymert, M. L., Worcester, Mass., Clark Univ. P., 1928.

(48) CARROLL, R. P. *The emotions, their nature and influence upon human conduct.* 208 pp. Washington, D. C., Daylion, 1937.

(49) LUND, F. H. *Emotions of men.* 348 pp. New York, McGraw-Hill, 1930.

(50) DEWEY, J. The theory of emotion. *Psychol. Rev.* 1: 553–569, 1894; 2: 13–32, 1895.

(51) ANGIER, R. P. The conflict theory of emotion. *Amer. J. Psychol.* 39: 390–401, 1927.

(52) KANTOR, J. R. The psychology of feeling or affective reactions. *Amer. J. Psychol.* 34: 433–463, 1923.

(53) DREVER, J. *Instinct in man; a contribution to the psychology of education.* 281 pp. Cambridge Univ. P., 1917.

(54) BERNARD, L. L. *Instinct. A study in social psychology.* 527 pp. New York, Holt, 1924.

(55) BORING, E. G., LANGFELD, H. S., AND WELD, H. P. *Introduction to psychology.* 652 pp. New York, Wiley, 1939.

(56) MURPHY, G. *General psychology.* 657 pp. New York, Harper, 1933.

(57) DARROW, C. W. Emotion as relative functional decortication: the role of conflict. *Psychol. Rev.* 42: 566–578, 1935.

(58) WHITEHORN, J. C. Physiological changes in emotional states. Pp. 256–270. In: *The interrelationship of mind and body.* 381 pp. Baltimore, Williams & Wilkins, 1939.

(59) McKINNEY, J. M. What shall we choose to call emotion? *J. Nerv. Ment. Dis.* 72: 46–64, 1930.

(60) WOODWORTH, R. S. *Experimental psychology.* 889 pp. New York, Holt, 1938.

(61) FREUD, S., AND BREUER, J. On the psychical mechanism of hysterical phenomena. Pp. 24–31. In: *Collected Papers,* Vol. I, 359 pp. London, Internat. Psychoanal. P., 1924.

(62) FREUD, S. The defense neuro-psychoses. Pp. 59–75. In: *Collected Papers,* Vol. I. 359 pp. London, Internat. Psychoanal. P., 1924.

(63) LANDAUER, K. Die Gemuetsbewegungen oder Affekte. Pp. 134–159. In: Federn-Meng, *Das Psychoanalytische Volksbuch,* Vol. I, Bern, Huber, 1939.

(64) FREUD, S. *The problem of anxiety.* 165 pp. New York, Psychoanal. Quart. P., 1936.

(65) FREUD, S. *The interpretation of dreams.* Pp. 179–548. In: *The basic writings of Sigmund Freud.* 1001 pp. Ed. Brill, A. A., New York, Modern Libr., 1938.

(66) FREUD, S. The unconscious. Pp. 98–136. In: *Collected Papers*, Vol. IV, 508 pp. London, Hogarth, 1925.

(67) FREUD, S. Repression. Pp. 84–97. In: *Collected Papers*, Vol. IV, 508 pp. London, Hogarth, 1925.

(68) KULOVESI, Y. Psychoanalytische Bemerkungen zur James-Langeschen Affekttheorie. *Imago.* 17: 392–398, 1931.

(69) BRIERLEY, M. Affects in theory and practice. *Internat. Psychoanal.* 18: 256–268, 1937.

(70) FREUD, S. *Beyond the pleasure principle.* 90 pp. Trans. Hubback, C. J. M. London, Internat. Psychoanal. P., 1922. *Jenseits des Lustprinzips*, 1920.

(71) JELGERSMA, G. Psychoanalitischer Beitrag zu einer Theorie des Gefuehls. *Internat. J. Psychoanal.* 7: 1–8, 1921.

(72) FREUD, S. Formulations regarding the two principles in mental functioning. Pp. 13–21. In: *Collected Papers*, Vol. IV, 508 pp. London, Hogarth, 1925.

(73) FEDERN, P. Die Ichbesetzung bei den Fehlleistungen. *Imago.* 19: 312–338; 433–453, 1933.

(74) FEDERN, P. Zur Unterscheidung des gesunden und krankhaften Ñarzismus. *Imago.* 22: 5–39, 1936.

(75) LANDAUER, K. Affects, passions, and temperament. *Internat. J. Psychoanal.* 19: 388–415, 1938; *Imago* 22: 275–291, 1936.

(76) FREUD, S. *New introductory lectures on psychoanalysis.* 257 pp. New York, Norton, 1933.

(77) MacCURDY, J. T. *The psychology of emotion. Morbid and normal.* 589 pp. New York, Harcourt, 1925.

(78) DEMBO, T. Der Aerger als dynamisches Problem. *Psychol. Forsch.* 15: 1–144, 1931.

(79) LEWIN, K., BARKER, R., AND DEMBO, T. *Frustration and Regression* 314 pp. Univ. Iowa P., 1941.

(80) DUNBAR, F. H. *Emotions and bodily changes.* 601 pp. New York, Columbia Univ. P., 2nd ed., 1938 (1st ed., 1935).

(81) PRESCOTT, D. A. *Emotion and the educative process.* 322 pp. Washington, D. C., Amer. Council on Education, 1938.

(82) ZACHRY, C. B., AND LIGHTY, M. *Emotion and conduct in adolescence.* 563 pp. New York, Appleton, 1940.

Chapter III

THE EXPERIMENTAL CONTRIBUTIONS OF GENERAL PSYCHOLOGY

1. Experimental Methods and Theories

Our survey of the experiments will organize them according to the experimental methods used; individual experiments will be viewed against a background of the theoretical influences from which they stem. It is thus necessary to review the main experimental methods used and the outstanding theoretical influences which have fostered these experiments.

Toward the end of the last century, when it was a young science, psychology used but few and simple experimental techniques. Investigations concerning memory employed two main methods: the learning method, and the association method. The learning experiments undertook to measure the abstract faculty called memory and were designed to investigate the characteristics of this faculty, such as the number of repetitions necessary to imprint entirely new material and the rapidity of forgetting. Nonsense syllables were employed in the belief that these have no prior associations; thus the imprinting of any of these was assumed to be of identical difficulty. Investigations were conducted to determine how the imprinting of nonsense syllables compared with the imprinting of series of single words, of meaningful texts, and of organized rhythmic texts or verses. The most notable of these experiments were those of Ebbinghaus (1). Later we shall discuss some of the conclusions reached through the use of this method. The other method investigated the associations, which were thought to constitute the immediate bases of memory. It was presupposed that if the emergence of an idea A is followed by the emergence of an idea B, there exists an associative bond between A and B by virtue of which the emergence of A "causes" the emergence of B. In the learning experiments it was assumed that the function of repetition was to create and reinforce the associative bonds. The aim of the first association experiments (Galton, 2, 3, and Wundt, 4) was to investigate the arrangement of these associative bonds in the human memory which was conceived as a kind of storehouse. It was assumed that the arrangement of the bonds might be investigated by asking the subject to respond to a spoken word with the next word that came to mind. The interest was centered in the logical and grammatical relations of the stimulus and reaction words: for example, the kind of reaction given to verbs, nouns, and adjectives, or whether the relation is a subordination, supra-ordination, and so on. Reaction time measurements were made to determine the ease of reaction to different categories of words, and there were attempts to establish standard and unusual reaction words. In addition to these two experimental methods psychology used the questionnaire method, which at present is used frequently in the younger sciences of experimental sociology and social psychology. The notion that psychological problems can be settled by asking many people for their opinion, though it now seems to us awkward, was at the time an accepted one. The experimentation relevant to our topic utilized mainly these three methods, though often with modifications and innovations.

Three factors influenced these experiments. First, the *fin de siècle* mood and the Schopenhauerian pessimistic philosophy exerted a great influence on humanistic science; the question of the essential optimism or pessimism of human beings was again at a zenith, and brought to the field of memory investigation the problem of determining whether pleasant or unpleasant experiences are better remembered. A second influential factor was the publication of the initial works of Freud. In the "Psychopathology of Everyday Life" (5) Freud analyzed certain phenomena of forgetting and of substitution of other material for the forgotten memories and actions; he showed that forgotten material which he analyzed was related to ideas significant and personally painful to the subject. Although his formulations were rather cautious, they nevertheless admitted of misunderstandings. Thus many investigators equated the Freudian *unconscious* motive for forgetting with *conscious* "unpleasantness" at large. The Freudian theory was regarded by many as conceiving that every "unpleasant" idea or experience is subject to repression; the Freudian "pleasure principle" was interpreted as teaching the facilitated recall of "pleasant experiences." A third influence was that of the "pleasure-pain theory of learning."[1] This theory was originated by Spencer (6) and elaborated by Bain (7). Spencer defined pleasure as "a feeling we seek to bring into consciousness" and pain as "a feeling we seek to get out of consciousness," and taught as a consequence that pleasant experiences are recalled frequently and unpleasant ones are forgotten. This theory has greatly influenced educational psychology and inspired Thorndike's (8, 9) "law of effect," according to which an experience followed by a satisfying state is "stamped in" and one followed by an annoying state is "stamped out." These theories were frequently equated with Freud's theory of forgetting, and contributed to the wide misunderstanding of it.

The superficial similarity of these theories has been in great part responsible for the inconclusiveness of the experimentation as a whole and

[1] See Cason (10).

the multiplicity of hasty unwarranted conclusions in many experiments. Actually, the three theories are basically different: the first is concerned with pessimism and optimism, and thus with the effect on memory of a general "personality trait"; the second considers the effect of a mechanism which in operation is personal, specific, and unconscious; the third deals with the effect of a "feeling tone," the presence, absence, quality and intensity of which in any group of subjects can, it is assumed, be generally agreed upon.

2. QUESTIONNAIRE STUDIES

In surveying the literature we shall follow a chronological order. The first investigations of our problem wore two questionnaire studies. Colgrove (11, 12) and Kowalewski (13) asked their subjects in questionnaires whether they remember better the pleasant (P) or unpleasant (U) experiences of their lives. Colgrove used different age and race groups; his results, varying to a considerable degree with race and age, were inconclusive. Kowalewski, who worked with children (10–13 years of age), used an improved questionnaire; he found that the group which remembered P experiences better than U ones was the larger. To express the difference between the group favouring P ness and the group favoring U-ness, he coined the concepts *memory optimism* and *memory pessimism*. Three decades later, Susukita (14, 15) used the method again with an elaborated questionnaire and with children as subjects. He asked not only whether P or U experiences were remembered better, but whether better meant "more" or "clearer" memories; moreover, he asked a series of such concrete questions as, "Which do you remember better, praise or scolding, play or injury?" He found that the memory type (pessimism-optimism) was dependent on the clarity and not on the quantity of remembering; that memory pessimism increased with age; that under poor social-cultural conditions memory optimism prevailed, but that under better social-cultural conditions memory pessimism was predominant.

These questionnaire studies inquired into peoples' *opinions* about remembering P and U experiences, and not into the *remembering* itself. Külpe's remark (16) that even he was unable to answer Kowalewski's questionnaire is in itself a most revealing criticism. In spite of the inadequacy of the method, these studies had the merit of having raised questions of individual, age, and cultural differences, which have had a role in the further experimentation on our problem. Washburn's studies, to be discussed later, attacked the question of personal differences; the first of these studies (Baxter, Yamada, and Washburn, 17) especially shows Kowalewski's influence.

3. Association Experiments

The origin and the problem of the association experiments have been described above. It was early recognized that feeling and emotion play a significant role in association-mechanisms. This realization may be ascribed in part to the fact that the pertinent theories of the philosopher-psychologists were not forgotten, and in part to immediate evidence revealed through the method of introspection, then in wide use. Another contributing factor was Kraepelin's attempt to apply to psychopathology the methods of the young science of psychology. In dealing with psychiatric patients who displayed abnormally active or torpid feeling reactions, Kraepelin (18), Aschaffenburg (19), and others became interested in the relation of these reactions to the peculiarities of memory and association phenomena. In this section we shall discuss four types of association experiments: first, general association experiments; second, diagnostic association experiments; third, feeling-tone association experiments; fourth, experience association experiments.

A. GENERAL ASSOCIATION EXPERIMENTS

In the general association experiments the introspective reports of the subjects drew attention to the role of "feelings," and we find casual references to this made by Wundt and other experimenters. Cordes (20) analyzed the psychic processes in the interval between the stimulus and reaction words, and found that feelings may accompany either word or may be a link between the two; and in either case may lengthen the reaction time. Ziehen (21) found that individual reactions of "relatively strong emotional accentuation" also lengthen the reaction time. On the basis of the introspective reports of the subjects, Wreschner (22) and Menzerath (23) established those associations which had pleasant or unpleasant feeling-tone. These tended to show longer reaction times than indifferent associations, and U-toned associations tended to show longer reaction times than P-toned ones. Similar findings were reported by Mayer and Orth (24). Wreschner emphasizes that in his experiment the feelings were reported by the subjects, and that "the reaction is usually deeply influenced, and only rarely is the emotional motif an epi-phenomenon" (p. 97). Menzerath stresses the point that "to say a priori that a certain sensation or presentation is pleasant is impossible, because on the one hand the feeling changes with the given conditions, and on the other hand the individualities are too different to agree on feeling tones; the same person may be stimulated at different times in different ways" (p. 63). Unfortunately, these valuable warnings remained unread or unheeded, and their truth was realized only after many inadequate experiments.

B. DIAGNOSTIC ASSOCIATION EXPERIMENTS

Although Kraepelin and his pupils made efforts to investigate the associations of psychiatric patients, Jung and Riklin (25) were the first to investigate systematically the diagnostic possibilities of association experiments. They compared associations of normals with those of patients of varied diagnostic groups. On the one hand, their interest was centered on differences between the formal relations[2]—that is, the grammatical and logical relations—of stimulus and reaction word.[3] With the exception of a few categories, the differences they found were without further consequences; the relation of logical and grammatical functions to emotions is a most obscure problem.[4] On the other hand, their findings concerning reaction time, reproduction-difficulties, and so on—called "complex-indicators"—aroused great interest. These findings have an immediate bearing on our problem for the growing interest in complex-indicators was accompanied by a shift in diagnostic aim from the diagnosis of psychiatric categories to the diagnosis of *individual* emotional problems or "complexes."

Jung's association experiment used a standard list of a hundred stimulus words; the subject was instructed to react to the stimulus word with the first idea that came to mind, and the reaction time was measured. A reproduction experiment followed, in which the same list of stimulus words was presented and the subject was instructed to react with the reaction words he had previously given.

Jung found several complex-indicators. Concerning one of these, the reaction time, he states:

"(1) The association has too long a reaction-time when the complex is aroused.

"(2) The association directly following the one arousing the complex has a prolonged reaction-time in consequence of the maintenance of the emotional tone." (p. 246)

The other complex-indicators will be discussed later.

The reproduction experiments, Jung concluded, are helpful in revealing

---

[2] The concept "formal relations" is in contradistinction to the content-relation of associations as investigated by psychoanalysis.

[3] Jung suggested the following categories: *I. Inner association:* 1. Coordination. 2. Predicate relationship. 3. Causal dependence. *II. Outer association:* 1. Coexistence. 2. Identity. 3. Verbal-motor forms. *III. Clang-reaction:* 1. Word-completion. 2. Clang. 3. Rhyme. *IV. Residual group:* 1. Indirect reactions. 2. Meaningless reactions. 3. Faults. 4. Repetition of stimulus-word. (A) *Egocentric reaction.* (B) *Perseveration.* (C) *Repetition.* (D) *Verbal Linking:* 1. Same grammatical form. 2. Same number of syllables. 3. Alliteration. 4. Consonance. 5. Same ending.

[4] See Schilder (26, 27); Vigotsky (28); Massermann and Balken (29).

the "complexes" of the subject. Erroneous reproductions, especially when given after a prolonged reaction time, and general failure of reproduction indicate the presence of a stimulus word connected with a "complex." Such failures sometimes occur not at the complex-connected stimulus word (critical stimulus), but at the word following it (postcritical stimulus). Sometimes a disturbance in reproduction starting at the critical or post-critical reaction perseverates. These results were the more significant in that the reproduction experiment investigated incidental remembering, the type which occurs in actual life situations.

The bearing of these experiments on our problem is shown by Jung's definition of complexes. A complex is defined as a set of ideas grouped around a strong emotion. Their influence on memory is explained as follows:

". . . the emotionally charged presentation complexes give rise to characteristic disturbances in the experiment; their presence and probable nature can be recognized from the disturbances themselves. The background of our consciousness (or the unconscious) consists of complexes of this kind. The whole material of memory is grouped around them. . . . They constellate the whole of our thinking and doing, hence the associations also." (p. 299)

Jung states that the rationale of his experiments is based upon the psychoanalytic theory, and especially on the concept of repression, interpreted in relation to the "complex" as follows:

"Repression arises from the critical presentations being so charged with pain (unpleasure) as to be insupportable to the conscious self." (p. 297)

"The chief characteristic of the complex is, at all events, its relative autonomy, which may find expression in two directions: by increased emphasis and stability in consciousness, and by repression—that is, resistance to reproduction in the *unconscious*. Hence the associations which belong to the complex lack the 'flexibility' of the remaining and more indifferent psychic material." (p. 397)[5]

"The complexes exhibited in the association experiment have usually a tone of unpleasure, so that the exceptional condition in which the complex stands during the test may be well qualified as 'repression.'" (p. 397)

Though it may seem surprising, these general suggestions comprise all of Jung's explanation of the rationale of the association experiment. The validity of the complex-indicators of the association experiment is derived from psychoanalytic practice:

"I discovered the complex-indicators empirically in the analysis:[6] I saw that in the associations which were distinguished by certain indications a complex was, as a

---

[5] An expression in this quotation appears to need explanation, as the translation may be misleading. "Resistance to reproduction in the unconscious" conveys that the resistance is unconscious.

[6] Namely, psychoanalysis.

rule, constellating with particular strength and had sometimes led to a 'disturbing' interference." (p. 396)

The validity of the complex-indicators of the reproduction experiment is established by comparing them with the complex-indicators of the association experiment:

"If these indicators are really characteristic, i.e. if the analytic method has led to a correct result which will stand proof, the indicators must be in close relation to one another. They will recur preferably at certain associations—for instance, at failures in reproduction and at delayed reactions." (pp. 396–397)

This manner of establishing indicators was sharply criticized by experimental psychologists. J. G. Schnitzler's (30) statement is representative of the attitude of these critics:

"Indicators of a very dubious value were used; the diagnosis was only apparently based on these, and nevertheless correct diagnoses were considered to have justified the use of these indicators. These complex indicators were again and again quoted in numerous publications for the purpose of explanation without the minimal fundamental clarification of their psychological significance." (pp. 53–54)

The justification for this criticism is limited by the fact that the stimulus-words eliciting complex-indicators *were* found to be connected with emotions or complexes discovered in the psychoanalysis of the subject; but the predictability of complexes from complex-indicators was doubtful, and subject to the experimenter's intuition. Jung felt this, and maintained that only the presence of several complex-indicators was sufficient warrant to assume the existence and to describe the quality of a complex. He even applied the psychogalvanic reflex to supplement the diagnostic procedure (31). He argued that the association experiment was not standardized but was considered by many to be an art, and thus every new means to "circumscribe the complex and its feeling-tone is useful."

Jung's work stimulated countless experiments and a ceaseless search for new complex indicators. Space does not allow for a detailed discussion of these experiments, but a reference to Kohs' (32) excellent survey[7] of the field may serve instead. He enumerated thirty qualitative, one quantitative, and fifteen physiological complex-indicators suggested by different experimenters.[8] As late as 1921, Hull and Lugoff (33) at-

---

[7] Kohs' survey gives an exhaustive bibliography.
[8] I. Qualitative: 1. Content. 2. Whispered Response. 3. Failure to Understand. 4. False Reproduction. 5. False Recall. 6. Perseveration. a. Response. b. Stimulus. c. Affect. 7. Inhibition. 8. Failure to Respond. 9. Quotations. 10. Titles. 11. Sentences. 12. Symbolism. 13. General Concepts Hiding the Meaning. 14. Addition of the Article. 15. Naming of an Object in the Examiner's Room. 16. Peculiar Form of the Response. 17. Unusual Response. 18. Errors in Response.

tempted to bring some order into the multiplicity of assumed complex-indicators. Using Jung's word-list, they investigated 10,000 associations of 100 subjects (Jung and Riklin reported 12,400 associations of 34 normal subjects). They proceeded on the assumption that

". . . other things being equal, two variables related positively to the same variable are positively related to each other . . . thus the strength of association found ultimately to exist between a given sign and all other signs taken together may be presumed to yield a useful indication to the closeness of association of the alleged sign with emotional complexes and hence of its diagnostic reliability." (pp. 123–124)

They investigated nine complex indicators,[9] and concluded:

"(1) Repetition of the stimulus word is decidedly the most reliable diagnostic sign of the five indicators examined.[10] (2) The first four are in all probability real complex signs. (3) Repeated use of the same reaction word is a complex sign of very doubtful diagnostic value, at least in the sense that the other signs are diagnostic." (p. 127)

"The computation shows that two given indicators are 64.8 per cent more likely to attract a given third indicator than either one of them is likely to attract it separately. This suggests that while two indicators are distinctly more significant than one, the second indicator adds by no means as much diagnostic potency as the first, to say nothing of more." (p. 136)

Summary

a. The diagnostic association experiments showed that "complexes" inhibit the associative reaction to stimulus words related to a complex, and

---

19. Assimilations. 20. Vacuum. 21. Unmeaning Responses. 22. Nonsense. 23. Incomplete Responses. 24. Supplementations of Stimulus Words. 25. Asymmetrical Responses. 26. Post-critical Responses. 27. 'Versprechen,' 'Verhoeren,' ('Verlesen'). 28. 'Komplexvertreter' (Complex-surrogate). 29. Translations. 30. Interjections or Single Letters. (pp. 573–579)
II. Quantitative: Time. (p. 579)
III. Physiological: 1. Psychogalvanic Reflexes. 2. Electro-motor Heart Flow. 3. Pulse. 4. Respiration. 5. Blood Pressure. 6. Involuntary Movements, or Tremors of the Hand or Limbs. 7. Ataxiagraph (Involuntary Bodily Sway). 8. Knee-Jerk. 9. Lifting Ability of the Finger (Ergograph). 10. Tapping Test. 11. Strength of Grip. 12. Facial Expression (Reddening, etc.). 13. Tone of Voice in Response. 14. Ability to Concentrate. 15. General Conduct and Behavior (Coughing, Clearing of the Throat, etc.). (p. 580)
[9] "(1) Long reaction time (over thirteen fifths of a second). (2) Inability to make any response whatever. (3) Extremely short reaction time. (4) Repetition of the stimulus word itself. (5) Assimilation (apparent misunderstanding) of the stimulus word. (6) Defective reproduction of original reaction at second presentation of the stimulus word. (7) Response with the same reaction word at two or more different stimulus words. (8) Strange or apparently senseless reactions. (9) Perseveration." (p. 114)
[10] Repetition, assimilation, reaction time, defective reproduction, repeated use of reaction word.

the reproduction of reaction-words to such stimulus-words. The symptoms of this inhibition were called "complex-indicators."

b. The influence of complexes on the memory-function seems to be established, but for the validity of complex-indicators only initial proof has been offered and their diagnostic value found to be uncertain.

c. The definition of "complex" implies the operation of a manifold "emotional factor," not adequately describable as simple "emotion" or "feeling-tone."

C. "FEELING-TONE" AND ASSOCIATION EXPERIMENTS

The diagnostic association experiment investigated the influence of complexes, and not of "feeling-tone" as such. The account of an experiment investigating the influence of feeling-tone on associations was published by Birnbaum (34). Experimenting with normal subjects, he found no differences of reaction time between stimulus-words generally considered feeling-toned and those generally considered indifferent. He concluded that

". . . mere isolated words, might they relate even to contents of ever so strong feeling-tones, do not necessarily elicit any of those feelings which they might elicit when they are presented in a meaningful connection." (p. 108)

In an attempt to create a situation in which the subject becomes more responsive emotionally, Birnbaum used psychiatric patients with "increased emotivity," "imagery strongly colored with feelings," "abnormal feeling disposition"; he selected stimulus-words designed to have individual significance for the subject, and endeavored to arouse him emotionally by means of a discussion before the experiment. This approach is of significance for our problem and may be useful in future experimentation, even though Birnbaum's results were rather meager and inconclusive. They indicated that feeling-tone when elicited might lengthen the reaction time, but that the conditions under which feeling-tone can be elicited vary with the psychiatric category of the subject.[11]

Birnbaum's findings indicate that the feeling-tone of the stimulus-word has influence only on persons with strongly accentuated affectivity

[11] Hysterics did not react to stimuli generally assumed to be feeling-toned, but reacted to some allegedly indifferent ones and were stimulated by initial discussion only when "special individually colored realms of ideas" were touched upon. Delusional psychotics showed some reaction to stimuli generally assumed to be feeling-toned. Depressives of the circular type were stimulated by stimuli generally assumed to be feeling-toned but not by individually toned stimuli or by initial discussion. Hysterical depressives reacted more to specific stimuli and were stimulated by initial discussion. Both groups reacted in a manner typical of depressed patients and had significantly elongated reaction times.

or in the context of an arousing discussion; but Tolman and Johnson (35) arrived at different results. Arbitrarily selecting words with pleasant, unpleasant, and indifferent feeling-tone, they used them as stimulus-words in an association experiment. The reaction time averages showed a UPI (Unpleasant, Pleasant, Indifferent) sequence, with U showing the longest reaction time. In order to exclude the possibility that these results might be ascribable to complexes connected with these stimulus-words, Tolman and Johnson undertook a second experiment in which the stimuli were P and U words; some referred to sense qualities, others—as "success," "failure"—to possible complexes. Their hypothesis was:

"If it should appear that the simple unpleasant sense qualities were just as provocative of length of reaction times as the words dealing with complexes such as failure, death, and disgusting objects, we should conclude that unpleasantness *as such* really lengthens association times." (p. 190)

They interpreted their results as follows:

"The . . . results . . . point very decidedly for longer times for the unpleasant words . . . for sense qualities the same is true as for all the words . . . it proves that simple unpleasantness as such lengthens reaction time." (p. 193)

Similar results were obtained by Carter (36).

W. W. Smith (37, 38) also reported an experiment investigating the influence of "affective tone" on associations. He equated "affective tone" with "emotions" and, like McDougall, described the latter as *"the affective aspect of the operation of an instinct"* (38, p. 24). He measured the affective tone with PGR, the use of which had already been introduced into the association experiment by Jung and elaborated by Binswanger. Using the Eder revision of Jung's word list, he obtained the greatest PGR deflections with those stimulus-words[12] considered to have the strongest "emotional" tone. He drew the following conclusions from his association and reproduction experiments:

"First, that memory for words is influenced by affective tone; secondly, that so far as the affective tone detected by the psychogalvanic reflex is concerned, its influence may be exerted into diametrically opposite directions; the fact that a given word evokes well-marked affective tone may lead to its being better remembered than a less intensely toned word, or may lead to its being forgotten more quickly. Affective tone as shown by the galvanometer deflexion should, therefore, be regarded as of two kinds, one of which facilitates, while the other impedes, the remembering of words which it accompanies. On the other hand, the kind of affective tone which is shown by Jung's reproduction test is uni-directional in its effects and tends to impede the remembering of the words concerned." (37, p. 250)

---

[12] Kiss, love, merry, divorce, name, woman, wound, dance, afraid, proud, money, fright, child, habit, state, despise, war, family, happy, prey.

This use of the PGR influenced later experimenters who, no longer concerned with the meaning of the "affective tone," nonchalantly identified it with "pleasantness" and "unpleasantness"—an error which Smith avoided.[13] Carter, Jones and Shock (39) obtained results strikingly similar to Smith's. Burtt and Tuttle (40) used the tendon reflex and Cason (41) used gross bodily movement to measure the feeling-tone of words in association experiments, and obtained positive correlations.

Summary

a. While the diagnostic association experiments investigated the symptoms of complexes in associative reaction, the experiments discussed in this section endeavored to demonstrate the influence of "feeling-tone" (affective tone) on associations.

b. No unitary concept of "feeling-tone" underlay these experiments. It was on occasion arbitrarily assumed (Birnbaum), or equated with sensory quality (Tolman, Johnson) or with emotions (Smith), or considered the factor measured by PGR or amount of gross bodily movement (Smith, Cason).

c. The results, although indicating some influence of feeling-tone on reaction time and reproduction, are inconclusive.

D. EXPERIENCE-ASSOCIATION EXPERIMENTS

Galton (2) observed that in the association-experiment reminiscences of experiences frequently emerged, rather than single reaction-words. Peters (42, 43, and 44)[14] reported experiments in which the subjects were instructed to react to stimulus-words with the first experience which came to mind; he called this method "experience association." Influenced by Freud and Jung this experiment investigated the role of feeling-tone in the recollection of experiences. The subjects were instructed to answer seven questions on the feeling-tone of the experiences.[15] Peters found that 80% of the experiences were feeling-toned; that 65% of these were P, 30% U, and 5% mixed (M);[16] that the percentage of the repeatedly-

[13] "I do not propose here to consider the relation of the two kinds of affective tone mentioned above to the varieties commonly described as 'pleasant' and 'unpleasant.' This is a question which would take us very far and I think it wiser to adhere strictly to the necessary inferences from the experimental results." (p. 250)

[14] A mass experiment of Peters and Nemecek.

[15] (1) Was the experience originally feeling-toned?   (2) What was the quality of the original feeling-tone?   (3) Is there a feeling-tone present at the moment of recollection?   (4) What kind of feeling-tone is this?   (5) When did this experience originally occur?   (6) How often has it been experienced since?   (7) How often has it been remembered since?

[16] It is noteworthy that most later experimenters neglected the possibility of M; only Lanier (45) made a special issue of it.

remembered experiences was highest among U experiences, and among the repeatedly-remembered experiences the percentage of U ones was highest; that avoidance of recollection of U experiences increases with the subject's age, and is a tendency manifested rather late in psychic development; and that among the experiences connected with complexes, the percentage of U was higher and the percentage of P lower than among the experiences not so connected. To explain his findings, Peters advanced the hypothesis that there is a general tendency, increasing with the subject's age, to "diminish the displeasure in consciousness," and:

"that . . . the remembered U experiences have a greater significance than the remembered P experiences is apparently due to the fact that the U experiences of little significance have less chance to be remembered than the P experiences of similar significance." (43, p. 218)

The second hypothesis, indicating that in remembrance the "personal significance" of an experience is at least as important as its feeling-tone, is of value in our problem. The nature of "personal significance" and its relation to the "feeling-tone" were not discussed by Peters. The mode of operation of the "tendency to diminish displeasure in consciousness" was described as follows:

". . . the fact that more P than U experiences are remembered means that the U experiences become repressed quicker and more easily than do P experiences. The will not to remember U experiences brings about a less frequent reproduction of them . . . According to the laws of memory, the fewer the repetitions the easier will forgetting ensue. Thus the influence of U-ness on memory is easily explained on the basis of one of the best established rules of the psychology of memory. And it is superfluous to assume a special mechanism of repression or blocking of U experiences, as was done by Freud." (43, p. 245)

The advantage of this unexplained "will to forget" over the repression-mechanism of Freud is incomprehensible. Moreover, the memory laws invoked here as the "best established rules" of psychology are laws which fail to explain the phenomena of reminiscence and of forgetting of quite familiar facts. This approach to Freud's theory characterizes many experimental studies.

Peters was the first to express the opinion that the effect of "feeling-tone" on immediate memory is slight; he was aware also that a "direct answer" concerning the difference in remembering P and U experiences could be obtained only if the experience itself, and not solely the memory of it, were known to us (43, p. 223). The difference between the questionnaire method and the experience association method is superficial. In the latter the questioning is more systematic and the experiences are recalled, but essentially the procedure is the same: the subject is asked for his opinion of the feeling-tone. Washburn and her pupils published a series of experience-association experiments (17, 46, 47, 48) which coupled the principle of experience-association with Kowalewski's notion of memory-types (memory-optimists, memory-pessimists). The aim of this series of experiments was to discriminate between pessimistic-optimistic, cheerful-depressive, emotional-phlegmatic, and more- or less-egotistic types. In each of the experiments the subjects were ranked, on the basis of self-judgment and the judgment of three friends, into one of these antinomic pairs. The subject was asked to react to stimulus-words with a sign as soon as the first recollection occurred, and to indicate whether the experience was P or U. The correlation of reaction time and type-ranking was found to suggest the possibility of discriminating between these personality types by means of reaction time. Griffitts (49) corroborated these findings; in a simultaneous reproduction experiment he found that any kind of feeling-tone supports reproduction.

Summary

a. The experience-association experiments differ only apparently from the questionnaire studies: both ask for judgments concerning past experiences.

b. The existence of a "tendency to diminish displeasure in consciousness" and of a greater likelihood for the recall of "personally significant" experiences was inferred from the judgments of the subjects.

c. Washburn suggested that the reaction times of P and U experiences tend to show differences between subjects with predominantly optimistic tendencies and those with predominantly pessimistic tendencies.

E. THE FACT-DIAGNOSTIC EXPERIMENT

The aim of the fact-diagnostic experiments was to develop the association-experiment into a reliable tool for the detection of crime. The laboratory investigations, preliminary to criminological application, attempted to determine the manner in which facts known to the subject influence his associations. The diagnostic association experiment developed in the field of psychopathology and, as we have seen, drew upon the theory of psychoanalysis; the fact-diagnostic experiment (Tatbestandsdiagnose) was based on the principles of general psychology, although it was precipitated by the Jungian experiments. The general psychology of the time was interested in cognitive processes, and explained psychic phenomena in cognitive terms; thus it had no understanding of psychoanalysis, and regarded it with a suspicion which was extended to the Jungian diagnostic association experiments. Experimental psychologists, who developed the fact-diagnostic experiment with a forensic aim, shared this attitude. Consequently, they framed the problem of "emotional influence" in cognitive terms.

Space limitations do not permit a discussion of the vast literature of fact-diagnostic experimentation; thus we shall discuss only Lipmann's (50) excellent survey[17] of the field. The title of his survey itself indicates the cognitive approach: "The Traces and Symptoms of Interest-Toned Experiences." Lipmann expounds the cognitive view as follows:

". . . it is beyond doubt that in the experiences concerned, not the emotional but mainly the intellectual processes play the decisive role. Thus I cannot share the opinion of Jung, that there are 'no other image complexes but feeling-toned ones.' " (p. 6)

Lipmann's view of memory-function shows the relation of the association experiment to the memory problem. Nowhere did Jung clearly express his opinion of this relation, and nowhere did he clearly indicate that he investigated "traces and symptoms" of ideas connected with complexes. Lipmann states the issue with classical clarity:

"The whole theory of memory images and of memory deals with symptoms of the traces of perceptions. It deals with two specific groups of problems: 1. Which psychic processes are apt to bring these traces from potentiality into actuality? 2. In which form do the revived traces appear and what are their symptoms and how can one recognize that in such symptoms revived traces reveal themselves?" (p. 2)

The criminological problem which the fact-diagnostic experiments attempted to solve was the detection of the actual criminal in a group of suspected persons. This required the psychologist to ascertain which subject had experienced the crime-situation. The theory involved was formulated by Lipmann as follows:

". . . we have the right to suppose that 'experiences,' i.e. interest-toned perception complexes, leave especially intense traces. The greater intensity exerts its effect in that: 1. The traces disappear less rapidly; 2. They are revived more easily; 3. They are not pure memory but reminiscence images[18] when revived, i.e. in their revival a conscious reminiscence of the whole interest-toned perception complex is reproduced." (p. 2)

Lipmann's conception of the driving forces of the memory-apparatus is intellectualistic; his idea of memory is that forgetting is a "disappearance of traces," and that vividness of memory is a matter of "intensity of traces." Surveying the literature, Lipmann concludes that the fact-

---

[17] Lipmann's survey gives an exhaustive bibliography. It deals mainly, however, with Wertheimer's work (51, 52) and Lipmann's own results (53).

[18] Reminiscence images differ from memory images, according to Lipmann, in that the former carry local and temporal signs.

diagnostic associaton experiment is reliable only if, first, the stimulus-words related to the crime situation are interspersed among *assuredly "neutral"* words; secondly, if a sufficient number of *assuredly innocent* subjects is used for control; and thirdly, if the experimenter decides in advance which reactions will be considered crime indicators. Lipmann characterizes Jung's procedure as diametrically opposite to this: Jung was primarily concerned with symptoms rather than with the original experience, and was interested in analyzing the subject's reactions rather than in introducing *assuredly reliable* control words and control subjects. The controversy centered on the predictability of crime-indicating reactions: the critical reactions being a matter of predetermined expectation, will the investigator find the criminal reacting with symptoms precisely to the predetermined stimuli? Birnbaum's experience, and the experience of many others, showed that reports on feeling-tone are frequently obtained where, according to the predetermined expectation, none was anticipated. The Jungian experiment is primarily concerned with symptoms wherever found, and endeavors to understand their genesis and significance. Yet understandability and predictability are not identical. Psychic dynamism is not a matter of one-to-one relations: as in meteorology, predictions can be only general but specific events may be readily understood. A psychic event which may be reasonably expected or predicted, can at any time be delayed, or replaced by an equivalent psychological event or even a physiological event. Nevertheless, cognitive psychology considers predictability as a *conditio sine qua non* of experimentation. This is probably the reason that it has not developed an adequate psychology of feelings and emotions; for here the multiple determination of psychic events and the consequent variability of reactions are the most striking. In the practice of fact-diagnosis the problem takes the following form: it is probable that a criminal, if he is neither a child nor a victim of a subsequent hysterical amnesia, will not forget the facts of the crime; it is also probable that he will be cautious enough to guard anxiously against any form of self-betrayal. The Lipmann-Wertheimer procedure apparently strives to elicit such a self-betrayal. The Jungian procedure, however, strives to elicit the symptoms of the anxiousness with which the criminal guards against self-betrayal, and of the guilt he feels when reminded of the crime. A person trained in cognitive psychology and logics will be more interested in the Wertheimer method than in the Jungian; people with some experience of the vicissitudes of the unconscious will be inclined to find greater interest in the Jungian method. It is to be regretted that neither method has been submitted to a test sufficiently valid to have made the methods subject to general practical, if not theoretical, agreement.

Lipmann concluded on the basis of his survey[19] that the nature of the memory traces of interest-toned experiences may be stated as follows:

"I. The traces of interest-toned experiences are more easily revived than those of others. This becomes manifest in the following phenomena: 1. Sensations become perceptions primarily by making use of these experience-traces.[20] These experience traces are easily revived associatively . . .

"II. These experience traces when revived come into consciousness as a reminiscence of the experience itself . . . Furthermore: 1. Since interest-toned ideas are characterized by a great number and variety of reproduction tendencies, the reproduction tendencies of different directions inhibit each other; thus the revival of experience-traces occurs always relatively slowly and the reaction is relatively easily forgotten. 2. Stimuli eliciting revival of experiences and the revived experiences themselves command special attention and consequently: (a) such stimuli have a strong distracting effect; (b) this concentration of attention might show up directly in certain physiological changes such as those of pulse, breathing, psychogalvanic reflex . . . etc. 3. Traces of experiences as a whole and of their parts are retained better than other events.

"III. The parts of these experiences are especially strongly associated with each other and consequently a revival of one of these parts makes for revival of other parts of the experience traces." (pp. 17–18)

Of even greater importance appear to be Lipmann's conclusions advancing the concepts of "amalgamation" and "overshadowing":

". . . the interest-toned experiences and their elements are retained better in memory and reminiscence than the indifferent ones; the images of indifferent experiences become more rapidly scattered and get more rapidly pale than those of

---

[19] Together with the "fact-diagnostic association experiment" Lipmann discussed a number of other fact-diagnostic experiments. Many of these were plans of suggested experiments rather than experiments reported in the literature. Some of these deserve to be discussed here as in them Lipmann anticipated some of the experimental methods which we shall discuss in Chapter VIII, inasmuch as they appear to promise further contributions to the knowledge of our field. Thus, for instance, Lipmann suggested that free reproduction of the description of the criminal act be obtained, because even such a narrative may reveal a subject's knowledge of the event when compared with the narrative of other assuredly non-involved subjects. The similarity of this procedure to the Thematic Apperception Test and to story-recall procedures (see Chapter VIII) is obvious. Also similar is Lipmann's suggestion of giving to the subject a story of the event on which he is being tested; the story contains gaps which are to be filled out by the subject. Resembling more closely the experiments on affective organization of visually perceived material (Chapter VIII) are the experiments in which words are presented tachystiscopically or acoustically; the words presented resemble words significant in the history of the event in question, and the involved subject is expected to mishear or misread the word presented for the word having a crucial significance. (pp. 47–60)

[20] By this expression Lipmann means the trace of the experience of interest-toned events (Erlebnis).

interest-toned experiences. If the indifferent and interest-toned experiences resemble each other, the traces become amalgamated at the expense of the indifferent experiences. The traces of these indifferent experiences suffer amendments and changes due to the traces of the interest-toned experiences; the reminiscence of the indifferent experience is 'over-shadowed' by that of the interest-toned. The validity of this theory was proved by Koeppen and Kutzinski. The symptomatological methods using the process of this amalgamation and over-shadowing . . . expose the subject first to an indifferent experience; the subject reads a story . . . the content of which is similar in certain items to the interest-toned experience, although it has been altered in parts and on certain points fails altogether to match.' It is assumed that the reminiscence of this 'experimental story' in a person who has participated in the experience will be amalgamated with the reminiscence of the experience: the identical parts will reinforce each other; and among the non-identical elements of the indifferent story, several will be substituted and amended by parts of the experience." (pp. 47–48)

It is assumed here that the traces of interest-toned experiences influence the traces of sufficiently similar, indifferent experiences. To use the language of Koffka and Koehler, an "aggregation" results. This "aggregation" takes the form of either a substitution by the interest-toned experience-trace for the indifferent experience-trace, a process called here "overshadowing," or a fusion of parts of the two traces, called here "amalgamation."

This function of "overshadowing" resembles in its formal structure the substitution found by psychoanalysts in slips of the tongue and other parapraxes. Similarly, the formal structure of the function of "amalgamation" resembles that of the "condensation" found in parapraxes. It is obvious, however, that in Lipmann's view amalgamation and overshadowing are due to interests; the psychoanalytic concepts of condensation and substitution are related not to intellectual but to more basic instinctual and affective dynamics. Although the relation of the two sets of concepts cannot be established at present, they appear to be similar functions on different levels of the psychological hierarchy ranging from instinctual to intellectualized functions.

Summary

a. The fact-diagnostic experiments were based on a cognitive theory and substituted "interest tone" for "emotional tone."

b. Lipmann's conception of memory, although still associationistic, is a definite contribution to memory theory in that it views memory in terms of traces and symptoms thereof which need not be direct recall.

c. The fact-diagnostic experiments insisted that the prerequisite of reliability was full predictability of those stimulus-words which would elicit reactions revealing the criminal. This expectancy was shown to be unwarranted in view of the great variety of ways in which a psychological reaction can be delayed, disguised, and displaced.

d. The concepts of "amalgamation" and "overshadowing" of indifferent experiences by "interest-toned experiences" appear to be similar to the Freudian concepts of "condensation" and "substitution"; the former, however, appear to be conceived on an intellectual level of the psychic hierarchy and are interest-determined, while the latter occur on a "deeper" level and are affect- or instinct-determined.

F. CONCLUSIONS

a. The association experiments of general psychology, the diagnostic association experiment, the association experiment investigating the influence of feeling-tone, the experience-association experiment, and the fact-diagnostic experiment all tended to show the influence of some emotional factor in the memory process.

b. This emotional factor was designated in the association experiments of general psychology and in experience-association experiments as "feeling-tone"; in the diagnostic experiment as a "complex"; and in the fact-diagnostic experiment as "interest." Usually these concepts were not defined by the experimenters.

c. All these experiments, as well as the reproduction experiments frequently associated with them, tended to show some influence of an "emotional factor" on reaction-time and reaction content. However, the relation of the emotional factor to its "symptoms" in reproduction was a variable one, dependent on the type of "emotional factor" investigated.

d. In investigating the influence of an "emotional factor" conceived to be intrinsically related to the "instinctive core" of the personality (such as the "complex" of Jung), the experimenter did not attempt to predict the symptom of the presence of a certain emotion in the association experiment; rather, he attempted to infer from the associative-disturbance (symptom) the nature of the emotion present. In investigating the influence of an "emotional factor" conceived to lie far from the "instinctive core" and to be arbitrarily predetermined (such as the "feeling-tone" or "crime indicator"), experimenters found it to be demonstrable only as a trend and only by statistical procedures.

e. It was clear to most of the investigators that the influence of these "emotional factors" showed great individual differences; these individual differences were sufficiently clear to encourage some experimenters to use them for investigating differences in personality type. Some investigators pointed out that the operation of these factors becomes more obvious in patients who have a pathologically vivid emotional life, or in situations calculated to arouse emotion.

4. Reproduction-experiments

The experiments to be reported on in this section employ the standard methods of memory-experimentation (recall, recognition, relearning[21]) to test the influence of emotions on memory. These experiments use a great variety of material, ranging from sensory impressions to organized verbal matter, and from nonsense material to personally meaningful material. Inasmuch as the variety of "emotional factors" investigated is rooted in the variety of the subject-matter used, we have organized the discussion according to the character of this subject-matter. First, we shall discuss experiments which attempt to determine "affective-tone" by associating P and U sensory experiences with indifferent verbal material, or introducing them during the learning of such material. Next, we shall discuss experiments which investigate affective-tone by obtaining recall of P and U personal experiences. Last, we shall discuss experiments which ask for recall of learned verbal material which has been judged P, U, and I.

The experiments on learned verbal material are here dealt with last because, despite their limited personal relevance, they were conducted with the best experimental techniques and thus led to relatively definite conclusions; the experience experiments, using what was apparently the most relevant material, failed of conclusiveness by reason of methodological difficulties.

Preliminary to our survey of these experiments, a brief discussion of the problem of P-ness and U-ness seems desirable. An extensive survey of the pertinent literature is given by Beebe-Center (55), who considers P-ness and U-ness as "attributes of sensations." He expresses his opinion by quoting Warren (56): "A feeling is an experience in which systemic sensations are the main elements" (pp. 203–204). His general point of view was also influenced by Troland's (57, 58) opinion that

"the affective intensity of any individual consciousness is proportionate to the average rate of change of conductance in the synapses the activities of which are responsible for that consciousness." (57, p. 377)

as well as by Nafe (59, p. 507) and Hunt (60, p. 87) who maintained that P-ness and U-ness are organic pressure phenomena. In general, however, Beebe-Center is inclined not to make a sharp differentiation between P-ness and U-ness on the one hand and emotions on the other. He does not clarify whether these two concepts are identical or wherein they differ. Indeed, the evidence provided by the literature is insufficient to permit a clarification of these relations by means of a simple survey.

Some theories advanced by others should be mentioned. James con-

[21] See Davis and Moore (54).

sidered "feelings" (under which term P-ness and U-ness might be subsumed) to be the "mental" aspect of emotions, the "reverberation of the
peripheral bodily changes on the cortex." According to this view the link
between P-ness and U-ness and emotions is an indirect one. The dependence of P-ness and U-ness on "conative tendencies" and "motivation" was
insisted upon by McDougall (61)[22] and Troland (58)[23] respectively. Krueger (62, 63) considered feelings to be the "whole-quality of experience"
in which *every* experience is embedded. Carr (64) and H. N. Peters (65,
66) set forth a "judgmental theory" of P-ness and U-ness which deserves
special attention. It was formulated by H. N. Peters (65) as follows:

"(1) Pleasantness and unpleasantness are dependent indirectly on reactions and
determinants of reactions; (2) pleasantness and unpleasantness are judgments; (3)
there are no conscious contents peculiar to pleasantness and unpleasantness."
(p. 384)

The implications of this formulation might be stated explicitly as follows.
The third statement stresses that there are no specific *conscious contents*
peculiar to P-ness and U-ness; but it permits the inference that there are
qualities of experience which allow for certain judgments, and these judgments according to the second statement are the essence of P-ness and
U-ness. This is expressed even more clearly in the first statement, according to which the motivating factors of reactions are the determinants of the
judgments of P-ness and U-ness. These judgments are not a purely
cognitive function, inasmuch as they are dependent on factors related more
or less indirectly to the deeper dynamics of personality which motivate
action and reaction. Thus this statement of the intellectual, judgmental
character of P-ness and U-ness does not imply that they have no relation
to their original "affective" source, although this relation remains an
indirect one.[24] P-ness and U-ness are thus rendered a derivative of a
general "emotional factor" on the level of judgment; this formulation
explains many of the contradictory findings on P-ness and U-ness, and sheds
some light on the cause of the frequent identification of P-ness and U-ness
with "emotions," a tendency we shall henceforth encounter frequently.

[22] ". . . pleasure and pain result from conation, are determined by the striving,
pleasure, when striving attains its natural goal or progresses towards it; pain, when
striving is thwarted or obstructed and fails to achieve or progress toward its goal
. . ." (p. 269)
[23] "Without committing ourselves at the moment to a definitely *hedonistic* theory
of motivation, we must . . . recognize the fact that feeling (P-ness, U-ness) is closely
bound up with the operation of desires and purposes." (p. 13)
[24] For a similar view see Freud (67, pp. 15–16)

A. EXPERIMENTS USING PLEASANT AND UNPLEASANT SENSORY MATERIAL

The experiments using sensory material to investigate the influence of an "emotional factor" on memory may be divided into four groups. The first group presented P-U sensory material to the subjects and asked for recall; the second group associated P-U sensory experience with neutral material; the third group interpolated P-U sensory experience into neutral material and tested the effect of the interpolation; the fourth group used the interpolation of an electrical shock, as in a conditioning experiment. In addition to these, we shall discuss two experiments which tested the recall of meaningful pictures previously judged on grounds of appeal. The idea underlying these experiments was that *sensory* P-ness and U-ness are the representatives of P-ness and U-ness in general; this idea was very popular among American psychologists in the first decades of this century. As we have seen, Nafe as late as 1924 attempted to reduce feelings to pressure sensations, and Beebe-Center in 1932 still adhered to a similar conception. It was believed that the introduction of P and U sensory qualities into memory experiments would decide whether P-ness and U-ness influence memory.

a. Remembering of P-U Sensory Material

Gordon (68) used simple drawings and combinations of nine colored squares: these were judged by the subjects P, U, and I; one recall test was given immediately, and another was given after three weeks. Tait (69) used a series of colors on which he asked for P, U, and I judgments, and gave an immediate recognition test. Gordon found no difference in the recall of P, U, and I material; but Tait found that 63.4% of the P, 47.2% of the U, and 27.3% of the I colors were recognized. The incidental results of Crosland's (70) experiments on the qualitative analysis of forgetting corroborated Gordon's findings. Whether the inconsistency of these results is to be attributed to the difference in the testing methods, and whether Tait's positive results are attributable to the use of the recognition test, which is accepted as highly sensitive, cannot be decided. These experiments have the merit that the "hedonic tone"[25] of the material was judged by the subjects themselves, but their validity is limited by the fact that in everyday life we do not usually experience colors and insignificant figures as P or U; people who experience them so are generally considered to have "aesthetic endowment" or morbid sensitiveness. Thus it is not surprising that Gordon in her report, and Külpe (16) in his "Remarks"

[25] "Hedonic tone" is Beebe-Center's (55) expression to describe P-ness, U-ness and I-ness (p. 5).

following the report, maintained that because of the "emancipation of intellect and will" from the feelings of P-ness and U-ness, the effect of feeling on memory is indirect, and acts by influencing the attention.

b. Remembering of Material Associated with P-U Sensory Impressions

All the experiments in this group used odors as hedonic sensory material, and associated them with the subject matter to be recalled; two experiments also used visual, auditory, and tactile sensory impressions. The use of odors was based on the assertion, frequently reported in the literature, that odors have an especially great associative power. The experiments were partly concerned with the problem of whether this special associative power is inherent in odors or attributable to their "affective value."

Heywood and Vortriede (71) paired magazine pictures with odors, and established the affective-tone on the basis of retrospective reports; they paired pictures and nonsense syllables in control experiments. Harris (72) associated two-digit numbers with odors, and obtained retrospective reports. Gordon (73) used the names and rank-order of odors as their associates which were to be recalled, and instructed her subjects to arrange the odors according to hedonic value; she used odorless liquids in her control experiments. Ratliff (74) associated numbers with odors, and his subjects made the hedonic rating. Heywood and Vortriede, and Harris used immediate recall tests; they found that odors had no special associative power, but that any kind of incidental affective-tone reported on the basis of introspection seemed to facilitate recall. There were two other similar studies; Bolger and Titchener's (75), which was inconclusive; and Kenneth's (76), which showed that in many cases olfactory stimuli, but not the affective-tone, aroused forgotten experiences. Gordon, who used immediate recall, found no preference for P over U, and concluded: "If any difference has been shown it is in favor of the unpleasant, but we are inclined to doubt the validity of this difference" (p. 239). Ratliff, who used delayed-recall tests—five and ten minutes' delay—found that U associates exceeded P associates in respect to speed of learning, amount and speed of recall, and errors.

These experiments have the merit that in them the hedonic tone was established by the subjects themselves. Although the studies in which hedonic tone was established by group ratings were carefully controlled and their results established statistically (Gordon, Ratliff), they did not show an advantage of P-ness over U-ness in the remembering of the investigated instances. The studies using hedonic tone established introspectively, but occurring incidentally, tended to show a facilitating effect of any hedonic tone, whether P or U. All these experiments agreed that odors showed no special associative power. The shortcomings of the experi-

ments lay in the use of small numbers of subjects (with the exception of
Gordon's 200 and Ratliff's 69) and in the use of immediate recall—or recall
after a very short delay—where, according to later investigations, the
influence of "emotional factors" is insignificant.

Ratliff (74) and Wuerdemann (77) were the only investigators to discuss
the nature of the emotional factor investigated. Also, they used other
sensory material in addition to the olfactory. Ratliff repeated his experiment, replacing odors by pitches and colors; in contrast to his previous
results, he found that the recall of numbers associated with P pitch and
color was superior to that of numbers associated with U pitch and color.
He attempted to explain this difference by referring to Cannon's (78)
thalamic theory of emotions.[26] His theoretical explanation deserves our
interest, as he is one of the few experimenters who attempted to connect a
theory of emotions with their findings on the effect of an "emotional factor"
on memory. Ratliff's conception of the thalamic theory is that ". . . the
neural mechanisms responsible for emotional expression are located at the
base of the thalamic region" and that ". . . the cortex exerts an inhibitory
control over these expressions"; "Lashley . . . raises doubts as to the
source of inhibition" (p. 700) On the basis of Lashley's doubts, Ratliff
localizes the repressing mechanism for U stimuli in the thalamus, and
explains that the discrepancy between the results obtained with the use
of olfactory stimuli and those obtained with the use of visual and acoustic
stimuli is due to the position of the corresponding lower centers, of which
the functions of the auditory and visual, but not of the olfactory, can be
repressed from the thalamus.[27] This argument implies several difficulties.
First, it does not clarify the relation of emotions to the subjects' PUI
judgments of the visual, auditory, and olfactory stimuli. Secondly, the
experiment deals with, at best, the emotion "felt," and yet is linked by
Ratliff with the thalamic theory described here as explaining the mechanism of "emotional expression";[28] emotion "felt" as a psychic phenomenon

[26] See also Bard's (79) discussion of this theory.
[27] Ratliff writes: ". . . results of the present experiment might be interpreted as
indicating that the repressing mechanism for U stimuli, as postulated by the Freud-
ians, is represented in the thalamus and therefore, operates in audition and vision
but not in olfaction. This position is taken because neurologists locate the lower
centers for audition and vision in the diencephalon and those for olfaction in the
rhinencephalon. If, however, the cortex is found to be the center for repression and
if it exerts greater and more direct control over the thalamus than over the uncus
and hippocampus, the difference between the auditory-visual inhibitions and those
of olfaction might be accounted for." (p. 700)
[28] It may be argued that Head's (80) and Wilson's (81, 82) clinical findings demonstrate that "emotion felt" is also localized in the thalamus. However, the evidence
for this is limited; and it can hardly be denied that emotion is a conscious experience.

obviously must be carefully differentiated from "emotional expression," which may imply simply somatic manifestations. Thirdly, no attempt is made to explain the relation of this theory to the memory function. This premature hypothesis reveals the gap between the standard theory of emotion and all that is frequently called "emotional" by academic, educational, and clinical psychologists. It also reveals that the endeavor to explain "the emotional influence on memory" on a physiological basis[29] leads to a fallacious identification of the source of "emotion felt" with the source of "emotional expression." If it were maintained that not only "emotional expression" but also "emotion felt" is localized in the thalamus, this theory would be subject to experimental proof or disproof.[30] If, however, this identity is tacitly assumed, it escapes scientific scrutiny.

Wuerdemann (77) of the Krueger school of "Ganzheit" psychology has reviewed previous experimentation. He points out that: (a) the procedures used in these experiments were much too simple, compared with the usual process of remembering in everyday life; (b) the feelings aroused were relatively weak and superficial; (c) the assumption that every feeling is ultimately either P or U was maintained dogmatically. Wuerdemann in his experiments used stereometric figures of different colors and varying tactile surfaces and presented them together with odors. The subjects were asked to accept passively the experience; thus the recall—after 24 hours, two weeks, and six weeks—tested incidental memory, the type of memory occurring in everyday life.[31] Moreover, as in a life-situation, the experience consisted of a complex of different qualities, rendering the recall a process of "redintegration."[32] The measure of retention was consequently not the quantity of recall, but the certainty and adequacy of redintegration.[33] The feeling-tone, its intensity, and its depth were established on the basis of introspective reports. A great variety of feelings was reported, but no attempt was made to classify them as P or U. Wuerdemann adopts Krueger's theory of feelings, according to which feeling is a "whole-quality" of experience.[34] Thus the influence of feelings on memory

[29] In this connection see Hunter (83, pp. 331–332).

[30] In Chapter II we have already discussed, and in Chapter V we shall discuss in greater detail, the relation of "emotion felt" to "emotional expression."

[31] Among the experiments reported so far, only the reproduction experiment in the diagnostic-association experiment tested incidental memory.

[32] An experiment by Stagner (84) also using the redintegration method will be reported later.

[33] "(a) 1 was the score when the two part-complexes were appropriately coordinated with a feeling of security. (b) 0 was the score of a bad coordination with a feeling of security. (c) $\frac{3}{4}$ was the score of good coordination with feeling of probability; (d) $\frac{1}{2}$ was the score of good coordination with labile feelings; (e) $\frac{1}{4}$ was the score of good coordination with considerable uncertainty." (p. 535)

[34] "The feeling is just the usual experience into which the others are embedded with more or less sharp contours." (p. 555)

becomes a tautology, inasmuch as a stronger "whole-quality" or "feeling"—which we would call a "memory-connection"—makes for a better retention. Wuerdemann summed up the results of his experiment as follows:

"(1) Experiences of great feeling-intensity and depth are remembered better than those weak and superficial in feeling. (2) An especially unique feeling-quality causes also better and longer retention. (3) That feeling promotes retention is explained by the fact that the remembering of part experiences becomes frequently possible only by their reviving whole-attitudes (Gesamthaltungen) or diffuse whole-qualities which we have shown to be identical with feelings. (4) Especially clear was the memory revival related to diffuse whole-qualities due to olfactory impressions. (5) The so-called associative power of odors is explained as a result of special emotionality of the impression." (pp. 567–568)

Among the experiments considered in this section, those which established feeling-tone from introspective reports made in the course of the experiment tended to show a dependence of recall on intensity of feeling, irrespective of P-U quality; those which established the P-U quality of the material by judgments of the subjects prior to the experiment proper found in general no superiority of the remembering of P associates over U associates. This discrepancy is parallel to that frequently found between the results of clinical observation and those of experimental-statistical treatment. We have discussed several attempts to explain the nature of the affective-tone on the basis of standard theories of emotion. These attempts have proved to be premature. Though lacking sufficient theoretical foundation, Ratliff's experiment aimed to prove the Freudian theory of "forgetting of the unpleasant," and Gordon's aimed to disprove it.

c. Remembering of Material with Interpolated P-U Sensory Impressions

The following experiments interpolated various allegedly disturbing or stimulating impressions into the course of learning neutral word material. The aim of this interpolation, originated by Tait (69), was to find an experimental miniature equivalent of shocks producing amnesias.[35] The fact that the interpolation of any material, whether emotional or not, operates according to the laws of retroactive inhibition[36] was apparently overlooked. The attempts to bring retrograde amnesia and retroactive inhibition to a common denominator[37] failed to justify Tait's idea, for they disregarded the emotional background of amnesia.

Tait (69) interpolated odors, the sound of a bell, the sound of a pistol shot, and experimentally-created dizziness into the course of learning, or in the interval between learning and recall. Robinson presented photo-

[35] See Tait (69, pp. 10–11).
[36] See Britt's (85) survey for the theories of retroactive inhibition.
[37] See e.g. Sears (86).

graphs of naked persons as interpolation.   Stone (87) presented pictures
of Russian famine victims and of Jesuits being tortured by Indians; he also
interpolated artificial blazes, and even asked his subjects to imagine that
their parents had died and to simulate the bodily expressions of grief (a
most effective way to elicit emotions, according to James).   Harden (88)
interpolated strong odors, the loss of bodily support, the crash of falling
objects, a brilliant flash of light, and electrical shock to elicit "emotional
interaction."   White (89) interpolated electrical shock.   These experiments used word lists for neutral material.   Measurements of emotions
were taken by Stone, who measured blood pressure, and White, who
measured P.G.R.   Tait found that although pistol shots have a marked
detrimental effect on recall, the effect of other interpolations is insignificant,
and the effect is greater when the interpolation occurs after learning.   The
results of Robinson's and Harden's experiments were indecisive, showing
only a slight tendency towards a detrimental effect on recall.   Stone and
White both found that interpolation sometimes facilitates and sometimes
inhibits recall.

Several of these experimenters refer to a theory on the basis of which
their findings may be explained, or their method justified.   Tait constructs the concept of a "psychophysical attitude," of which the physical
aspect is the arousal of an instinct and the psychological aspect is the corresponding emotion; these attitudes should determine the orientation of
the organism.   Stone, following James' theory of emotions, appears to
think that the imitation of expressive movements of emotion, or the in-
spection of pictures whose content if experienced would arouse emotion,
can elicit emotions sufficiently strong to exert a measurable effect on memory.   White endeavors to explain his results, similar to those of W. W.
Smith (36) by referring to Dashiel's (90) hypothesis that mild emotions
promote, but that strong emotions hinder, efficiency.   Frank and Ludwigh (91) were the only experimenters to be aware that they were measuring retroactive inhibition, and to ask their subjects for hedonic judgments
(absolute and relative) of the odors interpolated.   As neutral material,
they employed nonsense-syllables.   They found that interpolated P odors
facilitate, and that U odors inhibit, reproduction.   Whether this effect
was attributable to the hedonic tone of the odors or to the odors themselves, was left an open question.   Frank (92) investigated this problem.
He repeated the original experiment, and then introduced new odors
which changed the relative hedonic value of the odors used previously.
Frank expected that a change in the hedonic value of these odors would
result in a change in their effect on memory.   As the expected change failed
to occur, Frank concluded that the odors themselves were responsible for
the results.

Although these experiments used similar methods, their aims were variegated (as, to prove or disprove the Freudian theory of repression, or to investigate the effect of P-ness and U-ness on memory) and their results were contradictory. Most of them appear to demonstrate some influence of affective-tone on memory, yet the insufficient number of subjects used and the operation of the factor of retroactive inhibition make the issue somewhat nebulous.

d. *"Repression" Elicited by Electric Shock*

Two experiments fall into this category; both claim to have elicited "repression" experimentally by electric shock. Diven's (93) careful and stimulative experiment, which used a conditioning method, will be discussed in Chapter VIII. McGranahan's (94) aim was to test experimentally the Freudian theory of repression. In an association experiment the subjects were instructed to react with adjectives to nouns selected to arouse color associations, and were told that color-reactions would be punished with an electric shock. A control group was used without the restriction concerning colors or the electric shock. The results were matched with pursuit-meter performances of the subjects to compare "the capacity of subjects to carry out organized activity under a task motive" and their ability to "be uninfluenced by such conditions as fear" (p. 222). McGranahan stated the results as follows:

"Thus a tendency appeared for subjects who were most disorganized and overwhelmed by fear during motor performance to be least able to execute cognitive repression, and those least disturbed to be best able." (p. 222)

He included an extensive discussion of the Freudian theory of repression, giving a well-justified criticism of others' experiments on repression:

"Freud constantly remarks, particularly in his older writings, that repression deals with 'unpleasant thoughts' or 'painful ideas' or 'ideas that might awaken pain.' A number of American psychologists have taken this to mean any unpleasant experience whatsoever and have set out to 'test Freud's theory of repression' by seeing whether in experimental situations pleasant experiences are recalled better than unpleasant experiences." (p. 213)

Yet McGranahan's interpretation of repression as being in "close association" with "self-esteem and shame" (p. 218) is also questionable; instead of proving that he had investigated a repression phenomenon,—in the Freudian sense—McGranahan constructed on the basis of his experiment a repression theory of his own.[38] McGranahan did not measure repression

---

[38] "(1) Repression is conceived as a matter of *direct action and constraint upon the activity of consciousness* rather than upon non-conscious material viewed as trying to enter the 'chamber of consciousness.' (2) The material avoided in repression

as conceived of in psychoanalytic literature. According to Freud (5, p. 150), repression is an *unconscious* process; in McGranahan's experiment the avoidance of color-reactions was the result of *conscious* intention. The color-reactions given by some of the subjects, rather than the color-reactions avoided, are more pertinent to our problem: they reveal that, in spite of the conscious intention to avoid them, unconscious motives impel color-reactions. McGranahan demonstrated affect-determined remembering (performance) rather than forgetting (non-performance). This stress on individual differences is McGranahan's contribution.

e. Summary

α. In the experiments surveyed in this section, the source of the "emotional factor" ranged from P-ness and U-ness of sensory material to electrical shocks. In the latter, genuine emotional effects were evident; the former were recognized to be judgmental categories. The presence of an emotional factor was often arbitrarily judged by the examiner, sometimes introspectively by the subjects, but rarely by the subjects prior to the experiment.

β. Most of the experiments used a small number of subjects and insufficient controls; the verbal material employed was limited to nonsense syllables and isolated words. In one group of experiments, the factor of retroactive inhibition made the results dubious.

γ. Few attempts were made to link the experiments with a theory of emotion; and even these demonstrated only the schism between the theories dealing with bodily concomitants of emotion and those dealing with the psychological processes of emotions influencing memory. The experiments claiming to prove or disprove the Freudian theory of forgetting advanced either no justification for their claim or insufficient argument. Only Diven's experiment avoided most of these difficulties.

ϑ. Although the results were contradictory on the quality of the influence exerted by the "emotional factor," it seems safe to assert that they demonstrated the existence of some such influence on memory. No evidence was found sufficient to establish the dependence of this effect on the P-ness or U-ness of the emotional factor. This influence occurs on various levels and in various forms, and shows significant individual differences.

---

may be any material which if reported would be painful and frustrating to certain motivational conditions—typically the motive of self-esteem—which are primarily concerned with the having of one kind of conscious content and the avoiding of another kind. Repression is thus not limited to awareness of unsocial motives, but is considered to extend to any material that would fulfill these conditions. (3) Repression is considered to be a direct function of cognitive organization, rather than of fear or anxiety." (p. 224)

B. EXPERIMENTS ON THE REMEMBERING OF PLEASANT AND UNPLEASANT
LIFE-EXPERIENCES

The experiments to be surveyed in this section utilized the method of recalling life-experiences. In comparison with the memory experiments which employed sensory material to introduce an emotional factor, surveyed in the previous section, and with those which employed PUI words to the same end, to be surveyed in the next section, the experiments utilizing the recall of PUI life-experiences were considered more life-like. Meltzer (95), who gave the first exhaustive survey of the experiments dealing with the "relationship of feeling to memory," championed this view. He emphasized that memory is a function of the total personality, and that artificial laboratory experiments employing material irrelevant to the subject's interests are "not applicable to the study of feeling-reactions in everyday life" (p. 133). It was stressed by him that solely those experiments utilizing life-experiences are relevant to the Freudian theory of forgetting. We quote Meltzer's view, as it provides the opportunity to scrutinize the alleged advantages of utilizing life-experiences. Although life-experiences have a much greater personal relevance than arbitrarily-selected P and U words or P and U sensory material, skepticism regarding the optimism of Meltzer and other investigators on their use appears to be justified. First, it is questionable whether genuinely relevant, emotional experiences will be communicated by the subjects to the experimenter; it is also questionable whether the average subject is able to verbalize adequately the experiences of true emotional relevance.[39] Secondly, even if it is assumed that the experiences reported are emotionally relevant, their PUI classification will be but a judgment—in the sense of Carr and Peters—as was the PUI rating of words and sensory material. The memory of the emotional tone of the experience and the present hedonic judgment of it are so hopelessly intermingled that the rating becomes an "opinion," rendering

---

[39] In this respect, Whitehorn's (96) comments are elucidating:
"For a good many years I have been interested in listening to patient's accounts of their emotions. At one time I naively supposed that I might learn thereby just how the patient was feeling, perhaps even be able to label 'the emotions' which he was experiencing. I still listen with great interest to patient's statements along these lines, but not with the expectation of discovering what 'emotions' he or she is really experiencing—rather with the hope of understanding in some measure the conventionalized scheme of symbols by which the patient tries to represent himself to himself and to others. Not only are the words conventional symbols; the motor patterns of behavior are also conventionalized. Sometimes such conventionalized patterns of behavior and the corresponding verbalizations are used with the deliberate intension of deceiving others, but this is not the phenomenon of which I now speak. I refer to the degree of conventionality in the patterning of behavior by which one reacts overtly in an emotional experience." (p. 263)

the method similar to that of questionnaires. Thirdly, it cannot be expected that the U judgments will be applied to those experiences upon which repression, in the Freudian sense, has acted. Further, a principal difficulty in these experiments weakens their relevance to repression: the approach in them was a quantitative one, like that of the classical memory experimentation; but an investigation of repression, being an investigation of changes rather than of losses, requires a qualitative approach.[40] Forgetting as a result of repression is the extreme case of memory-changes effected by the repression process.[41]

The first studies to use the recall of experiences were published by Kowalewski (97) and by Henderson (98). Kowalewski asked school-children to report P and U experiences of a vacation-day on the day following, and ten days later. At the first test 62% of the children, and at the second test 61.4%, reported more P than U experiences; Kowalewski called this group "memory-optimists." Henderson asked his subjects to report one hundred experiences. Realizing that feeling-tone at the time of the experience might differ from the feeling-tone at the time of reporting it, he asked for the rating of the feeling-tone present at the time of the experience. More P than U, more U than I, and more intensive than superficial feelings were reported.[42]

Kowalewski concluded that the majority of people are "memory-optimists"; but failed to analyze whether the prevalence of reported P experiences corresponded to their prevalence in daily experience or whether the feeling-tone reported was merely a retrospective judgment. Henderson raised doubts as to whether the subjects related all the disagreeable experiences as recalled, whether their hedonic judgments were adequate, and whether the prevalence of P experiences in the reports was accounted for by a prevalence of P experiences in everyday life. After weighing these considerations, he concluded that his data, although roughly indicating a superiority of P experiences in remembering, did not warrant such a conclusion as Kowalewski's. Moreover, Henderson maintained that there was a difference between forgetting disagreeable experiences and discarding disagreeable memories: that is, the feeling-tone of an experience and the feeling-tone of a memory are two different matters. His general view of the problem of forgetting, had it attracted more attention, might have prevented many fruitless experiments. He wrote:

". . . when thought cannot cure the situation, we instead cure the thought by forgetting it. We forget not so much disagreeable ideas as useless ideas, ideas the distasteful quality of which stimulates us to know devices that modify their object

---

[40] See C. G. Crosland (70).
[41] See Chapter V.
[42] Henderson was the first experimenter to ask for intensity ratings.

. . . to forget the disagreeable would mean that we would be deprived of one of the principal sources of thinking."

The subjective-empirical truth of this statement deserves scientific attention; and it is regrettable that instead of this, the commonplace truth of the "forgetting of the disagreeable" was emphasized.

In the subsequent experimentation, the problem of the proportion of P-ness and U-ness and I-ness among life-experiences was attacked first. Fluegel (99, 100) reported an analysis of the diaries of nine subjects, highly trained in introspection. The diary-records were kept over a period of a month and contained notes written at sixty-minute intervals recording the intensity, duration, and quallty of the experiences. Fluegel found that *"pleasure occupies a very considerably larger proportion in human life than does unpleasure"* (100, pp. 328–329).

Several reservations must be made concerning these interesting results. First, the effect of concentrated attention on the feeling-tone of the experience, for the purpose of recording it, is problematic. Secondly, Fluegel's data refer to the duration of the experiences rather than to their quantity. Thirdly, Fluegel admitted that:

"There is unfortunately no means of estimating or measuring the extent of . . . these errors [which] . . . consist in a constant tendency for certain subjects to allot relatively high or relatively low marks for the affective intensity of their experiences or to be biased in favour of allotting + or − values." (p. 327)

However, Cason (101)[43] was able to demonstrate that:

"There was a tendency to exaggerate the number, duration, and strength of both the P and U scores; but a greater tendency to exaggerate the number, duration, and strength of the P scores." (p. 70)

Fourthly, Fluegel did not attempt to relate his findings to the personalities of the individual subjects.

His findings, corroborated in several later studies, apparently mean that subjects are inclined to report and judge experiences so that the majority is rated as P. Wohlgemuth (102) repeated Kowalewski's experiment and re-interpreted Kowalewski's data, taking Fluegel's results into consideration. He found no prevalence of P experiences in remembering, and felt he had disproved the Freudian theory of forgetting; he argued that the truth of this psychoanalytic theory can be settled only by experimental psychological investigation.[44] It can hardly be denied that the support of an experimental demonstration is valuable to any theory, even though

[43] Experiment No. V.
[44] "The statement that unpleasant experiences are more easily forgotten than pleasant ones is often found in psychoanalytic literature. Whether this is true or not can, I believe, only be settled by experimental psychological investigation;

many unquestionably useful theories were never experimentally validated (e.g., the theory of evolution). Experimental decision upon a theory, however, presupposes the proved relevance of the experiment to the theory in question. Neither Wohlgemuth, who undertook to disprove the Freudian theory of forgetting, nor most of the experimenters who undertook to prove it, attempted or were able to demonstrate this relevance. Gordon (103), for example, asked for the recall of earliest childhood experiences; finding that the majority of those reported was U, she stated that this result tends to disprove the existence of any general tendency to forget the disagreeable (p. 129). The psychoanalyst, however, would characterize the reported memories as "screen memories" designed to replace even more distressing and hence repressed childhood experiences; this explanation would use Gordon's results to prove what she attempted to disprove.[45]

In 1930 Meltzer published the first critical survey (95) of all the pertinent experiments,[46] and Meltzer and Koch each published reports of careful experiments, the results of which were interpreted rather cautiously. Meltzer in his survey criticized the lack of "life-likeness" of the previous experiments and emphasized that conclusive results could be reached only with "life-like" material, such as the remembering of experiences. He pointed out the insufficient number of subjects previously used, the unwarranted assumptions made, and the forced interpretations advanced in most of the studies.

Meltzer based his experiment on the conclusions of his survey. College students—77 men, 55 women—described their experiences of a Christmas vacation on the day following and six weeks later, judged these experiences as P, U, and I and rated them on a five-point scale as to vividness. Meltzer analyzed the data with regard first to individual differences (104), secondly to the relation of the results to I.Q. and school achievement (105), and thirdly to sex differences (106). Koch (107) asked each of her educational-psychology students to rate ten quiz-grades on a five-point scale of emotional reacton immediately upon receipt of the grades. Five weeks after the last quiz, recall of the ten grades was requested; the results were compared with I.Q. and a personality-questionnaire. These experiments had several advantages over the earlier experiments. Meltzer was able to establish the changes occurring between immediate and delayed recall

---

psycho-analysis does not, and cannot, furnish a scientific proof one way or the other. Nevertheless the above statement is postulated as a fact, and I have come across the assertion that 'the fact itself is beyond dispute, and has not been questioned by anyone who has seriously investigated the phenomenon, either experimentally or clinically.' " (p. 405)

[45] See Chapter V, section on infantile amnesia (pp. 155–156).

[46] Meltzer's review included all the types of experiments dealt with in this chapter.

of the experiences, while Koch established the emotional-tone at the time of the experience. Thus, both avoided the fallacy of assuming an equal proportion of P and U experiences in everyday life. Koch and Meltzer each found a prevalence of P experiences over U experiences in recall, and a prevalence of both P and U experiences over I experiences. They found great individual differences in these tendencies; Meltzer found individuals who forgot the P more than the U, but they were in a minority.[47] Neither Koch nor Meltzer found a significant correlation between intelligence and "influence of feeling-tone on memory." Meltzer's results were only suggestive of some sex differences.[48]

The reports of both Meltzer and Koch are distinguished in that they discuss the nature of the "affective factor." Also, they take a stand on the psychoanalytic theory of forgetting. Meltzer makes it clear that at present we have no proof that affective-tone conditions memory, and concludes that to speak of a causal relation between the two is an error; he suggests it would be more logical to suppose that both memory and feeling are conditioned by the same factors (104, p. 401). Koch describes a great variety of views on U-ness,[49] intermixing theories of emotion and feeling, and their physiological and introspective aspects. However, she points out the advantages of a judgmental theory, maintaining that the effect of the "affective factor" on memory is probably indirect; and she concludes:

"The problem will, doubtless, be given a more satisfactory answer after we have probed deeply into the question of the genesis and development of our values and the relation of these to such extra-organismal influences as social, moral, and philosophical traditions." (p. 186)

In spite of their advanced methodological thinking, neither Meltzer nor Koch avoided hasty conclusions concerning the relation of their results to the psychoanalytic theory. Meltzer thought he had investigated a phenomenon as lifelike and personal, although not so startling, as the repression phenomenon of the psychoanalyst; he considered his results to be in

---

[47] Meltzer found 56.4% optimists, 35.87% pessimists and 7.64% indifferentists.

[48] The problem of sex differences was also discussed by Colegrove (11), Gordon (73), and Tolman and Johnson (35).

[49] ". . . among the various views of unpleasantness that have been held—(a) that it is a psychic element, (b) an expression of the domination of the sympathetic nervous system over the cranio-sacral, (c) a pattern yielded by thalamic activity of a certain sort, (d) an instinctive reaction to thwarting, (e) an accompaniment of an energy deficiency, (f) a withdrawal reaction, (g) a value judgment upon stimuli, in terms of whether they normally arouse negatively adaptive responses—the latter seems to the author the most in keeping with the facts . . ." (p. 185)

harmony with the psychoanalytic theory. Koch, on the basis of the advantage in recall of both P and U experiences over I experiences, concluded: "It would be difficult to account for our results merely with an endopsychic censor" (p. 185).

These experiments were repeated by several investigators. Jersild (108) asked for reports of P and U experiences which had occurred in the three weeks immediately preceding the experiment. The time of reporting was limited; after twenty-one days a delayed-recall test was given. Cason (101) asked for reports of typical everyday incidents, and his subjects rated the intensity of P-ness and U-ness and the degree of perfection of the recall; the procedure was repeated three weeks later. Thomson (109) asked the subjects to keep diaries with P, U and I ratings over a period of five days, and gave recall tests after two and four weeks. Menzies (110, 111) asked for the report of P, U and I experiences of the day preceding the experiment, and gave delayed-recall tests after one and three weeks. Susukita (15) had children keep diaries of summer vacations, and asked for the recall of the contents on the first school day and after four weeks. Later Waters and Leeper (112) repeated Meltzer's experiment, with the aim of testing the fate of the experiences and their feeling-tone in delayed recall; they limited the time allowed for reporting and asked for intensity ratings, using eight groups of subjects and recall tests with delays ranging from 2 to 140 days. O'Kelley and Steckle (113) also repeated Meltzer's experiment, with recall after ten weeks.

Jersild found that more P than U experiences were reported, and that in delayed-recall the memory for P experiences was both absolutely and relatively better than for U experiences; he concluded that we forget U experiences either because they change in quality and are no longer U, or because they are less frequently rehearsed than P experiences. Cason found that in delayed-recall both P and U experiences tend to become I, though this is more marked in U experiences; the extremely P and U experiences are remembered equally well and somewhat better than mildly P and U or I experiences. He concluded that the intensity, not the quality, of the feeling-tone has an influence on memory. Thomson found an advantage of P over U experiences in recall, but this advantage was statistically not reliable. Menzies, like Cason, found that recall is influenced by the intensity of feeling-tone but not by its quality, and that the strength of affective-tone fades in time. Susukita's results supported Fluegel's (100) conclusion that P experiments constitute a greater part of daily life than U experiences; he found further that although the absolute number of remembered P experiences was greater than that of U experiences, in delayed-recall more P experiences were forgotten than U. He revived the "memory-optimist" and "memory-pessimist" classifications. Waters and

Leeper's results corroborated those of Cason and of Menzies, and disproved Jersild's contention that the difference between remembered P and U experiences is due to frequency of rehearsal. O'Kelley and Steckle compared their results with those of three other investigators who used varying periods of delay.[50] They concluded, from a very questionable comparison of material gathered from these different sources, that P events, although always more numerous, tend to be more quickly forgotten than U events. They emphasized the extent of individual differences, and found that while memory-optimists tend to forget P and U events equally, memory-pessimists more quickly forget P events.

Except for occasional perfunctory references to the "law of effect" and to the Freudian theory of forgetting, these experimental reports usually have been devoid of any explanation of the nature of the "emotional factor" involved. Waters and Leeper shed some light on the relation of the "law of effect" to this type of experimentation. This relation had been nebulous even to such acute investigators as Henderson and Meltzer: Henderson had identified the forgetting of U experiences, and Meltzer the Freudian theory of forgetting, with the law of effect. Waters and Leeper write:

> "The law of effect says simply that the subject will tend to avoid *performing* the act that formerly was followed by unpleasantness, it says nothing about his *remembering* his former experience and the unpleasantness connected with it. As a matter of fact, from ordinary observation, we would conclude that generally the reason a subject does not repeat his former unwise actions is because of the very fact that he does remember them and their consequences." (p. 214)

One more experiment, that of Stagner (84), should be mentioned in this connection, although its method differs greatly from that of the others and resembles rather Wuerdemann's experiment.[51] Stagner asked his subjects to write down a recent P and a recent U experience, with all trivial facts associated with each. In the delayed-recall test, the recall of the associated trivial facts was requested. The recall was rightly characterized as "redintegration," and was measured in terms of accuracy and completeness. The superiority of the "redintegration" of P experiences was established with statistical reliability. The number of associates given to P experiences was greater than that given to U experiences, but the difference only approached reliability; the average age of P experiences was reliably greater than that of U experiences. Stagner concluded that these data "indicate a trend towards the presence of an active process of repression" (p. 466).

Stagner's experiment has the advantage that it investigates not the for-

---

[50] They apparently were unacquainted with the many other experiments which attacked the problem of length of delay.

[51] See pp. 64–65.

getting of an experience but rather some of the changes which the experience undergoes in time. Stagner in this study shares Meltzer's view that the relation of retention to feeling-tone is one which does not imply causation. He attempts to explain the common factor underlying both: "Such a factor may be possibly found in the nature of an adaptive response" (p. 467). The U events, according to him, set up a tension "about which something must be done," while about the P events "nothing need be done." Adaptation is a release of tension, and as tensions involve changes in brain patterns they "must inevitably result in changes in the memory traces of the experience related" (p. 467). Such an attempted explanation would certainly be supported by the Lewinian and Gestalt psychology,[52] if not by the psychoanalytic theory to which Stagner refers.

Summary

   a. From the fact that the majority of reported experiences was P, the early experiments using experiences as material concluded that P experiences are better remembered. This was found methodologically erroneous, as it was demonstrated that a greater part of our experiences was judged P. Subsequent experimentation avoided this error and based its conclusions on the comparison of report and delayed-recall, or of experimentally-controlled immediately-judged experience and delayed-recall.

   b. These experiments were shown to measure the influence of judgmental P-ness and U-ness rather than of "emotions," and to have implied a confusion of the *memory* of the feeling-tone as experienced with the P-U *judgment* of the experience at the time of reporting. In addition, there was found a tendency to over-estimate the P-ness and U-ness of experiences.

   c. The experiments tended to show that experiences of intense P-ness or U-ness were better retained than those having mild feeling-tone, and only a minority of the experiments indicated a better retention of P than of U experiences. A decrease of intensity of feeling-tone with the lapse of time was found. Most investigators agreed that in spite of the frequent statistical reliability of the results, the individual differences are great.

   d. The significant theoretical advancements were: (*i*) The relation of P-ness and U-ness to advantages in remembering cannot be considered a causal relationship; rather, both depend on a common factor. (*ii*) The judgmental, rather than the emotional, theory of P-ness and U-ness was advanced. Nevertheless, references to the "law of effect" were abundant, and attempts were made to prove or disprove the psychoanalytic theory of forgetting by means of experiments whose relevance to the theory has not yet been clarified.

   e. Thus, these experiments, although using material more meaningful

[52] See Chapter IV, pp. 133-134, and in general the trace-theory of Koffka.

and lifelike than the experiments surveyed in the previous section, demonstrated still only a mediate influence of the emotional factor through judgmental P-ness and U-ness. Their value should not be under-estimated, even though it is observed that they claim to prove or disprove theories to which their relevance has not been established, and that their frequent theoretical inadequacy and inherent methodological difficulties reduce their cogency.

C. EXPERIMENTS ON THE REMEMBERING OF LEARNED MATERIAL

The apparently simplest way to investigate experimentally the influence of emotion on memory was suggested by the classical method of memory experimentation, which proceeded on the assumption that the properties of memory-functioning could be established by measuring the recall of nonsense-syllables, words, and texts learned by the subjects. It was a simple matter to assume next that if P, U, and I words were chosen for learning and the same method used, the recall would reflect the influence of these varied "emotional-tones" on memory functioning. Most of the experiments to be surveyed in this section employed this method. The means of establishing the "emotional-tone" of the words varied considerably: the feeling-tone was determined arbitrarily at first by the experimenter, in more recent experiments by judges, and most recently by the individual subject or by the experimenter on the basis of knowledge about the individual subject. Emotionally labile subjects were used in some instances to demonstrate the effect of the emotional-tone on memory; in other studies the learning-situation was so constructed as to reinforce the emotional-tone of the words.

Criticisms directed at the classical memory experiments are equally valid for the experiments discussed in this section. Gestalt psychology (Koehler, 114, Chapter IX) maintains that the method of learning word-lists disregards the essential factor in psychological functioning and in learning especially: namely, that of "meaning." The application of this learning-method to our problem was criticized by Meltzer (95), who characterized the method as lifeless and thus unable to measure an "emotional influence." In opposition to Meltzer's arguments, Barret (115) advances the following view:

"It is suggested that it might be easier to control and measure hedonic tone and its varying degrees in an experiment in which words rather than experiences are used. . . . Because of the difficulties involved in using pleasant and unpleasant experiences in studying the problem many investigators have made use of word lists. . . . The first difficulty in using lists of words appears to be that should negative results be obtained one would not be certain whether the results were due to the relatively innocuous nature of the materials used or whether there were really no differences which might be related to qualitative differences of hedonic tone to be found at any point on the scale.   If, however, differences could be established with simple, well-controlled methods one could feel confident of the results.   Further, with the simple situation it might be possible to vary the experiment in some way to obtain further information which could be helpful in interpreting the results." (p. 16)

Barret has been able to control strictly her experiments on the recall of words judged P, U, and I by the subjects, and to vary the experiment in such a manner as to glean further information useful in the interpretation of her results.   However, control and variation solely of the experimental situation are not sufficient to explain how the differences in recall of the words judged P, U, or I are related to the effect of emotions on memory, or how results obtained under artificial conditions and with meaningless material are relevant to the selective remembering observed in life situations.   Neither Barret nor the other experimenters using this method have clarified these relations.   All they have demonstrated is that even personally irrelevant and "lifeless" material judged P, U, and I elicits individual differences of recall.   The situation reminds one of Straus's (116) discussion of the Pavlovian reflexology: he endeavored to show that the Pavlovian conditioned reflex, far from being the archetype and basic element of psychological functioning, is the reaction of an animal deprived of its freedom of movement and set in an environment barren of all the conditions present in its everyday environment.[53]   Straus admits that Pavlov's description of the reactions of the experimental animals in this situation is adequate; but he shows that to draw conclusions concerning general laws of psychic functioning based on these observations is unwarranted, and that these conclusions were arbitrarily postulated by Pavlov. Likewise, the results of our next group of experiments will have validity only for the relatively meaningless learning-material used, and for P-ness, U-ness, and I-ness established by judgments.

If we will regard the psychic apparatus as a hierarchy, at whose foundation instinctual forces are the determining factors and in whose upper structure logical reasoning rules, with varied derivatives of the instinctual

[53] "We must not forget that during the experiment the animals are kept in an environment which is entirely different from their natural environment.   The laboratory is cut off from the outside world.   No light, no noise, no breeze penetrates from the outside.   The animal is kept in an atmosphere of monotonous, unchangeable silence.   After a period granted to the animal to become accustomed to this environment, the experiment begins.   The animals are put on tables, harnessed in frames; registering devices are fastened to them, and then they are left in the laboratory all to themselves.   The experimenter observes them from the adjoining room, without being seen by the animals.   All the 'stimuli' reach the animals in a mechanical way.   The utmost care is taken to shut out changes, that is stimuli with which the experimenter does not want to operate at the moment." (pp. 30–31)

forces between, then we may formulate more concretely our expectation concerning the results of the experiments to be surveyed. Any experiment using "emotional-tone" established by any method, and pertaining to any level of this hierarchy, may yield some information about the influence of the "emotional-tone" on memory. When a great distance exists between the "emotional-tone" investigated in the experiment and the instinctual forces of the hierarchy, and where its dependence on the instinctual forces is vague, the experiments will yield only quantitative measures of the differences in the recall; and the greater this distance, the less will they yield information on the dynamics of the influence of emotions on memory. It is a fact that the method of the classical memory experiment was *a priori* designed to measure only the quantitative aspect of memory, without reflecting its dynamics. Judgmental P-ness, U-ness, and I-ness, although certainly originating in basic affective attitudes, are but highly-intellectualized derivatives. We delineated the scope of the information which the experiments under discussion may be expected to yield. They gave rise, however, to several experiments whose results transcended this expectation.

a. Experiments on the Recall of P, U, and I Words

These experiments followed the classical method of memory experimentation more closely than any of the other experiments. They show a progressive improvement in that the experimental techniques became more adequate, although they retained the use of word-lists and of judgmental P-ness, U-ness, and I-ness. Although at first the P, U, and I words were arbitrarily selected, PGR measurements were later used to indicate the accuracy of this selection; still later, group judgments of the emotional-tone were obtained; finally, each subject judged the emotional-tone of the words he was to learn and recall. Other factors were also gradually subjected to control: the problem of partial and total learning, frequency, length of words, and so on.

Tait (69) and Tolman (117) published the first experiments of this kind; both determined arbitrarily the P, U, and I words. In Tait's experiments the words to be used were presented only once to the subjects; thus a memory phenomenon similar to the incidental memory which is common in everyday life was measured. Tait and Tolman both found a prevalence of P over U words and of P over I words, Tait measuring recall and Tolman learning. While Tait found that U words were favored over I words in recall, Tolman's results indicated the contrary; Tait found appreciable differences, and Tolman only a trend.

The reproduction experiments conducted as part of the diagnostic-association experiment have been previously discussed; although they may be considered as recall experiments, measuring incidental recall by the method of paired associates, we shall not discuss them again here. W. W. Smith's (37) reproduction experiment should be mentioned, however, as it introduced into these experiments the use of PGR measurements to establish the presence of an emotional-tone. Smith found that the emotional-tone as measured by the PGR influences memory. He called this influence —which he found might be positive or negative, favoring or impeding recall—"the bidirectional effect of emotions on memory"; but he did not associate these positive and negative influences with P-ness and U-ness. W. W. Smith's attempt was thus an improvement over Tait's and Tolman's arbitrary determination of the emotional-tone. His experiment was repeated, and his findings corroborated, by H. E. Jones (118). Later Lynch (119), accepting without question the word-lists and PGR measurements of Smith and Jones, gave his subjects immediate and delayed recognition tests. He found a high correlation between his results and those of Smith and Jones, but failed to find the bidirectional effect; his results in both tests showed a P-U-I sequence of recall-facility. Balken (120) and Stagner (121) investigated the relation of PGR measurements to the recall of learned material, and found a chance correlation. Later investigators used the PGR, not as the sole determiner of the emotional-tone and its intensity, but as a means of supporting the PUI judgments in selecting words to comprise the emotionally-toned material (Bunch and Wientge, 122; Carter, Jones, and Schock, 39). These experimenters gave no theoretical explanation of the functional interrelation between PGR and emotions influencing memory. It is doubtful whether at our present stage of knowledge such an explanation can be given, except for the postulation that the same factor conditions the PGR response and the differential memory response. That even such an explanation should be handled with caution is clearly stated by Stagner (121):

"Whatever else may be doubtful about the concept of 'affection,' it certainly is a conscious phenomenon and cannot be defined in physiological terms." (p. 130)

The arbitrary selection by the examiner of the words having an emotional-tone, and the use of PGR-measurements for this purpose, were followed in the course of experimentation by a tendency to establish the feeling-tone by group-judgments. Chaney and Lauer (123) had the PUI ratings of the words established by 150 judges, none of whom was in the experimental group. Under the influence of Meltzer's (95) survey, this was modified so that the PUI ratings were established by the experimental groups, and the experimental word-lists were selected from the words on whose rating there was maximal agreement (White and Ratliff, 124; Carter, Jones, and Schock, 39; Carter, 125; White, 126; Carter, 127; White and Powell, 128;

Carter and Jones, 129). A further step was taken by investigators who had each subject judge his own list of words (Thomson, 109; Stagner, 121; Silverman and Cason, 130). This procedure was carried still further by Thomson, who in one of his experiments asked his subjects to compose their own lists of PUI words, and by Bunch and Wientge (122), Cason (101), and Cason and Lungren (131), whose subjects selected words out of lists submitted to them. Establishing the emotional-tone by arbitrary judgments or by PGR measurements made for occasionally inconclusive results, but increasing conclusiveness was achieved as the experimental method approached comparing the individual's selective remembering with his own PUI judgments. Only one of the studies (Chaney and Lauer, 123), which used the judgments of a group other than the experimental group, was inconclusive. All the experiments basing the PUI rating on judgments of the experimental group, and all the experiments in which the subject selected his own PUI word-list, reported they had obtained positive results. Among the experiments in which the subject made his own PUI ratings, only the results of Cason and his pupils were interpreted as inconclusive; but the results of Cason's study, and of Silverman and Cason's study, indicate the presence of a trend towards better retention of P than of U words, and better retention of both than of I words. In these experiments, what is called a positive result is frequently only a statistical trend, the constancy of which indicates the presence of the effect.

Barret (115) selected the words for her experiment from lists used by previous experimenters, and had her subjects re-rate them PUI. She found that the difference between her selection and the average of the subjects' ratings was less than one per cent. This fact deserves attention, as it indicates wide social agreement regarding the so-called "emotional factor." This agreement in itself makes it obvious that here we are hardly dealing with a personal, deeply-rooted factor. Some understanding concerning the genesis of this "emotional factor" may be derived from Mueller's (132) explanation of the origin of the striving towards pleasantness, as distinguished from Freud's "pleasure principle." Mueller writes:

"The conscious search after pleasurable sensations is something which, in addition to the unconscious drives, plays a significant role in civilized man. *The more his being civilized inhibits him in satisfying his drives, the more obvious is his search for a substitute which he finds by exposing himself to pleasant stimuli.* The animals satisfy their drives or they face destruction in the struggle for satisfaction; they do not know this substitute, they rather know its opposite: the avoidance of disagreeable sensations. Man too tries to avoid pain, although he has the skill to learn to look for the pleasure itself; out of fear of pain he tries very early to rule his inclinations." (p. 265)

There were several other attempts to improve the experimental method. The problem whether the rank-order of favoredness in recall is P-U-I or

P-I-U—in other words, whether the quality or the intensity of the feeling-tone is of dominant importance in remembering—was a point of controversy in the experiments discussed. To investigate this problem, intensity-ratings of the feeling-tone were introduced. Earlier, Chaney and Lauer (123) had asked for intensity-ratings; Cason (101) made such ratings the nucleus of his investigations. This method, used also by White and Ratliff (128), was developed to its peak in Barret's experiment. The results reached by this method appeared to indicate that the difference in recall between more and less intensely feeling-toned words, and between feeling-toned and indifferent words, is much more significant than that between the recall of P and U words. As these findings indicated that not the disagreeable but the indifferent was most easily forgotten, several studies (especially Carter, Jones, and Shock's, 39, and Barret's, 115) concluded that this disproved the Freudian theory of forgetting. However, these experimenters made no attempt to prove the relevance of their experiments to the Freudian theory. In view of the position of P-ness, U-ness, and I-ness in the hierarchy of emotional factors, the possibility of proving such a relevance is slight. These experiments seem to indicate merely that any degree of judgmental "feeling-tone," but P-ness more than U-ness, lends an advantage in recall to the words to which it is attached. This interrelation could be otherwise described by the statement that the factors which make for P and U judgments of words also apparently enhance their availability for reproduction.

Another attempted improvement of the experimental method was the effort to measure incidental memory. We have already seen this effort in the reproduction-experiment employed in the association-experiments. It was well known that remembering in everyday life more often refers to an incidentally-perceived fact than to systematically-learned material: thus, to make the experiment more lifelike, the measurement of incidental memory for P, U, and I words was attempted (Silverman and Cason, 130; White and Ratliff, 128; Barret, 115; Lanier, 45, 133, 134). Barret emphasized the importance of testing incidental memory: ". . . word lists administered as memory tests permit mechanical associations to be forced into the material thus obscuring any factors which otherwise may be important" (p. 18). Silverman and Cason, Barret, and Lanier asked their subjects to make the PUI ratings while uninformed that recall would be requested. From an entirely different point of view, White and Ratliff came to doubt the adequacy of the learning procedure for testing the differential recall of feeling-toned material; they found that when time-limitation allowed for partial learning only, the advantage of P over U words was much more pronounced than when time allowed for full learning. The studies of Barret and of White and Ratliff were conclusive in demonstrating the advantage of P over U words; those of Silverman and Cason and of Lanier indicated only the presence of a trend in this direction. Barret's and Silverman and Cason's studies indicated an advantage of P and U words over I words. That incidental memory or recall after partial learning clearly shows a differential recall of feeling-toned material, and that complete learning equalizes the efficiency of recall, interlinks with Adams' (135) view that the learning process is too slow to permit observation of its dynamics.

The shortcut taken by investigating incidental memory and partial learning makes possible a glance into some processes of the learning of feeling-toned material. Among other attempts to exclude factors which might cloud the differential recall of PUI words, the following may be mentioned. There were attempts to use words selected as of equal frequency in usage, of equal length, and of identical grammatical category. Stagner (121) offered data to demonstrate that these factors do not exert a significant influence on the results of this type of experiment, and Carter, Jones, and Shock (39) agreed with this finding; but several of the later experiments, especially Barret's unusually careful study, made efforts to control these factors. Stagner (121) constructed an experiment to investigate the frequently disregarded effect of primacy and recency; Barret's (115) study also took this effect into account. The possibility that P words are better recalled because they have more associates had already been indicated by Griffitts's (49) association study. White (126) corroborated this finding, although he found great individual overlapping Barret's (115) results indicated only a slight relationship of the vividness of the hedonic-tone—the factor she considered important in eliciting differential recall—to the number of associations. The influence of the subjects' age on the superiority of P words in recall had been pointed out by Peters (42) in his experience-association studies; Thomson (109), Beebe-Center (55), and Carter (125) again called attention to this problem. Gilbert (136) investigated it experimentally and, like Peters (43, 44), found that the superiority of P words in recall is more evident in adults than in children.[54] The issue was not settled satisfactorily, because only Gilbert used

[54] "There is a development of hedonistic selectivity from childhood to adulty." (p. 435)
"The social restraint placed on hedonistic behavior in adults cannot be placed on natural thought habits, or tendencies, which are primarily hedonistic. On the contrary, it would serve to exaggerate them as a sort of compensation for the social restrictions on behavior. Children, however, finding their hedonistic impulses comparatively unrestrained, do not have to resort to such automatic measures of compensation . . . as other explanations might be that the distinction between pleasantness and unpleasantness in the higher mental processes have not been sufficiently well developed in children, simply because the higher processes themselves are still undergoing development." (p. 438)
These findings on the "development of hedonic selectivity" again demonstrate that the effect investigated is not that of "repression."

children under ten years of age; and Carter's studies with children above ten years of age and with adolescents, and Barret's and others' studies with college students, showed also a superiority of P over U words in recall.

Whether immediate or delayed recall is the better test of differential recall of P and U words has not been investigated so intensively here as in the experience experiments. White and Ratliff (124) came to the conclusion that the longer the delay, the more pronounced the effect. Gilbert (136) claimed that immediate recall is not a satisfactory test of superiority in recall.

Several surveys have contributed to the development of the experimentation described thus far, and that to be discussed in the remainder of this chapter. Meltzer's (95) positive criticism, Beebe-Center's (55) over-optimistic and Cason's (101, 137) over-pessimistic view of the results stimulated much of the technical improvement noted above. The surveys of Moore (138) and Gilbert (139) appraised the development that had taken place in the wake of the previous surveys. Also, most of the experimenters in their reports referred critically to previous experiments. But neither the surveys nor the historical comments of the experimental reports discussed the nature of the effect of emotional-tone on memory as investigated. It was not until 1937 that Young (140) published an experimental study in which he correlated the scores of genuine affective reactions to words—in place of the PUI judgments on them—with the scores indicating the differential recall of P and U words. He found no relation between the two, and concluded that the *meaning of P-ness and U-ness* and a *consciously felt experience of P-ness and U-ness* are entirely different considerations, and that his negative finding was "to be expected on the assumption that recalling *pleasant and unpleasant meaning* has little relation to *felt pleasantness and unpleasantness*" (p. 596). Young's theoretical explanation is that recall is a cerebral process, while it is assumed that the primary affective reactions are centered at the thalamic level. He maintains that although there are associatively aroused feelings, these are not necessarily present in the type of experiment discussed here.[55]

[55] "Recall is a cerebral process; the primary affective reactions are assumed to be centered at the level of the thalamus. There are, of course, cerebrally aroused feelings of pleasantness and of unpleasantness. Everyone knows that pleasantness and unpleasantness can be established by recalling past experiences and imagining possible situations. The report of felt pleasantness which is associatively aroused is one thing, but the mere listing of words with pleasant and unpleasant meanings is something different. Failure to recognize this distinction leads only to confusion.

"When the psychologist states that 'love,' 'beautiful,' and 'music' are *pleasant* words he knows that these words have associations which arouse or tend to arouse pleasant feeling. The awareness, however, of a pleasant *meaning* is not the same as

b. Recall of Liked Versus Disliked Material

The experiments in this small group used material which was more meaningful for the subject than that of the experiments with PUI words. Myers (141) and Laird (142) asked their subjects to write lists of names of people, foods, animals, colors, and so on. Later the subjects were asked to write down the names of items in these categories which they liked most and least. Myers found that the names of items liked most tended to appear early in the original lists, while those of items liked least tended either to appear late or to be omitted; he concluded that "from this it is pretty safe to infer that one intends to remember the agreeable rather than the disagreeable" (p. 90). Laird concluded that his results ". . . do not necessarily indicate the obliviscence of the displeasing" (p. 301); he obtained self- and group-judgments of the optimistic and pessimistic trends of his subjects, and found a marked tendency in the optimists to record the liked items first, and in the pessimists to record the disliked items first. These conclusions imply that the expressed is a measure of the remembered, and the unexpressed a measure of the forgotten; and that the position in the sequence of enumeration is a measure of the ease of remembering. Myers contended that "probably in the long run memory and expression are commensurate" (p. 91). Such a view would certainly contradict the classical conceptions of memory, which equated memory with the ability to recall, to recognize, or to save in relearning. If, however, memory is viewed as *one aspect of the organization of thought processes*, Myers' statement becomes self-evident and even the doubt he raises—namely, that social considerations inhibit the expression of the remembered—loses its pertinence.

A. Peters (143) showed portraits[56] to her subjects and asked for PUI judgments. Berliner (144) showed artistic post cards and asked for esthetic ranking. Both gave four delayed-recognition tests. The results of both experiments were positive. Peters found a P-U-I sequence of superiority in recognition, and a better recognition of greater P and U intensities than of lesser; Berliner found that cards ranked higher esthetically were better recognized than those ranked lower. Fox (146) asked his subjects to memorize two sonnets, and after the recall-test asked which of the two was preferred. Selz (147) asked his subjects to rank according to preference four lectures they had heard and reported on. Both Fox and Selz asked for recall after a week, and found a superiority of the preferred

---

an actual arousal of pleasant *feeling*. S may be aware of the meaning of pleasantness when no feeling is aroused; even in a thoroughly depressed mood he may be aware of the meaning of pleasantness without any trace of pleasant feeling." (p. 596)

[56] The significance of judgments of portraits has been discussed by Rapaport (145).

item in recall. A disadvantage of Fox's experiment was that the ranking was made after the recall, and success and failure may have directly determined the preference. Selz argued for an immediate dependence of retention on preference, and against a common factor determining both preference and retention. Fox's claims were somewhat pretentious, and were based on Ward's theory rather than on his own experiment:

"It follows from our investigation, that any experimental evidence about memory which does not take the subjective factor into account must be rejected . . . 'there is no pure passivity in experience; and even the association of ideas is determined, not mechanically, but by subjective selection and interest.' " (p. 403)

These experiments, using more meaningful material and so organized as to be psychologically relevant to the subjects, apparently support the findings of the experiments with PUI words; but the methodological flawlessness and statistical reliability achieved in the experiments with PUI words are here absent. The emotional factors—like-dislike, esthetic value, preference, interest—are still judgmental, although some appear to be nearer to the emotional core of the person than are P, U, and I judgments.

c. Experiments with Psychiatric Patients on the Remembering of P and U Verbal Material

The method used in the previous group of experiments marked an improvement in that the materials and procedures had some personal relevance for the subjects. They had also the advantage of showing not only quantitative differences, but some qualitative properties of the influence of preference on memory. The experiments to be discussed here also demonstrate some qualitative aspects of the relation of emotion to memory.

Birnbaum (34) had used psychiatric patients to investigate the influence of feeling-tone on associations. His underlying supposition was that if the affective-life is pathologically vivid, the effects on memory of even slightly feeling-toned material may be observable. This idea was applied by Waldberg (148) and by Sharp (149) in recall experiments. The application of the method was recommended also in Gilbert's survey (139).

Waldberg arbitrarily selected single words[57] frequently connected with complexes, without first considering whether they were P, U, or I. Sharp selected, on the basis of the subjects' case-histories, P, U, and I nouns meaningfully paired with P, U, and I adjectives. Waldberg gave no learning-instruction, asked only for attention, and presented her list of

---

[57] viz., unfaithfulness, bed-wetting, jealousy, bedroom, police, visit, physician, household, revenge, purgatorium, service, preacher, face, sister, aunt, father, fire.

words once; she then asked for reproduction and an introspective report. Sharp gave learning-instructions, three delayed-recall tests—after 2, 9, and 16 days—and then a re-learning test. Waldberg was interested in the influence of affects on memory; Sharp strove to verify experimentally Freud's theory of repression, and a facilitation-theory which maintained that Freud's "pleasure principle" implies a facilitation of remembering pleasant material. Waldberg used four experimental groups: normal adult, normal child, psychotic, and epileptic. Sharp used three groups of psychoneurotics and three control groups of normals.

Waldberg's results were purely qualitative. She found that the normal adult was inclined to reproduce the original sequence of words, interrupting it only at words having a personal feeling-value for him. The words connected with complexes contrary to self-esteem tended to be "repressed"; other complex-connected words, whether P or U, showed a special ease of recall. Children showed a smaller quantity of reproduction and a weaker inclination to follow the original sequence; both tendencies improve as the subject's age increases. Psychotics were found to disregard the sequence, and to reproduce words having an eminent "complex" connection or a connection to a recent experience; the most important of these recurred frequently in the course of recall, words given in reproduction but not present in the original series were always complex-connected words. Epileptics showed a very small quantity of reproduction, and tended to begin reproduction with words presented last—"just to be sure"—and to reproduce arbitrarily, with perseveration and distortion, "what had incidentally stuck in their memory."

Sharp summed up her results as follows:

"The unacceptable material is much more difficult to learn than the neutral list, but it is more poorly retained. The acceptable material is also more difficult than the neutral list, but it is more effectively retained for the longer intervals. The acceptable and unacceptable materials are approximately equal in difficulty, but they differ radically in respect to retention." (p. 410)

She concluded that:

"(1) The process of repression affects both the pleasant and the unpleasant materials but to unequal degree. (2) In both cases, the process of repression is limited to the first two days after learning. This fact suggests that repression is an autonomic process in that it takes place prior to the first recall. (3) The enhancement, on the other hand, is limited to the pleasant materials, and it does not occur until after the first recall. This fact suggests the possibility that the enhancement of the pleasant material may be a function of the prior recall." (p. 418)

Waldberg's experiment, although more clinical than experimental and somewhat arbitrary in its construction, is of value in that it shows some of the qualitative aspects of the influence of complexes and affects on re-production. Different types of affective organizations (child, adolescent, psychotic, epileptic), rather than the influence of specific affects, were investigated. Sharp's experiment is distinguished by the selection of the words based on the subjects' case-histories, and by the use of *meaningful* associations of nouns and adjectives. Her claim to have investigated "repression" is, however, not justified. The difference she found between the mechanisms of "repression" and "facilitation," and her relegation of "facilitation" to the realm of effects of repetition, appear to be significant. Sharp's experiment was repeated by Sears (150), with college-students as subjects; Sharp's word-pairs, and similar parallel series selected by a group of persons who had been psychoanalyzed, were used. In contrast to Sharp, whose control groups showed the same reaction as the psychoneurotic groups, Sears states:

"The only conclusion with reference to repression that seems reasonable to draw from these results is that if repression were operating the method described has not been appropriate for measuring it."

The significance of these experiments is that they used psychiatric patients, and that the word-material was related to the problems of the subjects. Sharp achieved this relation by taking her word-material from the case-histories; Waldberg achieved it by asking the subjects for intro-spective reports, and comparing her results with the case-histories.

d. The Influence of "Emotions" on Learning and the "Mental Set"

The group of experiments to be discussed here used a "mental set" to elicit the emotional-tone whose influence on memory was to be inves-tigated. In some of these experiments the "mental set" introduced the emotional effect; in others it was used to make the subjects more sensitive to the emotional-tone. The obvious advantage of these experiments over those using PUI words is that these take cognizance not only of the material learned and remembered, but also of at least part of the subject's relation to it. This is a step toward an experimental investigation of the "situa-tion as a whole."

Preliminary to reporting these experiments, we shall review what is meant by "mental set." Gundlach, Rotschild, and Young (151) experi-mentally analyzed the "mental set" and described it as follows:

"The word 'set' has several meanings. In the first place, it suggests something which is firmly established, as one's prejudices, fixed beliefs and habits. It is a fundamental biological principle that the nervous system retains its organization; that it becomes more or less permanently set. In the second place, the word 'set' suggests a bodily posture which an organism temporarily assumes. Thus the runner toeing the line and awaiting the gun is set. The cat crouching upon the floor prepared to spring upon a mouse is set. In these cases there is a temporary preparation for action which involves observable changes in the adjustment of muscles. In the third place, the word 'set' suggests a temporary preparation which is not directly dependent upon changes in muscular tonus. For example, after several hours of study I am *set* for my lecture. The pianist is set to play one of Beethoven's sonatas. Such neural preparation need not reveal itself in any particular bodily attitude. In the fourth place, the word suggests a temporary preparation for immediate action as determined by instruction." (p. 247)

McGeoch (152) describes the effect of the "mental set" on memory, and identifies it with the concept of "determining tendency" advanced by Ach (153):

"It is probable, although the experimental evidence in support of it is not yet conclusive, that forgetting also depends upon set or determining tendency. That interest or set in a given direction has a selective influence on recall is well known; if the set is in an incorrect direction, recall may fail, even though with a correct set it may occur." (p. 347)

G. Humphrey (154) defines the concept of "determining tendencies"[58] very much as Lewin in his theory defines "needs." The concept of "mental set" leads to the concept of "determining tendencies" and to the Lewinian concept of "needs"; and the experiments to be surveyed below lead to the Lewinian experiments. In another respect, the concept of "mental set" shades into that of "context." McGeoch (152) defines "context" as follows:

"One kind of context consists of the stimulation from the external environment, such as the furniture of the room, the experimenter and the apparatus. A second kind is the stimulation from the interoceptors which make up the feeling of the body, and a third is the ideational context which constitutes the unessential content of consciousness. These factors may be, and many of them are, connected with the material learned." (p. 347)

Pan's (155) experiment on the effect of "context" on memory showed that:

"The recall of any material is favored by the presence of an environmental factor which has some associative connection with that material. In the absence of such an association, the environmental situation is likely to be unfavorable to recall." (p. 490)[59]

---

[58] "It was found that when a subject is confronted with a problem, his behavior and thought are determined not only by the associations which past experience has attached to the problem, but also by what we now call a need that springs from the task the subject has set himself. It is these needs that give mental life its ordered and directed character, even though we are not conscious of them as such. They are called determining tendencies." (p. 389)

[59] See also Smith and Guthrie's (158), and Wong and Brown's (159) pertinent experiments.

"Determining tendency," "need," "context," and the four different types of "set" described by Gundlach, Rotschild, and Young, are the factors which introduce or reinforce the "emotional influence" in the experiments discussed in this section.[60]

Flanagan (156) and Sharp (157) used paired nonsense-syllables: Sharp's pairs had religious or profane connotations (as, jeh-sus, god-dum), and Flanagan's pairs had sexual connotations (as, piy-nis); both used control material with innocuous connotations. These experimenters proposed to investigate the Freudian theory of repression. Sharp was cognizant of the similarity of her experiment to Langfeld's (160, 161) on the suppressive effect of "negative set." Langfeld asked his subjects to make logical responses to a series of questions, but his additional instructions excluded certain types of response; this deliberate interference with a part of the logical response established the "negative set." In Sharp's experiment the "negative set" was the socially-unacceptable profane meaning, which acted against the efforts to recall. Flanagan was cognizant of the similarity of his experiment to Langfeld's, and to those of Pan (155) and Key (162) who investigated the effect of "context" on memory. Both Flanagan and Sharp found statistically-significant differences of learning and recall between material with socially-unacceptable (sexual, profane) connotations and material with innocuous connotations; both claimed to have demonstrated experimentally the Freudian theory of repression. The experiments appear to be related more intimately to the influence of "mental set" and social-unacceptability than to the repression theory; however, it is undeniable that the factor of social-unacceptability bears an emotional-tone rooted probably more deeply than the P-ness, U-ness, and I-ness of isolated words. The relevance of these experiments to the Freudian theory of repression cannot be considered proved; but Sharp describes reactions of her subjects, adopted in the situation of conflicting motivation, which resemble Freudian "mechanisms."[61]

[60] On "context" and "set," see also Woodworth (187).

[61] "In this study the subjects solved the difficulty in one of the following ways:

"1. Round-about methods, mispronunciation of an extreme nature to cover up the fact that the nature of the material is recognized. In about two-thirds of the cases the subjects pronounced the profane syllables correctly at first, but with the recognition of the sound of the taboo material they immediately changed and distorted the pronunciation.

"2. Systems of learning, other than accepting the obvious connection of meaning, were elaborately built up. One subject learned the response syllables vertically in serial order, disregarding the stimulus syllables.

"3. Openly, suddenly, and in strange tones of voice, with behavior exhibiting embarrassment, subjects gave up trying to conceal their knowledge of the nature of the material and quickly learned the material. This followed after a period in

Barret (115), in her experiment previously discussed, made an incidental observation which prompted her to investigate the influence of "emotional set" on remembering emotionally-toned material. A group of her subjects deviated from the others, in that they recalled U-material better than P. Investigation revealed that at the time of the recognition-test, this group was anticipating a school-examination; and Barret assumed that this anticipation operated to influence the recall. To test the effect of such "sets," she developed two experiments:

"Thirty students were asked to check the numbers of any of 10 adjectives which might apply to each of four descriptions of unpleasant behavior incidents. From 12 to 48 hours later, the subjects were tested for the recall of the 10 adjectives.

"Character sketches of pleasant, unpleasant, and both pleasant and unpleasant behavior incidents were prepared in order to distinguish, if possible, between a set involving logical relevancy and a set involving emotional congruity. After a single sketch, a group of subjects were to check from a list of 30 adjectives which were read to them, the numbers of any words which might apply to the characterizations in question. Forty-eight hours later the subjects were tested for the recall and recognition of the adjectives on the list." (p. 52)

Although a segment of the results was inconclusive,[62] the author concluded that the "emotional set" is important in the recall of P and U items. She advanced the theory that the superior recall of P words in her experiment, and probably in all other experiments yielding similar results, was due to the "happy frame of mind" of the subjects. It should be noted that the "mental set" which Barret had *incidentally* observed was operant at the time of reproduction, but that the set which she investigated *systematically* had been introduced at the presentation of the material; consequently, her final conclusion appears to be somewhat far-fetched. Her experiment, nevertheless, shares the advantage of those of Sharp and Flanagan, in that it controlled one component of the "total situation" of the subject. This component has a context-character, while that investigated by Sharp and Flanagan was "mental set" built on a rather constant attitude.

In the experiments of Sharp, Flanagan, and Barret, the setting was concrete and was associated with the material. The experiments of Sullivan (163) and McKinney (164) introduced a much less specific setting, and one independent of the experimental material. In Sullivan's experiment, two groups of children learned nonsense-syllables; after a test, one

---

which they would not admit the obvious and had been unable to learn or recall the syllables. In many cases the subjects would wait to within the merest fraction of the end of the two seconds allowed for the recall and then would blurt out the correct response, as if it were a great effort to bring out the condemning evidence of their thoughts." (pp. 20–21)

[62] The contrast of the P character sketch and U adjectives was so keenly felt by the subjects that it facilitated the remembering of the U adjectives.

group was told that it had been very successful and the other that it had failed completely. Sullivan found that:

> ". . . the time taken to learn a memory series is increased by the knowledge of failure in a previous performance and decreases by the knowledge of success in a previous performance." (p. 141)

> "The value for recall, measured by abbreviation of time taken to learn, is less in the case of the failure report and greater in the case of the success report." (p. 142)

In one of McKinney's experiments, the subjects were constantly reminded of the passage of time; in another, a time-limit inadequate for the task was set. McKinney found:

> ". . . that errors increase rather markedly when a time factor is introduced and increase still more when a time limit and a suggestion of inferiority is introduced." (p. 105)
> ". . . that time may increase or decrease as the result of an introduction of a time factor into the experimental situation, but the tendency seems to be more in the direction of an increase . . . that the number of trials required to learn is affected slightly by a time factor or a feeling of inferiority and more often in the direction of an increase." (p. 107)

Sullivan's and McKinney's procedures were based on everyday observations of the effect of success, failure, and timing. McKinney made observational records, on the basis of which he concluded that "there is little doubt that a genuine emotion was induced." (p. 110) Sullivan formulated his results in terms of the "law of effect." McKinney attempted an explanation in terms of the "emergency theory" of emotions:

> ". . . it might be well to remember that the physiological concomitant of emotion prepares the organism for overt behavior and not for ideational activity. The individual is energized and is impulsive; he finds it more difficult to represent his activity ideationally than to make the muscular response which vital processes prepare him to execute . . . Some authors have considered the emotions important motives . . . It is conceivable that as long as the emotion is just a mild but persistent stimulus it may act as a director or energizing force for ideational activity, but as soon as an emotion becomes so strong that impulsive behavior is unavoidable, it retards rather than directs activity . . . How this effect operates is a matter of speculation at present." (p. 112)

This explanation is built on Cannon's physiological theory of emotion, and is thus vitiated by the fallacy of inferring psychological phenomena from physiological phenomena; McKinney himself points out that the psychological mechanisms involved are obscure. The Lewinian school of psychology has attempted to develop a theory of these mechanisms on the basis of experiments somewhat similar to Sullivan's and McKinney's; these will be surveyed in the next section.

"Context," "set," conflicting feelings over socially-unacceptable words, effect of success and failure, observable emotional effects of "being timed" —all designate the "emotional factors" in the group of experiments described here. This list suggests that the abandonment of the simple judgmental P-ness, U-ness, and I-ness, the introduction of material and experimental situations of greater personal relevance, and the shift in emphasis to investigate not only the experimental-material but components of the "total situation," are accompanied by a growing multiplicity of the emotional-factors; and these factors pertain to quite different levels of the emotional hierarchy.

e. Summary

α. The experiments concerned with the "influence of emotions" on the remembering of learned material included the following: (i) those using P, U, and I material; (ii) those using liked and disliked material; (iii) those in which psychiatric patients were the subjects; (iiii) those introducing a "mental set" to sensitize the subject to the influence of the emotional-tone.

β. The first group of experiments was over-concerned with improving the technique and excluding disturbing factors: first, by improving the method of selecting the material; secondly, by considering the intensity of emotions as well as their "emotional-quality"; thirdly, by using incidental memory and delayed-recall, instead of learning and immediate recall; fourthly, by equating the material as to grammatical comparability, length, frequency of usage, and number of associates; fifthly, by controlling primacy and recency; and sixthly, by investigating the influence of the subject's age.

γ. The second group of experiments introduced a *qualitative* method. The subjects enumerated words belonging to a given category; they later stated the items of the category which were most liked and most disliked. The position in the original enumeration was viewed as the measure of remembering.

δ. The first two groups of experiments were little concerned with the nature of the "emotional factor" investigated; the third and fourth groups approached an understanding of this factor, and emphasized the need to dispense with superficial physiological references and to endeavor rather to understand the psychological mechanisms by which the emotions exert their influence on memory. The existence of the influence of "emotional factors" on memory had been established. As the "emotional factors" used in these experiments were highly intellectualized, and in the main judgmental entities, the need to "emotionalize" them was met by using psychiatric patients as subjects, and by creating a "setting" calculated to arouse emotion.

ε. The intensity of the "emotional factor" proved to be of more importance in its influence on memory than its quality; but some differences were found between the influence of P-ness and U-ness.

ζ. P-ness and U-ness, "emotional-tone," "affective-tone," "hedonic-tone," "interest," "like-dislike," "preference," "success-failure" are some of the designations of the "emotional factor" investigated.

η. Only McKinney's experiment explicitly reported emotions observed, although observations of emotions occurred in Sharp's and Flanagan's experiments. Many of the experiments claimed to have proved or disproved the Freudian theory of repression, purely on the basis of statistical results; but only Sharp's and Diven's experiments reported phenomena resembling the Freudian mechanisms.

5. The Lewinian Experiments

The two outstanding characteristics of the experimental material surveyed thus far were, first, the great concern for the experimental technique and its improvement, and second, the general lack of concern for the psychological function "emotion" whose influence on memory was being investigated. Most of those investigators who were concerned with the nature of this emotional factor referred to physiological theories of emotions; only a few (e.g., Stagner, 84, McKinney, 164) emphasized that "emotion" should be viewed as a psychological factor, and pointed out that this psychological function and the mechanism of its influence on memory are still obscure. Recently it has become customary to brand the differentiation between "psychological" and "physiological" phenomena as a dichotomy outdated in our period of "psychosomatic research." However, this differentiation does not necessarily imply a theoretical dichotomy; it is rather a matter of methodology. Today few persons will doubt the fact of psychosomatic unity; but most investigators will agree that some problems of this psychosomatic unity are to be attacked by psychological methods, and others by physiological   McKinney, Stagner, and others stressed the need to understand in psychological terms the nature of the "emotional factor" influencing memory. The only systematic attempt to investigate emotions experimentally—transcending pure description of them like Wundt's, Krueger's, and Stoerring's—has been made by Lewin and his pupils (165). Their investigations on emotions and on memory stimulated later experiments which claimed to investigate repression.

According to association psychology, associative-bonds cause the emergence of ideas into consciousness; when varied associative-bonds are at work, the strongest becomes effective. In opposition to this theory and its modifications (e.g., the "complex" theory of G. E. Mueller) Ach advanced the theory that the emergence of ideas is a result of "determining tendencies." Lewin (166, 167), in his experiments on "Associations and the Measurement of Will," demonstrated that the determinants of verbal reaction are neither associative bonds nor "determining tendencies." His final theoretical conclusions (168) were as follows: psychic occurrence, like physical occurrence, must be understood in terms of dynamics of forces; these forces are psychic "tension-systems" set up either by genuine physiological needs or by quasi-needs corresponding to intentions; the investigation of psychic life should be the investigation of these tension-systems and of their relation to the organization of psychological life-space.[63] His pupil, Ovsiankina (169), showed that in a series of tasks, in some of which the subject is interrupted and the remainder of which he is allowed to complete, the subject manifests a tendency to resume the interrupted tasks. She concluded that performance of the task discharges, and that interruption of the performance sustains, the tension-system urging towards the completion of the task. The relevance of this theory to memory has been experimentally demonstrated by Zeigarnik (170), who showed that the names of the interrupted tasks were better retained than the names of those completed. McKinney (171) showed that not only the name of the task, but also the skill of performance of the interrupted task as measured by re-learning, was better retained. Inasmuch as a summary of the details of these experiments has been given by Pachauri (172), they will not be discussed here.

It was found that only when the experiments were conducted in an informal fashion, so that they were not experienced as examinations, did there occur a better retention of the interrupted tasks, as a result of the corresponding tension-systems. A striking advantage in the remembering of interrupted tasks over completed tasks was observed in naïve unexcited subjects and children; excited subjects, however, showed little or no such advantage. These individual differences were explained by assuming that, in excitable subjects, the boundaries of the tension-systems have less solidity than in other subjects; thus, in these subjects the tension responsible for advantage in remembering decreases faster. The relation to remembering of these individual differences appears to be pertinent to our topic, inasmuch as Zeigarnik related them to the "emotional" make-up of the individual.

Before we turn to a specific finding of Zeigarnik which opened a new vein of pertinent experimentation, an experiment on the influence of affective phenomena on remembering by another pupil of Lewin, G. Biren-

---

[63] The psychological life-space, according to Lewin, is the "totality of facts which determine the behavior of an individual at a certain moment. The life-space represents the totality of possible events. The life-space includes the person and the environment." (173, p. 216)

baum (174), deserves mention, inasmuch as she also reports individual differences of the kind found by Zeigarnik. Birenbaum asked her subjects to put their signatures on their work-sheets upon completion of each of the tasks of the series given them. When the series consisted of tasks of a homogeneous nature, the subject's intention to sign his name, being apparently embedded into the tension-system of the series, was carried out. If, after a number of homogeneous tasks, strikingly different tasks followed, the intention to sign was forgotten and not carried out: the intention was part of the homogeneous series, but did not belong to the heterogeneous tasks. This forgetting was most obvious with the excited subjects, and least obvious with the naïve quiet subjects. Birenbaum observed that specific affects, as reported by the subjects, had at times the same effect of isolating the intention from the tasks; at other times they had the opposite effect of unifying the intention with the tasks, making for a better execution of the intention. Competition, which apparently increased excitement in all the groups of subjects, made for an easy forgetting of the intentions.

Zeigarnik, inquiring into the forgetting of certain interrupted tasks— a phenomenon contradictory to her general finding—showed that those forgotten had been experienced as failures. She called this phenomenon "isolation," implying that the tension-systems corresponding to these tasks had been not discharged but rather isolated from the whole field; this phenomenon was similar to that found by Birenbaum. Zeigarnik indicated that she considered this phenomenon analogous to "repression." To sum up, Zeigarnik discussed three types of forgetting: (a) forgetting of material not connected at the time to a psychic tension-system (as in completed tasks, where the corresponding tension-system has been discharged); (b) forgetting attributable to a lack of solidity of the boundaries of the tension-systems (as in emotionally excitable individuals); (c) forgetting due to "isolation" of the tension-system from the rest of the field (as in the case of the intentions of Birenbaum's subjects, where structural reasons made for isolation, and in the case of the Zeigarnik tasks experienced as failures, where emotional factors made for isolation). All three are related to the problem of "emotions and memory," and show mechanisms through which the variegated effects of emotions on memory may work. We have formulated these effects in terms of forgetting, but they may be formulated also in terms of mechanisms of remembering. The phenomenon of "isolation" as a result of the experience of failure was further investigated by Rosenzweig, and reported in a series of articles (175, 176, 177, 178, 179) and in a summary (180) of the tentative results. Rosenzweig gave his subjects jigsaw puzzles, and caused them to fail in one half and to succeed in the other. Thus, like Sullivan (163),[64] he introduced the element of success and failure, a procedure alien to Zeigarnik's experiment. The results of his first experiment on children (178) were summed up as follows:

"It would seem to be that, given an individual of sufficient intellectual maturity and a commensurate measure of pride, experiences that are unpleasant because they wound self-respect—perhaps it should be added in a *social* situation—are, other things being equal, less apt to be remembered than experiences that are gratifying to the ego. This is in keeping with the Freudian theory of repression." (p. 258)

"The group that recalled successes better than failures was differentiated from the group that recalled failures better than successes by a more advanced average mental age and a higher average rating for the trait of pride. Some important incidental results of the experiment were (a) that there was a distortion in recalling the outcome—success or failure—of the tasks attempted that ran parallel with the tendencies shown in recalling the names of the tasks; (b) that with increasing age there was an increase in self-critical answers to questions, "Do you feel that you did the puzzles well?" and (c) that the experiences of relatively shorter duration were more readily recalled than those of longer duration, presumably because of the prevailing dynamic conditions. The results of this experiment seem to support certain aspects of the Freudian theory of repression." (p. 264)

Experimenting on two groups of adults (180), he gave the puzzles to one group as an intelligence-test implying success or failure; the other group was asked to assist him in gaining more knowledge about the puzzles— a condition similar to that of Zeigarnik's experiments. He found that in the first group the finished puzzles were recalled more often than the unfinished ones; in the second group, in conformity with Zeigarnik's findings, the unfinished puzzles were recalled more often. Thus, interruption experienced as failure made for "isolation," or forgetting of the interrupted tasks; but informal interruption made for better retention, as a result of the operation of the undischarged tension-systems. Although the results were only tentative and showed great individual differences, Rosenzweig maintained that "the relationship of these results to the Freudian pleasure and reality principles is too obvious to require discussion" (180, p. 480). This statement apparently implies that where the experiment involved the pride of the subject and failure was felt, repression ensued; in the informal situation, where no such factor interfered, the tension-systems operated. However tempting this explanation may be, it is questionable whether the relation of Rosenzweig's findings to the Freudian principles is really "too obvious to require discussion." The Freudian "pleasure" and "reality" principles were derived from the relation of individuals to matters vital to them. Intelligence tests, or even tests in general, may or may not be vital in this sense. Rosenzweig corroborates Zeigarnik's

findings, and demonstrates experimentally an additional variation in the
functioning of memory which may be viewed as a result of emotional influence and as further material in bridging the gap between the Freudian
mechanism of repression and the functions investigated in memory experimentation. For the time being, however, there is no reason to assume
that his results constitute experimental proof of, or are more than an
experimental simile to, the repression mechanism. This is further indicated by the fact that Rosenzweig, on the basis of his results, felt it
necessary to suggest a revision of the concept of repression:

> "These results may thus be construed as indicating the repression as a mechanism
> of defense resorted to relatively late in the development of the child." (p. 481)

This statement is clearly in contradiction to the Freudian definition of
repression (181):

> "All repression takes place in early childhood, it is primitive defense of the feeble
> ego. In later years there are no fresh repressions but the old ones persist and are
> used by the ego for the purpose of mastering instinct. New conflicts are resolved by
> what we call 'after-repression'." (p. 383)

Some clarification of those cases in which the influence of emotions facilitates memory was provided by J. F. Brown's (182) experiment on the
relation of memory and "reality levels."   In this experiment, a portion of
the tasks was given as a college quiz and the remainder as occupation for a
rest-period; the recall-test showed that the names of the tasks given as a
quiz were remembered much better than those given in the rest-period.
It was concluded that the two groups of tasks were on different "reality
levels," and that on levels of unreality the boundaries of the tension-
systems are sufficiently fluid that the tensions responsible for recall are
not conserved in them.   It seems probable that these reality levels—that
is, the degrees of personal relevance—are essentially of an emotional
character.   However, the relation of these reality levels to the emotional
make-up of the personality is not clarified.

The experiments on anger by Dembo (183), a pupil of Lewin, shed light
on the influence of affects on tension-systems and on the organization of
the psychological field. She found that the influence of the affect is
characterized by a disorganization of the psychological field, and by disruption and elimination of the tension-systems. Dembo characterized
the affect as follows:

> "(1) a strong tension, i.e. a conflict of equal and strong field forces in every di-
> rection of the field, (2) a loosening or disruption of most of the boundaries in the
> whole-field. (a) The boundaries characteristic of the specific topology of the situa-
> tion in the field, and the specialties of the objects in it, appear to be dissolved or

eliminated. The field is homogenized and made primitive. The boundaries between reality and unreality also become fluid. (b) As a result of the total-tension the intrapsychic realms, layers, and systems are relatively homogenized, and the differentiation of surface and deep layers becomes less distinct. (c) The boundary layer between the intrapsychic systems and the psychic environment, the layer of action-motoric, is extraordinarily tense." (p. 144)

This may explain the mechanism by which the tension-systems responsible for recall are obliterated. In the light of these experiments it appears that recall depends on undischarged tension-systems and on their free communication with other systems at the time, and that emotions destructuralizing the psychic field and shattering the tension-systems may account for the detrimental influence of emotions on memory found by McKinney[65] and others. Although the phenomenon of "isolation" or "repression" was not linked with this conception of affect, its relation to the experience of failure makes its affective significance clear.

Summary

The bearing of the Lewinian experiments on the problem of "emotions and memory" may be summed up as follows:

a. The finding that facts pertaining to undischarged tension-systems are remembered better than those pertaining to discharged tension-systems may be interpreted as supporting a general motivational theory of remembering. The relation of this finding to emotions depends on the role attributed by any theory to emotional factors in motivation.

b. Emotions have an effect of disorganizing and homogenizing the psychological field; by loosening and disrupting the boundaries of tension-systems, they may result in forgetting.

c. The solidity of the boundaries of tension-systems shows great individual differences, varying with the emotional make-up of the subjects; the boundaries are more solid in naïve, unexcited and controlled individuals, and less solid in excited subjects. This finding would explain the individual differences in remembering.

d. Tension-systems do not always make for better remembering; those to which the experience of failure becomes attached are frequently "isolated" from the rest of the field. Although phenomenologically similar to Freudian "repression," this finding cannot be construed as proof, disproof, or basis for revision of the Freudian theory.

e. A facilitation of remembering by the personal relevance (reality level) of the material has been found. The relation of reality levels to emotions—especially of levels of irreality, where the boundaries of the tension-systems are assumed to be "fluid"—is a problem requiring further investigations.

[65] See pp. 91–92.

6. Discussion

The experimental material has been surveyed; it now remains to be considered whether a general conclusion is possible concerning the influence of emotions on memory. The critical reader will form his own opinion, and a final decision will be reached by future research. To us, this experimental material showed that "emotional factors" demonstrably influence memory. This demonstrable influence is not restricted to the quantity of recall of learned material but includes its recognition and re-learning, and affects as well the reproduction and recognition of personal experiences, the reaction-time of association and recall, the sequence of emergence of material in recall and in free enumeration, the redintegration of experiences, and associative reactions; it results in recall-errors, slips of tongue, and so on. The experimental material in itself suggests that the investigation of the influence of emotions on memory requires a concept of memory other than that of the classical association theory: memory must be viewed as one aspect of the organization of thought processes. Especially the results of association experiments, of redintegration experiments, of the analysis of enumeration sequences, errors, and slips in recall, suggest this; for they show that the emotional influence has not only a quantitative effect, in facilitating or inhibiting reproduction, but also a qualitative effect in organizing it.

What has been called in these experiments an "emotional factor" is a confusing multiplicity of factors. There are two methods of dealing with an unclarified situation in which a variety of factors is indiscriminately subsumed under one heading. One method would be to attempt a sharp scrutiny of each of these "emotional factors" to justify or reject its right to the term "emotional factor"; through this restriction of the term to a small group of phenomena, a sharply defined concept may emerge. The other method would be humbler in procedure but more ambitious in aim: it would accept as "emotional" all the factors thus designated, would endeavor to understand them as variegated expressions of a common factor, and would attempt to find their common denominator. Against the first method, so alluring in its fancied scientific exactness, there is the argument that we cannot be sure that, in excluding any of the factors designated as "emotional influence," we do not bar a way to the understanding of all of them. A procedure of exclusion has to be based on a theory much more developed than the theory of emotions we possess.[66] Against the other method, one may argue that it is hasty to assume that all the "emotional factors" in question have a common source. Yet this is the nature of all hypotheses: we can never be sure that their implications will stand the

---

[66] See the symposium on "Feelings and Emotions" (184).

scrutiny of time. The advantage of the second method over the first is that rather than exclude phenomena it applies hypotheses to link them. Any hypothesis advanced concerning the influence of "emotional factors" on memory must consider each of the reported "emotional factors" in the sense in which the individual experimenter used it. A hierarchy of these factors could be constructed in an attempt to determine how they relate to the central core of the personality. Such an attempt at constructing a hypothetical hierarchy must be arbitrary, and the following should be considered only as a suggestion. Let it be supposed that the emotional factor assumed to be active in the selective remembering of P, U, and I words is the intellectualized derivative, the representative on the judgmental level, of the affective instinctual core of the personality. Esthetic judgment would likewise be a representative of this core on a great variety of levels ranging from learned formal esthetic judgment to deep esthetic experience. Likes and dislikes, and preferences in general, would be representative of this core on a level more personal and perhaps less intellectual than that represented by P-ness and U-ness; these again would range widely.[67] Nearer to the core in this hierarchy would lie the manifold shadings of the "feelings" and "affects." Another group of factors in this hierarchy would be characterized by goal-directedness, and would range from the more intellectual factor of "logical relevance" to that of "interests" which lie nearer the core. Both these groups of factors would depend on still more central factors: the first group on those factors called "attitudes," "sentiments," "complexes";[68] the second group on those factors called "determining tendencies," "conative tendencies," "needs," "tension-systems."[69] This division of these factors into two groups is a recognition of the historical fact that the concepts of the first group were advanced by less intellectualistic investigators, and those of the second group by more intellectualistic investigators. The whole hierarchy would be founded on those basic factors at whose roots the "instincts" lie; "instinct" here is a borderline concept designating psychosomatic energies represented in the psychic life as drives and urges. The relation of these factors to each other, and their genesis from each other, is in itself a problem necessitating further hypotheses which may be either static or dynamic. The static hypotheses would maintain that the qualitative differences of these factors are defined by the levels on which they represent the

[67] See the like and dislike choices in the Szondi Test (141).
[68] "Attitudes" in Allport's sense, rather than in that of recent attitude measurements. "Sentiments" in Shand's sense. For the relation of attitudes and sentiments see Cattell (185). For the relation of complexes and sentiments see the Symposium on the topic (186).
[69] "Determining tendencies" in Ach's sense. "Conative tendencies" in McDougall's sense. "Needs" and "tension-systems" in Lewin's sense.

central emotional factor. The dynamic hypotheses would derive these factors from conflicts of more central factors: for instance, "affects" as an expression of conflicting drives. These hypotheses are necessarily vague, and disregard many facts and problems. The suggested hierarchy is not one in which every function is a necessary consequence of or in immediate relation to another.

Assuming that this hypothesis is of some heuristic value, it can be applied to the influence of emotional factors on memory. The experimental material surveyed in this chapter was divided into sections according to the nature of the emotional factors investigated. The material demonstrates that all emotional factors, on different hierarchic levels, have some influence on memory. This influence varies in quality and intensity. On some levels it can be established only by statistical probability in a great number of cases; on others by a qualitative analysis of any single case. Some varieties of this influence show great individual differences; others are present to a greater or lesser degree in every individual. Some may have either a favorable or a detrimental effect on memory; others have only a detrimental effect. The effect of some depends on their positive or negative quality, and that of others on their intensity; still others derive their power from their personal relevance for the individual. Some manifest themselves by transforming and distorting memories. Yet all of them necessitate the recognition that memory is not a storehouse of deposited engrams, but a stratification of a multiplicity of dynamic fields in which every experience enters into relation with related experiences on the varied levels of stratification. Thus there is no dividing line between memory and thinking: the same stratifying, connecting, and organizing influences which are active in thinking are at work in the memory organization; and this consideration makes memory one, and perhaps the most important, aspect of the organization of thought processes.

In this light repression would appear as a specific case of affective influence on memory, and one which can be demonstrated by qualitative clinical analysis of the memory material rather than by statistical probability. Accordingly, the evidence of repression in the experiments surveyed in this chapter was slight. In the field of experimentation surveyed here, the different emotional factors were arbitrarily equated with each other; and it may be that in future experimentation the intricacy of the hierarchic stratification discussed will still be neglected, in spite of the example of the great number of abortive experiments which failed, or unwarrantedly claimed, to prove or disprove the theory of repression.

A hypothesis such as that of the emotional hierarchy advanced here can be tested only by investigating the effects of the factors subsumed in the hierarchy on different psychic functions. The surveyed experiments on the influence of emotions on memory may be considered as one approach to the investigation of this hierarchy; there may be many other approaches. Much further experimentation is needed to reach a better understanding of this emotional hierarchy.

REFERENCES

(1) EBBINGHAUS, H. *Memory: A contribution to experimental psychology.* 123 pp. 1885. Trans. Ruger, H. A., and Busenius, C. E., New York, Teach. Coll., 1913.
(2) GALTON, F. Psychometric experiments. *Brain* 2: 149–162, 1892.
(3) GALTON, F. *Inquiries into human faculty and its development.* 387 pp. London, Macmillan, 1883.
(4) WUNDT, W. *Grundzuege der physiologischen Psychologie.* 3 vol., 811 pp. Leipzig, Engelmann, 1911.
(5) FREUD, S. *Psychopathology of everyday life.* Pp. 33–178. In: *The basic writings of Sigmund Freud.* Ed., Brill, A. A., New York, Modern Libr., 1938
(6) SPENCER, H. *The principles of psychology.* 635 pp. New York, Appleton, 2nd ed., 1873.
(7) BAIN, A. *The senses and the intellect.* 714 pp. London, Longmans, 3rd ed., 1868.
(8) THORNDIKE, E. L. *Educational psychology.* Vol. I. *The original nature of man.* 327 pp. New York, Teach. Coll. Press, 1923.
(9) THORNDIKE, E. L. The law of effect. *Amer. J. Psychol.* 39: 212–222, 1927.
(10) CASON, H. The pleasure-pain theory of learning. *Psychol. Rev.* 39: 440–466, 1932.
(11) COLGROVE, F. W. Individual memories. *Amer. J. Psychol.* 10: 228–255, 1899.
(12) COLGROVE, F. W. *Memory. An inductive study.* 369 pp. New York, Holt, 1900.
(13) KOWALEWSKI, A. Studien zur Psychologie des Pessimismus. *Grenzfragen des Nerven und Seelenlebens.* 4: 100–122, 1904.
(14) SUSUKITA, T. Ueber das Gedaechtnis fuer lust- und unlustbetonte Erlebnisse im Alltagsleben. *Tohoku Psychol. Folia.* 2: 43–55, 1934.
(15) SUSUKITA, T. Ueber das Gedaechtnis fuer lust- und unlustbetonte Erlebnisse im Alltagsleben. *Tohoku Psychol. Folia.* 3: 187–204, 1935.
(16) KÜLPE, O. Bemerkungen zu vorstehender Abhandlung. *Arch. ges. Psychol.* 4: 459–464, 1905.
(17) BAXTER, M. F., YAMADA, K., AND WASHBURN, M. F. Directed recall of pleasant and unpleasant experiences. *Amer. J. Psychol.* 28: 155–157, 1917.
(18) KRAEPELIN, F. Der psychologische Versuch in der Psychiatrie. *Psychol. Arbeiten,* ed. Kraepelin, E., 1: 1–91, 1896.
(19) ASCHAFFENBURG, G. Experimentelle Studien ueber Assoziationen. *Psychol. Arbeiten,* ed. Kraepelin, E., 1: 209-299, 1896; 2: 1-83, 1899; 4: 235–373, 1904.
(20) CORDES, G. Experimentelle Untersuchungen ueber Assoziationen. *Phil. Studien,* ed. Wundt, W., 17: 30–77, 1901.
(21) ZIEHEN, TH. *Leitfaden der physiologischen Psychologie.* 280 pp. Jena, Fischer, 1906.
(22) WRESCHNER, A. Die Reproduktion und Assoziation von Vorstellungen. *Z. Psychol. Erg. Bd.* 3, 599 pp., 1907–1909.

(23) MENZERATH, P. Die Bedeutung der sprachlichen Gelaeufigkeit oder der formalen sprachlichen Beziehung fuer die Reproduktion. *Z. Psychol.* 48: 1–95, 1908.

(24) MAYER, A., AND ORTH, J. Zur qualitativen Untersuchung der Assoziation. *Z. Psychol.* 26: 1–13, 1901.

(25) JUNG, C. G. *Studies in word-association. Experiments in the diagnosis of psychopathological conditions carried out at the psychiatric clinic of the University of Zuerich.* 575 pp. New York, Moffat, Yard, 1919.

(26) SCHILDER, P. Ueber Gedankenentwicklung. *Z. Neurol. Psychiat.* 59: 250–263, 1920.

(27) SCHILDER, P. Studien zur Psychologie und Symptomatologie der progressiven Paralyse. *Abhandl. Neurol. Psychiat. Psychol. Grenzgeb.* 58: 1–176, 1930.

(28) VIGOTSKY, L. S. Thought and speech. *Psychiatry* 2: 29–54, 1939.

(29) MASSERMANN, J. H. AND BALKEN, E. R. The language of phantasy. III. The language of the phantasies of patients with conversion hysteria, anxiety state, and obsessive-compulsive neuroses. *J. Psychol.* 10: 75–86, 1940.

(30) SCHNITZLER, J. G. Experimentelle Beitraege zur Tatbestandsdiagnostik. *Z. angew. Psychol.* 2: 51–91, 1909.

(31) JUNG, C. G. On psychophysical relations of the associative experiment. *J. Abn. Psychol.* 1: 247–255, 1907.

(32) KOHS, S. C. The association method in its relation to complex and complex indicators. *Amer. J. Psychol.* 25: 544–595, 1914.

(33) HULL, C. L., AND LUGOFF, L. S. Complex signs in diagnostic free association. *J. exp. Psychol.* 4: 11–136, 1921.

(34) BIRNBAUM, K. Ueber den Einfluss von Gefuehlsfaktoren auf die Assoziationen. *Monatschr. Psychiat. Neurol.* 32: 95–123, 194–220, 1912.

(35) TOLMAN, E. C., AND JOHNSON, I. A note on association-time and feeling. *Amer. J. Psychol.* 29: 187–195, 1918.

(36) CARTER, H. D. Emotional factors in verbal learning. Evidence from reaction time. *J. Educ. Psychol.* 28: 101–108, 1937.

(37) SMITH, W. W. Experiments on memory and affective tone. *Brit. J. Psychol.* 11: 236–250, 1921.

(38) SMITH, W. W. *The measurement of emotion.* 184 pp. London, Kagan, 1922.

(39) CARTER, H. D., JONES, H. E., AND SHOCK, N. W. An experimental study of affective factors in learning. *J. Educ. Psychol.* 25: 203–215, 1934.

(40) BURTT, H. W., AND TUTTLE, W. W. The patellar tendon reflex and affective tone. *Amer. J. Psychol.* 36: 553–561, 1925.

(41) CASON, H. Association in relation to feeling and gross bodily movement. *Amer. J. Psychol.* 46: 207–228, 1934.

(42) PETERS, W. Erinnerungsassoziationen. pp. 245–247. In: *Bericht ueber den 3. Kongress fuer experimentelle Psychologie.* 263 pp. Leipzig, Barth, 1909.

(43) PETERS, W. Gefuehl und Erinnerung. Beitraege zur Erinnerungsanalyse. *Psychol. Arbeiten,* ed. Kraepelin, E., 6: 197–260, 1914.

(44) PETERS, W., AND NEMECEK, O. Massenversuche ueber Errinnerungsassoziationen. *Fortschr. Psychol. Anwendungen.* 2: 226–245, 1914.

(45) LANIER, L. H. An experimental study of "affective conflict." *J. Psychol.* 11: 199–217, 1941.

(46) MORGAN, E., MULL, H. K., AND WASHBURN, M. F. An attempt to test moods or temperaments of cheerfulness and depression by directed recall of emotionally toned experiences. *Amer. J. Psychol.* 30: 302–304, 1919.

(47) WASHBURN, M. F., GIANG, F., IVES, M., AND POLLOCK, M. Memory revival of emotions as a test of emotional and phlegmatic temperaments. *Amer. J. Psychol.* 36: 456–459, 1925.

(48) WASHBURN, M. F., HARDING, L., SIMMONS, H., AND TOMLINSON, D. Further experiments on directed recall as a test of cheerful and depressed temperaments. *Amer. J. Psychol.* 36: 454–456, 1925.

(49) GRIFFITTS, C. H. Results of some experiments on affection, distribution of associations, and recall. *J. exp. Psychol.* 3: 447–464, 1920.

(50) LIPMANN, O. Die Spuren interessenbetonter Erlebnisse und ihre Symptome. (Theorie, Methoden und Ergebnisse der "Tatbestandsdiagnostik.") Beihefte *Z. angew. Psychol.* vol. 1, 96 pp., 1911.

(51) WERTHEIMER, M. Experimentelle Untersuchungen zur Tatbestandsdiagnostik. *Arch. ges. Psychol.* 6: 59–131, 1906.

(52) WERTHEIMER, M., AND KLEIN, J. Psychologische Tatbestandsdiagnostik. *Arch. Kriminol.* 15: 72–113, 1904.

(53) LIPMANN, O., AND WERTHEIMER, M. Tatbestandsdiagnostische Kombinationsversuche. *Z. angew. Psychol.* 8: 119–128, 1907.

(54) DAVIS, R. A., AND MOORE, C. C. Methods of measuring retention. *J. gen. Psychol.* 12: 144–155, 1935.

(55) BEEBE-CENTER, J. G. *The psychology of pleasantness and unpleasantness.* 427 pp. New York, Nostrand, 1932.

(56) WARREN, H. C. *Elements of human psychology.* 416 pp. New York, Mifflin, 1922.

(57) TROLAND, L. T. A system for explaining affective phenomena. *J. Abn. Psychol.* 14: 376–387, 1920.

(58) TROLAND, L. T. *The fundamentals of human motivation.* 521 pp. New York, Nostrand, 1928.

(59) NAFE, J. P. An experimental study of the affective qualities. *Amer. J. Psychol.* 35: 507–544, 1924.

(60) HUNT, W. A. The relation of bright and dull pressure to affectivity. *Amer. J. Psychol.* 43: 87–92, 1931.

(61) McDOUGALL, W. *An introduction to social psychology.* 459 pp. London, Methuen, 1908.

(62) KRUEGER, F. Das Wesen der Gefuehle. Entwurf einer systematischen Theorie. *Arch. ges. Psychol.* 65: 91–128, 1928.

(63) KRUEGER, F. The essence of feeling. Pp. 58–88. In: *The Wittenberg symposium.* 454 pp. Ed. Reymert, M. L., Worcester, Clark Univ. Press, 1928.

(64) CARR, H. A. *Psychology: a study of mental activity.* 432 pp. New York, Longmans, 1925.

(65) PETERS, H. N. The judgmental theory of pleasantness and unpleasantness. *Psychol. Rev.* 42: 354–386, 1935.

(66) PETERS, H. N. A note on verifications of the judgmental theory of pleasantness and unpleasantness. *Psychol. Rev.* 44: 533–535, 1937.

(67) FREUD, S. Formulations regarding the two principles in mental functioning. Pp. 13–21. In: *Collected Papers.* IV. 508 pp. London, Hogarth, 1925.

(68) GORDON, K. Ueber das Gedaechtnis fuer affektiv bestimmte Eindruecke. *Arch. ges. Psychol.* 4: 437–458, 1905.

(69) TAIT, W. D. The effect of psycho-physical attitudes on memory. *J. Abn. Psychol.* 8: 10–37, 1913.

(70) CROSLAND, H. R. A qualitative analysis of the process of forgetting. *Psychol. Monogr.* 29: 159 pp. 1921.

(71) HEYWOOD, A., AND VORTRIEDE, H. A. Some experiments on the associative power of smells. *Amer. J. Psychol.* 16: 537–541, 1905.

(72) HARRIS, J. W. On the associative power of odors. *Amer. J. Psychol.* 19: 557–561, 1908.

(73) GORDON, K. The recollection of pleasant and of unpleasant odors. *J. exp. Psychol.* 8: 225–239, 1925.

(74) RATLIFF, M. M. The varying function of affectively toned olfactory, visual, and auditory cues in recall. *Amer. J. Psychol.* 51: 695–701, 1938.

(75) BOLGER, E. M., AND TITCHENER, E. B. Some experiments on the associative power of smells. *Amer. J. Psychol.* 18: 326–327, 1907.

(76) KENNETH, J. H. An experimental study of affects and associations due to certain odors. *Psychol. Monogr.* 37: 64 pp. 1927.

(77) WUERDEMANN, W. Ueber die Bedeutung der Gefuehle fuer das Behalten und Erinnern. *Neue Psychol. Studien.* 1: 507–573, 1926.

(78) CANNON, W. B. *Bodily Changes in pain, hunger, fear, and rage.* 404 pp. New York, Appleton, 2nd ed., 1929.

(79) BARD, P. The neuro-humoral basis of emotional reactions. Pp. 264–311. In: *Handbook of general experimental psychology.* 1125 pp. Ed. Murchison, C., Worcester, Clark Univ. Press, 1939.

(80) HEAD, H. *Studies in neurology.* Vol. I, 329 pp.; vol. II, 862 pp. London, Frowde, 1920.

(81) WILSON, S. A. K. Pathological laughing and crying. *J. Neurol. Psychopath.* 4: 299–333, 1924.

(82) WILSON, S. A. K. *Modern problems in neurology.* 364 pp. New York, Wood, 1929.

(83) HUNTER, W. S. *General psychology.* 368 pp. Chicago, Univ. Chicago Press, 1923.

(84) STAGNER, R. The redintegration of pleasant and unpleasant experiences. *Amer. J. Psychol.* 43: 463–468, 1931.

(85) BRITT, S. H. Theories of retroactive inhibition. *Psychol. Rev.* 43: 207–216, 1936.

(86) SEARS, R. R. Functional abnormalities of memory with special reference to amnesia. *Psychol. Bull.* 33: 229–274, 1936.

(87) STONE, A. R. The reaction of memory to affective states. *Amer. J. Psychol.* 36: 112–123, 1925.

(88) HARDEN, L. M. The effect of emotional reactions upon retention. *J. Genet. Psychol.* 3: 197–221, 1930.

(89) WHITE, M. M. Influence of an interpolated electric shock upon recall. *J. exp. Psychol.* 15: 752–757, 1932.

(90) DASHIEL, J. F. *Fundamentals of objective psychology.* 588 pp. New York, Mifflin, 1928.

(91) FRANK, J. D., AND LUDWIGH, E. J. The retroactive effect of pleasant and unpleasant odors on learning. *Amer. J. Psychol.* 43: 102–108, 1931.

(92) FRANK, J. D. Affective value vs. nature of odors in relation to reproduction. *Amer. J. Psychol.* 43: 479–483, 1931.

(93) DIVEN, K. Certain determinants in the conditioning of anxiety reactions. *J. Psychol.* 3: 291–308, 1937.

(94) McGRANAHAN, D. V. A critical and experimental study on repression. *J. Abn. Soc. Psychol.* 35: 212–225, 1940.

(95) MELTZER, H. The present status of experimental studies on the relationship of feeling to memory. *Psychol. Rev.* 37: 124–139, 1930.

(96) WHITEHORN, J. C. Physiological changes in emotional states. Pp. 256–270. In: *The interrelation of mind and body*. 381 pp. Baltimore, Williams & Wilkins, 1939.

(97) KOWALEWSKI, A. *Arthur Schopenhauer und seine Weltanschauung*. 237 pp. Berlin, Halle, 1908.

(98) HENDERSON, E. N. Do we forget the disagreeable? *J. Phil., Psychol. Sci. Methods* 8: 432–437, 1911.

(99) FLUEGEL, J. C. A quantitative study of feeling and emotion in everyday life. *Brit. Psychol. Soc.* 24: 408, March, 1917.

(100) FLUEGEL, J. C. A quantitative study of feeling and emotion in everyday life. *Brit. J. Psychol., Gen. Sec.* 15: 318–355, 1925.

(101) CASON, H. The learning and retention of pleasant and unpleasant activities. *Arch. Psychol.* vol. 21, no. 134, 96 pp.

(102) WOHLGEMUTH, A. The influence of feeling on memory. *Brit. J. Psychol. Gen. Sec.* 13: 405–416, 1923.

(103) GORDON, K. A study of early memories. *J. Delinq.* 12: 129–132, 1928.

(104) MELTZER, H. Individual differences in forgetting pleasant and unpleasant experiences. *J. educ. Psychol.* 21: 399–409, 1930.

(105) MELTZER, H. The forgetting of pleasant and unpleasant experiences in relation to intelligence and achievement. *J. Soc. Psychol.* 2: 216–229, 1931.

(106) MELTZER, H. Sex differences in forgetting pleasant and unpleasant experiences. *J. Abn. Soc. Psychol.* 25: 450–464, 1931.

(107) KOCH, H. L. The influence of some affective factors upon recall. *J. gen. Psychol.* 4: 171–190, 1930.

(108) JERSILD, A. Memory for the pleasant as compared with the unpleasant. *J. exp. Psychol.* 14: 284–288, 1931.

(109) THOMSON, R. H. An experimental study of memory as influenced by feeling tone. *J. exp. Psychol.* 13: 462–467, 1930.

(110) MENZIES, R. N. Memory for pleasant, unpleasant, and indifferent events of the recent past. *Psychol. Bull.* 30: 574, 1933.

(111) MENZIES, R. N. The comparative memory values of pleasant, unpleasant, and indifferent experiences. *J. exp. Psychol.* 18: 267–279, 1935.

(112) WATERS, R. H., AND LEEPER, R. The relation of affective tone to the retention of experiences of daily life. *J. exp. Psychol.* 19: 203–215, 1936.

(113) O'KELLEY, L. T., AND STECKLE, L. C. The forgetting of pleasant and unpleasant experiences. *Amer. J. Psychol.* 53: 432–434, 1940.

(114) KOEHLER, W. *Psychologische Probleme*. 252 pp. Berlin, Springer, 1933.

(115) BARRET, D. M. Memory in relation to hedonic tone. *Arch. Psychol.* vol. 131, no. 223, 61 pp., 1938.

(116) STRAUS, E. *Vom Sinn der Sinne*. 314 pp. Berlin, Springer, 1935.

(117) TOLMAN, E. C. Retroactive inhibition as affected by conditions of learning. *Psychol. Monogr.* 25: 50 pp., no. 107, 1917.

(118) JONES, H. E. Emotional factors in learning. *J. gen. Psychol.* 2: 263–272, 1929.

(119) LYNCH, C. A. The memory values of certain alleged emotionally toned words. *J. exp. Psychol.* 15: 298–315, 1932.

(120) BALKEN, E. R. Affective, volitional and galvanic factors in learning. *J. exp. Psychol.* 16: 115–128, 1933.

(121) STAGNER, R. Factors influencing the memory value of words in a series. *J. exp. Psychol.* 16: 129–137, 1933.

(122) BUNCH, M. E., AND WIENTGE, K. The relative susceptibility of pleasant, unpleasant, and indifferent material to retroactive inhibition. *J. gen. Psychol.* 9: 157–178, 1933.

(123) CHANEY, R. M., AND LAUER, A. R. The influence of affective tone on learning and retention. *J. Educ. Psychol.* 20: 287–290, 1929.

(124) WHITE, M. M., AND RATLIFF, M. M. The relation of affective tone to the learning and recall of words. *Amer. J. Psychol.* 46: 92–98, 1934.

(125) CARTER, H. D. Effects of emotional factors upon recall. *J. Psychol.* 1: 49–59, 1935.

(126) WHITE, M. M. Some factors influencing recall of pleasant and unpleasant, words. *Amer. J. Psychol.* 48: 134–139, 1936.

(127) CARTER, H. D. Emotional correlates of errors in learning. *J. Educ. Psychol.* 27: 55–67, 1936.

(128) WHITE, M. M., AND POWELL, M. Differential reaction time for pleasant and unpleasant words. *Amer. J. Psychol.* 48: 126–133, 1936.

(129) CARTER, H. D., AND JONES, H. E. A further study of affective factors in learning. *J. Genet. Psychol.* 50: 157–163, 1937.

(130) SILVERMAN, A., AND CASON, H. Incidental memory for pleasant, unpleasant, and indifferent words. *Amer. J. Psychol.* 46: 315–320, 1934.

(131) CASON, H., AND LUNGREN, F. C. Memory for pleasant, unpleasant, and indifferent pairs of words. *J. exp. Psychol.* 15: 728–732, 1932.

(132) MUELLER, F. B. Gefuehlstheoretisches auf psychoanalytischer Grundlage. *Imago*, 12: 263–267, 1926.

(133) LANIER, L. H. Memory for words differing in affective value. 8 pp. Paper read at the 1940 meetings of the *Amer. Psychol. Assoc.*, State Coll., Penn., 1940.

(134) LANIER, L. H. Incidental memory for words differing in affective value. *J. Psychol.* 11: 219–228, 1941.

(135) ADAMS, D. K. A restatement of the problem of learning. *Brit. J. Psychol.* 22: 150–178, 1931.

(136) GILBERT, G. M. The age difference in the hedonistic tendency in memory. *J. exp. Psychol.* 21: 433–441, 1937.

(137) CASON, H. Methods of studying the learning and retention of pleasant and unpleasant activities. *J. exp. Psychol.* 16: 454–459, 1933.

(138) MOORE, E. H. A note on the recall of the pleasant vs. the unpleasant. *Psychol. Rev.* 42: 214–215, 1935.

(139) GILBERT, G. M. The new status of experimental studies on the relationship of feeling and memory. *Psychol. Bull.* 35: 26–35, 1938.

(140) YOUNG, P. T. A study upon the recall of pleasant and unpleasant words. *Amer. J. Psychol.* 49: 581–596, 1937.

(141) MYERS, G. C. Affective factors in recall. *J. Phil., Psychol. Sci. Methods.* 12: 85–92, 1915.

(142) LAIRD, D. A. The influence of likes and dislikes on memory as related to personality. *J. exp. Psychol.* 6: 294–303, 1923.

(143) PETERS, A. Gefuehl und Wiedererkennen. *Fortschritte der Psychologie und ihrer Anwendungen.* 4: 120–133, 1917.

(144) BERLINER, A. Zusammenhang zwischen aesthetischem Wert und Wiedererkennen. *Arch. ges. Psychol.* 41: 401–410, 1921.

(145) RAPAPORT, D. The Szondi test. *Bull. Menninger Clinic* 5: 33–39, 1941.

(146) FOX, C. The influence of subjective preference on memory. *Brit. J. Psychol., Gen. Sec.* 13: 398–404, 1923.

(147) SELZ, O., AND BAUMANN, A. Ueber die Abhaengigkeitsbeziehungen zwischen Lernlust und Lernerfolg. *Z. Psychol.* 109: 191–209, 1929.

(148) WALDBERG, L. Zur Wirkung der Affekte auf die Erinnerungsfaehigkeit bei gesunden Erwachsenen, bei Kindern und bei Geisteskranken. *Allg. Z. Psychiat.* 77: 29–57, 1921.

(149) SHARP, A. A. An experimental test of Freud's doctrine of the relation of hedonic tone to memory revival. *J. exp. Psychol.* 22: 395–418, 1938.

(150) SEARS, R. R. Recall of free associations to anxiety-inducing phrases. Paper read to the 1940 meeting of the *Amer. Psychol. Assn., Penn. State Coll.,* 1940.

(151) GUNDLACH, R., ROTHSCHILD, D. A., AND YOUNG, P. T. A test and analysis of "set." *J. exp. Psychol.* 10: 247–280, 1927.

(152) MCGEOCH, J. A. Learning. Retention. pp. 290–350. In: *Introduction to psychology,* 652 pp. ed. Boring, E. G., Langfeld, H. S., and Weld, H. P. New York, Wiley, 1939.

(153) ACH, N. *Ueber die Begriffsbildung.* 343 pp. Bamberg, Buchner, 1921.

(154) HUMPHREY, G. Thought. Pp. 381–410. In: *Introduction to psychology.* 652 pp. Ed. Boring, E. G., Langfeld, H. S., and Weld, H. P. New York, Wiley, 1939.

(155) PAN, S. The influence of context upon learning and recall. *J. exp. Psychol.* 9: 468–491, 1926.

(156) FLANAGAN, D. *The influence of emotional inhibition on learning and recall.* 13 pp. Unpubl. thesis on file Univ. Chicago Libr., 1930.

(157) SHARP, A. A. The influence of certain emotional inhibitions on learning and recall. 22 pp. *Unpubl. thesis* on file Univ. Chicago Libr., 1930.

(158) SMITH, B., AND GUTHRIE, E. R. *General psychology in terms of behavior.* 270 pp. New York, Appleton, 1921.

(159) WONG, H., AND BROWN, W. Effects of surroundings upon mental work as measured by Yerke's multiple choice method. *J. comp. Psychol.* 3: 319–331, 1923.

(160) LANGFELD, H. S. Suppression with negative instructions. *Psychol. Bull.* 7: 200–208, 1910.

(161) LANGFELD, H. S. Suppression with negative instructions. *Psychol. Rev.* 18: 411–424, 1911.

(162) KEY, K. B. Recall as a function of perceived relations. *Arch. Psychol.* 13: 106 pp. 1926.

(163) SULLIVAN, E. B. Attitude in relation to learning. *Psychol. Monogr.* 36: 1–149, 1927.

(164) MCKINNEY, F. Certain emotional factors in learning and efficiency. *J. gen. Psychol.* 9: 101–116, 1933.

(165) LEWIN, K. *A dynamic theory of personality.* 286 pp. New York, McGraw-Hill, 1935.

(166) LEWIN, K. Die psychische Taetigkeit bei der Hemmung von Willensvorgaengen und das Grundgesetz der Assoziation. *Z. Psychol.* 77: 212–247, 1916.

(167) LEWIN, K. Das Problem der Willensmessung und das Grundgesetz der Assoziation. *Psychol. Forsch.* I. 1: 192–302; II. 2: 65–140, 1922.

(168) LEWIN, K. *Vorsatz, Wille und Beduerfnis. Vorbemerkungen ueber die psychischen Kraefte und Energien und ueber die Struktur der Seele.* Berlin, Springer, 1926.

(169) OVSIANKINA, M. Die Wiederaufnahme unterbrochener Handlungen. *Psychol. Forsch.* 11: 302–379, 1928.

(170) ZEIGARNIK, B. Das Behalten erledigter und unerledigter Handlungen. *Psychol. Forsch.* 9: 1–85, 1927. Cf. Lewin, K. *A dynamic theory of personality.* Trans. Adams, D. K., and Zener, K. E., pp. 243–247. New York, McGraw-Hill, 1935.

(171) McKINNEY, F. Studies in the retention of interrupted learning activities. *J. comp. Psychol.* 19: 265–296, 1935.

(172) PACHAURI, A. R. A study of Gestalt problems in completed and interrupted tasks. *Brit. J. Psychol.* 25: 365–381, 447–457, 1935.

(173) LEWIN, K. *Principles of topological psychology.* 247 pp. New York, McGraw-Hill, 1936.

(174) BIRENBAUM, G. Das Vergessen einer Vornahme. Isolierte seelische Systeme und dynamische Gesamtbereiche. *Psychol. Forsch.* 13: 218–284, 1930.

(175) ROSENZWEIG, S. *The dependence of preferences upon success and failure.* Doctoral thesis. Cambridge, Mass., Harvard Univ. Libr., 1932.

(176) ROSENZWEIG, S. Preferences in repetition of successful and unsuccessful activities as a function of age and personality. *J. Genet. Psychol.* 42: 423–441, 1933.

(177) ROSENZWEIG, S. The recall of finished and unfinished tasks as affected by the purpose with which they were performed. *Psychol. Bull.* 30: 698, 1933.

(178) ROSENZWEIG, S., AND MASON, G. An experimental study of memory in relation to the theory of repression. *Brit. J. Psychol.* 24: 247–265, 1934.

(179) ROSENZWEIG, S. The preferential repetition of successful and unsuccessful activities. *Psychol. Bull.* 33, 797, 1936.

(180) ROSENZWEIG, S. The experimental study of repression. Pp. 472–490. In: *Explorations in personality.* 761 pp. Ed. Murray, H. A. New York, Oxford Univ. Press, 1938.

(181) FREUD, S. Analysis terminable and interminable. *Internat. J. Psychoanal.* 18: 373–405, 1938.

(182) BROWN, J. F. Ueber die dynamischen Eigenschaften der Realitaets- und Irrealitaetsschichten. *Psychol. Forsch.* 18: 2–26, 1933.

(183) DEMBO, T. Der Aerger als dynamisches Problem. *Psychol. Forsch.* 15: 1–144, 1931.

(184) REYMERT, M. L. (ed.) *Feelings and emotions. The Wittenberg symposium.* 454 pp. Worcester, Clark Univ. Press, 1928.

(185) CATTELL, R. B. Sentiment or attitude? The core of a terminology problem in personality research. *Character and Personality* 9: 6–17, 1940.

(186) RIVERS, W. H. R., TANSLEY, A. G., SHAND, A. F., PEAR, T. H., HART, B. AND MYERS, C. S. The relations of complex and sentiment. A symposium. *Brit. J. Psychol.* 13: 107–148, 1922.

(187) WOODWORTH, R. S. *Dynamic psychology.* 206 pp. New York, Columbia Univ. Press, 1922.

CHAPTER IV

THEORETICAL CONTRIBUTIONS OF GENERAL PSYCHOLOGY

Epistemological discussions for centuries attempted to solve the question of whether, and how, our knowledge reflects the true nature of the world. The question has been formulated as that of the relation of "reason" and "reality," of "verité du fait" and "verité de la raison," and so on. Hume thought that the nature of our world lay in the recurrence of events, and that the nature of the human mind lay in the imprinting in it of ideas and connections of ideas as the recurrence of external events strengthened the associations. It has frequently been shown that Hume's philosophy as epistemology was sterile; although it may explain how we understand the world, it can yield mere statistical probabilities and not causal laws, because any change of repetition sequences would make the concept of law senseless. Yet this momentous attempt to account for our mental life in terms of passive dependence on the outside world profoundly influenced the development of psychology in general, and of English and American psychology in particular. Out of it grew the mechanistic conception of psychology, in which ideas and presentations were but reproductions of impressions. It would be an exaggeration to say that a thoroughbred psychology of this stock still exists. In the last few decades we have witnessed concessions made by all schools of thought, and at present every psychology and every science is more or less eclectic. The different schools of science did not teach solely a theory; most of them discovered facts as well, some of which were accepted by and influenced the theories of the other schools.

Today even conservative textbooks of psychology recognize that the human mind is not purely passive and receptive. Nevertheless, Ebbinghaus's theory, and the recent attempts at a mechanistic explanation of memory-functioning, show that the influence of Hume's philosophy is still active.

Many schools of thought are built on a principle opposed to Hume's: for example, the vitalistic schools of biology and psychology. Yet to demonstrate in psychology this opposed principle one need not resort to the arguments of the vitalist. A historical analysis[1] shows that the main philosophical influence on psychology, issuing in the recognition of the self-activity and autonomy of the human mind, was the philosophy

[1] See Rapaport (1).

111

of Kant; this was the true antithesis of Hume's mechanistic theory. Kant propounded his theory in the *"Prolegomena To All Future Metaphysics,"* and in the *"Critique of The Pure Reason."* In the *"Critique"*[2] he suggested that both the laws of nature and our knowledge of them are rooted in the self-activity of the reason; that time and space are modes of experiencing and that causality is a category of the pure reason: in other words, that the pure reason synthesizes experience according to its own nature, and that the understanding of the outside world is possible only in terms of our modes of perception—space and time—and in terms of the categories of pure reason. His essential thesis may be stated in brief thus: to understand our knowledge of the outside world, we must investigate the nature of human thinking. Although Kant's transcendental idealism was not a purely "psychologistic" philosophy, it maintained that the laws of man's thinking determine what laws of nature he can discover. Whether this philosophical contention is tenable is a question beyond the scope of our discussion; but the enormous influence on psychology of this "Copernican turn" of philosophy constitutes the historical background of the modern theory of memory and especially of the theory of the influence of emotions on memory. It was a momentous discovery that the facts or processes as perceived by us are not necessarily identical with the facts or processes as they "exist," and that our perceptions follow the laws of our mind. The influence of this theoretical discovery is reflected in the most original investigations of modern psychology. Uexkuell (2) demonstrated that animals, insects, children, and adults of the western civilization all see the world in a manner peculiar to themselves. Werner (3) summarized the available experimental findings and observations concerning the mental life of native peoples, brain-injured men, psychotic patients, children, and animals; and showed that on these varied developmental levels the organization of time, space, imagery, memory, thought, and personality greatly differs. Piaget (4), in a series of meticulous investigations, explored the child's organization of the world.

An early modern formulation of the memory function as an active organization by the mind of external phenomena has been made by Dewey (5):

"Memory is not a passive process in which past experiences thrust themselves upon the mind, any more than perception is one where present experiences impress themselves." (p. 177)

The investigations and theories reflecting this idea are countless. In our field this discovery is represented by theories conceiving of memory not as an ability to revive accurately impressions once obtained, but as the

[2] See especially the first edition: the chapter on "Transcendental Dialectics."

integration of impressions into the whole personality and their revival according to the needs of the whole personality. These theories imply that the impressions are products of an active psyche, that revival depends on their relation to the whole of the individual's organized experience, and that in recall the impressions reappear as modified by this relation.

The recognition of the autonomous activity of the human mind, and of memory as an aspect thereof, set the stage for the investigation of the influence of emotions on memory, an investigation which otherwise would have remained impossible. The recognition of the active nature of memory, however, was pregnant with the further recognition that the emotional influence is the core of this autonomous activity. The material to be presented below will represent an incomplete but probably fruitful process of birth rather than a completed, well-formed creation. To date, the fact of the emotional influence on memory is recognized rather than explored fully, and its laws are indicated rather than proved.

The classical association psychology stated its laws of memory and thinking in terms of the relative strength of associations derived from the frequency of contiguous occurrence and the degree of similarity of the associated elements. It was early recognized that the frequency-principle was insufficient, that the meaning of similarity was vague and that its degrees were lacking objective criteria. To cope with these difficulties Ziehen assumed that the interaction of all the aroused associations—or "constellation"—has a role in determining the emerging idea. A similar concept, "complex,"[3] was introduced by G. E. Mueller. Ach of the Marburg school introduced the concept "determining tendency" to designate a selective psychic function in contrast to the merely quantitative strength of association. The Graz school of psychology introduced the concept "Gestalt Qualitaet" to designate a similarly qualitative selective function. These concepts, however, were vague and were defined only in terms of their effects; they were coined in a search for a selective function to complement the associationists' concept of the passive receptivity and mechanical responsiveness of the human mind. The association theory was destined to failure, as it lacked a concept of "psychic force" on the basis of which a theory of psychic dynamics could be developed. Even the attempts of Ziehen, Mueller, Ach and others to find a selective function failed to reach such a concept. "Emotions" and "feelings" were assigned the role of such a selective force only recently, and with

[3] This concept of "complex" must be carefully distinguished from the "complex" of Jung and early psychoanalysis. The latter consists in a group of ideas centered on and held together by an affect; the former is simply an idea and all others connected with it by virtue of associative bonds.

partial success; for in regard to both memory and the emotions, a theory based on the dynamics of forces is still in an early stage of development.

We have selected for discussion only a few outstanding newer theories concerning these selective forces and their influence. It is our opinion that each of the contributions to be quoted adds a new shading to the problem. The method of extensive quotation was considered justified, as the material here collected has never, to our knowledge, been systematically surveyed. The discussion will be divided into four parts: (1) the nature of the selective force suggested; (2) the role played by the selective force in determining the original registration; (3) the effect of the selective force in the period between registration and reproduction; (4) the role of the selective force in the process and result of reproduction.

1. THE NATURE OF THE SELECTIVE FORCE

Investigators have grasped and described varied aspects of the selective force operating in remembering and forgetting. In this section we shall collect the descriptions of the selective force by these authors in the hope that a synopsis of them will contribute to the knowledge of the nature of the selective force whose operation we have designated as the "influence of emotions on memory."

Mueller-Freienfels (6, 7) calls the selective force "feeling." Criticizing the associationistic view which regarded feeling-tone as one of the factors determining memory function, he states his own point of view:

"The introduction of feeling-tone means a disruption of the associationistic principle which wants to explain everything on-the basis of the associations of ideas, because feeling is either considered as an accompanying tone—an attribute of the idea, in which case it is hard to understand how it would work—or it is considered to be different from the idea in which case the associationistic principle is disrupted." (7, p. 76)

In discussing the relation of "feelings" and associations, he elaborates on the differences between the associationist theory and his:

" . . . the spatial-temporal association of individual ideas is not the objective unity in which the experiences originally occur, but rather a subjective one built by the feeling background." (6, p. 407)

" . . . our ideational life is dependent on our affective life, our feelings, and will. It is the common basic mood, the affective attitude, which creates the constellations, since ideas alone never constitute a state of the ego. By modifying our affective life through a dose of alcohol we are able to disrupt any constellation without this effect being due to the idea of alcohol." (6, p. 417)

He suggests further that the "feeling" is not an associated element but rather the mediator of associations:

"Words and concepts . . . are not the elements of reproduction. It is rather the movements and attitudes which in verbal thinking allow the words to be more than flatus vocis." (6, p. 398)

He stresses the intimate relation of "feelings" to kinaesthesis:[4]

"In the controversy concerning the nature of feelings we join those who assume an interrelation of feelings and kinaesthetic experience. Without making final statements, we only point out that in every feeling there is a motoric tendency, a readiness for action." (6, p. 395)

He also identifies "feelings" with attitudes:

" . . . Most psychologists designate only pleasure-displeasure as feeling. The reduction to this pair of all subjective reactions is a momentarily useful, but in the long run insufficient and negative, selection. 'The state of consciousness,' 'character' are some of the concepts that were used to denote the subjective reactions. We consider the concept 'attitude' (Stellungnahme) to be the most useful." (6, pp. 392–393)

Finally, Mueller-Freienfels provides an imaginative description of the role of "feeling" as a selective force:

"We call the constitutive feelings, which have their effect rather through their constancy than by their intensity, mostly interest. In point of fact, it is the interests which shape the constitution of our thinking. These feelings act like a magnet which selects the iron pieces from a heap of dust. The interests, these feeling-dispositions existing in the consciousness like an undercurrent, draw into their realm everything they can use. The fate of what is thus attracted depends on many things, first of all on their control by the judgment . . . " (6, p. 429)

Crosland (10), the only experimenter to precede Bartlett in giving a qualitative analysis of the functioning of memory, finds that the content of remembering is embedded in a general "attitude complex." This "attitude complex" consists mainly of kinaesthetic, organic, and affective components, and is very stable:

"It was found that this . . . *added* component was remembered more fully than the *received* component." (p. 73)

Pear (11), in his undogmatic and rich treatise on "Remembering and Forgetting," considers logical and affective relevance to be the selective power (p. 136). He defines this relevance as follows:

"Relevant memories are those which consciousness at the moment admits and incorporates with its present experience." (p. 138)

---

[4] See also Muensterberg (8) and Washburn (9).

This relevance is discussed in connection with "sentiments"[5] and "complexes," the affective nature of which is obvious:

" . . . [one] aspect of forgetting . . . has scarcely been touched by any writer: its relation to the sentiments . . . If sentiments . . . differ from complexes . . . only in degree, then we must grant that repression may play a part in the formation of both . . . Probably forgetting will never be satisfactorily explained until the relations between sentiments and complexes are made clearer." (p. 175)

Thus, Pear sought to explain normal remembering and forgetting by assuming that they are determined by the sentiments—that is, the normal counterpart of complexes, whose determining role in pathological memory phenomena he accepted.

William Stern's "personalistic" psychology (15, 16) also recognizes a selective memory function, which is labelled "personal determination." However, this concept is frequently identified by him with "personal reference," "attitude," and "set." The "personal determination" in memory works through "selection" and "modeling" (15, p. 360).

"The modeling ensues directly under the influence of personal affects and strivings." (15, p. 362)
"This selectivity is retraceable to a dispositional readiness of the person." (16, p. 223)

McDougall (17) maintains that "like other thinking, remembering is a conative activity" (p. 310). He defines conation as one of

" . . . the three aspects of all mental processes—the cognitive, the affective, and the conative aspects; that is to say, every instance of instinctive behaviour involves a knowing of something . . . a feeling in regard to it, and a striving towards or away from that object." (p. 27)

Szymanski (18) considers "interests," "driving-forces" (Antriebe), "basic-needs" (Lebensbeduerfnisse), to be the selective forces (p. 182). As he defines affects as expressions of the knowledge (Erkenntnis) of "driving-forces," his theory resembles McDougall's.

[5] A definition of sentiments is given by McDougall (12): "Mr. Shand points out that our emotions, or more strictly, our emotional dispositions, tend to become organized in systems about the various objects and classes of objects that excite them. Such an organized system of emotional tendencies is not a fact or mode of experience, but it is a feature of the complexly organized structure of the mind that underlies all our mental activity. To such an organized system of emotional tendencies centered about some object Mr. Shand proposes to apply the name 'sentiment' " (p. 126). See also "The Relations of Complex and Sentiment: A Symposium" (13), and Cattell (14) on attitudes and sentiments.

K. Gordon (19) maintains that "memory is selective" as

"It cannot be separated from social life . . . social interests . . . Those things are memorable which are apprehended as having bearing on the personal welfare of the individual . . . and those which have a more general value and logical or esthetic coherence of their own . . . " (p. 121)

Lewin, in his experiments reported in "The Problem of Measurement of Will and of the Associations" (20), finds that tendencies—such as the "tendency to identify," the "tendency to reproduce,"—are indispensable factors in remembering, recognition, and so on. A similar opinion is voiced by Cason (21) who, challenging the "law of effect,"[6] quotes examples to show that without an "intention to learn" no learning ensues. In 1926 Lewin (23) came to the conclusion that these "intentions" generally determine our remembering and other actions. He showed that in their structure these intentions resemble "needs," and he named them "quasineeds"; these "needs" and "quasi-needs" differ from wishes in that they imply activity directed towards satisfaction. He considers the "quasineeds" and the tension systems[7] created by them as the selective forces active in memory functioning. Bartlett (24) finds the "attitude," or "active organized setting," to be the selective force and describes it as:

" . . . a complex psychological state or process which it is very hard to describe in more elementary psychological terms. It is, however, as I have often indicated, very largely a matter of feeling, or affect. We say that it is characterized by doubt, hesitation, surprise, astonishment, confidence, dislike, repulsion and so on." (pp. 206-207)

Moreover, Bartlett's "attitude" is identical with "interests" on the level of human remembering:

"The active settings which are chiefly important as the level of human remembering are mainly 'interest' settings; and, since an interest has both a definite direction and a wide range, the development of these settings involves much reorganization of the 'schemata' that follow the more primitive lines of special sense differences, of appetite and of instinct." (p. 214)

Because of the "attitudes"—which are identified with the "affective setting"—remembering is not a mechanical revival of "engrams," but an active process of reconstruction:

" . . . in many cases the main conditions for the occurrence of images appear to be found in their affective setting. This functions as an 'attitude,' and the attitude is best described as an orientation of the agent towards the image and its less ar-

---

[6] See also Tolman (22).
[7] See pp. 95-96 for a detailed discussion of "tension-systems."

ticulated 'schematic' surroundings. If, then, as in specific recall, we are called upon to justify the image, we do so by constructing, or reconstructing, its setting. Thereupon the attitude acquires a rationalisation. Social grouping, with its accompaniment of conventionalised and relatively permanent traditions, institutions and customs, has been shown to play a great part in the development of interests, in the determination of the affective setting which is often at the basis of image formation, and in the provision of material for the constructive processes of recall." (p. 303)

For comparison, we insert here the definition of "attitudes" as given by Allport (25). Unlike Bartlett, Allport derived his definition of attitudes from personality and socio-psychological investigations:

"An attitude is a mental and neural state of readiness, organized through experience, exerting a directive or dynamic influence upon the individual's response to all objects and situations with which it is related." (p. 810)

The concept "attitude" of sociology and social psychology so frequently used at present—as, attitudes toward war, attitudes of college freshmen toward Russia, and so on—is only a distant relative of the concepts of "attitude" discussed on these pages. Although it is hard to draw up a comprehensive definition, it appears that the concept of "attitude" dealt with here refers to a more general, and psychologically more elementary, factor.

Gestalt psychology maintains and has shown experimentally, that percepts and memories do not have an independent existence, but rather are determined by the "field" in which they are embedded. Thus, to the Gestalt psychologist the structure or organization of the "field" is itself the selective factor. To clarify this statement, it may be advisable to expound the Gestalt psychological conceptions underlying it. According to the Gestalt psychologist, underlying every psychological process—perception, judgment, remembering, thinking, and so on—there occurs in the brain an electro-chemical process, the structure of which is similar—isomorphous—to that of the psychological process. It is maintained, and inditial experimental proof is adduced,[8] that these electro-chemical changes in the brain are partly processes corresponding to current psychological processes, and partly traces of these processes which underly memory functions.

In terms of such a trace theory the selective role of the whole field may be expressed as follows: (*a*) No isolated stimulus is preserved, since all the parts of the whole field elicit electro-chemical changes in the brain, and these changes are not isolated but interact; thus their interaction plays the role of a selective factor. (*b*) Not only do the simultaneous processes—the whole field—interact, but the processes occur in a medium in which traces of previous processes also exert an effect; the interaction of these

[8] See Koehler (26), Koffka (27).

traces with the current processes constitutes another selective factor. In addition to these, Koffka describes a selective factor which he designates "attitude." To understand Koffka's view of "attitudes" we must understand his view of the psychological field. The psychological field is conceived as including both the environment and the ego of the experiencing person. Corresponding to this psychological field there is an isomorphous brain field consisting of traces and processes, which have a "core" corresponding to the ego and a "shaft" corresponding to the environmental field. Remembering is conceived as the communication of a process with a trace; and the problem is how such a communication comes about. The organization of the current processes and their relation to the traces have thus far been discussed without regard to the role of the ego; Koffka's (27) concept of "attitude" takes the role of the ego into consideration. Koffka views "attitudes" as similar in their nature to Lewin's "quasi-needs," and integrates them into his trace theory. The mechanism of their influence is explained as follows:

"In the first place this attitude has the character of a quasi-need, it corresponds to a tension in the Ego part at the tip of the column. This tension can be relieved only through that part of the trace column which contains yesterday's figures, since a linking up of today's with yesterday's is possible only if these traces influence the new process. In other words, the attitude requires the reaction of a field which in cludes these particular traces." (p. 609)

Koffka raises the question of whether the presence of "attitudes" is indispensable for the "communication of traces"—that is, for remembering and recognition. After analyzing Bartlett's and Lewin's theoretical position, he arrives at the following conclusion:

"It is possible to interpret both Lewin and Bartlett as asserting that communication between process and trace as an event entirely within the shaft of the trace column does not occur. Whether such a claim is true or not, experiments will have to decide. Personally I do not believe it. Again I hold that dynamic relations within the shaft, i.e., within the environmental field, and between core and shaft, may be effective, and not only dynamic relations within the core, the Ego system. Despite this belief, which, as I just said, will have to be tested by experiments, I recognize the enormous importance of attitudinal factors. *As I envisage the problem, the alternative, either spontaneous recognition or recognition always mediated by attitude, does not exist.*[9] That intra-shaft forces are necessary even where an attitude made communication possible, we have seen above. Thus a frank acceptance of the effectiveness of all the forces that may come into play seems the safest position to adopt before new experimental evidence is adduced." (p. 611)

Koffka's warning that it is necessary to accept all the forces that may come into play must not be forgotten by one who attempts to develop a

[9] Italics mine.—D. R.

theory of memory with the "emotional influence on memory" as its core. To attempt to deduce all the memory functions only from emotional influences without regard to the meaning and the frequency of experiences would be repeating the historical errors of associationists and Gestaltists. In general, however, Gestalt psychology disregards other factors, and considers field-structure to be the sole selective principle. Thus Katona (28) shows that the "eclatant"[10] and "better organized"[10] parts of the experience are the ones which leave traces or, in other words, are selected for survival:

"Series 1: A A A A X A A A A
Series 2: X X X X A X X X X
Series 3: X Y Z W A V U T S
"The configuration of A in Series 1 is called "accumulation" and in Series 2 "isolation." In Series 3 we have only isolated members. The letters A, X, Y, and so forth can represent any material. Suppose A represents nonsense syllables, X numbers, and the other letters miscellaneous material—small geometrical drawings, words, and so forth." (p. 184)
"Restorff obtained unequivocal results in various experiments. The recall, reconstruction, and recognition of A was best in Series 2, not quite as good in Series 3, and least good in Series 1. Isolation appears to be more favorable for learning than is monotonous accumulation, and isolation appears best when the isolated object is surrounded by uniform objects." (p. 185)

Wheeler and Perkins (29), who advocate a "traceless" Gestalt theory of memory, express the following opinion:

" . . . the social and emotional tone of he original situation for the observer emphasizes those facts which harmonize best with his attitudes and purposes; the observer tends to recall past events as he thinks that they should have taken place." (p. 401)

In psychological text-books and experimentation the selective factor is called at times "set," at times "context." We have quoted the definition of these concepts from Boring's (30, 31) text-book. Characteristically, several recent text-books, such as that of E. Freeman (32) or of Guilford (33), fail to mention these concepts and phenomena. Accounts of pertinent experiments on human subjects are also rather scarce; those of Langfeld (34, 35), Wong and Brown (36), Pan (37), and Gundlach, Rotschild and Young (38) deserve mention in this connection.

Though not explaining the role of selective functions in memory, the

---

[10] The concepts "eclatant," "better organized," "meaningful," "prägnant-principle," "better form," and "good continuation," so often found in Gestalt literature, are unquestionably useful. They disregard, however, the dependence of the properties designated by these concepts on the interests, attitudes, and affects of the subject.

aged theory of "emergence" at least set the background for such an explanation. How did human memory emerge phylogenetically? Edgell (39) summed up the early pertinent theories, of which S. Butler's (40) is especially interesting; in modern general psychology those of Buehler (41), Stern (16), and Allport (42) deserve mention.

Buehler (41) considers instinct, habit, and intellect to be the three consecutive evolutionary levels of mental functioning in general, and of memory functioning in particular. These three levels interact in man's mental life, each lower level serving as a basis for the higher (pp. 2–10). Stern (16) voices a similar opinion:

"(The mneme) is conservative and progressive, in the same time, for *its function is conservation of progress* . . . [the] mneme occupies the middle-ground between instinct which is of a generally conservative nature, and intelligence, which is progressively directed." (p. 191)

Allport (42) writes:

"The significance of memory is found in the mid-position it occupies in personal life between the function of instinct (the conservational factor) on the one hand and the function of intelligence (the progressive factor) on the other." (p. 555)

Whatever the meaning here of "conservation" and "progress," the ideas of Allport and Stern seem to be similar to Buehler's. According to the kind of interpretation of which these three are samples, human memory emerged from instinctive functioning as a result of a delay of action. At this point the tempting hypothesis offers itself that the selective influencès to which memory is subject are of instinctual origin.

Some contributions of developmental psychology may be interpreted to point in a similar direction, as shown in the following statement of Heinz Werner (3):

" . . . in the primitive sphere there is a very close connection between *emotion* and memory image. Reality, in retrospect, is shaped strongly by the affective need. The boastful revision of accounts of martial exploits found everywhere among primitive and naïve people are evidence of a mnemonic reality formed through affective influence. Pechuel-Loesche reports that the Loangos incline to the most extravagant forms of exaggeration even when referring to events to which they have been eye-witnesses. Anyone struck by a bullet or anyone on whom blood is running is reported as killed, and anyone who suffers a slash from a weapon is reported as dead after being horribly cut to ribbons. We find this phenomenon again in the exaggeration of affectively conditioned drawings from memory. If the Brazilian Indian draws a picture of a battle between a jaguar and a tapir, the jaguar—as the more powerful member of the situation—will be represented in a size out of all proportion . . . The drawings of Bushmen in which they represent themselves as giants and their enemies as dwarfs are well known. The objective representation is determined to a large degree by an affective evaluation. We might speak here of 'emotional perspective,' a common feature, as we shall see, of children's drawings."

"It is a generally recognized fact that the *child's* memory is often radically transformed under the influence of affect. This is true, for example, of the memory of
size. Such a metamorphosis can be followed most clearly in representations of the
eidetic type. In eidetic children, transformation according to affective compulsion
may even reach out into the immediate perceptual reality. For example, one of
Jaensch's subjects, a schoolboy, sees certain scenes from a play which impress him
so deeply that the actors grow to enormous proportions before his eyes. Kroh tells
of an interesting case of an eidetic youth who always saw the cigars which chanced
to suit his taste as much larger than all the rest in the cigar-store window." (pp.
148–149)

2. The Role of the Selective Factor in the Process of Registration

The concept of "registration" is by no means an unequivocal one,
and thus requires some discussion before we present the material relevant
to the role of the selective factor in registration. One attempting to
define what is meant by registration must consider a number of concepts,
such as those of stimulation, perception, apperception, understanding, and
experiencing; it would not be difficult to find additional concepts which
belong in the same category. For the present we limit ourselves to these
five, which will serve our purpose. Some theories, especially the mechanistic theories which conceived of the mind as a passive agent, emphasized
the stimulus; others, especially those which conceived of the mind as an
autonomous active agent, emphasized the process current in the mind
while being stimulated. The expressions "stimulus," "perception,"
and even "registration," generally pertain to the former group of theories;
the concepts "apperception," "understanding," and "experiencing"
pertain to the latter group. In recent years it has become increasingly
evident that perception and registration are active processes of the mind,
and that the incoming stimulation is organized under the influence of the
past experiences and strivings of the organism; thus the original passive-
receptive connotation of the concepts "perception" and "registration"
has been changed to a more active one. Accordingly, in the following
discussion the context in which these concepts occur, rather than the
expressions themselves, will indicate the school of thought adhered to
by the author quoted.

Mueller-Freienfels (6) maintains that already in the process of registration the subjective selection is active:

"The imprints—which, according to the older teaching, are effective in our psyche
—are primarily of a subjective nature . . .
"Thus, it is quite unessential whether or not contiguity exists objectively; the
problem is whether or not contiguity is subjectively experienced." (p. 407)

He explains further this "subjective experiencing":

"Only when they elicit . . . attitudes in us, do we understand words. These attitudes may be of an affective nature towards poetry, of a practical nature towards questions and comments . . . in all cases they are responsible for understanding." (p. 408)

Pear (11) characterizes registration as a process dependent on the state of consciousness:

" . . . the sensation is a *modification* of consciousness. It is merely a change in the subject's experience, not something which drops into a previous nothingness." (p. 30)

W Stern's (16) view of this question is similar to that of Mueller-Freienfels:

"We saw that *associations by contiguity* originate in the temporal coincidence of stimulation. But not everything that is experienced once—or even frequently— together with something else, is thereby coupled with it in such a way that both will necessarily be reinstated as an associative combination. A high degree of *selection* is operative that isolates only a very few pairs and groups of temporally contiguous experiences in mneme and thus establishes their associations. This selectivity is traceable to a disposition readiness of the person, to his *susceptivity to mnemic stimuli* . . . no association can originate in the individual without having personal relevance . . . To be sure, the concept of 'personal relevance' must be given sufficient breadth of scope." (p. 223)

Szymanski (18) maintains that the presence of the "driving force"—his expression for the selective factor—is more important than the frequency of experiencing, in bringing about registration:

"The frequency of experiencing alone, without the presence of a 'driving force,' is not enough to gain knowledge of an object . . . Conversely, an object may affect a person but once or a few times, and knowledge may still be gained if the object is connected with driving-forces (Antriebe) in the subject." (p. 183)

Gordon (19) compared changes and distortions in perception with changes in memory. She maintains that neither percepts nor memory images are merely photographic records, and that the material of both is transformed according to the interests of the experiencing subject. Cason (21) cites the following example to show the role of intention in registration: a student read and re-read a series of nonsense syllables and when asked to recall it, was surprised, and stated that he did not know that he had to learn it, and could not recall it, thus showing that use alone does not account for learning.[11] Bartlett's (24) theory of selection in registration

[11] See Cason, pp. 399–400.

is similar to Pear's; he maintains that the process of perception implies two factors:

" (a) that of the sensory pattern, which provides a physiological basis for perceiving; and
" (b) that of another factor which constructs the sensory pattern into something having a significance which goes beyond its immediate sensory character. The latter appears to be a specifically psychological function in the total perceptual response and, for the moment, I purposely leave it vague and undefined." (p. 188)

He emphasizes that the incoming impulse is organized by and integrated with previous ones, and does not persist as an isolated trace:

"All incoming impulses of a certain kind, or mode, go together to build up an active, organized setting; visual, auditory, various types of cutaneous impulses and the like, at a relatively low level; all the experiences connected by a common interest: in sport, in literature, history, art, science, philosophy and so on, on a higher level. There is not the slightest reason, however, to suppose that each set of incoming impulses, each new group of experiences persists as an isolated member of some passive patchwork." (p. 201)

The second factor—which he designated as "effort after meaning" (43)—is described further as

" . . . an attitude, or orientation, which we cannot ascribe to any localized physiological apparatus, but which has to be treated as belonging to 'the whole' subject, or organism, reacting." (p. 191)

The effect of this factor may be seen in the difference between hearing and listening:

" . . . under no circumstances whatever does hearing without listening provide a sufficient basis for recognition . . . Selective listening is determined mainly by the qualitative differences of stimuli in relation to predispositions—cognitive, affective and motor—of the listener." (p. 190)

Gestalt psychology with its *prägnant-principle*, one of its basic concepts, refers to the organization of the percept under the influence of the whole field.   Wulf (44), who demonstrated the autonomous changes which take place during the retention period, called attention to the fact that a part of these changes is initiated in the act of perception.   This point was also stressed by Gibson (45), but was denied by Hanawalt (46).   Katona (28) maintains that the meaning, the whole-character of the percept, leaves traces—"structural traces"—qualitatively different from that of specific items—"individual traces"—; and he advances the following hypotheses regarding the structural traces, which correspond to the selective factor called by the Gestalt-psychologists "meaning":

"Hypothesis I: Traces referring to specific items of past experience and those connected with and derived from the whole-character of a process can be distinguished from each other. We shall call the first 'individual traces,' the latter 'structural traces.'

"Hypothesis II: Individual traces are characterized by a certain degree of fixation and rigidity, while structural traces are more readily adaptable and flexible.

"Hypothesis III: The formation of individual traces is usually a long and strenuous process, while under certain conditions understanding may lead quickly and with less effort to the formation of structural traces.

"Hypothesis IV: Structural traces persist longer than individual traces, which vanish soon unless reinforced." (pp. 194–195)

Eidetic imagery has frequently been considered to be a primitive kind of memory, a transitional form between perception and memory. Its dependence on "interests" was already known to Urbantschitsch and Jaentsch. Concerning the relation of the eidetic-imagery (E I) to the memory image (M I) and after image (A I) *and other kindred* phenomena, we read in Kluever's (47) survey of the pertinent literature:

"It is apparent that E I are more or less related to phenomena such as after-images, memory-images, projected memory-images (Martin), memory after-images (Fechner), subjective visual sensations (G. H. Meyer), pseudo-memory-images (Gruenbaum), illusions, hallucinations, pseudohallucinations, re-perceptions (Ebbecke), phantastic visual phenomena (J. Mueller), *Sinnesgedaechtnis*, hypnagogic images, synesthesia, and subjective visual phenomena produced by hypnotic methods or by drugs; but it is at present often extremely difficult to say in what way some of these phenomena are different from E I." (p. 700)

"The assumption of the Marburg school that there is a sufficiently large number of criteria at hand for differentiating the A I and the M I from the E I is merely an assertion and not a fact." (p. 705)

Concerning the dependence of the E I on the "interest" or "set," Kluever writes:

"The appearance of an E I, or of a certain part of an E I, often depends on the 'interests' or the 'set' of the subject. A child may be able to reproduce an object, but not the picture of this object, eidetically." (p. 715)

Stern (16) voices a similar view:

"Particular eidetic-types are distinguished according to resemblance of eidetic images, as in flexible, uncontrollable, and involuntary infringements upon the person, to after-images (tetanoid, or T-type for Jaentsch), rather than to states embedded in the total person so that he is able to produce, utilize, and alter them according to his interests and inclinations (Basedow or B-type)." (p. 202)

The literature of these types of eidetic imagery which is relevant to the problem of the influence of emotions on memory, and especially of individual differences therein, is voluminous but too technical to be dealt with here at greater length. Further material concerning the role of selective emotional factors in registration will be found in Chapter VIII.

3. THE ROLE OF THE SELECTIVE FORCE AND THE FATE OF MEMORIES IN THE "RETENTION" PERIOD

What happens between experiencing and remembering is the essential riddle of the theory of memory. In fact, the concept "memory" refers to this happening as do the terms "retention," "engram," and "trace." There is, however, no way to learn what happens in the retention-interval other than to investigate what has been experienced and what is remembered, and then thus to infer the intermediate happenings. The organization of the material which takes place in the retention period, and the changes resulting in the material, show the operation of selective forces.

Mueller-Freienfels (6) maintained that the traces of impressions are not unconscious ideas, but are motor and feeling "dispositions":

"We readily admit that in the psyche there are *dispositions* which under certain *conditions* can lead to ideas; it is, however, by no means proved that these states are essentially identical with the ideas." (p. 388)

"We assume only such dispositions as under certain circumstances elicit reproductions from within, just as sensations are stimulated by external impressions. However, we do not consider these dispositions to be unconscious ideas, but rather . . . motoric dispositions which, when entering the field of consciousness, become apparent as feelings, tendencies, etc., although they frequently arouse ideas as secondary effects." (pp. 388–389)

"One will admit, even when he wants to maintain the theory of unconscious ideas, that the dominant content in them is the feeling while the ideas are—at best—secondary, and that we deal here with psychic happenings which we cannot dispose of by considering them just another link in the chain of ideas." (p. 400)

The feelings are considered to account also for the automatic formation of concepts:

"Thus, we emphasize again that what is retained and effective in the psyche is not a reproduction . . . it is the attitudes, 'sentiments generiques,' which are retained, as was proved experimentally by Abramowski. We assume that a certain attitude (Stellungnahme) corresponds to each percept, especially to what is typical in it, and that this attitude is what is primarily retained . . . These attitudes . . . are subjective adaptive factors, mostly of an affective and motoric nature and constitute all that is called concept, thought, consciousness, etc." (p. 408)

The attitudes, however, not only account for retention and concept formation, but play an active role in organizing the content of experience in general:

"We assume that feelings and attitudes schematize and generalize the impressions, and that their immense significance for each percept is precisely this. If we were always to take an entirely specific subjective attitude to each individual percept, no general experience would be possible. In fact, the generalizing attitudes are the ones primarily effective in memory, as every impression is typified and only dull people create entirely atypical memories." (p. 409)

The constellations result from the organizing effect of the attitudes:

"As it is not the ideas which constitute the constellations, one must descend more deeply to understand them. The continuity of our life, actions, and thinking is determined primarily by our affective life, our feelings and our will. It is only the common basic mood, the affective orientation, which creates the constellations, since ideas alone never constitute a state of the ego." (7, p. 78)

Crosland (10), on the basis of his experiments, characterizes the process taking place in the "retention period" as a process of losing details, with a characteristic typifying and disintegrating of the image; and as a process of subjective selecting, interpolating and clarifying (p. 67). Also, Crosland reports to have found in his experiments memory changes resembling Freudian mechanisms, occurring in the period of retention. Pear (11) raises the question:

"Does the image ever completely vanish, or does it merely become so unsubstantial as to defy discovery by untrained introspection?" (p. 55)

He favors the second possibility, in accordance with the psychoanalytic theory. W. Stern (16) describes the role of emotional selection in the "retention" period:

"Every person has the peculiar property of being lastingly impressed by external and internal events; this personal factor influences not only the intensity and persistence of mnemic stimuli, but also—what is more important—their *selection*. It would be hopeless to attempt to derive the unconscious choice of mneme predominantly from qualities of the items chosen; it is the deeper strata of the person, in which emotion and striving are rooted, that mark out certain life patterns with a mnemic accent while others remain neglected . . . The same proves true of the *second phase*: the re-actualization of a mnemic effect is the work of the whole person." (pp. 194–195)

Stern maintains that the result of selectivity is a retention of the personally relevant meaning, which is independent of wording, and suggests that:

"Such phenomena conclusively disprove the 'trace' theory of the mnemic processes. No 'traces' whatever of the words heard are left behind in the form of corresponding word images . . . " (p. 205)

Szymanski (18) writes:

"With the change of the 'driving-forces' (Antriebe), our knowledge of the object, dependent on these 'driving-forces,' also changes." (p. 183)

Purdy (48), opposing the old theory of the fading of traces with the lapse of time, maintains, quoting Stoerring, that

"It is not the time itself but the impressions occurring in it, which normally contribute to the forgetting of old impressions." (p. 340)

His theory, although one-sided in its disregard of internal selective factors, is supported by experiments comparing retention in sleeping and waking states.[12] Lewin and his pupils demonstrated that a change in the field-conditions—as, for instance, the introduction of new intentions—may isolate the tension system responsible for the remembering of an intention (Birenbaum, 49) and that the lapse of time also diminishes the intensity of the tension (Zeigarnik, 50).   Bartlett (24), on the basis of his and H. Head's (51) experiments, took a stand in opposition to the classical memory theory:

> "The traces are generally supposed to be of individual and specific events. Hence, every normal individual must carry about with him an incalculable number of individual traces. Since these are all stored in a single organism, they are in fact bound to be related one to another, and this gives to recall its inevitably associative character; but all the time each trace retains its essential individuality, and remembering, in the ideal case, is simple re-excitation, or pure reproduction . . . The actual facts of perceiving and recognizing suggest strongly that, in all relatively simple cases of determination by past experiences and reactions, the past operates as an organized mass rather than as a group of elements each of which retains its specific character." (p. 197)

Gestalt psychology contends on the basis of the experimental results of Wulf (44) that, in the retention period of visually perceived figures, processes operate resulting in autonomous changes such as in "leveling" and "pointing," which change the figure to a "better" one.   Hanawalt's (46) results oppose Wulf's.   The studies of Gibson (45), Allport (52), Perkins (53), W. Brown (54), Zangwill (55), and Irwin and Seidenfeld (58) partially support Wulf's conclusions.   On the basis of Restorff's (59) and Harrower's (60) findings, Koffka (27) maintains that another process occurring in the retention period is an "aggregation" of traces which results in loss of their individuality.   In the case of heterogeneous traces, this loss of individuality may result in a loss of retention; in the case of homogeneous traces, it may result in the emergence of a common schema which strengthens retention.   Wheeler and Perkins (29) object to the assumption of persisting traces:

> "Consider the air in a room. . . . Light a candle and a current of air will be set up.   Introduce more candles and the air will be chopped into many currents all of which must adjust to each other.   Now blow out a candle, the currents disappear. The brain is like the air and the candles are like stimuli.   Remove the organism from stimuli and an analogous process takes place.   There are no traces left in the atmosphere.   There are none left in the brain, for the brain, in principle, is a fluid field of energy like the air.   In one case the air is necessary for air currents; in the other case brain substance is necessary for brain currents, but in no case are traces involved." (p. 388)

---

[12] See the experiments of Dahl (56) and of Jenkins and Dallenbach (57).

4. The Role of the "Selective Factor" in Remembering

"Remembering," "reproduction," "recollection," "recall," "memory revival," "recognition," "knowing," and "feeling of familiarity" are different expressions used to designate the process of past experiences becoming effective in the present. "Remembering," "reproduction," and "recollection" are terms used for the most part to express a direct and active conception of the process. "Recall" and "memory revival" are used rather to express a passive though direct conception of the process. "Recognition," "knowing" and "feeling of familiarity" are used to refer to active though indirect effects. These terms, however, like those designating registration, were so loosely used that their exact meaning can be inferred only from the context in which they are found. Recent investigators prefer to use the terms connoting activity, in order to indicate the creative, selective nature of the process of remembering.

Mueller-Freienfels (6) maintains that goal-directedness alone does not account for remembering:

"... in general, ideas without any attitudes, feelings, or motoric tendencies do not exist. The more goal-directed thinking is, the more apparent the attitudes are." (p. 398)

He suggests that the mediators of associations are sets of moods, and describes the method he uses in the effort to remember:

"I try to enhance, revive by every possible means, the mood of that time. I surround the first thoughts with such an atmosphere of mood, and in this way I often manage to arouse the idea concerned." (p. 407)

Applying this theory to obsessive ideas, which may be described as ideas that cannot be forgotten, he writes:

"Here too the word is only the incidental clothing of the feeling hidden in it . . . We might state for all the obsessive phenomena . . . that what proves, by its constancy, to be their real content is an affective phenomenon, while the intellectual content is of secondary nature selected by the feeling or drive to act in them and through them." (p. 420)

Of the availability of contents for remembering, he states:

"The availability of a content depends first of all on its feeling-tone, by which we do not mean only its pleasure or displeasure character in general, but that feeling-excitability which allows for its getting into connection with our interests. Interests, however, are feeling-attitudes, and the availability of memory-contents depends on their relations to these. Thus, in order to make a content available we have to connect it first of all with our interests, in other words, we have to keep its feeling-tone fresh and lively. A content strong in feeling always strives toward the foreground, especially when it is feeling-charged in the direction of the dominant interests." (7, pp. 79–80)

Crosland (10) found in his experiments that what is remembered is the "dominant meaning." Details close to this dominant meaning tend to change in order to fit it; the peripheral details are easily forgotten, but when remembered appear as isolated discrete images relatively undistorted:

> "The closer the relation of the details to the general dominant meaning of the material, the more augmented was the effect of this . . . assimilative or generalizing forgetting upon it . . ." (p. 76)

Pear (11) maintains that the selective function is the essence of remembering:

> ". . . a good memory should be serviceably selective . . . The art of forgetting is but the inner aspect of the art of remembering." (p. 13)

Accordingly, the old dichotomy is dead; forgetting and remembering are but two aspects of the same process. Recognition of this is regarded to be a crucial development in psychology:

> ". . . selective omission . . . must be regarded . . . as one of the starting points of the newer psychology." (p. 52)

The selective function is determined by the personality make-up:

> ". . . our mind never photographs, it paints pictures. And those pictures, if interpreted with understanding, portray not only the external, impersonal objects which they profess to depict, but the personality too, of their owner, who is also their maker." (p. 35)
> "And it is just this selective nature of memory, favouring and welcoming what it wants at the moment, pushing out what at just that point of time is irrelevant for it . . . Not only, however, is the image the result of selection, but on examination it often shows unmistakable evidence of the type of filter through which it has passed." (p. 34)

Like Stern and Crosland, he also stresses the significance of meaning in selection. This meaning appears here, however, in a new light:

> "To declare that meaning is personal is to imply that it is relative to the *whole* personality, and it is not a pure intellectual affair." (p. 48)

Like Stern, he includes dreams among the memory phenomena; he states that memory, imagery, and dreams are all shadings of one continuum, and differ only in the freedom of operation of the selective factor:

> "Usually, perhaps always, the dream is composed of recalled experience. It can therefore be included among the phenomena of memory. While all memory is selective, the dream usually exhibits the results of this picking and choosing in a pronounced form." (p. 107)

"The dream displays in an exaggerated form all the advantages and drawbacks oı concrete imagery; and so it resembles—perhaps even it is—the thinking of the primitive mind." (p. 109)

Stern (15) characterizes the role of "remembrance"—his expression for conscious remembering—as follows:

"In the remembrance, I—as I had been—belong to myself as I am now and as I tend to be later; my present and my readiness for the future are filled, made rich, influenced and restrained by my past; . . . I strive to settle it, to rule it . . . and by these personal strivings remembrance-experiences are awakened, formed, even created . . . An essential function of remembrance is to secure one's past in a form appropriate and necessary for him." (p. 359)

He describes the positive role of emotional factors in remembering:

". . . [the] emotional condition in the present, . . . [the] hopes, fears and expectations directed toward the future, determine the appearance in which events of the past are revived or are prevented from reviving (so called 'repression')." (16, p. 195)

Forgetting and false memory productions are explained by him as follows:

"That which lacks this relation to the present is 'forgotten,' i.e., it does not come to revival, because it is personally meaningless. The fact that there is no absolute forgetting speaks clearly for this personal relation; that which is apparently lost, completely settled, can under certain circumstances have an unexpected revival when a personal situation or phase of life favors it . . ." (15, p. 360)

"A satisfactory explanation of . . . [the fausse reconnaissance] has never been contrived, but one thing, which is brought out . . . is certain: that the principle is to be sought in an alteration of the person's feeling-attitude. It is not at all necessary for the objective stimulus situation as such to acquire something that resembles a former stimulus and is now falsely identified with it; on the contrary, the individual feels himself misplaced in a mental condition that saturates with the feeling of familiarity whatever may be perceived through the senses." (6, p. 209)

"It is a counterpart of that form of disorientation called 'alienation,' in which familiar situations and persons known intimately suddenly appear unfamiliar and uncanny." (16, p. 209, footnote)

In Stern's Psychology of Early Childhood (61, pp. 241–261) we find a description and interpretation of a series of false memory productions. He ranks dreams among memory phenomena, and maintains that dreaming is the only state in which the selective and organizing tendencies operate freely:

". . . the dreams are the only [memory functions] in which wishes and drive-tendencies come to a realization in the present . . . Reminiscences create reality out of wish, drive, and need—but in . . . the past." (15, p. 361)

"[in dreams] the modeling follows immediately under the influence of personal affects and strivings . . . It develops a wish-representation in the form of remembered reality." (15, p. 362)

Szymanski (18) describes the dependence of remembering on needs and interests:

"One can maintain in general that an element of knowledge stored in memory can be reproduced as it suits the interest of the subject . . . When the interest expires, e.g. in consequence of the satiation of the 'striving-force' (Antrieb), the corresponding idea is less and less frequently experienced, until reproduction is no longer possible." (p. 191)

"It occurs frequently that an allegedly forgotten . . . idea emerges spontaneously, when the 'driving-force' (Antrieb) for the satisfaction of which this knowledge was gained, or another 'driving-force' for which it is useful, suddenly emerges." (pp. 192–193)

Gordon's (19) opinion about remembering is similar to Szymanski's:

"Our theory is that good memory depends upon the skillful organization of interests. Memory cannot be forced, because interest cannot be forced . . . a person who wishes to improve his memory must study his own interests and aims." (p. 124)

She also maintains that distributed practice and other rules of learning are of great help, though secondary to the content which determines the interest, which in turn organizes remembering. Lewin and his pupils find that facts connected with intentions are remembered (Zeigarnik, 50), and that intentions are executed (Birenbaum, 49) if the tension system corresponding to the intention remains charged. They also find that emotional excitements disorganize the tension systems and thus influence memory (Dembo, 62). In unbalanced, "excited" persons the tension systems appear to be less persistent than in balanced, "unexcited" persons (49, 50). Bartlett (24) stresses the active creative character of remembering:

"Consider particularly the case in which a subject was remembering a story which he heard, say, five years previously, in comparison with the case in which he was given certain outline materials and constructs what he calls a new story. I have tried the latter experiment repeatedly, and not only the actual form and content of the results, but what is of more significance for the moment, the attitudes of the subject in these two cases were strikingly similar. In fact, if we consider evidence rather than presupposition, remembering appears to be far more decisively an affair of construction rather than one of mere reproduction." (pp. 204–205)

The selectivity of the remembering is characterized as follows:

"A new incoming impulse must become not merely a cue setting up a series of reactions all carried out in a fixed temporal order, but a stimulus which enables us to go direct to that portion of the organized setting of past responses which is most relevant to the needs of the moment." (p. 206)

Bartlett finds that in his experiments selection of the relevant material is ascribable to attitudes:

"Ask the observer to characterize this general impression psychologically, and the word that is always cropping up is 'attitude.' I have shown how this 'attitude' factor came into nearly every series of experiments that was carried out. The construction that is effected is the sort of construction that would justify the observer's 'attitude.' " (p. 206)

"It may be that what then emerges is an *attitude* towards the massed effects of a series of past reactions. Remembering is a constructive justification of this attitude . . ." (p. 208)

Zangwill (63) demonstrated the influence on recognition of an experimentally created attitude. His "attitude" appears, however, to be a superficial one, resembling a "mental set." Koffka (27) crystallized the memory theory of Gestalt psychology. In his terms, remembering, reminiscence, recognition occur when a process set up by incoming stimuli and a trace of an old process *communicate*. We have already discussed the role of attitudes in this communication.[13] When there is no communication, no remembering occurs. Lack of communication may come about in three ways: (1) The disappearance of the trace through "lack of cohesion," through "communication with a new process," or through "communication with other traces"; (2) the momentary unavailability of the trace because of isolation, such as occurred in the "repression" cases of Zeigarnik already discussed,[14] or because of a lack of the proper relation between the Ego and the trace-field,[15] or because of a change of interests;[16]

[13] See pp. 118–120.

[14] See p. 96.

[15] The role of the relation between the Ego and the trace-field was characterized by Koffka as follows:

"Availability of the trace, in cases considered at the moment, depends upon proper connection between the trace system and the Ego. Now this connection depends upon a host of factors, among which the so-called conative ones are probably of paramount importance. If a trace is derived from a process which was directly connected with a person's interests, then it will have its place in a field formed by processes of high intensity and will be in particularly close connection with the Ego system. Such traces then are favored for many reasons. Belonging to a sphere of interest, these traces will find ready a trace system with which they will communicate, and ever new traces will be formed which communicate with the same system, enlarging and stabilizing it continually." (p. 526)

[16] Concerning the change of interests he wrote:

"When the interest dies all this is changed. The large system which has been gradually built up may disintegrate because parts of it may become connected with other interests. The original trace will become more and more isolated and more and more separated from the stratum of the present. In this sense we can therefore subscribe to Bartlett's thesis that traces are 'interest-determined, interest-carried.' " (p. 526)

(3) the failure of a process to communicate with an otherwise available trace, the causes of which are, according to Koffka, not known as yet (pp. 522–28). The role attributed in this theory to the Ego, "interests" and "attitudes," is limited but still significant. This dynamic theory recognizes the role of selective forces in remembering, and attributes them more to processes in the trace-field than in the Ego.

Katona's (28) views appear to be more flexible. He attempts in his theory to give some place to mechanical memory and its affective factors, which in his conception, however, appear to be limited to those of the type of "mental set" (pp. 290–306):

> "We called the carriers of relatively inflexible remembering individual traces, which refer to specific items of past experience. Such traces are effective, or, to state it less technically, "raw facts" are retained as such, if the items are: (a) reconstructed (that is, if they are derived from an integrated whole); (b) carried by the whole as essential parts; (c) impressed upon the learner by memorization; or (d) impressed upon the learner by affective factors." (pp. 229–230)

Wheeler (64) maintains that reproduction is actually production:

> "What, you are now asking, does explain recall? The same organization of potentials in the nervous system and the same stimulus-pattern that accounted for the original observation, except that (1) maturation has taken place meanwhile, and (2) there is only a partial duplication of the original stimulus-pattern." (p. 168)

He considers "meaning" to be the essence of perception and recall:

> "Each perception and each recall (for recall is incomplete perception) involves an interpretative factor, a discovery, an invention. It is the perceiving of some detail in its relation to a total situation. It is an emergent phenomenon." (p. 169)

Wheeler's opposition to the trace-theory is clearly expressed by his pupil F. H. Lewis (65) who advances the argument used by Stern[17] that, since a meaningful story or sentence can be reproduced by means of sentences and expressions other than the original, it is senseless to attribute the reproduction to surviving traces of the original word-images. This argument is rendered invalid if Katona's (28) conclusion on the conveyance of the meaning by the structural traces be accepted.[18]

5. The Theory of Memory: A Discussion

There is no doubt at present that the days are past when it was believed that an impression or learned material was retained and revived in a form true to the original. The "machine theory" of associationism—as the psychologists of the Gestalt school like to call it—is, in its pure form, now

---

[17] See p. 127.
[18] See pp. 124–125.

discarded. Its influence can be best appreciated if we review the classification of memory theories made by the Gestalt school, the most bellicose and most direct antagonist of associationism. Psychologists of this school maintain that there are three types of memory theory:[19] (1) the type of theory according to which every memory function is based on mechanical association, and those memory phenomena which do not seem based on it are but complicated variations of it; (2) the type of theory according to which memory function is essentially based on mechanical association, but the association-mechanism is directed by additional organizing factors such as the "Gestalt-qualities" of the Graz school, the "determining-tendencies" of Ach, attitudes, feelings, emotions, and so on; (3) the type of theory according to which memory-function depends on meaningful and appropriate organization, and the common arbitrary associations are only an extreme case of minimal organization.

For Gestalt psychology, the pioneer of modern memory theory, only the third of these approaches is acceptable: the first is mechanistic; the second is vitalistic in the sense that the organizing factors in it are extraneous to, and superimposed upon, the memory mechanism. The organization-theory of memory built by Gestalt psychology assumes the unity of the organizing principle and the organized material, inasmuch as the contents of the entire psychological field determine its organization. Katona mentions the possibility that even affective factors may be determined by a specific kind of organization[20] present in the learning or recall situation. In such views, however, the intrinsic weak point of the Gestaltist memory-theory becomes obvious. The "organization," "meaningfulness," "embeddedness," "isolation" of the material are observed under experimental conditions, where the observable attitudes—affective factors—are of a rather intellectual character. This led to a disregard of the "influence of emotions on memory" in Gestalt psychological theory. The possibility of a fourth and perhaps comprehensive theory of memory has been left out of consideration.

Gestalt psychology pointed out that memory experiments using nonsense material could produce only memory laws pertaining to the extreme case of nonsense-memorizing; and accordingly, memory experiments using meaningful material were introduced. Remembering as encountered in everyday life, however, works with material not only logically and grammatically meaningful, but also personally—emotionally—important and relevant. It is true that Gestalt psychologists endeavored to show that there is no qualitative difference between remembering, problem-solving,

[19] I am indebted to G. Katona for suggesting in a private communication this trichotomy. The responsibility for its formulation rests, however, solely with me.
[20] 28, pp. 299, 306.

and discovering. But this was a cold insight. Remembering, problem-solving, and discovering are qualitatively similar not only because they involve meaningful organization, but also because they are directed by our strivings and their success or failure depends on the interplay of these strivings. One might even go so far as to hypothesize that, in the same way that "associations" are extreme cases of minimal "meaningful organization," so is "meaningful-logical" organization only a special case of emotional-affective organization. Such a hypothesis implies a memory theory in which memory phenomena depend on the emotional-affective organization. It is hoped that the following chapters will be contributions to the development of such a memory theory.

6. Summary

a. The material surveyed in this section shows that in the literature of psychological theory there was an ever-increasing realization that memory was not merely a process of mechanical imprinting on a wax plate, of retention or fading of this imprint, and of isolated resuscitation of the material thus registered and retained. There appears to be considerable agreement that memory processes are subject to the activity of selective forces related to deep strata of the personality, and to the field conditions under which registration and remembering take place and which exist in the retention period.

b. It was recognized that the selective forces are active in perception, and also in after-images, eidetic-images, and other phenomena frequently considered to be primitive memory phenomena. The retention-period was recognized to be a period in which incoming impressions, as well as changes in the person's life and strivings, actively influence and change the memory trace. Remembering was understood to be an active process of reconstruction, in which selective forces appear to be of greater importance than the elements of the material.

c. A great variety of selective forces influencing memory organization has been surveyed. Some contributors have considered them to be of instinctual, emotional, or affective origin; others have identified them with attitudes and interests, emphasizing their intellectual rather than their emotional aspect; finally, some recognized only the context and the influence of past experiences as selective forces. In general, however, there was abundant evidence that the selective forces were related more or less intimately to the emotional make-up of the personality. Thus, these selective forces may justly be considered representatives of the emotional influence on memory.

d. Certain investigators suggested that the influence of these selective forces in the functioning of man's memory is indicative of the genesis of memory. It is suggested that memory has emerged from the primitive instinctual response and developed through the level of "habit" to its present character; selective forces of instinctual origin and processes of habituation are interlaced in memory function, producing the magnificent and well-nigh impenetrable complexity of man's memory.

e. The outlines of a memory theory, centered in emotional-affective organizing factors, were suggested. Such a theory would embrace the associationist and the Gestalt theories of learning as descriptive of extreme instances of minimal organization.

REFERENCES

(1) RAPAPORT, D. *The history of the association concept.* 92 pp. (In the Hungarian language.) Budapest, Roy Hung. Univ., 1937.
(2) UEXKUELL, J. VON. *Theoretical biology.* 362 pp. New York, Harcourt, 1926.
(3) WERNER, H. *Comparative psychology of mental development.* 510 pp. New York, Harper, 1940.
(4) PIAGET, J. *The child's conception of the world.* 397 pp. New York, Harcourt, 1929.
(5) DEWEY, J. *Psychology.* 427 pp. New York, Amer. Book, 3rd revised ed., 1891.
(6) MUELLER-FREIENFELS, R. Der Einfluss der Gefuehle und motorischen Faktoren auf Assoziation und Denken. *Arch. ges. Psychol.* 27: 381–430, 1913.
(7) MUELLER-FREIENFELS, R. Studien zur Lehre vom Gedaechtnis. *Arch. ges. Psychol.* 34: 65–105, 1915.
(8) MUENSTERBERG, H. *Psychology, general and applied.* 486 pp. New York, Appleton, 1914.
(9) WASHBURN, M. F. *Movement and Mental Imagery.* 252 pp. Boston, Houghton Mifflin, 1916.
(10) CROSLAND, H. R. A qualitative analysis of the process of forgetting. *Psychol. Monogr.* 29: 159 pp., 1921.
(11) PEAR, T. H. *Remembering and forgetting.* 242 pp. New York, Dutton, 1922.
(12) McDOUGALL, W. *An introduction to social psychology.* 459 pp. London, Methuen, 1908.
(13) RIVERS, W. H. R., TANSLEY, A. G., SHAND, A. F., PEAR, T. H., HART, B., AND MYERS, C. S. The relations of complex and sentiment. A symposium. *Brit. J. Psychol.* 13: 107–148, 1922.
(14) CATTELL, R. B. Sentiment or attitude? The core of a terminology problem in personality research. *Character and Personality* 9: 6–17, 1940.
(15) STERN, W. Personalistik der Erinnerung. *Z. Psychol.* 118: 350–381, 1930.
(16) STERN, W. *General psychology from the personalistic standpoint.* 589 pp. Trans. Spoerl, H. D., New York, Macmillan, 1938.
(17) McDOUGALL, W. *Outline of psychology.* 456 pp. New York, Scribner, 1923.
(18) SZYMANSKI, J. S. *Psychologie vom Standpunkt der Abhaengigkeit des Erkennens von den Lebensbeduerfnissen.* 349 pp. Leipzig, Barth, 1930.
(19) GORDON, K. Memory viewed as imagination. *J. gen. Psychol.* 17: 113–124, 1937.
(20) LEWIN, K. Das Problem der Willensmessung und der Assoziation. *Psychol. Forsch.* 1: 191–302, 1922. 2: 65–140, 1922.

(21) CASON, H. Criticisms of the laws of exercise and effect. *Psychol. Rev.* 31: 397–417, 1924.

(22) TOLMAN, E. C. Retroactive inhibition as affected by conditions of learning. *Psychol. Monogr.* 25, 50 pp., no. 107, 1917.

(23) LEWIN, K. *Vorsatz, Wille und Beduerfnis. Vorbemerkungen ueber die psychischen Kraefte und Energien und ueber die Struktur der Seele.* 92 pp. Berlin, Springer, 1926.

(24) BARTLETT, F. C. *Remembering, a study in experimental and social psychology.* 317 pp. Cambridge, Univ. Press, 1932.

(25) ALLPORT, G. W. Attitudes. Pp. 798–844. In: *Handbook of social psychology.* Ed. Murchison, C. Worcester, Clark Univ. Press, 1935.

(26) KOEHLER, W. Zur Theorie des Sukzessivvergleichs und der Zeitfehler. *Psychol. Forsch.* 4: 115–175, 1923.

(27) KOFFKA, K. *Principles of Gestalt psychology.* 720 pp. New York, Harcourt, 1935.

(28) KATONA, G. *Organizing and Memorizing. Studies in the psychology of learning and teaching.* 318 pp. New York, Columbia Univ. Press, 1940.

(29) WHEELER, R. H., AND PERKINS, F. T. *Principles of mental development. A textbook of educational psychology.* 529 pp. New York, Crowell, 1932.

(30) HUMPHREY, G. Thought. Pp. 381–410. In: *Introduction to psychology.* 652 pp. Ed. Boring, E. G., Langfeld, H. S., and Weld, H. P. New York, Wiley, 1939.

(31) McGEOCH, J. A. Learning. Retention. Pp. 290–350. In: *Introduction to psychology.* 652 pp. Ed. Boring, E. G., Langfeld, H. S., and Weld, H. P. New York, Wiley, 1939.

(32) FREEMAN, E. *Principles of general psychology.* 530 pp. New York, Holt, 1939.

(33) GUILFORD, J. P. *General psychology.* 630 pp. New York, Nostrand, 1939.

(34) LANGFELD, H. S. Suppression with negative instructions. *Psychol. Bull.* 7: 200–208, 1910.

(35) LANGFELD, H. S. Suppression with negative instructions. *Psychol. Rev.* 18: 211–424, 1911.

(36) WONG, H., AND BROWN, W. Effects of surroundings upon mental work as measured by York's multiple choice method. *J. Comp. Psychol.* 3: 319–331, 1923.

(37) PAN, S. The influence of context upon learning and recall. *J. exp. Psychol.* 9: 468–491, 1926.

(38) GUNDLACH, R., ROTHSCHILD, D. A., AND YOUNG, P. T. A test and analysis of "set." *J. exp. Psychol.* 10: 247–280, 1927.

(39) EDGELL, B. *Theories of memory.* 174 pp. London, Univ. Oxford Press, 1924.

(40) BUTLER, S. *Life and habit.* 310 pp. London, Fifield, 1910.

(41) BUEHLER, K. *The mental development of the child. A summary of modern psychological theory.* 170 pp. New York, Harcourt, 1930.

(42) ALLPORT, G. W. *Personality; a psychological interpretation.* 588 pp. New York, Holt, 1937.

(43) BARTLETT, F. C. An experimental study of some problems of perceiving and imaging. *Brit. J. Psychol.* 8: 222–266, 1916.

(44) WULF, F. Beitraege zur Psychologie der Gestalt; Ueber die Veraenderung von Vorstellungen. *Psychol. Forsch.* 1: 333–373, 1922.

(45) GIBSON, J. J. The reproduction of visually perceived forms. *J. exp. Psychol.* 12: 1–39, 1929.

(46) HANAWALT, N. G. Memory trace for figures in recall and recognition. *Arch. Psychol.* 31: 1–89, 1937.

(47) KLUEVER, H. Eidetic imagery. Pp. 699–722. In: *A handbook of child psychology.* 956 pp. Ed. Murchison, C. Worcester, Clark Univ. Press, 2nd ed., 1933.

(48) PURDY, D. M. The theory of forgetting. *Amer. J. Psychol.* 46: 339–340, 1934.

(49) BIRENBAUM, G. Das Vergessen einer Vornahme. Isolierte seelische Systeme und dynamische Gesamtbereiche. *Psychol. Forsch.* 13: 218–284, 1930.

(50) ZEIGARNIK, B. Das Behalten erledigter und unerledigter Handlungen. *Psychol. Forsch.* 9: 1–85, 1927. Cf. Lewin, K. A. *A dynamic theory of personality.* Trans. Adams, D. K., and Zener, K. E. Pp. 243–247. New York, McGraw-Hill, 1935.

(51) HEAD, H. *Studies in neurology.* Vol. I, 329 pp.; vol. II, 862 pp. London, Frowde, 1920.

(52) ALLPORT, G. W. Change and decay in the visual memory image. *Brit. J. Psychol.* 21: 133–148, 1930.

(53) PERKINS, F. T. Symmetry in visual recall. *Amer. J. Psychol.* 44: 473–490, 1932.

(54) BROWN, W. Growth of 'memory images.' *Amer. J. Psychol.* 47: 90–102, 1935.

(55) ZANGWILL, O. L. An investigation of the relationship between the processes of reproducing and recognizing simple figures, with special reference to Koffka's trace theory. *Brit. J. Psychol.* 27: 250–276, 1937.

(56) DAHL, A. Ueber den Einfluss des Schlafens auf das Wiedererkennen. *Psychol. Forsch.* 11: 290–301, 1928.

(57) JENKINS, J. G., AND DALLENBACH, K. Obliviscence during sleep and waking *Amer. J. Psychol.* 35: 605–612, 1924.

(58) IRWIN, F. W., AND SEIDENFELD, M. A. The application of the method of comparison to the problem of memory changes. *J. exp. Psychol.* 21: 363–381, 1937.

(59) RESTORFF, H. VON. Ueber die Wirkung der Bereichsbildung in Spurenfeld. *Psychol. Forsch.* 18: 299–342, 1933.

(60) HARROWER, M. R. Organization in high mental processes. *Psychol. Forsch.* 17: 56–120, 1932.

(61) STERN, W. *Psychology of early childhood up to the sixth year of age.* 612 pp. New York, Holt, 1930.

(62) DEMBO, T. Der Aerger als dynamisches Problem. *Psychol. Forsch.* 15: 1–144, 1931.

(63) ZANGWILL, O. L. A study of the significance of attitude in recognition. *Brit. J. Psychol.* 28: 12–17, 1937.

(64) WHEELER, R. H. *The laws of human nature. A general view of Gestalt Psychology.* 235 pp. New York, Appleton, 1932.

(65) LEWIS, F. H. Note on the doctrine of memory traces. *Psychol. Rev.* 40: 90–97, 1933.

CHAPTER V

THE CONTRIBUTIONS OF PSYCHOANALYSIS

1. PSYCHOANALYTICAL THEORY; FORGETTING VS. REMEMBERING

The field of affects and emotions—in other words non-sensory and non-intellective processes—has been generally an isolated field within the sphere of general psychology. The exploration of them has remained unsatisfactory,[1] and in the main has attempted to reduce them to physiological, sensory, or at best intellective processes. Thus, as has been demonstrated in the preceeding chapters, the influence of emotions on memory phenomena has remained insufficiently attacked and elucidated by general psychology.

In view of this situation, the psychoanalytic contributions to the knowledge of this influence appear to be of great importance. In psychoanalytic theory, affects and emotions are not an isolated terrain; no concept is more central to it than that of emotion, affect, drive. The importance of the psychoanalytic contributions to our topic is increased by another feature of this theory: its underlying postulate of strict psychic determinism. Psychic determinism signifies that the present is determined by the past. Psychic phenomena of the present can be determined by the past only to the degree that the past survives; the survival of psychic events is, however, the phenomenon usually subsumed under the concept memory.[2] In the psychoanalytic theory of the etiology and therapy of psychic disturbances, the central significance of forgetting and remembering is a basic tenet.

We may accordingly expect rich contributions to our topic from psychoanalytic investigations. In order to avoid exaggerated expectations, we must be alert to several difficulties. First, the theory and concepts of psychoanalysis were developed independent of, and generally without regard for, the theoretical and conceptual development of general psychology; thus it is questionable whether the concepts and conclusions of the two are directly comparable. Secondly, psychoanalytic theory, having been built upon clinical experience, underwent frequent revisions, resulting in a fusion of old and new concepts and contents which was unfavorable to the development of a homogeneous conceptual framework; thus its conclusions were capable of misinterpretations which, in turn, are responsible in part for the

---

[1] See Hunt (1).

[2] The concept "memory" as used here is conceived broadly; it includes registration, retention, and recall, and their implications.

confusion prevailing in our field.[3] Thirdly, the psychoanalytic contributions must be inferred from material based on the study of pathological cases, which constitute the main topic of psychoanalytic investigation. Freud (2) himself cautioned us that the function of memory proper is an unsolved problem; his caution will give a proper background to our survey of the pertinent contributions.

"Since the time when we recognized the error of supposing that ordinary forgetting signified destruction or annihilation of the memory-trace, we have been inclined to the opposite view that nothing once formed in the mind could ever perish, that everything survives in some way or other, and is capable under certain conditions of being brought to light again, as, for instance, when regression extends back far enough. One might try to picture to oneself what this assumption signifies by a comparison taken from another field. Let us choose the history of the Eternal City as an example." (pp. 15–16)

"Now let us make the fantastic supposition that Rome were not a human dwelling-place, but a mental entity with just as long and varied a past history: that is, in which nothing once constructed had perished, and all the earlier stages of development had survived alongside the latest. This would mean that in Rome the palaces of the Caesars were still standing on the Palatine and the Septizonium of Septimus Severus was still towering to its old height; that the beautiful statues were still standing in the colonnade of the Castle of St. Angelo, as they were up to its siege by the Goths . . ." (p. 17)

"There is clearly no object in spinning this fantasy further; it leads to the inconceivable, or even to absurdities. If we try to represent historical sequence in spatial terms, it can only be done by juxtaposition in space; the same space will not hold two contents. Our attempt seems like an idle game; it has only one justification: it shows us how far away from mastering the idiosyncrasies of mental life we are by treating them in terms of visual representation.

"There is one objection, though, to which we must pay attention. It questions our choosing in particular the past history of a city to liken to the past of the mind. Even for mental life our assumption that everything past is preserved holds good only on condition that the organ of the mind remains intact and its structure has not been injured by traumas or inflammation." (pp. 18–19)

"We admit this objection; we will abandon our search for a striking effect of contrast and turn to what is after all a closer object of comparison, the body of an animal or human being. But here, too, we find the same thing. The early stages of development are in no sense still extant; they have been absorbed into the later features for which they supplied the material." (p. 19)

"The fact is that a survival of all the early stages alongside the final form is only possible in the mind, and that it is impossible for us to represent a phenomenon of this kind in visual terms.

"Perhaps we are going too far with this conclusion. Perhaps we ought to be content with the assertion that what is past in the mind *can* survive and need not necessarily perish. It is always possible that even in the mind much that is old may be so far obliterated or absorbed—whether normally or by way of exception—that it cannot be restored or reanimated by any means, or that survival of it is always connected with certain favourable conditions. It is possible, but we know nothing about it. We can only be sure that it is more the rule than the exception for the past to survive in the mind." (p. 20)

Even earlier Freud (3) had indicated his belief that:

"Today, forgetting has perhaps grown more puzzling than remembering . . ." (p. 95)

Jones (4) quoted Brough to the effect that:

". . . psychologists may be divided into two schools as regards the subject of memory, . . . those who hold that the facts in most need of explanation are those of remembering, and those who hold that they are the facts of forgetting." (p. 131)

Jones suggested that psychoanalysts belong to the latter school. The psychologist who familiarizes himself with psychoanalytic literature will find in it two general trends supporting this conclusion. First, psychoanalytic investigations tend to show that perhaps nothing once experienced is lost; consequently, the problem is rather how forgetting is possible. Forgetting in this sense means a "non-emergence in consciousness." Secondly, in psychoanalytic literature no attempt has been made to advance a systematic theory of remembering. One undertaking to define remembering in the spirit of psychoanalytic theory, and in conformity with this definition of forgetting, would designate it as "emergence into consciousness." Although lacking a systematic treatment of it, psychoanalytic literature implies a theory of remembering. Freud also discussed directly[4] the function of memory, and gave us a sketch of a memory functioning in reference to dreamwork. We lack, however, an integrated presentation of these discussions with other psychoanalytic findings contributing to a theory of memory. It is hoped that psychoanalysts will systematize this theory in furthering Freud's attempt to create a psychoanalytical psychology, which he called "metapsychology." Being far from attempting any such systematization, we shall only gather material sufficient to show the role of affects in memory functioning as it is conceived in psychoanalytical theory. First we shall survey the problem of forgetting and of parapraxis. Next we shall consider the bearing on our topic of dreams and of other psychic phenomena investigated by psychoanalysts. Finally, we shall deal with the psychoanalytic explanatory principle of forgetting, "repression."

2. THE PARAPRAXES

The history of modern science includes many examples of the exceptional case making possible the understanding of the general. Thus, the theory of evolution found its most important support in the discovery of animals

---

[4] See (5), pp. 487–497, and (6)

which unite characteristics of different species, and the first facts to support the theory of relativity were obtained by observing comparatively rare astronomical phenomena. Accordingly, Freud's attempt to understand the function of memory by analyzing striking cases of forgetting, of memory-errors, of lapses in speaking, reading, and writing, of actions carried out erroneously, and of so-called "chance actions" should not be alien to scientific taste. The phenomena enumerated here were termed by Freud "Fehlleistungen"; Jones suggested the designation "parapraxis."[5] After two preliminary articles (8, 9), Freud incorporated his theory of these phenomena in "The Psychopathology of Everyday Life" (3). The unusual wealth and variety of examples—which increased in the later editions—formed a mosaic picture rather than propounded the theory in a continuous chain of arguments. This method of presentation, though probably warranted by the nature of the material, admits of no simple summarizing and leads easily to misunderstandings and misrepresentation. "The Psychopathology of Everyday Life" did not escape this fate.

Undoubtedly, the clearest and most unequivocally formulated point of the book is the strict validity of *determinism* in psychic life. Applying the principle of determinism to his investigation on forgetting and parapraxis, Freud (3) wrote:

"*Certain inadequacies of our psychic functions . . . and certain performances which are apparently unintentional prove to be well motivated when subjected to psychoanalytic investigation, and are determined through the consciousness of unknown motives.*" (p. 150)

It is maintained that nothing is due to chance or is incidental in psychic life. Chance and incident—or, as it was frequently expressed, "spontaneity"—were long maintained to be the inherent properties of psychic happening only because of the failure to recognize the determining unconscious motivation. Thus, the theory that forgetting is not chance happening but strictly determined by unconscious motives, links it with other inadequacies and unintentional activities of our psychic functions. Several questions emerge at this point, the answers to which may clarify the implications of this theory for our problem:

(a) Does the theory apply to all forgetting? or if not, to which kinds of forgetting and to what extent?
(b) What is the motivation and the mechanism operating in forgetting, as conceived of by the Freudian theory?
(c) What is the justification for including forgetting with the other "inadequacies" and "unintentional" actions of our psyche?

The answer to the first question will clarify the degree of generality which

[5] The term was modelled after the term "apraxis." See Jones (7, p. 57, footnote).

was claimed for the Freudian mechanisms of forgetting. The answer to the second will help clarify the issue of "forgetting of the disagreeable" which has kept many an experimenter busy; it will clarify the paradoxical question of whether everything disagreeable is forgotten or whether everything forgotten is disagreeable. The answer to the third question will show that forgetting is but a special case of parapraxis, which in turn is a variety of "motivated" or "affectively" determined memory phenomena. Finally, the discussion of these three points will give us a glimpse of the psychoanalytic conception of memory functioning.

A. THE SCOPE OF THE FREUDIAN THEORY OF FORGETTING

In order to clarify the claim for generality of these mechanisms of forgetting, we must survey the different kinds of forgetting discussed by Freud. In "The Psychopathology of Everyday Life" Freud analyzed three kinds of forgetting: (1) that of proper names, foreign words, names, order of words, impressions and experiences (knowledge); (2) that of intentions; (3) that of childhood experiences. The third kind was dealt with only parenthetically in this work. In "The Interpretation of Dreams" (5, p. 470), a fourth kind of forgetting—that of dreams—is discussed. We shall consider the forgetting of childhood experiences and of dreams later, and turn our attention now to the first two groups.

It may be asked, when one considers the comprehensive enumeration in the first category, whether any memory-content is excluded. The indefiniteness of the concepts might allow for inclusion of every possible type of memory. This enumeration was apparently due to Freud's reluctance to apply his findings to *every* phenomenon of forgetting. He expressed this reluctance directly when writing.

"We shall represent this state of affairs carefully enough if we assert that *besides the simple forgetting of proper names, there is another forgetting which is motivated by repression.*" (3, p. 40)

"If in the determinations of faulty and symptomatic actions, we separate the unconscious motive from its co-active physiological and psychophysical relations, the question remains whether there are still other factors within normal limits which, like the unconscious motive, or a substitute for it, can produce faulty and symptomatic actions on the path of these relations. It is not my task to answer this question." (3, p. 172)

The hypothesis that "all forgetting is due to repression" was advanced much later by Jones (4, p. 141, ff.). It is only in regard to the forgetting of intentions that Freud's claim appears to be general; he considered this type of forgetting to be the best demonstration of the thesis that "lack of attention does not in itself suffice to explain faulty acts..." (3, p. 106) "... they could invariably be traced to some interference of unknown and

unadmitted motives . . ." (3, p. 108).   Freud maintains that there is a
general tendency to forget childhood experiences and dreams.   Thus we
see that he was reluctant to claim a general validity of his theory for the
forgetting of isolated words, facts, and knowledge, but readily claimed
it for the tendency to forget childhood memories, dreams, and intentions.[6]

B. THE FREUDIAN THEORY OF FORGETTING

Forgetting is explained as a result of the tendency "to avoid *the awakening of pain*" through memory . . ." (3, p. 61).   Elsewhere in the same
work (p. 101), however, we read: ". . . *The tendency to forget the disagreeable*[7] seems . . . to be quite general; the capacity for it is naturally differently developed in different persons."

"To avoid the awakening of pain through memory" and "to forget the
disagreeable" are two different matters.   "To forget the disagreeable"
implies that what is forgotten is consciously disagreeable, since the term
disagreeable obviously refers to conscious content;[8] thus, it does not fit
the Freudian conception of the unconscious motivation of forgetting and
parapraxis.   "To avoid the awakening of pain through memory" refers
directly to those unconscious motivating factors whose awakening is prevented by the forgetting of ideas which stand even in a distant relation to
them.   The expression "the awakening of pain" implies that if those unconscious factors to which the forgotten idea is related were to gain access
to consciousness, a conscious conflict would result.   The ideas distantly
related to prohibited unconscious tendencies need not be unpleasant, and
may be altogether innocuous.   We shall now attempt to go further into
this theory of forgetting and into the method whereby it was developed,
to show that only the formulation "to avoid the awakening of pain through
memory" is consistent with it.

The method evolved by Freud in investigating the nature of forgetting
is that of free association.   The person in whom the forgetting has occurred
is asked to associate freely, and to relate without selection the whole chain
of his associations.   This chain of associations usually leads to a personally
important and prohibited group—"complex"—of ideas of which the person
was not conscious at the time of forgetting.   The link in this chain of
associations is at times a superficial similarity of words or parts of words,
and at times a meaningful and logical interrelation.   In either case, these
links appear in the final analysis to have an intimate relation to a painful

---

[6] The experimental investigations of Lewin pertinent to this point were already
discussed on p. 94ff.

[7] Italics mine.—D. R.

[8] The term disagreeable in this sense appears to be parallel to that of unpleasantness, which was discussed from many angles in Chapter III.

set of unconscious ideas (3, p. 39).   The forgotten material itself can be of two kinds: either it "touches something unpleasant, or. . . it is brought into connection with other associations which are influenced by such effects" (3, p. 61).   That the painful idea motivating the forgetting must be reached through free associations demonstrates that it is an unconscious one; and that the forgotten material either touches upon this unconscious idea or is in an associative connection with it proves sufficiently that only the statement "to avoid the awakening of pain through memory" is adequate.   The thesis of "the tendency to forget the disagreeable" is guilty of two contradictions: the first is that the unconscious and avoided idea is designated as "disagreeable," an adjective usually applied to a conscious content; the second is that it suggests that the forgotten idea itself is disagreeable.

Here we have arrived at the core of the misunderstanding which we found so widespread among the experimenters whose work was discussed in Chapter III.   That which is consciously disagreeable is easily available for experimental manipulation; but the unconscious idea to avoid whose emergence forgetting ensues—according to Freud—eludes the usual methods of the memory experimenter.   While the thesis of the "forgetting of the disagreeable" seems to be a logical statement of cause (disagreeableness) and effect (forgetting), that of "avoiding the awakening of pain through memory" appears to be a teleological statement in which the future seems to exert its effect on the present.   We have attempted to show that the first thesis is fallacious.   The apparently teleological implication of the second cannot be discussed here.[9]

The painful set of ideas of which the subject is not conscious is designated as "repressed," and the process of forgetting is described as follows: the repressed ideas ". . . associatively gain control over the desired name and take it along into the repression"[10] (3, p. 39).   Freud's final presentation of his theory is again cautious:

"The principal conditions of the normal process in forgetting are unknown.   We are also reminded of the fact that not all is forgotten which we believe to be.   Our explanation deals here only with those cases in which the forgetting arouses our astonishment, in so far as it infringes upon the rule that the unimportant is forgotten, while the important matter is guarded by memory.   Analysis of these examples of forgetting, which seems to demand a special explanation, shows that the motive of forgetting is always an unwillingness to recall something which may evoke pain-

---

[9] For a discussion of this point see Weber and Rapaport (10, pp. 71 ff.).

[10] In connection with this, it may be mentioned that the distinction previously quoted from Freud—that the forgotten material either touches upon or is in associative connection with the unconscious painful idea—is not a classificatory distinction, but designates rather the "length" of the associative chain.

ful feelings. We come to the conjecture that this motive universally strives for expression in psychic life, but is inhibited through other and contrary forces from regularly manifesting itself. The extent and significance of this dislike to recall painful impressions seems worthy of the most painstaking psychologic investigation. The question as to what special conditions render possible the universally resistant forgetting in individual cases cannot be solved from this further connection." (pp. 174–175)

Before summing up the Freudian theory of forgetting, other points deserve mention. The kind of forgetting discussed occurs more frequently under conditions which are favorable for it: for example, in foreign-language material (3, p. 39), in states of fatigue (Silberer, 11), or with neurotic and psychotic subjects (3, p. 104).   One might say that the repressive forces attack at the point of least resistance.   Further, in discussing the forgetting of an intention—that is, of ". . . an impulse for an action which has already found approbation, but whose execution is postponed for a suitable occasion" (3, p. 106)—Freud again relates our topic to motivation.   He compares intention with posthypnotic suggestion, and points out that neither need emerge in consciousness before the moment of performance. He explains their forgetting on the basis of ". . . a recent change in the adjustment of motives" (3, p. 106), and states further "that they could invariably be traced to some interference of unknown and unadmitted motives" (3, p. 108).   These motives are sometimes termed "counter-will," and can be either related directly or transferred associatively to the intention.   As Freud puts it:

". . . in the forgetting of resolutions; the supposed conflict resulting in the repression of the painful memory becomes tangible, and in the analysis of the examples one regularly recognizes a counter-will which opposes but does not put an end to the resolution. As in previously discussed faulty acts, we here also recognize two types of the psychic process: the counter-will either turns directly against the resolution (in intentions of some consequence) or it is substantially foreign to the resolution itself and establishes its connection with it through an outer association (in almost indifferent resolutions)." (3, p. 175)

Thus far we have seen that forgetting is motivated by the tendency to avoid the emergence of painful ideas. "To forget the disagreeable" has proved an inadequate and misleading formulation. The painful ideas underlying forgetting are at the time personal and unknown (unconscious) to the subject and in a state of "repression."   We see the presence of affective factors, but as yet we do not know enough about their nature and their exact function in "repression."   Recently there has been a tendency to identify this "painfulness" with that which "diminishes self-esteem" or is "socially unacceptable."   A careful analysis of Freud's writings does not bear out the specific import of these considerations.   First, there are many cases which do not primarily involve self-esteem or do not involve it at all. Self-esteem, and factors militating against what could diminish it, do not— according to Freudian theory—belong to the basic "unacceptables" governing forgetting. Secondly, "socially unacceptable" appears to be a psychological tautology, inasmuch as it can be reversed: an individual considers what he has repressed as socially unacceptable.

C. FORGETTING AND PARAPRAXES: BOTH MEMORY PHENOMENA

"Forgetting," other "inadequacies," and "unintentional" actions of our psyche were dealt with as similar phenomena for two reasons. First, prior to Freud all these were considered the products of chance and inattentiveness; Freud was the first to endeavor to demonstrate that determinism is valid for all of them. Secondly, both forgetting and parapraxes are attempts to deal with a prohibited striving, whose emergence into consciousness in the form of ideas would give rise to a conflict. In forgetting, even distant associates of these ideas are eliminated from consciousness. Parapraxes, on the other hand, are *unsuccessful* attempts at forgetting; the prohibited striving asserts itself indirectly by distorting the word or idea which is in an associative connection with it. However the prohibitive forces be conceived, forgetting and parapraxes appear to be memory phenomena which are "affectively" motivated. Thus, in a memory theory in which the emergence or non-emergence of memories depends on the interplay of affective forces, memory errors, slips of the tongue, incidental actions—in short, the parapraxes—may be considered specific memory phenomena.

In general psychology, memory phenomena have been investigated with the restricted methods discussed in the previous chapters, and were rarely dealt with as one aspect of the organization of thought-processes. The emergence of the proper memory in a thought-process was treated in a perfunctory manner. Association psychology contended that the emergence of the memories in thought-processes results from the strength and the constellation of associations. When this had been proved an untenable simplification, the problem was excluded from the realm of memory-psychology and relegated to a newly-created branch of psychology, the psychology of thinking (Hoenigswald, 12; Selz, 13; Duncker, 14). Only the trace theory of Gestalt-psychology attempted to re-unite the two fields. Parapraxes are memory phenomena embedded in thought processes: instead of the emergence of a memory fitting the chain of thoughts, either the memory fails to emerge or one not fitting the chain of conscious thoughts emerges, or the relevant memory forms a compromise with a seemingly irrelevant memory. This compromise results from the interplay of the prohibited but upsurging strivings and others which strive to prevent it from entering consciousness.[11] If, then, prohibited strivings may distort ideas or replace them by others, there is sufficient reason to assume that memories in general are brought to consciousness by those strivings which they express. It is, however, only in parapraxes and other extreme cases that this becomes palpable. If this interpretation of parapraxes is correct, psychoanalytic theory and experience have implications concerning the role of "affective factors" not only in forgetting but also in remembering. It will be worthwhile to quote Freud's formulation of the conditions which parapraxes must fulfill, as it states the unity of the group of phenomena we are discussing here:

"In order to belong to the class of phenomena which can thus be explained, a faulty psychic action must satisfy the following conditions:

"(1) It must not exceed a certain measure, which is firmly established through our estimation, and is designated by the expression 'within normal limits.'

"(b) It must evince the character of the momentary and temporary disturbance. The same action must have been previously performed more correctly or we must always rely on ourselves to perform it more correctly . . . if we are corrected by others, we must immediately recognize the truth of the correction and the incorrectness of our psychic action.

"(c) If we at all perceive a faulty action, we must not perceive in ourselves any motivation of the same, but must attempt to explain it through inattention' or attribute it to an 'accident.' " (3, p. 150)

---

[11] Had the general psychological investigators considered the close relation between parapraxis and forgetting, they would never—in spite of some ambiguous statements of Freud—have come to the idea that he maintained that a general tendency exists to forget the unpleasant. The same factor, of which the attempted expulsion from consciousness results in forgetting, occurs as a causing factor of the slip; instead of being totally prevented from expression, it manifests itself indirectly. A more recent development of the theory of slips militates further against the idea of the forgetting of "the unpleasant."

Eidelberg (15) pointed out that while in forgetting the interfered-with idea was analyzed, the analysis of it in slips of the tongue was neglected. He found:

"Analytical investigation shows that in studying slips of the tongue it is important to examine the hitherto-neglected 'intention interfered with,' because it has not only a conscious and harmless, but an unconscious and prohibited significance." (p. 470)

On the basis of this he formulated:

"The mechanism of slips of the tongue is the following: A phrase or word which was to have been pronounced has not only a conscious, but an unconscious, significance, the latter representing the gratification of infantile instinctual wishes. These emanate from the id and the unconscious part of the ego sets up a defense to prevent their being satisfied. This defense is a two-fold process: (a) The instinct-fusion which is pressing for gratification is turned against the self and (b) the opposite type of instinct-fusion is mobilized." (p. 470)

In other words, two unconscious strivings and a conscious goal-pursuit struggle here. It is a relief to learn from the author that it is not yet determined whether or not this mechanism is present in every slip of the tongue.

The unity of the phenomena is further discussed in another statement by Freud:

"If the lapse in speech, which is without doubt a motor function, admits of such a conception, it is quite natural to transfer to the lapses of our other motor functions the same expectation. I have here formed two groups of cases; all these cases in which the faulty effect seems to be the essential element—that is, the deviation from the intention—I denote as erroneously carried out actions or defaults; the others, in which the entire action appears rather inexpedient, I call 'symptomatic and chance actions.' Again, no distinct line of demarcation can be formed; indeed, we are forced to conclude that all divisions used in this treatise are of only descriptive significance and contradict the inner unity of the sphere of manifestation." (3, p. 113)

Clearly, by referring to the unity of the material of his treatise, Freud equates the origin and psychological significance of forgetting and parapraxes.

The connection of these phenomena with other psychic phenomena gives us a broader view of memory-functioning as conceived by psychoanalysis. Thus, for example, the chance activities are a link to the field of expressive movements of emotions, the symptomatic actions[12] are a link to psychopathology, the defaults[13] are a link to the field of symbols. From the different parapraxes, manifold threads lead to the dream-work. This is not surprising, for we have seen that the parapraxes—and shall see that the dream-work—may be considered specific memory functions. The similarity of the mechanisms of slips to certain dream-mechanisms, with special emphasis on the function of condensation common to both, is stated by Freud as follows:

". . . in my *Interpretation of Dreams*, I have shown the part played by the process of *condensation* in the origin of the so-called manifest contents of the dream from the latent thoughts of the dream. Any similarity of objects or of word-presentations between two elements of the unconscious material is taken as a cause for the formation of a third, which is a composite or compromise formation. This element represents both components in the dream content, and in view of this origin, it is frequently endowed with numerous contradictory individual determinants. The

---

[12] *Symptomatic or chance actions* are characterized as follows:
"We can undertake a grouping of these extremely frequent chance and symptomatic actions according to their occurrence as habitual, regular under certain circumstances, and as isolated ones. The first group (such as playing with the watch-chain, fingering one's beard, and so on), which can almost serve as a characteristic of the person concerned, is related to the numerous tic movements, and certainly deserves to be dealt with in connection with the latter. In the second group, I place the playing with one's cane, the scribbling with one's pencil, the jingling of coins in one's pocket, kneading dough and other plastic materials, all sorts of handling of one's clothing and many other actions of the same order." (3, p. 131)
[13] *The defaults* are described as: "a symbolic representation of a definite thought which was not accepted consciously as serious" (3, p. 114).

formation of substitutions and contaminations in speech-mistakes is, therefore, the beginning of that work of condensation, which we find taking a most active part in the construction of the dream." (3, pp. 71–72)

In a summarizing description of the mechanism of forgetting, Freud discusses the functions operating in active remembering and brings them into close parallel with the dream work:

"I can perhaps give the following outline concerning the mechanism of actual forgetting. The memory material succumbs in general to two influences, condensation and distortion. Distortion is the work of the tendencies dominating the psychic life and directs itself above all against the affective remnants of memory traces which maintain a more resistive attitude towards condensation. The traces which have grown indifferent, merge into a process of condensation without opposition; . . . these processes of condensation and distortion continue for long periods, during which all fresh experiences act upon the transformation of the memory content. . . . It is quite probable that in forgetting, there can really be no question of a direct function of time. From the repressed memory traces, it can be verified that they suffer no changes even in the longest periods. The unconscious, at all events, knows no time limit. The most important, as well as the most peculiar character of psychic fixation consists in the fact that all impressions are, on the one hand, retained in the same form as they were received, and also in the forms that they have assumed in their further development. This state of affairs cannot be elucidated by any comparison from any other sphere. (3, p. 174, footnote)

In the course of this discussion, we have gained some understanding of the mechanisms involved in forgetting and parapraxes. The nature of the unconscious ideas underlying these phenomena has not yet been clarified. The fact that the disturbing factors were designated as unconscious, and as a tendency to avoid the emergence of pain, makes it fairly clear that we deal here with "affective" factors influencing memory function. A final summarizing statement from "The Psychopathology of Everyday Life" sheds some light on the nature of these "affective factors":

"The . . . question (as to the origin of the thoughts and emotions which find expression in faulty actions) we can answer by saying that in a series of cases, the origin of the disturbing thoughts can be readily traced to repressed emotions of the psychic life. Even in healthy persons, egotistic, jealous and hostile feelings and impulses, burdened by the pressure of moral education, often utilize the path of faulty actions to express in some way their undeniably existing force which is not recognized by the higher psychic instances. Allowing these faulty and chance actions to continue, corresponds, in great part, to a comfortable toleration of the unmoral. The manifold sexual currents play no insignificant part in these repressed feelings." (3, pp. 175–176)

Did any of the experimenters whose work we surveyed in the previous chapters produce experimentally conditions relevant to the mechanisms or qualitatively comparable to the phenomena discussed here? Among those referred to in Chapter III, Flanagan (16) and Sharp (17) elicited phenomena comparable to slips of tongue. Diven (18), whose work we shall discuss in detail in Chapter VIII, found displacement phenomena. The diagnostic association experiments had shown quantitative differences in the ease of reaction and reproduction. The most important pertinent experiments were those of Erickson[14] (19), who succeeded in eliciting parapraxes under posthypnotic suggestion.

We have begun this chapter with Freud's colorful analogy advancing a wise and skeptical warning on our hopes of understanding the intricacies of the memory function. We should like to conclude this section with Stekel's (20) enthusiastic allegory which paints a picture of the memory-function rather than discuss its problem:

". . . the phenomenon of slip proves only that there exists a permanent struggle between contradictory energy streams. All the energies originate in the drive-life. Speech and thought also derive their energies from it. One of the deepest thoughts of Nietzsche was: 'Denken ist nur ein Verhalten der Triebe zueinander.'[15] The affect, the intellectual elaboration of the drives, gives a specific coloring to the thought process . . .

"This relation between speech and thought, or better the relation between what we want to express and what we are able to express, originates mostly in the fact that we never have one thought but many thoughts, a whole polyphony of which the language expresses only the melody, while the middle voices and the counterpoints remain hidden. The usual concept of thinking as flowing in one direction is no more sustainable . . . I maintain that the thought process shows quite an extraordinary condensation. Verbalization is preceded by a struggle ending in most cases with the victory of the reality principle. I believe that thinking is a stream of which we see only the surface . . ." (pp. 1–2)

D. SUMMARY

Our survey of the parapraxes has shown us that:

a. Although the psychoanalytic theory deals in the main with the problem of *forgetting*, it implies a clear-cut theory of *remembering*.

b. This theory can be inferred when it is realized that forgetting and parapraxis constitute one group of phenomena, describable as the disturbance of the usual memory-function as observed in its natural setting in the thought processes.

c. These memory phenomena are elicited whenever an unconscious, repressed, affect-charged tendency strives for expression, and interferes with the emergence of the goal-relevant idea.

d. Sufficient indication has been found that the psychoanalytic theory implies that the unconscious or preconscious affect-charged tendencies effecting "parapraxis" are also present in "praxis"—in other words, are the

---

[14] See Chapter VI and VIII, pp. 179–180, 253ff.
[15] "Thinking is but the interaction of drives."

carriers of the memory-function in general as encountered in its natural setting in thought processes.

e. There has been no doubt that the tendencies eliciting parapraxis are "affective" in character, but the nature of these "affective" factors has not yet been clarified. It appeared to be clear that not the conscious "unpleasantness" attached to the forgotten idea but the connection of this idea to a set of unconscious ideas, which in turn are expressions of prohibited drive-tendencies, is responsible for forgetting.

3. The Fundamental Rule of Psychoanalysis; Infantile Amnesia; the Dream

In order to gain further insight into the memory theory of psychoanalysis, we shall discuss three other points of psychoanalytic theory: the "fundamental rule of psychoanalysis," the problem of "infantile amnesia" and of "screen memories," and the "dream-work."

A. THE FUNDAMENTAL RULE OF PSYCHOANALYSIS

The reader will remember that Spinoza[16] warned against hatred, lest it influence and inhibit the free flow of associations; and that Gordon[17] suggested that good memory depends on the skillful organization of interests. The "fundamental rule of psychoanalysis"—whose aim is to make it possible for the patient to arrive at his repressed memories—demands that he

"put himself into the position of an impassionate and attentive observer, reading always only the surface of his consciousness and making it his duty to be perfectly frank, not failing to communicate any emerging idea, not even if he should (1) find it too painful, judge it (2) senseless, (3) all too insignificant, or (4) not belonging to what he sought for. It usually proves true that just these ideas eliciting the attitudes mentioned here are of particular value in discovering the forgotten material." (21, pp. 204–205)

Thus the patient is asked to renounce any goal-directed thinking and, figuratively speaking, spell out passively what his memory brings to the surface. Our discussion of the genesis of parapraxes has already made it clear why the psychoanalyst expects to learn about the forgotten material from "the free associations" of the patient following the "fundamental rule." The following statements of Freud shed further light on the point:

"For it is demonstrably incorrect to state that we abandon ourselves to an aimless excursion of thought when, as in the interpretation of dreams, we renounce reflection and allow the involuntary ideas to come to the surface. It can be shown that we are able to reject only those directing ideas which are known to us, and that with the cessation of these the unknown—or, as we inexactly say, unconscious—

---

[16] See p. 4.
[17] See p. 132.

directing ideas immediately exert their influence, and henceforth determine the flow of the involuntary ideas. Thinking without directing ideas cannot be ensured by any influence we ourselves exert on our own psychic life; neither do I know of any state of psychic derangement in which such a mode of thought establishes itself." (5, p. 482)

Are these statements pertinent in a discussion of the "affective influence in memory functioning"? To answer this question we must remind ourselves that the association-experiment was accepted in general psychology[18] as a means of exploring memory; here also the associations are considered to reveal the nature of memory. But in the psychoanalytic conception of memory, it is not the formal connection of stimulus and reaction words which is important, but the affective factor or underlying striving which couples the links of the associative chain.   These links are all representatives of the striving which underlies the chain and which brings these links— memories—into consciousness to find, through them, expression.

The issue of "free associations" and the "fundamental rule," and of their bearing on our problem, becomes even clearer in another application. Freud, in a paper making recommendations to the physician on the psychoanalytic method of treatment, discusses how the analyst who treats several patients daily may remember the material.   He explains his procedure as follows:

"The technique, however, is a very simple one. It disclaims the use of any special aids, even of notetaking, as we shall see, and simply consists in making no effort to concentrate the attention on anything in particular, and in maintaining in regard to all that one hears the same measure of calm, quiet attentiveness—of 'evenly-hovering attention,' as I once before described it. In this way a strain which could not be kept up for several hours daily and a danger inseparable from deliberate attentiveness are avoided. For as soon as attention is deliberately concentrated in a certain degree, one begins to select from the material before one; one point will be fixed in the mind with particular clearness and some other consequently disregarded, and in this selection one's expectations or one's inclinations will be followed. This is just what must not be done, however; if one's expectations are followed in this selection there is the danger of never finding anything but what is already known, and if one follows one's inclinations anything which is to be perceived will most certainly be falsified. It must not be forgotten that the meaning of the things one hears is, at all events for the most part, only recognizable later on . . .

"What one achieves in this way will be sufficient for all requirements during the treatment. Those elements of the material which have a connection with one another will be at the conscious disposal of the physician; the rest, as yet unconnected, chaotic and indistinguishable, seems at first to disappear, but rises readily into recollection as soon as the patient brings something further to which it is related, and by which it can be developed." (22, pp. 324–325)

---

[18] See pp. 41, 44ff.

This "fundamental rule" and the "recommendations" are part of the technique rather than of the "psychological theory" of psychoanalysis. Yet in a certain respect they represent the outlook of the psychoanalyst on memory function and its "affective" motivation.

B. INFANTILE AMNESIA

The general forgetting of childhood experiences is another phenomenon which Freud first pointed out as requiring explanation. He called attention to this phenomenon as early as 1899, and discussed it in the "Psychopathology of Everyday Life" (3) and in "Three Contributions to the Theory of Sexuality" (23). He formulated the problem thus:

"I refer to the peculiar amnesia which veils from most people (not from all) the first years of their childhood, usually the first six or eight years. So far, it has not occurred to us that this amnesia should surprise us, though we have good reasons for it. For we are informed that during those years which have left nothing except a few incomprehensible memory fragments, we have vividly reacted to impressions, that we have manifested human pain and pleasure and that we have expressed love, jealousy and other passions as they then affected us. Indeed, we are told that we have uttered remarks which proved to grownups that we possessed understanding and a budding power of judgment. Still we know nothing of all this when we become older. Why does our memory lag behind all our other psychic activities? We really have reason to believe that at no time of life are we more capable of impressions and reproductions than during the years of childhood." (23, p. 581)

Freud integrated this forgetting with his theory of infantile sexuality. According to this theory, infantile sexuality reaches its peak of manifestation in the third and fourth years of life, and later succumbs to a progressive suppression. The instinctive affective forces inhibiting sexual manifestation are considered to account also for the initial repression,[19] the forgetting of childhood experiences. Further, this forgetting is brought into connection with neurotic forgetting:

"Hysterical amnesia which serves the repression can only be explained by the fact that the individual already possesses a sum of memories which were withdrawn from conscious disposal [the infantile memories] and which by associative connection now seize that which is acted upon by the repelling forces of the repression emanating from consciousness. We may say that without infantile amnesia there would be no hysterical amnesia.

"I therefore believe that the infantile amnesia which causes the individual to look upon his childhood as if it were a *prehistoric* time and conceals from him the beginning of his own sexual life—that this amnesia, is responsible for the fact that one does not usually attribute any value to the infantile period in the development of the sexual life." (23, p. 582)

---

[19] See p. 166.

The problem of remembering childhood experiences has still another bearing on our topic. In the earlier contributions already mentioned (8, 9), Freud called attention to the fact that the few memories one has of childhood are apparently insignificant; he demonstrated that these are only "screen memories" (Deckerinnerungen) hiding significant experiences. In other words, their relation to the significant childhood memory is similar to the relation to the forgotten idea of the substitute ideas which emerge in the subject's effort to remember; and similar also to the relation of parapraxis to forgetting. Screen memories like parapraxes are compromises, results of unsuccessful attempts at forgetting. Thus, we encounter another memory phenomenon determined by strong unconscious affective forces. This phenomenon of substitution is called displacement, in reference to the affect-cathexis (charge) which is displaced from the significant (hidden) memory to the insignificant (screen) memory. Along with the mechanisms of condensation and distortion, already mentioned in discussing slips of the tongue, the mechanism of this displacement will be further discussed in the section on dream-work. It now becomes obvious that Gordon's[20] attempt at investigating "early memories" and their "feeling-tone" was not relevant to the psychoanalytic conception of the theory of early memories, for this theory does not require that screen memories have either pleasant or unpleasant feeling-tone.

C. THE MECHANISMS OF DREAM-WORK

The material to be surveyed in this section may at first glance seem remote from our topic, and many a detail may seem an unnecessary burden. But we are obliged first to define the concepts in terms of which the contribution of dream-work to our topic may be expressed.

In the section on the theoretical contributions of general psychology, it was mentioned that Pear[21] and Stern[22] considered dreams to be memory phenomena, and even maintained that in them the subjective selective function of memory appears in an exaggerated manner. Thus, we may hope that by learning about the organization of the dream we shall be in a position to draw further conclusions on the affective organization of memory.

According to Freud, the manifest form of the dream carries the latent dream content. The essence of the dream is wishfulfilment, and its form of appearance is a composite memory image, usually visual.[23] The appar-

---

[20] See p. 72.
[21] See p. 130.
[22] See p. 131.
[23] It is beside our point to discuss the accidental presence and significance of other images.

ently logical form of the dream is effected by a process due to partially-awakened consciousness and similar to our waking thinking. We are not concerned here with proving or discussing these conclusions; our aim is only to extract the implications for our problem of this theory and the findings on which it is based. To this end we shall attempt to answer the following questions: (a) Did Freud have a specific view of memory functioning, and if so what was it? (b) What mechanisms are at work in organizing individual memories into the manifest form of the dream, so as to express the latent dream content? (c) What is the nature of the "wish" which is claimed to be the organizing essence of the dream, and what is its relation to the affect which is claimed to be genuine and identical (5, p. 435) in both the manifest dream and its latent content?

a. Freud's View on Memory Functioning

Freud illustrates his memory theory in the following scheme (p. 491):

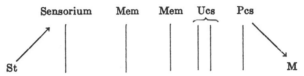

The stimulation (St) reaches the psychic apparatus through the system to which the function of perceiving (P) is attributed: "The P-system, which possesses no capacity for preserving changes,[24] and hence no memory, furnishes to consciousness the complexity and variety of the sensory qualities"[25] (5, p. 490). Behind this lie the memory systems (Mem) of which, according to Freud, there are many:

"On further investigation we find it necessary to assume not one but many such *mem*-systems, in which the same excitation transmitted by the P-elements undergoes a diversified fixation. The first of these *mem*-systems will in any case contain the fixation of the association through simultaneity, while in those lying farther away the same material of excitation will be arranged according to other forms of combination; so that relationships of similarity, etc., might perhaps be represented by these later systems. It would, of course, be idle to attempt to express in words the psychic significance of such a system. Its characteristic would lie in the intimacy of its relations to elements of raw material of memory . . ." (5, p. 490)

---

[24] Freud suggests: " . . . obvious difficulties arise when one and the same system is faithfully to preserve changes in its elements and skill to remain fresh and receptive in respect of new occasions of change." (5, p. 489)

To the same effect see Freud: A Note Upon the 'Mystic Writing-Pad.' (6)

[25] The symbols Ucs, Pcs and M stand for Unconscious, Preconscious, and Motor System. The course of excitation, according to Freud, proceeds in the waking state from the stimulation to the motor-system, while in the dream it follows the opposite course.

These memory systems transform the momentary excitations of the P-system into lasting traces (5, p. 489). These memories may become conscious; as a rule, however, they are unconscious[26] and exert their influence while in this state. The so-called "normal" organization of memories is not specifically explained; as far as their organization in dreams is concerned, it is maintained that the "impetus" (5, p. 491) to dream formation originates in the system Ucs (unconscious). Intrapsychic censors on the border of the systems Ucs and Pcs (preconscious) prevent the penetration of these impulses into consciousness in the waking state. In the sleeping state they are admitted to dream-consciousness, for the path to the motor system is blocked and there is no danger of executing the impulses. Accordingly, the impulse takes an opposite—"regressive"—course:

"It communicates itself not to the motor end of the apparatus, but to the sensory end, and finally reaches the system of perception" (5, p. 492).

Freud explains the process as follows:

"We call it regression if the idea in the dream is changed back into the visual image from which it once originated. . . . *In regression the structure of the dream-thoughts breaks up into its raw material*" (7, p. 493)

This raw material consists of visual and acoustic memory images. It seems important to add here that, according to Freud, a process similar to the dream process accounts for hallucinations.[27] A similar phenomenon of thoughts breaking down into their raw material was discovered by Silberer (11) who, in attempting to observe his own intellectual work in a state of fatigue, found that his thoughts were transformed into visual hallucinatory symbolic pictures (hypnagogic-hallucinations).[28]

The implications for our problem of the psychoanalytic theory of dreams may be stated as follows: the experience is deposited in the memory systems

[26] The attribute *unconscious* (ucs) is to be distinguished from the system *Unconscious* (Ucs).

[27] "As an example I will cite the case of one of my youngest hysterical patients—a boy of twelve, who was prevented from falling asleep by 'green faces with red eyes,' which terrified him. The source of this manifestation was the suppressed, but once conscious memory of a boy whom he had often seen four years earlier, and who offered a warning example of many bad habits, including masturbation, for which he was now reproaching himself. At that time his mother had noticed that the complexion of this ill-mannered boy was *greenish* and that he had *red* (i. e. red-rimmed) *eyes*. Hence his terrifying vision, which merely determined his recollection of another saying of his mother's, to the effect that such boys become demented, are unable to learn anything at school, and are doomed to an early death." (5, p. 494)

Similar processes, found in "primitive" and "autistic" thinking as well as in daydreams will be discussed in Chapter VII (p. 224ff) in connection with the Korsakow syndrome.

[28] For examples, see p. 242.

in a manner influenced by its relation to other deposited material. Instinctual impulses originating in the organism become active in the Unconscious, and use memories for their representation and expression. This
organization of memories to represent instinctual impulses can come about
on the level of any one memory system or several memory systems so as
either to enter consciousness directly—as in the normal waking state—if
the impulse is "acceptable," or revert into the original sensory form of
perception—as in dreams or daydreams—if the impulse is "unacceptable."
We shall see that this reversal does not, however, bring to consciousness
isolated and undistorted perceptions corresponding to single memories.
In this memory theory instinctive-affective factors play a central role,
organizing memories and using "memory traces" to assert and express
themselves. Among the memory theories discussed, only Bartlett's[29]
approached such a view.

b. Dream-Work

In order to obtain a more concrete picture of the operating mechanism
of the organizing affective-instinctive factors as viewed by Freud, we must
discuss in some detail what he calls "the dream work." The latent dream
thought is elaborated into manifest dream content chiefly by means of the
"primary processes" of condensation, displacement, and symbolism, and
by the "secondary processes." The two regulative principles of the operation of the dream-work are first, the organizing of the latent dream thought
into a form acceptable to the censor and suitable to enter consciousness;
and secondly, the regard for the "regressive" course of the dream impulse
which requires a representation in terms of sensory images. These two
principles determine the appearance of the latent dream thought in the
manifest dream content. The regard for the censor is specially important
as the latent dream thought is always unacceptable to the consciousness, a
fact which is responsible for the tendency to forget dreams. However, the
censor should not be conceived anthropomorphically but rather as an
expression designating all the strivings that oppose the emergence into
consciousness of a certain striving. Thus, the functions to be described
are the effects of interfering strivings on the organization of memories in the
dream. *Condensation* is described as

". . . a selection of those elements which occur several times over in the dream-
content, the formation of new unities (composite persons, mixed images), and the
production of common means . . ." (5, p. 330)

Displacement means that

". . . essential components of the dream content do not by any means play the
same part in the dream thoughts. . . . The dream is, as it were, *centered elsewhere;*

---

[29] See pp. 117–118, 123–124, 132–133.

its content is arranged about elements which do not constitute the central point of the dream-thoughts." (5, p. 336)

Symbolism is defined as "indirect representation." It is maintained that

"In a number of cases the common quality shared by the symbol and the thing which it represents is obvious, in others it is concealed. . . ." (5, p. 370)

It is pointed out that although there are general symbols, as documented by ethnopsychological research, the choice of symbols of a dream is determined by the context.[30]

These three functions serve the purpose of withdrawing the dream thought from "censorship." The finishing touch to the material thus prepared is given by the *secondary elaboration*, which is the work of the partly-awakened conscious thinking; it attempts to connect the parts of the dream material in terms of conscious logic (5, p. 456).[31] Thus, the reversal of the dream thought into its raw material does not result in isolated memory images, because the primary and secondary processes reorganize the material. Accordingly, all these may be considered specific memory functions which are motivated by "affective factors." These "affective factors" become obvious if one considers that the manifest form of the dream is essentially a compromise resulting from the struggle of the dream-wish which strives for expression and those strivings which are symbolized by the expression "censorship."

These four functions change only the ideational but not the affective content of the dream.

". . . the ideational contents have undergone displacements and substitutions, while the affects have remained unchanged. . . . In a psychic complex which has been subjected to the influence of the resisting censorship, the affects are the unyielding constituent, which alone can guide us to the correct completion." (5, pp. 434–435)

It may appear that we have strayed from our topic, but to arrive at the conclusion that in the course of the dream-work the affect remains unchanged is, we feel, a step forward. While the memories are reorganized, the affect—like the "meaning" of Wheeler[32] and Stern,[33] or the "attitude" of Bartlett[34]—remains the unchanged constant core of the memory organization. The reader will remember that Mueller-Freienfels characterized the affect as the factor which selects the words for its "cloth," making them more than "flatus vocis," and that Bartlett maintained that reproduction originates from the attitude and is a "justification" of it.

[30] See also Jones (4, pp. 154–211)
[31] See also 5, p. 467
[32] See p. 128.
[33] See p. 131.
[34] See pp. 117–118.

As the reader has perhaps been impressed disagreeably by the anthropomorphic "censor" and the "tricky" methods applied to compromise with it, it may make for a more adequate understanding to insert here Jones' view of the point:

"Freud himself seems to place what he terms the 'censorship'—an expression covering the sum total of the repressing forces in question—at the place of transition between the unconscious and the preconscious, with a less important one at the place of transition between the preconscious and the conscious. While it may be agreed that the action of repression is mainly exhibited at these points of junction, the evidence, in my opinion, induces one rather to picture the inhibiting tendencies as being distributed, in a streaming fashion, throughout the whole mind, conscious as well as unconscious, increasing in strength, however, as one proceeds from the level of consciousness to the lowest layers of the unconscious." (4, p. 129)

Jones' approach means a new and less anthropomorphic development of the theory. It may well be that in such a new development, the "tricky" mechanisms of condensation, displacement, and symbols will be recognized as mechanisms on different levels of representation of memories, the visual representation characteristic of dreams being one among many. In this new development the "censor" will appear as the effect of interfering strivings, and the mechanisms of memory organization on different levels will probably be expressed as properties and functions of "memory-traces." A theoretical development of this sort would be supported by the findings of H. Werner (24) concerning the developmental levels of the memory function, of Varendonck (25) concerning "preconscious phantasying thinking," and of Silberer (11) concerning "hypnagogic hallucinations." The findings of these investigators all indicate the presence of a great variety of levels of representation in our psychic life—in other words, a great variety of forms of organization of memory and thinking. On each level of organization the affect is the unchanging, and probably the organizing, factor; but the mechanisms of organizing appear to change from level to level. The form of appearance of the unchanging affect is also a varying one, ranging from genuine affects to their intellectualized derivatives, such as P-ness and U-ness. We still do not know enough about this "affect"; our next step must be to collect more material concerning its role in the dream.

c. Wishfulfilment

The function of wishfulfilment is explained in Freud's description of the dream-function:

"The dream is a psychic act full of import; its motive power is invariably a wish craving fulfilment; the fact that it is unrecognizable as a wish, and its many peculiarities and absurdities, are due to the influence of the psychic censorship to which it has been subjected during its formation. Besides the necessity of evading the censorship, the following factors have played a part in its formation: first, a need for condensing the psychic material; second, regard for representability in sensory images; and third (though not constantly), regard for a rational and intelligible exterior of the dream-structure. From each of these propositions a path leads onward to psychological postulates and assumptions. Thus, the reciprocal relation of the wish-motives, and the four conditions, as well as the mutual relations of these conditions must now be investigated; the dream must be inserted in the context of the psychic life." (pp. 485–486)

The meaning of the concept "wish" is clear only if we remember that Freud has adopted a biological theory which maintains that a living organism strives to keep itself as free as possible from stimulation—that is, excitation or tension (5, p. 508); Freud equates the accumulation of excitation with pain, its discharge with pleasure.[35] He writes:

". . . the accumulation of excitation . . . is felt as pain, and sets the apparatus in operation in order to bring about again a state of gratification, in which the diminution of excitation is perceived as pleasure. Such a current in the apparatus, issuing from pain and striving for pleasure, we call a wish. . . . The first occurrence of wishing may well have taken the form of a hallucinatory cathexis of the memory of gratification." (5, p. 533)

It is explained that as the hallucinatory performance cannot bring about the cessation of needs, in reality a detour is made to find the gratifying object; the dream, however, remains on the hallucinatory level, and in it the wish is the representative of the drive-forces. This definition of wish leaves no doubt of its intimate relation to affective factors. It is questionable whether pain and pleasure, as identified with the increase or decrease of excitation, can still be equated with the identical terms in general psychology. We have earlier[36] advanced the hypothesis that the different motivating or "affective" factors are manifestations of a common basic factor on different levels of psychic functioning; Freud's definition of the role of the wish in dream-work would comply with such a hypothesis. Freud expressed this point even more clearly:

". . . this wish impulse, . . . essentially represents an unconscious instinctual demand and in the Pcs has taken on the guise of a dream-wish, a wishfulfilling phantasy." (28, p. 142)

The relation of wishfulfilment to the processes of dream-work, discussed in the previous section, is defined thus:

"The primary process strives for discharge of the excitation in order to establish with the quantity of excitation thus collected *an identity of perception;* the secondary

---

[35] To the same effect see Jelgersma (26); also Freud (27).
[36] See p. 100ff.

process has abandoned this intention, and has adopted instead the aim of an *identity of thought*. All thinking is merely a detour from the memory of gratification (taken as a purposive idea) to the identical cathexis[37] of the same memory, which is to be reached once more by the path of motor experiences. Thought must concern itself with the connecting-paths between ideas without allowing itself to be misled by their intensities. But it is obvious that condensations of ideas and intermediate or compromise-formations are obstacles to the attainment of the identity which is aimed at; by substituting one idea for another they swerve away from the path which would have led onward from the first idea. Such procedures are, therefore, carefully avoided in our secondary thinking." (5, pp. 535-536)

This definition also implies that on the level of conscious thinking and acting, the gratification to be reached by motor activity can no longer be expressed as "wishfulfilment" but rather should be expressed in terms of a purposive idea.

In view of the fact that a wish is a striving for pleasure and that dreams are wishfulfilment, anxiety dreams—since they seem to contradict the thesis of "avoiding the awaking of pain through memory"—require an explanation. It is explained that the wish belongs to the Ucs, but the Pcs rejects and suppresses it. This suppression is normally successful; when it is unsuccessful, a conflict of the two systems ensues and results in anxiety dreams. Thus we are taught by the function of the "dream-work" that wishfulfilment is not necessarily a direct gain of pleasure.[38] This complicated state of affairs must be kept in mind when judging the effect of pleasantness and unpleasantness on memory, especially in the case of experiments which propose to offer proof or disproof of the Freudian theory of forgetting. ' Conscious pleasantness and unpleasantness are phenomena which of themselves do not indicate the nature of the process which gives rise to them. The effect on memory phenomena of the process indicated by the presence of pleasantness and unpleasantness may be manifold. This state of affairs is well characterized in Freud's discussion of the nature of affects:

"We will therefore affirm the proposition that the principal reason why the suppression of the *Ucs.* becomes necessary is that if the movement of ideas in the *Ucs.* were allowed to run its course, it would develop an affect which originally had the character of pleasure, but which, since the process of *repression*, bears the character of pain. The aim, as well as the result of the suppression is to prevent the development of this pain. The suppression extends to the idea-content of the *Ucs.*, because the liberation of pain might emanate from this idea-content. We here take as our

[37] "Identical cathexis" means here identical strivings. In other words, in this detour, memories different from those of the original gratification are revived by the striving toward this gratification in the course of the attempt to attain the gratification by planning action in reality.

[38] ". . . it is certain that all neurotic 'pain' is of this kind, is pleasure which cannot be experienced as such." (27, p. 6.)

basis a quite definite assumption as to the nature of the development of affect. This is regarded as a motor or secretory function, the key to the innervation of which is to be found in the ideas of the *Ucs*. Through the domination of the *Pcs*. these ideas are as it were strangled, that is, inhibited from sending out the impulse that would develop the affect. The danger which arises if catexis by the *Pcs*. ceases thus consists in the fact that the unconscious excitations would liberate an affect that—in consequence of the repression that has previously occurred—could only be felt as pain or anxiety." (5, p. 521)

D. SUMMARY

a. "The fundamental rule of psychoanalysis" and the "recommendations to the psychoanalyst" express a knowledge concerning one type of "affective influence on memory." They state that to abandon conscious directing ideas—those which usually bring to our consciousness the memories leading to our goal—results not in a chaos in our mind, but rather gives free reign to unconscious directing ideas which lead to repressed affect-cathexed memories.

b. The wholesale forgetting of childhood memories, according to the psychoanalytic theory, results from the progressive repression which occurs concomitantly with the latency period in the sexual development of the child; it is an amnesia determined by the inhibition imposed on the evolving infantile sexuality. The few apparently insignificant childhood memories are "screen memories" for significant affect-charged experiences, to which they are related as substitute ideas are related to forgotten ones, and as parapraxes are related to forgetting.

c. In the dream, memories are organized by the dream-wish, which is defined as a striving to diminish the accumulation of excitement. This organization comes about on a level where the memories are reverted into their original sensory images. The wish, the affective organizing principle, uses the mechanisms of condensation, displacement, symbolism, and secondary elaboration to express itself—that is, the latent content of the dream—in a form acceptable to consciousness. The ideational content, the memory material, is thus transformed, while the affect remains the unchanged core of the dream out of which it can be reconstructed.

d. The material surveyed indicates a number of phenomena in which the "affective influence" in memory functioning is present in a variety of forms.

4. INSTINCTS, AFFECTS, AND REPRESSION

In surveying the contributions of psychoanalysis to our problem we have repeatedly encountered instinct (Trieb), affect, and pleasure-principle as the motivators and determiners of memory functioning, and "repression" as the explanation of forgetting. The aim of this section is to clarify the meaning and interrelation of these concepts and functions in the hope that their clarification will shed further light on the nature of the "affective factors" in memory functioning.

The Instinct. In his paper on "The Instincts and Their Vicissitudes" (29) Freud wrote:[39]

". . . an 'instinct' appears to us as a borderland concept between the mental and the mental and the physical, being . . . the mental representative of the stimuli emanating from within the organism and penetrating to the mind . . ." (p. 64)

Freud explains that the instinct as such can never be the content of consciousness; in consciousness, and even in the unconscious, it can be represented only by an idea (30, p. 109). This statement, however, needs some amplification, for instincts, as we learn from Freud, also have representations other than ideational ones. Besides the ". . . idea or group of ideas which is cathected with a definite amount of the mental energy (libido, interest) pertaining to an instinct," there exists the ". . . *charge of affect* [which] . . . represents that part of the instinct which . . . finds proportionate expression, according to its quantity, in processes which become observable . . . as affect" (31, p. 91).

The Affect. The affects are thus one of the representatives of the instincts. The "*charge of affect*" is variously referred to as the "instinctual energy attached to the idea" (31, p. 91) or "the quantitative factor in the instinct presentation" (31, p. 92). The "*affect*" itself, however, is conceived of as a "process of discharge, the final expression of which is perceived as feeling" (30, p. 111). The essence of the affect is that it is consciously experienced. The term "unconscious affect" is, according to Freud, a misnomer; when it is used, it refers to an affect which, though consciously experienced, is displaced from the idea to which it originally pertained. The discharge process called "affect" is distinguished from "discharge through *motility*" by Freud as follows:

"Affectivity manifests itself essentially in motor (i.e. secretory and circulatory) discharge resulting in an (internal) alteration of the subject's own body without reference to the outer world; motility, in actions designed to effect changes in the outer world." (30, p. 111, footnote)

Here a sharp distinction is made between "charge of affect" as instinctual energy, and affects or emotions[40] as discharge processes. In general, however, the expression "affect" is used loosely in psychoanalytic literature. Jones, for example, writes:

"Accompanying every mental process is a varying amount of psychical energy, which roughly corresponds with what we term the affect." (4, p. 21)

---

[39] See also Bibring (32) and Jones (33).
[40] "Affekt" is the German term for emotion.

It appears that one must distinguish between three notions of affect: one is the energy component of the instinct representation, of which the other two—the affects as discharge processes, and their perception, the feeling—are but expressions.

The Principles. The problem of the "Principles" arises out of the formulation of the instincts,[41] given above. Bibring (32) expresses this rather clearly:

"According to this view instinct, whatever may be the form in which it becomes a tension of psychical energy, is always, as being a stimulus, contrasted with the mental apparatus with its postulated methods of functioning . . . we must bear in mind . . . that the principles or regulative mechanisms regulate the mental apparatus, while the instincts continually impose fresh demands for work upon that apparatus, so regulated." (p. 105)

There are two such regulative principles:[42] the "pleasure principle," according to which the psychic apparatus strives to diminish its tension; and the "reality principle," according to which the present attainment of a dangerous pleasure is postponed in the effort to pave the way towards a more secure pleasure—that is, it follows the line of greatest advantage instead of that of least resistance (34, p. 18). These principles are not causal factors, but expressions of empirical observations couched, unfortunately, in a teleological language. Although they are extremely useful in practice, their teleological coloring does not make for scientific clarity. Thus, the "pleasure-principle" gave rise to the misunderstanding that the psychoanalytic theory is a hedonistic one, and that it promulgates a "forgetting of the unpleasant." Yet more thorough scrutiny of the theory shows that in it "pleasure" and "pain" are relative terms: the aim of attaining "pleasure" is usually relinquished because of the dangers attached to it, and "pain" is often endured as being the lesser evil.

Repression. Repression is one of the vicissitudes of the instincts (29, p. 69); its essence lies ". . . *in the function of rejecting and keeping something out of consciousness,*"—that is, something which might awaken painfulness. In *primal repression*—always, according to Freud, a childhood repression—it is the ideational presentation of the instinct which is denied entry into consciousness: in *repression proper*, the derivatives of this instinct-presentation are denied such entry (31, p. 86). The closer the connection of the idea to the repressed instinct-presentation and the stronger its cathexis, the more likely is it to succumb to "repression proper" (31, p. 88). It is shown, however, that the work of repression is *variable*, *specific*, and *mobile*

[41] The expression "drive" is used interchangeably with "instinct."
[42] A number of suggestions have been made which imply the existence of a third principle: "death instinct," "destrudo," "mortido," "repetition-compulsion." A discussion of these is beyond our scope.

—in fact, unpredictable (31, p. 89); it is not general and capable of statistical treatment, as most of the experimenters whose work was surveyed in
Chapter III would have it.   The repressed idea is not lost; it becomes unconscious.   What makes it unconscious?   According to Freud, the *primal
repression* comes about by anti-cathexis[43] applied by the preconscious in
guarding itself against the intrusion of the unconscious idea (30, p. 113).
In *repression proper* the cathexis of the idea is withdrawn; this withdrawal
renders the idea unconscious, and the cathexis is used as anti-cathexis to
keep it unconscious.   Freud came to the conclusion that the differcnce
between the unconscious and the preconscious is that the former has only
ideas of *things* and the latter has ideas of *words* deposited as memory traces
(30, p. 133).[44]   Thus, he concludes that repression "denies to the rejected
idea . . . translation of the idea into words." (30, p. 134)   The same idea is
expressed positively in "The Ego and the Id":

> ". . . anything arising from within (apart from feelings) that seeks to become
> conscious must try to transform itself into external perceptions: this can be done by
> way of memory-traces," and "by coming into connection with the verbal images
> that correspond to it." (35, p. 21)

Jones (4) advanced a different theory, according to which emotions (Affekt-
betrag) spreading over the mcmory-traces like an electric charge vitalize
them and so bring the memories into consciousness.
   Thus far, we have discussed the ideational representation of the instinct.
Let us turn now to the other representation of the instinct, the "energy-
cathexis"—in other words, the "affect-charge" and its *fate in repression*.
Concerning this, Freud wrote:

> "The fate of the quantitative factor in the instinct-presentation may be one of
> three . . . [if repressed]: either the instinct is altogether suppressed, so that no trace
> is found, or it appears in the guise of an affect of a particular qualitative tone, or it is
> transformed into anxiety." (31, pp. 91–92)

In other words, it is through repression that the "affect charge" is transformed into "affect"—that is, feeling or peripheral discharge process.
   Repression, striving to prevent the penetration into consciousness of
instinct-representations which would result in conflict, deprives the instinct-representations or their derivatives of their preconscious cathexes,
separates them from verbal images, splits the instinct-representation into
idea and "affect charge," and manages to keep now one, now the other, in

---

[43] "Anti-cathexis" designates those strivings, connected with an idea, which prevent its entering consciousness.
[44] This assumption is supported by Freud's observation that communication to a
patient of an idea he has repressed usually does not result in his recognizing it; it is
as though two different traces of the idea were simultaneously present.

repression. This results in the forgetting of the idea or in the displacement of the affect to other ideas. Thus, the fate of the "affect charge" is closely connected with the fate of memories. But this "affect charge" is, as we saw, the source of the discharge process designated as "affect" or emotion. Thus, memory phenomena and affects appear to be parallel expressions of the same factor—namely, the regulative dynamics which dispose of the psychic tension set up by instincts. Freud, describing the role of the "reality principle" in memory functioning, again discusses the role of the "affect":

"In place of repression, which excluded from cathexis as productive of 'pain' some of the emerging ideas, there developed an impartial *passing of judgment*, which had to decide whether a particular idea was true or false, that is, was in agreement with reality or not; decision was determined by comparison with the memory-traces of reality.

"A new function was now entrusted to motor discharge, which under the supremacy of the pleasure-principle had served to unburden the mental apparatus of accretions of stimuli, and in carrying out this task had sent innervations into the interior of the body (mien, expressions of affect); it was now employed in the appropriate alteration of reality. It was converted into *action*.

"Restraint of motor discharge (of action) had now become necessary, and was provided by means of the process of *thought*, which was developed from ideation. Thought was endowed with qualities which made it possible for the mental apparatus to support increased tension during a delay in the process of discharge. It is essentially an experimental way of acting, accompanied by displacement of smaller quantities of cathexis together with less expenditure (discharge) of them. For this purpose conversion of free cathexis into 'bound' cathexes was imperative, and this was brought about by means of raising the level of the whole cathectic process. It is probable that thinking was originally unconscious, in so far as it rose above mere ideation and turned to the relations between the object-impressions, and that it became endowed with further qualities which were perceptible to consciousness only through its connection with the memory-traces of words." (34, pp. 15–16)

We may conclude that not the emotions but their source, the instinctual tension, exerts the paramount influence on memory phenomena.

Summary

a. Instincts are forces which originate in the organism, and enter consciousness only through their quantitative and ideational representations.

b. The "affect charge" is the quantitative representative of the instinct; it has an energy character, and feeling as well as emotion—peripheral discharge—are but manifestations of it.

c. The "pleasure principle" and the "reality principle" are convenient but, as a result of their teleological terminology, frequently misleading empirical descriptions of the dynamics of instincts.

d. Repression is twofold. While primal—infantile—repression expels and keeps out of consciousness *an instinct representation*, repression proper affects the derivatives of instinct representations. To keep material out of consciousness means to deprive it of its preconscious verbal images or its energy-cathexis, or both.

e. The effect of repression consists not only in expelling and keeping a memory out of consciousness, but also in displacing its "affect charge" to another idea or in suppressing it entirely.

f. The "affect-charge" is the energy-source of which feeling and emotion are but expressions; it is not feeling or emotion, but the "affect charge" itself which plays a determining role in memory function.

5. Conclusions

a. The survey of the pertinent psychoanalytic literature has shown us the fallacy of the widespread notion that Freud taught the forgetting of the disagreeable. What Freud discovered was the function preventing the emergence into consciousness of an unconscious idea which, if it became conscious, would give rise to a conflict. This function, called repression, proved to be a specific and variable one, hardly amenable to the statistical treatment adopted by experimentalists.

b. Forgetting has appeared to be one of the many "inadequacies of our psychic functioning" which are the result of the conflict between the "censor" and the prohibited unconscious tendencies which strive to assert themselves.

c. The mechanisms encountered in analyzing these inadequacies— mechanisms which produce screen memories in the place of amnesized infantile experiences, mechanisms which underlie the dynamic flow of free associations, mechanisms of dream work—have been found to be specific memory functions. These functions are displacement, condensation, substitution, symbolization, and secondary elaboration.

d. Remembering as emergence into consciousness, and forgetting as non-emergence, have been recognized as expressions of memory dynamics, in which instinctual strivings use individual memories—deposited in strata according to their connection with other deposited material—for their representation. This representation may come about on various levels, the mechanisms described being the forms of memory organization on these levels. The dream is an extreme example in which the instinctual component—the wish—organizes memories to represent itself on a primitive perceptual level.

REFERENCES

(1) Hunt, W. A. Recent developments in the field of emotion. *Psychol. Bull.* 38: 249–276, 1941.
(2) Freud, S. *Civilization and its discontents.* 144 pp. New York, Cape, 1930.

(3) FREUD, S. *Psychopathology of everyday life.* Pp. 35–178. In: *The basic writings of Sigmund Freud.* 1001 pp. Ed. Brill, A. A. New York, Modern Libr., 1938. First publ. in *Monatschr. Psychiat. Neurol.* X.

(4) JONES, E. *Papers on psycho-analysis.* 731 pp. New York, Wood, 3rd ed., 1923.

(5) FREUD, S. *The interpretation of dreams.* Pp. 181–542. In: *The basic writings of Sigmund Freud.* 1001 pp. ed. Brill, A. A. New York, Modern Libr., 1938. First publ. *Die Traumdeutung.* Leipzig-Wien, Deuticke, 1900.

(6) FREUD, S. A note upon the "Mystic Writing-Pad." *Internat. J. Psychoanal.* 21: 469–474, 1940. Notiz ueber den "Wunderblock." In: *Gesammelte Schriften. Wien. Internat. Psychoanal. Verl.* 6: 415–420, 1925.

(7) JONES, E. *Papers on psycho-analysis.* 643 pp. Baltimore, Wood, 1938.

(8) FREUD, S. Zum psychischen Mechanismus der Vergesslichkeit. *Monatschr. Psychiat. Neurol.,* 4: 436–443,1898.

(9) FREUD, S. Ueber Deckerinnerungen. *Monatschr. Psychiat. Neurol. G. S.* 1: 465–488, 1899.

(10) WEBER, A. O., AND RAPAPORT, D. Teleology and the emotions. *Phil. Sci.* 8: 69–82, 1941.

(11) SILBERER, H. Bericht ueber eine Methode gewisse symbolische Halluzinationserscheinungen hervorzurufen und zu beobachten. *Jhb. Psychoanal. Psychopath. Forsch.* 1: 513–525, 1909.

(12) HOENIGSWALD, R. *Die Grundlagen der Denkpsychologie: Studien und Analysen.* 416 pp. Leipzig, Teubner, 2nd ed., 1925.

(13) SELZ, O. I.: *Ueber die Gesetze des geordneten Denkverlaufs.* 320 pp. Bonn, Cohen,1913. II: *Zur Psychologie des produktiven Denkens. Eine experimentelle Untersuchung.* 688 pp. Bonn, Cohen, 1922.

(14) DUNCKER, K. A qualitative (experimental and theoretical) study of productive thinking (solving of comprehensible problems). *Ped. Sem.* 33: 642–708, 1926.

(15) EIDELBERG, L. A contribution to the study of the slips of the tongue. *Internat. J. Psychoanal.* 17: 462–470, 1936. *Imago.* 22: 196–202, 1936.

(16) FLANAGAN, D. *The influence of emotional inhibitions on learning and recall.* 13 pp. Unpubl. Thesis on file Univ. Chicago Libr., 1930.

(17) SHARP, A. A. An experimental test of Freud's doctrine of the relation of hedonic tone to memory revival. *J. exp. Psychol.* 22: 395–418, 1938.

(18) DIVEN, K. Certain determinants in the conditioning of anxiety reactions. *J. Psychol.* 3: 291–308, 1937.

(19) ERICKSON, M. H. Experimental demonstration of the psychopathology of everyday life. *Psychoanal. Quart.* 8: 338–353, 1939.

(20) STEKEL, W. Polyphonie des Denkens. *Fortschritte der Sexualwissenschaft und Psychanalyse* 1: 1–16, 1924.

(21) FREUD, S. "Psychoanalyse" und "Libidolehre." In: *Gesammelte Schriften.* Wien. Internat. Psychoanal. Verl. 11: 201–273, 1928.

(22) FREUD, S. Recommendations for physicians on the psycho-analytic method of treatment. Pp. 323–333. In: *Collected Papers,* vol. II. London, Hogarth, 1924. First publ. in *Zentralblatt Psychoanal.* 2: 483–489, 1912.

(23) FREUD, S. Three contributions to the theory of sex. Pp. 553–629. In: *The basic writings of Sigmund Freud.* 1001 pp. Ed. Brill, A. A. New York, Modern Libr., 1938.

(24) WERNER, H. *Comparative psychology of mental development.* 510 pp. New York, Harper, 1940.

(25) VARENDONCK, J. *The psychology of day-dreams.* 367 pp. New York, Macmillan, 1921.

(26) JELGERSMA, G. Psychoanalytischer Beitrag zu einer Theorie des Gefuehls. *Internat. Z. Psychoanal.* 7: 1–8, 1921.

(27) FREUD, S. *Beyond the pleasure principle.* 90 pp. Trans. Hubback, C. F. M. publ. London, Internat. Psychoanal. Press, 1922. *Jenseits des Lustprinzips.* Vienna, Internat. Psychoanal., 1920.

(28) FREUD, S. Metapsychological supplement to the theory of dreams. Pp. 137–151. In: *Collected Papers,* vol. IV, 508 pp. London, Hogarth, 1925. First publ. in *Internat. Z. Psychoanal.* 4: 277–287, 1916–1918.

(29) FREUD, S. Instincts and their vicissitudes. Pp. 60–83. In: *Collected Papers,* vol. IV. 508 pp. London, Hogarth, 1925. First publ. in *Internat. Z. Psychoanal.* Bd. 3, 1915.

(30) FREUD, S. The unconscious. pp. 98–136. In: *Collected Papers,* vol. IV. 508 pp. London, Hogarth, 1925.

(31) FREUD, S. Repression. pp. 84–97. In: *Collected Papers,* vol. IV. 508 pp. London, Hogarth, 1925.

(32) BIBRING, E. Zur Entwicklung und Problematik der Triebtheorie. *Imago.* Heft. 2. 22: 147–176, 1936. The development and problems of the theory of the instincts. *Internat. J. Psychoanal.* 22: 102–132, 1941.

(33) JONES, E. The classification of the instincts. *Brit. J. Psychol.* 14: 256, 1924.

(34) FREUD, S. Formulations regarding the two principles in mental functioning. Pp. 13–21. In: *Collected Papers,* Vol. IV. 508 pp. London, Hogarth, 1925.

(35) FREUD, S. *The Ego and the Id.* 88 pp. London, Hogarth, 1927. First publ. Wien, Internat. Psychoanal. Verl., 1923, 77 pp.

Chapter VI

THE CONTRIBUTIONS OF HYPNOSIS

Hypnotic experimentation called attention to a great variety of memory phenomena; hypnotic hypermnesia, posthypnotic amnesia, posthypnotic suggestion—specifically, the "remembering" implied in the execution of the suggestion—are the general names under which many of these phenomena have been subsumed. We shall not enter into a detailed discussion of the field of hypnosis, most of which is still a no-man's land.[1] We shall summarize briefly the investigations, facts, and opinions which seem to have a bearing on our problem. Our discussion will revolve around five questions:

(1) Are hypnotic phenomena emotional phenomena, and thus may hypnotic memory phenomena be considered as effects of emotions on memory?

(2) What is the relationship of the phenomenon of posthypnotic amnesia to our problem?

(3) What is the relationship of the phenomenon of hypnotic hypermnesia to our problem?

(4) What is the relationship of posthypnotic suggestion to our problem?

(5) What have the experiments on drug hypnosis contributed to our problem?

1. Affective Factors in Hypnosis

Whether the spectacular memory phenomena of hypnosis can contribute to our knowledge of the "emotional influence on memory" depends on the nature of hypnotic phenomena in general. Hypnosis has been considered on the basis of three explanatory theories: "transference," "dissociation," and "conditioning." Of these, the first and second suggest that hypnosis is an affective phenomenon. A discussion of the nature of these theories will clarify the role of emotions in hypnotic phenomena.

Transference. Bernheim[2] (5) and Forel (6) asserted that suggestion is

---

[1] See Young's three surveys (1, 2, 3) and Hull's work (4).

[2] "Hypnosis is not a pathological state nor does it create new functions or supernatural phenomena; it simply exaggerates what is already happening in the waking state, and it reinforces by means of the psychic changes connected with it, the suggestibility which we all possess normally to a certain degree." (p. 140)

the essence of hypnosis.[3] Bleuler (7) maintained that "suggestion is an affective process" (p. 53); by this he meant to characterize the relation of the two persons, the first giving and the second receiving the suggestion. Jones (8), discussing Bleuler's views, stated that not the content of the "verbal suggestion" but the affective process, which may be termed "affective suggestion," is the more fundamental of the two and the necessary basis of the former (p. 342). Freud, in his "Three Contributions to the Theory of Sex" (9), expressed this relation in psychoanalytical terms:

"... the blind obedience evinced by the hypnotized subject to the hypnotist causes me to think that the nature of hypnosis is to be found in the unconscious fixation of the libido on the person of the hypnotizer (by means of the masochistic component of the sexual instinct)" (p. 564, footnote).

Ferenczi (10) attributed the dominant affective factor in hypnosis to the 'parental complex." He wrote:

"The capacity to be hypnotized and influenced by suggestion depends on the possibility of transference taking place, or—more openly expressed—on the positive, although unconscious, sexual attitude that the person being hypnotized takes up in regard to the hypnotizer; the transference, however, like every 'object love,' has its deepest roots in the repressed parent complex." (p. 57)

Jones (8) was even more blunt: " ... suggestion and hypnosis ... are merely examples of transference"[4] (p. 353). Schilder (13) stated the psychoanalytic point of view in a manner more familiar to the psychologist, and in a terminology similar to that used in this survey; he stressed the affective nature of hypnotic phenomena:

"The phenomena of hypnosis have not the significance of isolated peculiarities ... all the phenomena elicited by hypnosis may be elicited by affects. ... One can say that the drive-attitudes (Trieb-Einstellung) and affects are responsible for the phenomena of hypnosis. Our drives are phylogenetic survivals. Biological facts lead to the conclusion that in hypnosis it is a special drive attitude which elicits the phenomena which otherwise are elicited by affective life." (p. 10)

---

[3] Both Hull (4) and Young (3) found in their surveys no unanimity of opinion in this respect, although a great number of experiments favored this view. Of special interest are Young's (11, 12) experiments attempting to disprove the importance of rapport.

[4] Jones defined transference as follows:
"By the term 'transference' is meant that displacement on to the physician of various affects (feelings) that really belong to some other person." (p. 309)
This definition is a simplification, disregarding the fact that not simple affects but affect-constellations are displaced and that this displacement lacks an objective basis.

Concerning the nature of these affects he maintained:

"Many people seek in vain the passions which would fully absorb them . . . hypnosis creates the pleasure of conditionless devotion, and puts into reality the ideal of wishless slavery (Hoerigkeit). The hypnotizer is for the subject but a pretense, but an occasion to fulfill his wishes." (p. 24)

R. W. White (14) formulated the problem of the affective nature of hypnosis as one of "motivation in hypnosis." Expressing views similar to those of psychoanalysis, he stated them in terms of Murray's "need and press" theory. He emphasized especially that the needs of the hypnotic subject, rather than the hypnotist's power, are the basis of hypnotic phenomena.[5]

Dissociation. Janet, Charcot, Sidis, Prince, McDougall, and others were in agreement in regarding hypnosis as a dissociation phenomenon. It is well known that these authors considered dissociation to be the basis of hysteria, and thus its relation to affective processes need not be further discussed here.[6] It should be mentioned that the dissociation-theory was applied to the so-called "dual-personalities," which present an unusually interesting memory problem.

The *conditioned-reflex theory* of hypnosis[7] would probably not agree that hypnosis is an affective phenomenon. As this theory does not consider any of the emotional aspects of hypnosis, it does not concern our topic and will not be discussed here.

This brief discussion has made it evident that hypnotic phenomena have been viewed in the main as affective phenomena; we may therefore expect that the following discussion of hypnotic memory phenomena will shed some light on the "influence of emotions on memory."

[5] "If we divest from these theories the language of the libido hypothesis, we may restate them substantially as follows. The hypnotic situation, with its general atmosphere of strangeness, its special press of dominance, and its peculiar relation between subject and operator, tends to arouse latent needs which were more active in childhood than they can be at the subject's present age. One of these motives is the need for *love* such as might have been gratified by adoring parents when their child behaved well. The subject momentarily loves the hypnotist as he once loved one or both of his parents, and he wants the hypnotist, as he wanted the parents, to return this love. Another motive is the need for *abasement* or *compliance*, the echo of a relation with parents of a more stern, forbidding disposition. The subject momentarily stands in awe of the hypnotist, and yields to his demands rather than risk his displeasure and wrath. The active agent in hypnotic behavior is the motive force of these latent needs rather than any power in the hypnotist, who serves at most as a kind of projection screen. It is safe to add that if the situation awakens latent anxiety or aggression hypnosis is effectually prevented." (p. 155)
[6] For the discussion of the concept "dissociation," see pp. 212–214.
[7] See Hull (4).

2. POSTHYPNOTIC AMNESIA[8]

The term "posthypnotic amnesia" designates the general tendency of the hypnotic subject to forget the events of the trance after having emerged from it.. Several reservations to this statement should be made explicit, however. (1) The hypnotist can successfully suggest that no posthypnotic amnesia develop.[9] (2) The hypnotist's insistence in the posthypnotic state may also make the subject remember the happenings of the trance state.[10] (3) The amnesized experiences have a tendency to recur in dreams, fantasies, etc.[11] (4) The relearning in the normal state of material learned in the trance state shows a significant saving.[12] (5) In paired-associate recall, and in recognition and relearning experiments, the amnesized experience sometimes recurs "from nowhere."[13] (6) The amnesized material may be remembered in a subsequent trance state.[14] (7) Spontaneously-emerging trance states in which posthypnotic suggestions are executed and in which the material originally amnesized is remembered are themselves later amnesized.[15]

Schilder and Kauders (15) maintain that posthypnotic amnesia is due to the affective factors underlying the hypnotic state:

"... the motive of amnesia ... must be sought in peculiarity of content. Obviously, the hypnotized is ashamed of his infantile-masochistic adjustment and denies the hypnosis in order to conceal the adjustment. Very frequently, therefore,

---

[8] The results described in the following sections are dependent on the depth of hypnosis, and in general are valid only with subjects who are able to reach the somnambulistic stage of hypnosis.

[9] Schilder and Kauders (15): "Amnesia may cease as a result of a new hypnosis ... together with the simultaneous shout of an order not to forget the content of the hypnosis after waking, or the order may simply be issued in hypnosis that everything be remembered after waking." (p. 60)

[10] Schilder and Kauders (15): " ... post-hypnotic amnesia may yield as a result of persistent questioning, questioning accompanied by suggestive procedures (such as laying the hand on the forehead or stroking the latter." (p. 60) For similar facts see Erickson (16, Account II).

[11] Schilder and Kauders (15): "Not infrequently, the content of the hypnosis will reappear in a dream, although the patient may not always be able to indicate precisely the origin of this content. The content of the hypnosis may also come to light in the form of a spontaneously arising notion." (p. 60)

[12] Strickler (17) demonstrated that a relearning test in the normal state reduces the amnesia by fifty per cent.

[13] Strickler (17) demonstrated that while amnesia is a hundred per cent for general recall, paired-associate recall which gives clues reduces this amnesia to ninety-seven per cent.

[14] See Erickson (16, Accounts I and III).

[15] See Erickson and Erickson (18)

we find hypnotized persons indignantly denying that they have been hypnotized." (p. 60)[16]

A further contribution to the understanding of the nature of posthypnotic amnesia is given by Freud in his *"History of the Psychoanalytic Movement"* (19), where he explains that the repression encountered in the psychoanalytical procedure in the form of resistance is concealed by hypnosis for the duration of the trance.[17] He maintains that the cause of the amnesia is the repression which is temporarily lessened by the trance and then reinstated upon emergence from the trance; the trance happenings are included in this reinstatement. The nature of repression and its relation to affects have been discussed in Chapter V.

According to the material surveyed, the phenomenon of posthypnotic amnesia is similar to the process of repression. It is maintained that the infantile masochistic adjustment in the hypnotic trance is, for the subject, sufficiently intolerable to account for the forgetting of all the experiences accompanying it. The hypnotist is able to dissolve this amnesia by another suggestion which makes for a change in affective attitude; the suggestion of the hypnotist probably appeals to strong affective tendencies —that is, the masochistic adjustment—which revive the forgotten experiences in consciousness. In other words, the rejection by the subject of his masochistic tendencies results in the forgetting of the trance experiences; the acceptance of them—when enforced by the hypnotist— results in the remembering of them. The fact that posthypnotic amnesia can be resolved demonstrates that the forgotten material is not lost; it is inhibited by "emotional factors" which under certain conditions may yield to other "emotional factors," and allow for the reappearance of the forgotten material in consciousness.[18]

[16] Experimental evidence to this effect seems to be offered by P. C. Young (11), who concluded: "It seems . . . that in absence of a suggestion to remember, posthypnotic amnesia is directly proportional with the amount of *rapport*, and consequently inversely proportional to the number of autosuggestions carried out in hypnosis." (p. 139)

[17] "One is then confronted with a resistance which opposes and blocks the analytic work by causing failures of memory. This resistance was always covered by the use of hypnosis; the history of psychoanalysis proper, therefore, starts with the technical innovation of the rejection of hypnosis. The theoretical value of the fact, that this resistance is connected with an amnesia, leads unavoidably to that concept of unconscious psychic activity which is peculiar to psychoanalysis . . . " (p. 939)

[18] The fate of the amnesized memories during the posthypnotic state, and their influence on thought and behavior, have been but rarely investigated. The pertinent demonstrations of Erickson and of Brenman will be mentioned in the section on posthypnotic suggestion in this chapter and in the section on "Affective Organization of Behavior" in Chapter VIII. To our knowledge, the first methodical experimental investigation of the nature of posthypnotic amnesia, and of the effects of the am-

3. Hypnotic Hypermnesia

The phenomenon of hypnotic hypermnesia is described by Hull (4) as follows: " ... the alleged capacity of subjects in the hypnotic trance to recall events which are completely lost to the ordinary waking memory ... is called *hypermnesia*" (p. 105). The phenomenon was originally observed by psychiatrists. Bernheim made extensive use of it for therapeutic purposes. Freud and Breuer (20) maintained that a hysterical symptom could be traced back to an original traumatic experience, and made use of hypnotic hypermnesia to obtain an account of that experience.[19] Some investigators advanced doubts as to the actual occurrence of the traumatic events thus recollected, and correctly argued that the therapeutic effect of such "recollections" of traumatic experiences is no proof of their experiential verity.[20] In some reported cases, the hypnotic recollections could be checked against diaries of the subject's relatives, and were found authentic;[21] in other cases, systematic historical investigation found the occurrence of the "recollected" event to be improbable.[22] Erickson (24) reports a case in which a subject re-experienced hypnotically a significant experience in every detail. Re-experiencing or hypnotic reorientation—or, as it is recently referred to, hypnotic regression—is considered by Erickson to be the most reliable method in obtaining hypnotic hypermnesia.[23]

The phenomenon of hypnotic hypermnesia does not seem to be limited

---

nesized material on behavior and memory, is being conducted at present by M. Brenman. This experimentation employs the topological techniques of Lewin, aiming at the establishment of the topology of the hypnotic state in order to derive from it the topology of posthypnotic amnesia and its effects.

[19] "Stimulated by a chance observation, we have for a number of years been investigating the most varied types and symptoms of hysteria with reference to the exciting cause, the event which evoked the phenomenon in question for the first time, often many years before. In the great majority of cases it is impossible to discover this starting-point by straightforward interrogation of the patient, be it ever so thorough; partly because it is often a matter of experiences which the patient finds it disagreeable to discuss, but chiefly because he really does not remember and has no idea of the causal connection between the exciting occurrence and the pathological phenomenon. As a rule it is necessary to hypnotize the patient and under hypnosis to arouse recollections relating to the time when the symptom first appeared; one can then succeed in revealing this connection in the clearest and most convincing manner." (20, p. 24)

[20] See Hull (4).

[21] See Young (21); also Hadfield (22).

[22] See Freud (23).

[23] Erickson (24): " ... neither detailed questioning in the normal waking state nor instruction to recall fully these past events in a state of ordinary deep hypnosis served to secure the same degree of accuracy and amount of detail as did the process of reorientation." (p. 1282)

to traumatic events.   Moll (25), Bramwell (26),[24] Wingfield (27) and Mc-
Dougall (28) maintained, and reported supporting evidence, that early
childhood experiences long forgotten are recalled in the hypnotic trance;
the experiments on hypnotic regression[25] also appear to confirm these
findings.   Hull stated that these phenomena could be explained on the
basis of either of two hypotheses:

"It is very generally believed by psychopathologists that the memory traces in
the case of hysterical amnesias are not particularly weaker than those which mediate
ordinary waking recall.   It is supposed, rather, that the trauma or emotional complex, whatever its nature, somehow inhibits or blocks the recall; that it interferes
with the action of excitatory tendencies which would otherwise bring about perfectly
normal recall.   On this hypothesis, then, hyponosis merely removes the block or
inhibition in the case of hysterical or traumatic amnesias and thus permits the ex-
istent excitatory tendencies to function in a normal manner.

"It is possible, however, to frame an alternative, or at least a supplementary,
hypothesis.   According to this second supposition, the greater facility of recall
alleged in cases such as are cited by Wingfield and Bramwell . . . as well as the results reported by Stalnaker and Riddle, may be accounted for by assuming a genuine
lowering of the threshold of recall in the trance.   If such a general lowering of the
recall threshold takes place automatically in the trance, on some primitive physiological basis, it should operate to facilitate the recall of recently learned material as
well as of relatively remote material.   Fortunately, we have in the very carefully
controlled work of Huse, an experimental test of this lower-threshold hypothesis."
(pp. 115–116)

Huse's experiment (29), to which Hull refers, used nonsense material and
showed no hypnotic hypermnesia.   Neither Mitchell's (30) experiment,
which used number material and the method of retroactive inhibition,
nor Young's (21) experiment, which asked for recall of the furnishings of a
room incidentally seen, showed hypermnesia.   Stalnaker and Riddle's
(31) experiment asking for recall in trance and waking states of poetry
learned in the remote past, and Young's (21) experiment asking for recall
of early childhood experiences, demonstrated significant hypnotic hypermnesia.   To explain this discrepancy of results, Hull concluded that
the "threshold of recall is lowered" for remotely-learned, but not for
recently-learned, material; however, he finds this result paradoxical.   The
material seems to allow for a different interpretation: the nonsense material did not show hypnotic hypermnesia, but the meaningful material
did.   This conclusion is supported by the findings of White, Fox, and Harris (32), who tested hypnotic and waking recall of recently-learned and
remotely-learned meaningful and nonsense material.[26]   We have already

[24] See Hull (4, p. 110)
[25] See Young's (3) survey of the pertinent experiments.
[26] "In view of such considerations we do not believe that our results can be explained in terms of an hypnotic lowering of retroactive inhibition." (p. 100)
"Bartlett has proposed that remembering is typically the reconstruction of past

seen in the experimental material surveyed in Chapter III that the operation of the "emotional factor" was always more obvious in relevant material than in nonsense material.

In this connection, Freud's view that hypnosis lessens and conceals repression is again pertinent. The manner in which this temporary diminishing of repression makes for hypermnesia is evident, if the role of repression in forgetting is considered.[27] Freud's conception of the relationship between hypnosis and the lessening of repression sheds some light on the affective character of hypnotic hypermnesia.

4. Posthypnotic Suggestion

The term "posthypnotic suggestion" describes a subject's execution in the waking state of a command given by the hypnotizer during the trance state; this execution occurs at a given time or signal, without the subject's being aware of the actual origin of his behavior. Erickson and Erickson (18) maintain that the execution of posthypnotic suggestion takes place during a short revival of the trance state.[28] This statement implies the affective background of the unconscious remembering which is displayed in the execution of a posthypnotic suggestion. The phenomenon of posthypnotic suggestion was used by Erickson (33) to produce parapraxes experimentally. The relevance of parapraxes to our problem, and the manifestation in them of unconscious strivings—"affective tendencies"— have already been discussed. In Erickson's experiments, and in Bren-

experiences out of such images and fragments of 'schemata' as are retained. Obviously there is little scope for such reconstruction if the experimenter has already given the whole cue for a strictly limited response. If this be a correct interpretation, the choice by Huse of paired nonsense associates for a crucial experiment on hypnotic hypermnesia was indeed unfortunate. It is possible that recall can be improved by hypnosis only so far as opportunity is offered for the active reconstruction described by Bartlett." (pp. 100–101)

"One of our subjects, in an unsolicited introspection, declared that under hypnosis, in contrast to the wide-awake state, the poetry 'seemed to flow together nicely.' He thereby acknowledged that the material underwent a certain spontaneous reconstruction while he himself remained relatively passive." (p. 101)

"We do not believe that the hypermnesia obtained by hypnosis is unique for this state . . . It would be interesting to parallel our procedure with experiments in which relaxation took the place of hypnosis and suggestion was kept at a minimum. Until then, we doubt the wisdom of further speculation." (p. 102)

[27] New investigations on the subject of hypnotic hypermnesia are being conducted by M. Brenman. These investigations use the recollection of well-known fairy-tales for material. See p. 252.

[28] " . . . the posthypnotic response consists of the *spontaneous and invariable development, as an integral part of the performance of the suggested posthypnotic act, of a self-limited, usually brief, hypnotic trance.*" (18, p. 104)

man's similar experiment, parapraxes were produced by the hypnotic suggestion to the subjects of socially-unacceptable ideas; it was demonstrated experimentally that the parapraxes were a result of the interference of these unacceptable ideas, and that hypnotically-implanted ideas—that is, posthypnotic suggestions—influence memory processes just as affects do. These experiments will be discussed in greater detail in Chapter VIII.

5. Drug Hypnoses

Some contribution to our problem has been made by the experiments with drug hypnosis. Lindeman's (34) experiments with sodium amytal are pertinent: he showed that while the sodium amytal "twilight-state" did not change the personality, it relieved inhibitions—though only temporarily—and thus made possible the communication of information about conflicts of emotional import which could not be communicated in the normal state.[29] Merloo (35), Berrington (36), and others reported similar findings with sodium amytal, other barbiturate derivatives, and alcohol.

Whether the effect of these drugs can be justifiably called hypermnesia remains questionable. Their contribution to our problem is that the removal of affective inhibition brings into consciousness and makes possible the communication of affectively-toned material which was previously not communicated. To speak of non-communication as a memory phenomenon may seem far-fetched; but reports of some non-communicative patients after their recovery often reveal that they felt "blank" and could remember nothing in the course of their illness.

Drug hypnosis was also used by Schilder, Kauders and others to resolve amnesias. This application was frequently successful and is another contribution to the hypermnesia elicited by drug hypnosis. The pertinent literature will be summarized in Chapter VII.

Although the immediate effect of drugs is obviously physiological, their influence on repression, memory, and communication is psychological. Thus drug hypnosis leads to a psychosomatic problem of memory functioning. This field still awaits exploration.

6. Summary

a. Hypnosis has been shown to be an affectively-motivated phenomenon, whether a transference or a dissociation theory is adopted. Thus, hypnotic memory phenomena have a bearing on the problem of the influence of emotions on memory.

---

[29] Lindeman wrote: "The shifting of the emotional state along the depression-elation scale in the direction of elation was quite evident in each case." (pp. 1087–1088) "Patients, as well as normal individuals, under the influence of the drug are freed from *that* factor which prevents them from communicating their thoughts and from reaching out for human contacts." (p. 1089)

b. Posthypnotic amnesia, hypnotic hypermnesia, and the execution of posthypnotic suggestions are the memory phenomena of hypnosis. The literature pertaining to their affective motivation has been discussed.

c. It has been indicated that posthypnotic amnesia can be resolved by sufficiently strong affective influence; that hypermnesia refers only to meaningful material and increases with its affective relevance; that the execution of posthypnotic suggestion occurs in a spontaneous brief revival of the trance state, and that such suggestion influences memory as do affects.

d. The contributions of drug hypnosis lead into the field of the psychosomatic implications of memory processes.

REFERENCES

(1) YOUNG, P. C. A general review of the literature on hypnotism. *Psychol. Bull.* 24: 540–560, 1927.

(2) YOUNG, P. C. A general review of the literature on hypnotism and suggestion. *Psychol. Bull.* 28: 367–391, 1931.

(3) YOUNG, P. C. Experimental hypnotism: a review. *Psychol. Bull.* 38: 92–104, 1941.

(4) HULL, C. L. *Hypnosis and suggestibility. An experimental approach.* 416 pp. New York, Appleton, 1933.

(5) BERNHEIM, H. *Die Suggestion und ihre Heilwirkung.* Trans. Freud, S. 218 pp. Leipzig, Wien, Deuticke, 2d ed., 1896.

(6) FOREL, A. *Hypnotism; or suggestion and psychotherapy: a study of the psychological, psycho-physiological and therapeutic aspects of hypnotism.* 382 pp. Trans. Armit, H. W. London, Rebman, 1906.

(7) BLEULER, E. *Affectivity, suggestibility, paranoia.* 121 pp. Trans. Ricksher, C. Utica State Hosp., 1912. Also *N. Y. State Hosp. Bull.*, 4, 481–601, 1912.

(8) JONES, E. *Papers on psychoanalysis.* 731 pp. New York, Wood, 3rd ed., 1923.

(9) FREUD, S. *Three contributions to the theory of sex.* Pp. 551–629. In: *The basic writings of Sigmund Freud.* 1001 pp. Ed. Brill. A. A. New York, Modern Libr., 1938. *Drei Abhandlungen zur Sexualtheorie*, 101 pp. Leipzig, Wien, Deuticke, 3rd ed., 1915.

(10) FERENCZI, S. Introjektion und Uebertragung. *Jhb. Psychoanal.* I. *Contributions to Psychoanalysis.* 288 pp. Boston, Badger, 1916.

(11) YOUNG, P. C. Is *rapport* an essential characteristic of hypnosis? *J. Abn. Soc. Psychol.* 22: 130–139, 1927.

(12) YOUNG, P. C. The nature of hypnosis: as indicated by the presence or absence of post-hypnotic amnesia and *rapport*. *J. Abn. Soc. Psychol.* 22: 372–382, 1928.

(13) SCHILDER, P. *Ueber das Wesen der Hypnose.* 32 pp. Berlin, Springer, 1922.

(14) WHITE, R. W. An analysis of motivation in hypnosis. *J. gen. Psychol.* 24: 145–162, 1941.

(15) SCHILDER, P. AND KAUDERS, C. *Hypnosis.* 118 pp. Trans. Rothenberg, S. New York, Nerv. Ment. Dis. Publ., 1927.

(16) ERICKSON, M. H. Clinical forms and varieties of hypnotic amnesia. 9 pp. Unpubl. paper, by courtesy of the author, 1941.

(17) STRICKLER, C. B. A quantitative study of post-hypnotic amnesia. *J. Abn. Soc. Psychol.* 24: 108–119, 1929.

(18) ERICKSON, M. H., AND ERICKSON, E. M. Concerning the nature and character of post-hypnotic behavior. *J. gen. Psychol.* 24: 95–133, 1941.

(19) FREUD, S. *The history of the psychoanalytic movement.* Pp. 931–977. In: *The basic writings of Sigmund Freud.* 1001 pp. Ed. Brill, A. A. New York, Modern Libr., 1938. Zur Geschichte der psychoanalytischen Bewegung. *Jhb. Psychoanal.* 6: 207–259, 1914.

(20) FREUD, S., AND BREUER, J. On the psychical mechanism of hysterical phenomena. Pp. 24–41. In: *Collected Papers*, vol. I. London, Internat. Psychoanal. Press, 1924. First publ. in *Neurol. Zentralbl.* 1893, Nos. 1 and 2.

(21) YOUNG, P. C. An experimental study of mental and physical functions in the normal and hypnotic states. *Amer. J. Psychol.* 36: 214–232, 1925.

(22) HADFIELD, J. A. The reliability of infantile memories. *Brit. J. Med. Psychol.* 8: 87–111, 1928.

(23) FREUD, S. *From the history of an infantile neurosis.* Pp. 473–605. In: *Collected Papers, vol. 3.* 607 pp. London, Hogarth, 1925. *Aus der Geschichte einer infantilen Neurose.* Pp. 439–567. In: *Gesammelte Schriften.* Vol. 8, 567 Pp. Vienna, Internat. Psychoanal. Verl., 1924.

(24) ERICKSON, M. H. Development of apparent unconsciousness during hypnotic reliving of a traumatic experience. *Arch. Neurol. Psychiat.* 38: 1282–1288, 1937.

(25) MOLL, A. *Hypnotism, including a study of the chief points of psychotherapeutics and occultism.* 610 pp. Trans. Hopkirk, A. F. New York, Scribner, 1909.

(26) BRAMWELL, J. M. *Hypnotism.* 480 pp. Philadelphia, Lippinscott, 3rd ed., 1930.

(27) WINGFIELD, H. E. *An introduction to the study of hypnotism, experimental and therapeutic.* 195 pp. London, Baillière, 1920.

(28) McDOUGALL, W. *Outline of abnormal psychology.* 572 pp. New York, Scribner, 1926.

(29) HUSE, B. Does the hypnotic trance favor the recall of faint memories? *J. exp. Psychol.* 13: 519–529, 1930.

(30) MITCHELL, M. B. Retroactive inhibition and hypnosis. *J. gen. Psychol.* 7: 343–359, 1932.

(31) STALNAKER, J. M., AND RIDDLE, E. E. The effect of hypnosis on long delayed recall. *J. gen. Psychol.* 6: 429–440, 1932.

(32) WHITE, R. W., FOX, G. F., AND HARRIS, W. W. Hypnotic hypermnesia for recently learned material. *J. Abn. Soc. Psychol.* 35: 88–103, 1940.

(33) ERICKSON, M. H. Experimental demonstration of the psychopathology of everyday life. *Psychoanal. Quart.* 8: 338–353, 1939.

(34) LINDEMAN, E. Psychological changes in normal and abnormal individuals under the influence of sodium amytal. *Amer. J. Psychiat.* 11: 1083–1091, 1932.

(35) MERLOO, A. M. On the action of barbituric acid compounds. A contribution to the prolonged narcosis treatment of mental symptoms. *J. Ment. Sci.* 79: 336–367, 1933.

(36) BERRINGTON, W. P. A psycho-pharmacological study of schizophrenia, with particular reference to the mode of action of cardiasol, sodium amytal and alcohol in schizophrenic stupor. *J. Ment. Sci.* 85: 406–488, 1939.

CHAPTER VII

CONTRIBUTIONS OF THE STUDY OF PATHOLOGICAL MEMORY PHENOMENA

1. AMNESIA—A PSYCHOSOMATIC PROBLEM

The thesis that pathology of the organism is our best informant concerning the normal functions of the organism is generally accepted in medical science. Janet (1) applied it to the problem of memory when he wrote:

"The psychologists in their descriptions admit of no other elementary phenomena of memory than conservation and reproduction. We think that they are wrong, and that disease decomposes and analyses memory better than psychology." (p. 102)

It will not surprise us to find that the relation of emotions to memory, to which experimental psychology has only recently paid attention and of whose existence the experimental proof must be pieced together painstakingly, was accepted as obvious by psychiatrists and those physicians who dealt with pathological memory phenomena. Pathological memory phenomena are probably more multifarious than the memory phenomena dealt with by general psychology; yet our systematic understanding of these pathological phenomena is much less developed than our understanding of memory phenomena in general. The previous chapters have shown that our systematic knowledge of memory was until recently limited to those phenomena which were amenable to investigation in terms of association-psychology. Psychopathological memory phenomena in general, however, have hardly been thus amenable.[1] The organismic and Gestalt points of view have not yet penetrated it deep enough to give us a systematic view of pathological memory phenomena, even though the memory investigations conducted from these points of view contribute toward systematizing the field of memory-pathology.

A general non-mechanistic theory of psychopathological memory phenomena has not yet been developed; but the realization that these phenomena are at least partly due to pathology of emotions was recognized by psychiatrists, and became a commonplace after the discoveries of the French psychiatrists Charcot, Janet, and Bernheim, and of Freud and the

[1] In this regard consider the fruitless experiments of Barnes (2) and Liljencrants (3), and those surveyed by Hunt (4), which attempted to investigate the memory functioning of psychotics by methods of classical memory experimentation.

psychoanalytic school.   The Freudian discoveries made many phenomena
of the pathology of memory meaningful.   Specific forgettings, wholesale
amnesias, peculiar memory distortions, fixed false rememberings, all have
lost their incidental character and have become understandable in psycho-
dynamic terms.   It would be an exaggeration to state that the field of
pathology of memory has been systematically explored in the wake of the
Freudian discoveries; but the opinion that many memory disturbances are
of "functional" or "emotional" origin has become accepted.   It might
even be said to have been accepted too facilely, and uncritical application
of this view frequently made for an indifference to search into the authentic
nature of the phenomena to which the view was applied, with the result
that even the mechanism of the assuredly "emotional" disturbances of
memory has not been investigated with sufficient care.

The etiology and dynamics of psychogenic amnesias are problems to
which the answer of current psychiatric and psychological literature can
hardly be considered conclusive.   The pertinent literature consists chiefly
of more or less detailed case-histories, interpreted in terms of some current
theory of psychodynamics.   These case-histories culminate in the onset
of the amnesia.   They do not differ significantly from case-histories which
culminate in a psychosis, a neurotic breakdown, or a suicide.   Excepting
the work of a few pioneering authors, these investigations are neither
intensive nor extensive enough to show a *specific* and *necessary mechanism*
of amnesia in addition to demonstrating merely the presence of sufficient
"emotional" reason for its development.

Even less satisfactory is the situation in those cases where the traumatic
event immediately precipitating the amnesia is of a somatic nature.   In
spite of the somatic etiology, recovery or at least demonstration of
the presence of lost memories is frequently possible; thus arose the question of whether in these cases also a functional-emotional and reversible
element is involved, and whether and how organic amnesias can be differentiated from functional-emotional ones.   It was asked whether the
organic amnesia could be defined as an irreversible memory-loss, and the
functional amnesia as a reversible memory-loss.   The question is whether
an amnesia is reversible even though precipitated by the somatic trauma,
or whether it is reversible because the emotional shock caused by the
somatic trauma is what precipitates the memory disturbance.   No conclusive answer could be given to this problem: on the one hand, amnesias
were encountered which to all appearances were of functional-emotional
origin, and were found to resist all attempts aimed at relieving them;
on the other hand, many amnesias precipitated by somatic traumata
proved to be reversible.   Further complications appeared upon investigation of the life-histories of the subjects of amnesia.   One expected to find
generally a history of maladjustment serving as a basis for the develop-

ment of an amnesia in the wake of the traumatic event. There were many amnesias, organic as well as functional, in which the subject's past history was of an emotional lability discernibly pathogonomic; but also there were amnesias of both types—naturally more of organic—in which no such clear-cut pathogonomic past history could be established. A further complication was contributed by the fact that somatic as well as psychic traumata which precipitated amnesias were frequently found as events precipitating neuroses and psychoses; and there arose the question of what factors in personal history and make-up determine the specific outcome of the traumatic event. Finally, there appears to be an intimate link between hysterical conversion symptoms and functional-hysterical amnesias;[2] such a link would indicate that not only the organic but also the functional amnesias constitute a psychosomatic problem.

Thus, not only the theoretical-methodological immaturity of the investigating methods, but the extreme intricacy of the problem itself made clarification of the role of the emotional factor extremely difficult. It appears that in these disturbances psychic and somatic, functional and organic etiology shade imperceptibly into each other; and where this is the case, the problems are at present least amenable to investigation, inasmuch as the proper methodology has not been developed to attack this interrelation of the psyche and the soma.

2. THREE SURVEYS OF THE PHENOMENA OF MEMORY-PATHOLOGY

Memory functioning is usually viewed as having three phases—registration, retention, and reproduction; and theories explaining memory disturbances had the choice of attributing the disturbance to one of these. As the disturbance becomes perceptible only in reproduction, the choice was determined always by the theoretical viewpoint of the individual investigator. Organically-oriented, non-psychological, and mechanistic investigators chose registration and, to a more limited extent, retention as the disturbed functions; psychologically- and dynamically-oriented observers were inclined to choose the process of reproduction. The extremists of the former group sought the cause of forgetting in an original lack of registration or a decay of traces; the extremists of the latter group maintained that nothing once experienced is truly lost.

We possess three surveys of the field of pathological memory phenomena. Ribot's (6), Schneider's (7), and Gillespie's (8) surveys represent three steps in the development of a psychological understanding of the pathology of memory. Ribot expressed the physiologically-oriented associationist view; Schneider's survey showed the effects of the impact of psycho-

---

[2] See to this effect Jones (5); also pp. 204–205 of this chapter; Janet (1) for instance writes: "In a word, certain amnesias seem to be dependent on anesthesias." (pp. 112 ff.)

analytic discoveries; Gillespie attempted to interpret amnesias by utilizing discoveries of modern general and experimental psychology.

Ribot viewed memory as an emergent phenomenon in which conscious memory is but a special case of biological-organic memory. He accordingly attributed the amnesia of fugue states to a lack of, or extreme weakness of, consciousness in those states.[3] This explanation naturally did not account for the frequent recovery of the memories of the experiences of the fugue states. He attributed the amnesias of organic etiology to the destruction of the traces or of their associative bonds.[4] Only in explaining the reciprocal amnesias of multiple personalities[5] does Ribot overstep his framework to include an emotional factor in explaining the memory disturbance. In this connection, he states that memories are organized around an Ego; he denies the mechanistic view that the identity of this Ego is entirely dependent upon the accumulated body of memories; and he maintains that the core of the Ego is the *coenaesthesis*, a vital, instinct-like, emotional factor, whose periodic alternation explains the reciprocal amnesias of multiple personalities.[6] Ribot does not apply this explanation to other amnesias, but proceeds to a discussion of "progressive amnesias" wherein he states his final conclusion, known as "Ribot's law." According to this law, the destruction of memory is progressive from labile recent memories to fixed old memories, from more unstable conscious memories to more stable organic memories.[7] This law is based on a theory of

[3] "As to its psychological interpretation, there are two possible hypotheses. We may conclude, either that the period of mental automatism is not accompanied by consciousness, in which case the amnesia does not need explanation, as, nothing having been produced, nothing could be conserved or reproduced; or consciousness does exist, but in so weak a form that amnesia ensues. I believe that the second hypothesis is the true one in the majority of cases." (pp. 73–74)

[4] "The physiological cause of amnesia in this group is only amenable to hypothesis; probably it varies with each case. At first, the faculty for registering new impressions is temporarily suspended; as they appear, states of consciousness vanish and leave no trace. But preceding recollections, registered for weeks, months, years— where are they?" (p. 96)

"Thus two suppositions are possible: either the registration of anterior states is effaced, or, the conservation of anterior states persisting, their power of revivification by association with the present is destroyed. It is impossible to decide arbitrarily between these two hypotheses." (pp. 96–97)

[5] For a discussion of these amnesias see pp. 206 ff., 211 ff.

[6] "It would seem, according to this view, that the identity of the *Ego* depended entirely upon the memory. But such a conception is only partial. Beneath the unstable compound phenomenon in all its protean phases of growth, degeneration, and reproduction, there is a something that remains: and this something is the undefined consciousness, the product of all the vital processes, constituting bodily perception, and which is expressed in one word—the *coenaesthesis*." (p. 108)

[7] "We thus see that the progressive destruction of memory follows a logical order —a law. *It advances progressively from the unstable to the stable.* It begins with the

destruction and again leaves unexplained the frequent recovery of the "losses," although Ribot described recoveries and knew that they follow the opposite route, from stable to labile. Ribot included among memory disturbances what he called losses of organic memory, such as aphasias and agnosias. Janet, Charcot, and others were also inclined to such a classification, and in their writings on hysterical aphasia, agnosia, and kindred phenomena, they offered ample proof that emotional factors play a significant role in these disturbances; we shall not discuss them here, however, as we have attempted to limit our investigation so as to make it possible to view memory as one aspect of thought processes.

Schneider's survey, both in its material and in its implicit theoretical view, stresses disturbances of reproduction rather than of registration. Material is adduced to show that typical anterograde amnesia—the type in which disturbance of registration and retention was considered prevalent, since it is the recent experiences which are lost—is extremely rare. Material is juxtaposed to show that the Korsakow syndrome is not merely a disturbance of registration and retention. The literature on hypnotic and drug-hypnotic restoration of amnesias is surveyed, showing that much of what was considered lost can be recovered. Learning experiments which measured saving in relearning are quoted, showing that even irrecoverable memory material cannot be considered totally lost. Schilder's experiments and views, according to which nothing once experienced is ever lost, are given eminence in the views implied in the material thus surveyed, and even more clearly in the organization of the survey the impact of Freudian psychology is perceptible. Thus, Schneider differentiates between quantitative and qualitative memory disturbances. His views of the quantitative disturbances have been described. The qualita-

most recent recollections, which, lightly impressed upon the nervous elements, rarely repeated and consequently having no permanent associations, represent organization in its feeblest form. It ends with the sensorial, instinctive memories, which, become a permanent and integral part of the organism, represents organization in its most highly developed stage. From the first term of the series to the last the movement of amnesia is governed by natural forces, and follows the path of least resistance—that is to say, of least organization. Thus pathology confirms what we have already postulated of the memory, viz., that the process of organization is variable and is comprised between two extreme limits: the new state—organic registration.

"This law, which I shall designate as *the law of regression or reversion*, seems to me to be a natural conclusion from the observed facts. However, that all doubts and objections may be removed, it will perhaps be well to subject the law to further test. If memory in the process of decay follows invariably the path just indicated, it should follow the same path in a contrary direction in the process of growth; forms which are the last to disappear should be the first to manifest themselves, since they are the most stable and the synthesis progresses from the lower to the higher." (pp. 121–122)

tive disturbances—allomnesias and pseudomnesias[8]—are dealt with in a manner implying, but not stating explicitly, their "emotional origin."

Gillespie in his survey, conceived in the framework of the concepts of the psychologist Bartlett (9), views registration disturbances as unimportant, retention disturbances as of peripheral importance even in the Korsakow syndrome, and reproduction disturbances as focal. In addition to this emphasis on reproduction, his taking into consideration other factors which play an important role in memory functioning marks his attempt to utilize as much as possible of the present-day knowledge of psychology and psychopathology to elucidate the problem of amnesia. These other factors enumerated by Gillespie[9] may be condensed into the following three

[8] Allomnesias are defined as memory disturbances "in which the memories, although not altogether false, are distorted, being 'different' from what they ought to be according to the facts." (p. 521)   Pseudomnesias are defined as memory disturbances "in which presentations carry falsely a memory character." (p. 522)

An especially lucid example of allomnesia was described by Pick (10): a patient while talking with the physician suddenly jumped on a passing attendant and after assaulting him severely tumbled back holding his head, pale in face, crying: "Jesus Maria, this guy killed me, he broke my skull." Afterwards he did not remember having assaulted the attendant and complained of him, stating that he would murder and stab the man who assaulted him. (pp. 256–257)

[9] In the following table Gillespie summarized the memory factors, and enumerated the psychiatric conditions in which these are disturbed and become recognizable as individual factors in memory functioning.

Factors in Remembering	Conditions in Which These Factors Are Interfered with or Appear in Isolation
(a) Registration	Acute organic reaction type (delirium); manic excitement (inattention); hysteria (global inattention)
(b) Retention	Organic reaction type in general
(c) Recall	
(1) simple and elementary	Organic reaction type (severe degree)
(2) as a voluntary act	Psychogenic conditions, e.g., hysteria; certain forms of organic reaction type, e.g., trauma to the head; Korsakow's psychosis; epilepsy
(d) Time Sense	Various psychoses with depersonalization (?); Korsakow's psychosis (amnestic symptom-complex)
(e) "Pastness"	Epilepsy (dèja vue); anesthetic states
(f) Associations determined by (sense organs) (appetites) (instincts) (interests)	Organic reaction types in general; psychogenic conditions
(g) Imagery ("extracted images" of Bartlett)	Korsakow's psychosis; early senile dementia
(h) Personal Identity (awareness of)	Hysteria; depersonalization in various psychoses

(pp. 750–751)

categories: (a) awareness of personal identity; (b) associations determined by sense organs, appetites, interests, instincts and Bartlett's "schemata"; (c) time sense and "pastness." The first of these categories, the awareness of personal identity which may be lost in psychogenic emotional disturbances, is obviously affect-charged, and designates something similar to what Ribot endeavored to express by "Ego" and "Coenaesthesis." The second of these categories may be elucidated by quoting Gillespie:

"Remembering . . . is the imaginative reconstruction built out of the relation of our attitude towards a whole mass of organized past reactions of experience. . . .
"These reconstructions Bartlett called 'schemata.' It is likely that the earlier schemes follow the line of demarcation of the special senses. Thus, appetites, like food seeking and sleeping, and instincts, like fear, determine the form of the schemata. Temperament—which evidently Bartlett believed, and I agree, is best regarded as a matter of pattern of relative strengths of the appetites and instinctive tendencies—and character are next involved." (p. 748)

The individual, deeply-rooted character of these schemata, as well as their being organized around appetites, interests, and instincts, makes it obvious that they are considered to be in intimate relationship with those factors subsumed in this monograph under the term "emotional influences"; Gillespie, however, only implies this bearing. The third category is the "time-ordering of experiences," the relation of which to emotional factors we shall discuss in connection with the Korsakow syndrome.[10]

Ribot's survey cannot be expected to be up to date; the two other surveys, in spite of their distinct values, neither summarize exhaustively our present knowledge of the pathology of memory nor—though they imply it frequently—elucidate explicitly the role of the affective factor in pathological memory phenomena. We shall attempt this in the following pages.

3. The Plan of Our Survey

We must first delimit our topic and then state the manner in which we propose to organize our discussion. When in this chapter we speak of the "pathology" of memory, we do not include all phenomena that might be so designated. We have excluded those which Freud called the phenomena of "psychopathology of everyday life," the slips of tongue, forgettings, and parapraxes; we have already discussed these in Chapter V, and what we propose to discuss in this chapter is "pathological" in a stricter sense. Secondly, we have excluded allo- and pseudomnesias, hallucinations, projective delusions, and so on; they are in a certain sense pathological exaggerations of the phenomena of the psychopathology of everyday life, and are memory phenomena occurring as one aspect of pathological thought processes, but their theory and in it the influence of affect on memory is related to the theory of the psychopathology of everyday life and has been

10 See p. 226 ff.

discussed in Chapter V. Thirdly, we have excluded the hypermnesias. The hypnotic hypermnesias have already been discussed; as to the others. neither the objectivity of reporting nor the availability for systematic investigation of the emotional factor involved is sufficient to warrant discussion beyond the following enumeration:

(a) The survival of memories of danger (Stratton, 11), and the "panoramic memory" of people who on the brink of death relive their whole life in a few terrific seconds, seem to bear on our topic but have never been substantiated by careful investigation.

(b) The phenomenal memories of "mathematical wizards" and of such persons as Cardinal Mezzofanti,[11] who allegedly spoke fifty languages, seem similar to the memories of some compulsion neurotics, but have not been investigated.

(c) Neither the general poverty of memory in mental deficients nor the phenomenal memory of a few of them has been qualitatively investigated.

Fourthly, we shall mention only in connection with the Korsakow syndrome, and not in detail, the proverbial weakness of memory of the aged; the literature of this problem is extremely meager, and contains little that may be usefully evaluated from the point of view of our topic.

These reservations limit our topic to the phenomena showing a gross pathology of memory; that is to say, to states which include amnesia in some form. Even so, we deal with a field of enormous variety.[12] We shall not discuss all the varieties, and shall limit our discussion to the dynamically significant categories. We shall first discuss the amnesias of functional —that is, psychogenic—origin. Secondly, we shall survey the problem of those amnesias in the genesis of which organic brain changes play a significant role, excluding only one group of these. Thirdly, we shall discuss the Korsakow syndrome and kindred disturbances, which—despite a fluid transition from them to the cases of the second group—constitute a characteristic group.

[11] See the Encyclopaedia Britannica: Guiseppe Carper, Cardinal Mezzofanti. Vol. 15, page 402.

[12] Leavitt (12), for instance, recorded nine types of temporary amnesia. He classified as follows 104 cases of amnesia which he had investigated: (1) trauma group; (2) toxic group (toxic psychosis from renal disease, acute alcoholism with complete memory ablation, diabetic hyperglycemia with amnesia); (3) psychotic group (paranoid, schizophrenic, senile, involutional melancholia, manic depressive psychosis); (4) amnesia in constitutional mental inferiors; (5) epileptics (post-epileptic fugue states); (6) psychoneurotic group (most frequently hysterical); (7) undiagnosed (atypical); (8) organic neurological group (non-luetic cerebral vascular disease, motor aphasia with word-deafness, or word-blindness); (9) malingering.

4. The Functional Amnesias

Within the limits of our discussion there may be discerned three types of functional amnesias: (*a*) retrograde and anterograde amnesias; (*b*) the amnesias of fugue states, and of the loss of personal identity; (*c*) the amnesias of multiple personalities. Each of these types has its counterpart in amnesias of organic etiology; thus our discussion will also bear partly on the problem of the latter.

A. Retrograde and Anterograde Amnesias

A retrograde amnesia is one in which a person loses the memories of a period of his life which at the time he had experienced consciously and which, prior to the amnesia, he had remembered as fully as those other periods of his life which he still remembers. The definition implies that neither a clouding of consciousness nor any other limitation of conscious experiencing was present in the period later subject to retrograde amnesia.[13] This implication necessarily is difficult to substantiate. We shall see, in discussing loss of personal identity, fugue states, and mono- and polyideic somnambulism, that the transition from "limited" to "full" consciousness is a fluid one. It seems probable that the periods later subject to retrograde amnesia are not abruptly and arbitrarily segregated from the continuum of experience, nor are their memory-traces eliminated by reason of their recency and lability, as Ribot thought; rather, the manner in which they are experienced appears different from the rest of the experiential continuum. Sollier arguing against Ribot's theory, maintained that— we quote this after Janet (1)—" . . . the accident which caused the amnesia must be associated with the facts that preceded and prepared it, and it carries them with it into the same forgetfulness" (p. 109). Early writers— Janet, Charcot, and even Freud[14]—referred to this difference in experienc-

---

[13] C. Munn's (13) paper is an example of misuse of the term amnesia. Having announced in her title that she will describe an amnesia of ten years' duration, she then describes the bewilderment of a patient upon awaking from a stupor of ten years. Not an amnesia, but a limitation of conscious experiencing, was here responsible for the patient's bewilderment.

[14] Freud (14) wrote:

" . . . Indeed, the more we occupied ourselves with these phenomena the more certain did our conviction become that splitting of consciousness, which is so striking in the well-known classical cases of *double conscience*, exists in a rudimentary fashion in every hysteria and that the tendency to this dissociation—and therewith to the production of abnormal states of consciousness, which may be included under the term 'hypnoid'—is a fundamental manifestation of this neurosis." (p. 34)

" . . . There is one thing common to all these hypnoid states and to hypnosis, in spite of all their differences—namely, that the ideas which emerge in them are marked by great intensity of feeling but are cut off from associative connection with the rest

ing as being "a hypnoidal state." Freud assumed that such a state is sensitive for traumatization, and is easily "forgotten." Later Freud adopted a dynamic theory for explaining these phenomena; Fenichel (15) summarizes this theory as follows:

"Freud . . . favored a conception which was to become the basis of psychoanalytic theory and which is known as the dynamic point of view. He maintained that given a special force within the ego which is engaged in defending the latter against the impact of certain experiences, it repels them, as it were, and they stay isolated in the individual's psychic life because they are unpleasant; hence they are purposely eliminated from consciousness—they are *repressed*. Consequently, there is a constant conflict between the memories which are striving to break into consciousness, and the forces within the ego which are directed against them and repressing them. The hysterical symptoms should thus be understood as a sign and outcome of a conflict of this order. This theory, according to which hysterical amnesias are the result of a purposive (unconscious) desire to ignore, was confirmed by Freud's discovery of the purposive nature of slips of memory, so-called 'unintentional' forgetting, and also by the fact that forgotten ideas could be recovered by means of psychoanalysis." (pp. 11–12)

Clearly, this is a statement of the "emotional" origin of these amnesias. But even earlier, under the influence of Janet and Charcot, these amnesias were characterized as "hysterical," a term implying their "emotional" character.

These retrograde amnesias of functional origin, devoid of a clouding of consciousness during the period subsequently forgotten, are not as frequent as is generally assumed; cases as clear-cut as those reported by Wechsler (17)[15] and Janet (1) are rather rare. Border-line psychosomatic cases,

---

of the content of consciousness. These hypnoid states are capable of association among themselves and the ideas belonging to them may in this way attain different degrees of psychical organization." (p. 35)

"If such hypnoid states exist before the manifest illness, they provide a foothold upon which the affect establishes itself with its pathogenic recollection and its subsequent somatic manifestations. This situation corresponds to dispositional hysteria." (p. 35)

On this point see also Henderson and Gillespie (16, pp. 425–426).

[15] "S. S., a school teacher, twenty-three years of age, suffered from total amnesia for a period of about one year and a half. Following the death of her father from heart disease several years before, she began to complain of precordial distress and other vague symptoms. Then her sister died, also of heart disease, and the patient began to manifest definite neurotic traits. Meanwhile she had been teaching in school. About a year and a half following the death of her sister her mother died. It was then that her amnesia set in and covered the period between the death of the sister and that of the mother. I saw her at the time of the circumscribed amnesia. She remembered everything up to the death of her sister but nothing which followed. She was unaware that her mother and sister were dead, did not recall that she was being treated by a physician all that time, although she knew him well and recalled every visit she made to him before the onset of amnesia, was astonished to learn that

in which effects of shell explosions, cave-ins, and asphyxiations act as precipitating events, are more common.[16] Cases precipitated by this type of experience cannot be considered as of purely "organic" etiology: concerning the war amnesias, war-neuroses, and "shell shocks," psychiatrists are inclined to agree at present that on the whole they are of emotional origin;[17] case-histories such as those published by Thom and Fenton (19) show emotional factors; psychoanalysts maintain that the life histories of the victims of war-neuroses and amnesias show discernible neurotic trends.[18] As evidence of their psychogenic origin, we may adduce, first, their relatively easy hypnotic restoration (Thom and Fenton, Rivers); secondly, the fact that according to reports, amnesias following head

she underwent an operation in the interim, and insisted that her mother was in Europe. Compelled by her illness to give up teaching she yet went to the school principal begging to be given back her class and not realizing that she had not been teaching for three terms. One day she bought a steamship ticket to go to Europe and would have made the trip had not the family learned by chance of her intended voyage to see her mother whom she imagined to be living in Vienna. Indeed she was writing letters to her and wondering why she got no replies. During the consultation in the office she seemed perplexed by everything, denied knowledge of facts which her family physician confronted her with, and was curious to know why the examiner was interested in her at all, seeing that there was nothing wrong with her. She subsequently bought a railroad ticket to go to a sister in California and after being stopped once she succeeded in getting away. She stayed there for some time and finally returned to New York. One day she telephoned to ask whether I was the neurologist who saw her before going to California. She had been told that she had visited my office, but had no recollection of the fact. She made several appointments which she did not keep, and the family physician informed me that she repeatedly did the same thing to him. I have been informed that she has recovered the memory of death of her mother and sister and has gone over into a state of depression." (pp. 201–202)

[16] See Rivers (18, pp. 14–15) and the three cases reported by Thom and Fenton (19).

[17] See A. Kardiner (20).

[18] In "Psychoanalysis and the War Neuroses" (21) Abraham wrote:

"The previous history of such people, and naturally, still more, a penetrating analysis, teaches us why the one in spite of the severest physical and mental influences of the war remains to all intents and purposes healthy, and why the other reacts to relatively trifling stimuli with a severe neurosis. It transpires with great regularity that the war neurotics already before the trauma were labile people— to designate it, to begin with, by a general expression—and especially so as regards their sexuality. Many of these men were unable to carry out their tasks in practical life, others that were capable of doing this, however, showed little initiative and manifested little impelling energy. In all of them sexual activity was diminished, their sexual hunger (libido) being checked through fixations; in many of them already before the campaign potency was weak or they were only potent under certain conditions. Their attitude towards the female sex was more or less disturbed through partial fixation of the sexual hunger (libido) in the developmental stage of narcissism. Their sexual and social capacity of functioning was dependent on their making certain concessions to their narcissism." (pp. 23–24)

injuries are in extent and duration more limited than functional amnesias (Russel, 22); and thirdly, the fact that the period forgotten in the retrograde amnesia is usually the war period in war cases, and the period preceding and leading up to the attempted suicide in asphyxiation cases— in other words, the period in which the event precipitating the amnesia occurred.   In cases where an organic involvement is present, according to Thom and Fenton's findings, an irreversible amnesia covering a short period usually persists after recovery.   Thus in this group we see a continuous transition from the psychogenic to the organic cases.

Another continuous transition is to be noted from cases of retrograde amnesia to those of the fugue states.   In the rather clear-cut case of retrograde amnesia reported by Wechsler,[19] there are features resembling a fugue state.   The patient, having forgotten the deaths of her sister and mother and the whole period between them, acts as though the events had never occurred: unlike typical retrograde-amnesia patients, she refuses to recognize the fact of her amnesia and the reality of her memory-losses, even after being informed of them; she is possessed by the idea of communicating with and travelling to her mother who, she believes, lives in a far-off land.   Her behavior is similar to that of subjects described by Janet as being in fugue states.   In the following section we shall discuss the fugue states; and it will then be clearer that Wechsler's case, although clearcut as a retrograde amnesia, may be interpreted as a peculiar fugue state. There are two reasons that it is difficult to recognize the case as a fugue state: first, the patient instead of forgetting her *relatives*—as is usual in fugue states—forgot their *deaths*; secondly, the fugue-like state was present at the time of the observation, and the investigator did not see it in retrospect as fugue states are customarily seen, when the victim has "snapped out of it" and has a retrograde amnesia for the period of the fugue.

Before discussing further the fugue state, we must consider the anterograde amnesias.   These were called by Ribot "progressive," and by Janet "continuous," amnesias.   They are amnesias in which events are forgotten soon after having been experienced.   Again, the necessary implication of this definition is that no clouding or other limitation of consciousness—in the usual sense of the term—is present at the time of the original experiencing.   We say "in the usual sense" because the state of consciousness from which the new experiences soon irrevocably disappear[20] can hardly be considered a normally unclouded and unlimited consciousness; yet the term "anterograde amnesia" should not be applied to a period of experiencing in which a deep clouding of consciousness has made normal registration impossible.   These amnesias shade in a fluid fashion into the Korsakow

[19] See pp. 192–193.
[20] See Stoerring (23) and Syz (24) to this effect.

syndrome; the retention of recent impressions in certain of them is extremely short-lived, which gives the impression that registration or at least retention is vitally afflicted; most of them show some organic etiology, and not a selective but a wholesale forgetting of the recent experiences: for these reasons, this type of amnesia has been generally considered organic.[21] Purely psychogenic cases of anterograde amnesia, such as those of Marcelle, Maria, and Mme.D. described by Janet (1), are extremely rare, if the frequency of literature-reports of the malady can be considered a measure of the frequency of its occurrence. The cases of Marcelle[22] and Mme. D.[23] appear to be retro- and anterograde; that of Maria,[24] as far as

[21] Bonhoeffer (25) was the psychiatrist to give the weight of his authority to this view.

[22] "When she relates the incidents of her past life, we observe that her story is clear, exact, rich in details, but only so long as it runs over her childhood, before she was fifteen, the beginning of her malady. From that moment the remembrances decrease and become vague; at nineteen they fail almost entirely and are limited to some few salient events. Finally, if you question her touching the last months or weeks just elapsed, you will discover to your surprise an absolute forgetfulness. Her old remembrances are preserved, but she herself has become more and more incapable of acquiring anything new, any new remembrances. This forgetfulness regarding recent events is very curious for its rapid occurrence and completeness. Marcelle cannot tell us what happened the day before; often at noon the whole morning has slipped from her mind. A word from her tells the situation: "Is it possible that I have been here a whole year? What a strange year in which nothing has happened!" In a young girl of twenty-two, such a memory is an old man's who can recite the *Aeneid* and cannot remember what he has done in the morning. . . ." (pp. 88–89)

[23] "Mme. D. has not a feeble memory: she has none at all. In the spring of 1892, —that is, eight months after the initial emotion,—she forgets entirely and in less than a minute a name, a fact; and indeed what lasts longer, is the perception of objects, the effort she seems to make to retain the initial impression; but she has no recollection, properly so called, for she is incapable of reproducing an image of the sensations she has allowed to become extinct. Let us add that this profound and fast-travelling amnesia was continuous and invariable, a thing we had not seen in the previous observations. We never saw Mme. D. show more memory at any time. Let us say, moreover, that this strange psychological perturbation was prolonged into the month of May, 1892—that it lasted, consequently, nine complete months without modification—and we shall have shown that it is the most curious case of continuous amnesia that has ever, to our knowledge, been pointed out." (pp. 90–91)

[24] ". . . Maria, for example, undertakes to read a novel, but her neighbours call our attention to the fact that she spends the whole day reading the same page; when she comes to the bottom she stops a moment and regularly begins again at the top. Besides, when we asked her what she had read, she was not even able to tell the title of the novel. She could never, though we insisted, and she did not mind the work, learn by heart a few lines. Sometimes the forgetfulness was immediate. She could answer only questions rapidly put to her; otherwise she remained amazed and said: 'What is it you asked?' She would forget her own questions and say: 'What is it I was talking about?' " (p. 89)

described, appears purely anterograde: all three cases are described as hysterical. In the cases of organic etiology—for instance, that of Syz (24), to be discussed later—the effect of psychogenic or emotional factors is obvious. A case of psychogenic loss of personal identity observed by M. Gill and the present author (26), in which the emotional factors precipitating the amnesia were rather clear, revealed a peculiar anterograde amnesia in the period of the loss of personal identity. The patient, whose case will be described later, forgot immediately, in the course of this period in which he was possessed by one idea, events and facts which were contrary to that idea. We found no other case of selective anterograde amnesia described in the literature, although it is true that the anterograde-like amnesia of the Korsakow syndrome shows selectiveness.

Janet's (1) theoretical explanation of amnesias is rather vague:

"Hysterical amnesias, like anesthesias, may be represented as troubles of this kind. The elements of remembrance, the conservation and the reproduction of the images are intact; but there is a lack of the real synthesis of the psychological elements which suppresses, more or less completely, the assimilation of the remembrances to the personality." (p. 106)

This explanation is based on the concept of "dissociation."[25] The views of Henderson and Gillespie (16) are based on psychoanalytic concepts:

". . . the production of symptoms at all means a partial failure of repression; if repression has partly failed, conscious conflict exists, and conflict is the condition that led to the formation of symptoms in the way already set forth. These theories hold for the physical symptoms of hysteria.

"With the mental symptoms of hysteria a similar process occurs. In hysterical amnesia, for example, there has been a period of conflict; then emotional preoccupation prevents the subject's noticing events in the ordinary way, consequently the memory of them, when the conflict has died down (they are registered marginally), is vague; vagueness of memory suggests complete failure of it, the patient does not wish to remember in any case—again the emotional symptom coincides with the wish—we accept what we wish to believe, and so does the hysterical patient—and an amnesia results." (pp. 425–426)

Further theoretical discussion of psychogenic amnesias will be found in the following two sections; attention here is called to the tacit assumption in the views quoted that amnesias are hysterical in origin. This assumption was the background of Freud's endeavor to find a forgotten event relevant to every hysterical, and later to every neurotic, symptom.

The attempts by Sears (27) and Ray (28) to compare retrograde amnesia with its experimental simile, retroactive inhibition,[26] were not successful. McGeoch (29) showed that the locus of action of retroactive inhibition

---

[25] For a discussion of the concept of "dissociation" see pp. 174, 212–214.
[26] See Britt's survey of the pertinent theories (30).

lies in the process of reproduction, just as in functional amnesias the disturbance is also of reproduction rather than of registration or retention. Nevertheless, retrograde amnesia and retroactive inhibition are hardly comparable. These attempts at comparison failed to take cognizance of the complexity of amnesia, and were satisfied to state the obvious but superficial analogies of two phenomena which were known to different degrees, described in different terms, and observed in different settings by people of different backgrounds.

B. PSYCHOGENIC LOSS OF PERSONAL IDENTITY AND FUGUE STATES

Fugues and "loss of personal identity" are states in which, although knowledge of general matters is retained, the subject is unaware of his personal identity, and the knowledge which could give him clues concerning that identity—knowledge of relations, home, profession, life history—is also generally forgotten. Retrograde amnesia covers usually only a part of the life history; in fugues and losses of personal identity, the amnesia appears to cover all of it. However, on closer scrutiny the amnesia occurring in these cases proves to vary in degree and in the cues it leaves open, such as profession, name and so on.[27] These amnesias, although spectacular and implying considerable change in personality organization, are often rather easily recovered, either spontaneously, by suggestion, by meeting familiar people, or by hypnosis and drug hypnosis. The fugue state and the loss of personal identity are not sufficiently differentiated in the literature, and the terms are to a certain extent used interchangeably. Scrutiny of a great number of cases published in the literature suggests that one reason for the lack of a proper definition is that not sufficient distinction has been made between "loss of personal identity" and "awareness of loss of personal identity."[28] Loss of personal identity is unquestionably present and is an important factor in fugue states; but no awareness of it is present, and the subject usually gives a fictitious identification. Where the subject is puzzled and bewildered by becoming aware of having lost his personal identity, the state is usually called "loss of personal iden-

[27] Abeles and Schilder (31) wrote: "One of our patients was unusual because she knew her name but not her address. Frequently the patient can give some approximate information and isolated details about himself, which is of little or no use in identifying him or locating relatives. Not infrequently he hints at the cause of the absence of memory; he may mention money or some conflict of opinion. One case was unique in that the loss of memory was not so much in the foreground as was the inability of the patient to remember the circumstances of his life, i.e., whether he was married and details about his business. Sometimes the memory is spotty, so that it reminds one of a Ganser syndrome. In most cases the condition is not amnesia in the sense of loss of personal identity but amnesia in the sense of loss of memory of the past." (p. 594)

[28] I am indebted to M. Gill, for suggesting the formulation of this distinction.

tity." It would appear that fugues and losses of personal identity thus defined are two phases of one process. This process starts usually with the phase in which the subject acts and thinks without being aware, and without making others aware, that something is wrong with him and that he is not acting in accordance with the set of behavior patterns usually called his "personality." His "personal identity" is changed or lost, but he is not aware of it. What he thinks and does in this period is in few cases learned by the psychiatrist and psychologist, for it is later forgotten. This phase, usually called a "fugue state," may end in either of two ways: in a sudden awakening to personal identity; or in a sudden awareness that he does not know who he is, where he is, or what to do next—in other words, in a state of "loss of personal identity." The fugue state is characterized by a loss of personal identity of which no awareness exists, and in which a single idea possesses the person and directs his behavior; the state of "loss of personal identity" implies an awareness of the loss, resulting in total perplexity. The fugue state has, as we shall soon see, other characteristics which differentiate it from the period of loss of personal identity. Whether a state of loss of personal identity may occur without a preceding fugue state is a question to which no conclusive answer is available in the literature. It must be remembered that the first period of these states is covered by amnesia.

In the literature this amnesia is as a rule not sufficiently distinguished from retrograde amnesias, although there are significant differences. In a fugue state, the subject if questioned—and subjects have rarely been questioned—cannot give true information about himself; but during the period later covered by retrograde amnesia, no such disturbance apparently exists.[29] In cases of loss of personal identity, the efforts of the psychiatrist are usually directed toward restoring the patient to his personal identity, and only rarely is memory of the course of the fugue state also recovered[30] or does a subject after recovering his personal identity still feel a need to recover memory of the lost period.[31] It is generally conceded that such

----

[29] The case described by H. A. Grierson (32) may be for instance interpreted, in the absence of sufficient detail, both as a fugue state with ensuing amnesia and as a retrograde amnesia. Grierson chose the latter explanation: "J. C. T.—male, aet. 39. Charged with cutting the throat of his child and afterwards his own. On reception he said he did not remember cutting his own throat, and that he did *not* cut his child's throat. His history showed a certain amount of depression following unemployment. The depositions revealed a statement from the accused showing that at the time of the crime he knew what he had done, and regretted it. Repeated examinations showed amnesia from repression, and retrograde expansion to cover the first crime." (p. 369)

[30] See the cases of M. Gill and the author (26), Bennet (33), and Bryan's (34) fourth case.

[31] See Naef (35).

a loss of personal identity is of emotional origin and is frequently accompanied by depressive manifestations, and that the recovery of the memories is accompanied by an emergence of various somatic complaints. Nevertheless Abeles and Schilder (31),[32] as well as Gordon and Lawrence (36), report cases of undoubtedly organic origin. The similarity of epileptic fugues[33] to the psychogenic loss of personal identity is also a commonly known fact. Thus this group also shades into the organic disturbances, although it is the most clear-cut in its emotional origin.

The psychological significance and explanation of this type of amnesia is still a great problem, although there have been several attempts to explain it. We shall discuss here three such attempts, those of Janet, E. Jones, and Abeles and Schilder.

Little attention has been paid recently to Janet's (37) theory; his terminology of "monoideic" and "polyideic somnambulism" and "fugue states" has been replaced by "amnesia" and "loss of personal identity." This is regrettable, for Janet's approach had focussed on the memory function more sharply than the theories that replaced it. Janet's view, stressing the emotional origin of these amnesias, was that the fugue state belongs to the continuum of the hysterical somnambulistic states.[34] Somnambulism was described by Janet (37) as follows:

"What, then, exactly, is a somnambulist? Popular observation has answered long ago: it is an individual who thinks and acts while he is asleep. Without a doubt that answer is not very clear, for we don't know very well what sleep is. That answer means only that the person spoken of thinks and acts in an odd way, different from that of other people, and that at the same time that person is in some way like a person asleep." (p. 24)

The thoughts and acts of the somnambulist constitute a closely-knit but isolated system:

"Normally, in good health, the little system must be connected with the large one, and must in great part depend on it. Generally the partial system remains subject to the laws of the total system; it is called up only when the whole consciousness is willing, and within the limits in which this consciousness allows it.

"Now, to picture to ourselves what has taken place during somnambulism, we may adopt a simple provisional *resume*. Things happen as if an idea, a partial system of thoughts, emancipated itself, became independent and developed itself on

---

[32] See pp. 599–601.

[33] The organic origin of at e ast some epilepsies may be safely assumed.

[34] Janet (37) wrote: "Fugues of this kind, exactly characterized, usually appear in the life of some subjects who have had already, or who will have later on, other phenomena connected with the accidents we know as hysterical ones. In one word, this kind of fugues appears usually in hysterical people." (p. 58) On the other hand, K. A. Menninger (38) describes a cyclothymic fugue.

its own account. The result is, on one hand, that it develops far too much, and, on the other hand, that consciousness appears no longer to control it." (p. 42)[35]

Mention of the Freudian theory of somnambulism is relevant here. According to this theory, the dream expresses an unconscious wish; this dream-wish cannot penetrate into waking consciousness nor can it find expression in motor activity while the person is awake, for the wish is unacceptable to the person. During sleep, the pathway through which thoughts and wishes find motor expression and regulate action are blocked, and there is no danger that an unacceptable wish will be executed; thus these wishes are permitted to enter dream-consciousness. Somnambulism is that unusual case in which the blocking which prevents the dream-thought from finding motor expression is weakened, and the dream-wish becomes translated into the somnambulistic activity.[36]

To those somnambulistic states whose unity of ideational content is the result of the prevalence of a single dream-thought, Janet gave the name "monoideic"; those in which the subjects are possessed by a multiplicity of ideas he called "polyideic" somnambulisms. The difference between somnambulistic states and fugues is explained thus:

". . . First, during the abnormal state, the idea that develops has certainly not the same power as during monoideic somnambulism; true, it directs the conduct, but it does not bring on the hallucination and deliriums that it produced in the preceding case. When Irene had the idea of committing suicide and of getting herself crushed by a locomotive, she had not patience enough to go to the railway track and compass a real suicide; she immediately had the hallucination of the railway track, and, with-

---

[35] Janet (37) quotes the sleep-walking scene from Shakespeare's Macbeth and a number of cases he observed. One of his descriptions may be given here as illustration:

"A young woman, twenty-nine years old, called Gib., intelligent, sensitive, hears one day abruptly some disastrous news. Her niece, who lives next door, has just died in dreadful circumstances. She rushes out, and comes, unhappily, in time to see the body of the young girl lying in the street. She had thrown herself out of the window in a fit of delirium. Gib., although very much moved, remains to all appearance calm, helping to make everything ready for the funeral. She goes to the funeral in a very natural way. But from that time she grows more and more gloomy, her health fails, and we may notice the beginning of the singular symptoms we are going to speak of. Nearly every day, at night and during the day, she enters into a strange state; she looks as if she were in a dream, she speaks softly with an absent person, she calls Pauline (the name of her lately deceased niece), and tells her that she admires her fate, her courage, that her death has been a beautiful one. She rises, goes to the windows and opens them, then shuts them again, tries them one after another, climbs on the window, and, if her friends did not stop her, she would, without any doubt, throw herself out of the window. She must be stopped, looked after incessantly, till she shakes herself, rubs her eyes, and resumes her ordinary business as if nothing had happened." (p. 27)

[36] See Freud (39).

out more ado, lay down on the floor of the room. Remember that difference: there is no real hallucination in the fugue. The development of the idea is less intense. Secondly, the idea is not absolutely isolated as in somnambulism; this is the most characteristic fact. Our great somnambulists, you remember, do not see or hear anything but what concerns the idea rooted in their mind; and it could not be otherwise, for, if Irene saw the beds in the room, if she heard my voice, she would not believe herself alone on a railway track. On the contrary, the patients who make fugues need a great many perceptions and recollections to enable them to travel without any mishaps. 'What is most wonderful in fugues,' Charcot said, 'is that these individuals contrive not to be stopped by the police at the very beginning of their journey.' In fact, they are mad people in full delirium; nevertheless, they take railway tickets, they dine and sleep in hotels, they speak to a great number of people. We are, it is true, sometimes told that they were thought a little odd, that they looked preoccupied and dreamy, but after all, they are not recognized as mad people; whereas Irene could not take two stops in the street, when she was dreaming of her mother's death, without being immediately taken to the asylum. So you see that the range of consciousness is not at all the same, that the mind is not distinctly reduced to a single idea. We can make the same remark concerning the state called normal: the oblivion of the fugue is total, but the oblivion of the directive idea and of the feeling connected with it is by far less distinct, and the restoration of the normal self is much more complete." (pp. 59–60)

The polyideic somnambulism theoretically constitutes the transition between the monoideic and the fugue state,[37] and completes the continuum of these states. There appear to have been two reasons that Janet considered somnambulistic and fugue states to lie in a continuum: first, it was commonly known that both states are attended by an amnesia; secondly, in both states one idea or a limited system of ideas possesses the subject and he acts as though only what pertains to this exists for him. This second phenomenon has been less frequently observed in states of loss of personal identity. It is obvious that the theory of dissociation is the basis of Janet's reasoning.

M. Gill and the present author (26) investigated an "amnesia" case in which it became obvious why the relation between fugues and monoideic somnambulisms stressed by Janet is frequently overlooked. In this case the loss of personal identity occurred in the presence of the subject's relatives, and thus information was obtained not only of the fugue-like character but also of the somnambulistic monoideic content of the state. This state was precipitated by financial trouble, and in the period of the loss of personal identity the subject was possessed by the idea that he was "out to find a job," which if attainable in reality would eventually have extricated him from his financial difficulties. This subject was in touch with his surroundings, but did not recognize them; his personal identity was forgotten, but he was not concerned over this loss and appeared to be una-

[37] For the connection of amnesias, fugues, and somnambulistic states, and for further examples, see Dorcus and Schaffer (40, pp. 281–282).

ware of it; instead, a single striving—"to get a job"—regulated his behavior.   Up to this point, he acted as a person in a fugue state would act,
and the monoideic character of this fugue state was obvious.   Later,
when brought to the hospital where we observed him, he apparently en-
tered the state which Janet would call a hallucinating somnambulism: he
behaved as though working on a job; the noise of the heating system was
misrecognized by him as that of the machines of the work shop, and the
doctor as the owner.   Upon his spontaneous recovery, he forgot everything
that had happened in both periods; it was *as if* the striving "to find a new
job" were no longer psychically present, and thus the experiences grouped
around it had lost the propelling power that could have brought them into
consciousness.   So far our observation appears to bear out the dissociation
theory, advocated by Janet.   Yet closer scrutiny, revealing certain features
of the striving "to find a new job," sheds new light on the process underlying these states.   The case-history shows that the striving in this case was
equivalent to getting away from a father figure on the one hand, and from
the responsibility for the patient's wife and children on the other; these
strivings were guilt-laden for they implied murderous thoughts, as shown
by the suicidal ideas[38] which precipitated the fugue.   Thus his striving
"to get a new job" expressed, in a condensed fashion, many guilt-laden and
so forbidden strivings.   It appears as though—perhaps because of this
guilt—he was able to carry out the single striving only if at the same time
he forgot the memories expressing the implicit forbidden strivings.   This
striving became so powerful that it gained control of the motor and perception systems as well as of the memory and thought processes.   Older
psychology would probably have stated that "the striving filled the whole
field of consciousness"—implying a limited amount of space.   Such a
spatial conception of consciousness, however, makes impossible the understanding of consciousness as a process.

If our interpretation is correct, the case itself is a sturdy support to those
theories according to which memory organization is determined by strivings, affects, and attitudes.   The few carefully-described fugue states
which we found in the literature seem to confirm our conclusions.[39]   Addi-

[38] Psychoanalytic and psychiatric experience and theory assert that suicidal
ideas and acts are the result of the murderous aggressive impulses which have been
diverted from fellow-humans and are directed toward the self. See K. A.
Menninger (41).

[39] See the case reported by Bennet (33). His conslusions are:
"Each fugue, in addition to the state of mental strain, had been foreshadowed by
a period rich in phantasy construction.   These phantasies seem to afford a key as to
the motive of the fugue, for in the fugue many of the phantasies are realized.   For
example, before the last fugue he had a recurring phantasy of inheriting, or acquiring
in some romantic fashion, a sufficiency of money.   There were also the phantasies of

tional support can be derived from other observations on this case. Only after the patient was able to remember the suicidal ideas which, as well as his desire to find new employment, possessed him immediately prior to the fugue, did the recovery of the memories of the fugue state begin. Step by step, and with obvious labor, he recovered and described them. His story was rather lifeless: the people and places which had been encountered in his fugue state were at first simply described and either not identified or identified only by rational inference. Apparently at the time of experiencing he had not recognized them. The single striving which dominated the fugue state made for non-identification and even misidentification of the environment. When this striving was again controlled, amnesia ensued for the period in which the striving had been the organizer of experience. It was not until one more key-experience was recovered that the patient was able to give his full story. In the course of a conversation with his wife, he suddenly recalled that immediately prior to the fugue his wife had offered to help him in his financial trouble and he had answered, "It is too late." Previously he had not remembered and denied even the possibility of such a conversation. But after remembering it, he saw his story in a new light: he identified the places and persons without the necessity of rational inference; he described facts in true and vivid detail. It was as though a dammed-up river had been released suddenly, and flowed again in its banks. The attitude of personal identity now permeated the memories; in other words, the normal interplay of strivings now allowed full reproduction of the experiences of the fugue period. Significantly enough, when in the course of this new narration we interrupted the patient and asked him to skip to later events, we again obtained a lifeless account of them; but when he proceeded in his own sequence he produced the newly animated and detailed story.

This case sheds some light on the nature of amnesia. The theory of dissociation merely describes these memory phenomena, emphasizing the isolation—"dissociation"—of a set of memories from the rest. Our case shows that these "isolated" memories are organized around a striving, and that the striving is one which condenses and expresses symbolically a set of unacceptable strivings. Ribot's law[40] also appears now in a new light. Ribot witnessed such cases and yet maintained that the older memory trace is more stable and thus is lost later. He knew that the older traces are

---

actual flight from his problems. Both these phantasies were realized in the fugue state, as were many others." (p. 147)

"In each fugue, therefore, there is this return to an unfinished train of thought and there is the effort to bring it to completion." (p. 148)

See also the fourth case in Bryan's report (34).

[40] See the discussion of this law on pp. 186–187.

recovered first; he attributed this to their greater stability. Our case shows that not greater stability, but position and role in the organization of memory determine the fate and sequence of a memory in forgetting and recall. Ribot's law thus remains unsubstantiated, and will yield to a theory which replaces the age and strength of memories by their relation to each other in the architectonics of memory organization and to the strivings or other dynamic factors which organize memory.

Let us turn now to Jones' contribution to the problem of loss of personal identity or, as he called it, "complete autopsychic amnesia." Jones (5) in describing and analyzing a case observed by him, advanced one of the few theoretical explanations which psychoanalysts have ventured concerning generalized amnesia. Psychoanalytic theory explains partial amnesias[41] or "forgettings" by the concept of repression, and extends this explanation to wholesale amnesias; but the difference between spotlike forgetting and wholesale amnesia remains still unexplained. It is a problem why the organization of memory by strivings is of such a nature that, in general, "repression" affects only the few memories through which an unacceptable striving may enter consciousness, but that in some "abnormal" cases a whole period of experiences or the entire personal past is forgotten. Jones shows first that his patient is a hysterical case; he then proceeds to analyze the nature of hysterical symptoms. It is maintained, in accordance with psychoanalytic theory, that physical symptoms of hysteria are based on forgotten traumatic events; the conversion symptoms are based on a series of amnesias and are a *somatic reproduction* of those events on whose amnesia they are based; behind each of these forgotten traumatic events lie several others, on different levels of psychic development. Hysterical wholesale amnesia is, like any other hysterical symptom, built on an extensive series of partial amnesias which have not been converted into physical symptoms. Jones reported that in his case the clearing up of the general amnesia resulted in an occurrence of conversion symptoms; this finding seems to be corroborated by several other reports, and was seen also in the case investigated by M. Gill and the present author.

Jones' theory that the total amnesia is built upon partial amnesias, and facts found in other reports of fugue states which indicate that some kinds of memories are always preserved in such cases, appear to be of considerable significance. The speculation arises that the miraculous completeness of classical amnesias may be a fable of a time when methods of investigating amnesias were even less complete than those of today. It is possible that, when sufficiently strong and numerous strivings can find expression through one striving and when the nature of these strivings is such that the relevant memories must be repressed, then the full body of

[41] See Erickson (42).

memories, containing the meaning of the various strivings expressed now by a single striving, is forgotten. The striving which condenses the various strivings becomes paramount and rules consciousness, and thus is the motif around which the fugue state is built. Total forgetting is more appearance than fact in these cases where memories organized around strivings emerge or recede with the predominance or repression of the strivings.

Abeles and Schilder (31) were the first to recognize that loss of personal identity is a specific disturbance. They segregated it from other amnesias,[42] and gave a detailed phenomonological description of it. This was a step ahead, for neither Janet nor Jones had sharply segregated loss of personal identity from other amnesias. But Abeles and Schilder's work was in other respects a step backward. Neither the relation of loss of personal identity to fugues and somnambulistic states, nor its dynamic— non-descriptive—difference from other amnesias was investigated by these authors. Their theoretical view of amnesia is indicated by Schilder's designation of amnesia, in a later paper (43) discussing the disappearance of the classical "grande hysterie," as one of the new forms hysteria chooses.[43] Abeles and Schilder make no direct reference to hysteria; but in discussing two cases quoted from the literature, the authors indicate their orientation:

"In both cases there was intense parental repression followed by rebellion in the form of amnesia." (p. 588)

Even more explicit is their description of the emotional background they consider to be the basis of amnesia:

". . . the amnesia is self-punishment arising from a feeling of guilt; it is a partial suicide. The psychogenic blindness in 2 cases preceding the amnesia probably had a similar meaning.

"In many cases one finds a deep disappointment in the love object. It is a going away from the love object. One is dead for the love object. One removes oneself (suicide), but one removes the others at the same time. The tendency to punish them is often obvious.

"Economic problems are often given as the cause of amnesia. One should be skeptical about such a possibility. One finds easily that there are usually deeper

---

[42] "In psychopathology every state of forgetting is called amnesia. We are interested here merely in cases of amnesia in which the subjects forget their own identity. To one's own identity belongs the connection with a specific social structure. One has relatives, friends, a place where one works and another where one lives. But the name and address are symbols of one's identity. In every-day life one identifies people by these criteria and they identify themselves in this way. A person's knowledge, insight and faculties are much less important in this respect." (p. 587)

[43] 36% of the hysterical cases reported by Schilder here are amnesias. (p. 139)

motives. A man had to sell a valuable picture and became amnesic, but he needed
the money for the defense of his mother, who was accused of murder.
"Amnesia is often a giving in to a stronger force. One of our patients became
amnesic after being robbed of money he needed for the family. It is seemingly a
simple way out. In another case the patient became amnesic when pushed by a
car, but in this case a deep love conflict was in the background." (pp. 602–603)
"On the whole, amnesia is a weak attempt of a weak personality to escape conflicts which are chiefly conflicts of actual life, but of course these conflicts have relation to the more infantile reaction types, especially to the Oedipus complex. It is
the fear of being punished by the family, by the father and mother or their representatives, which leads to an escape which does not harm the person too much." (p. 603)

Although its emotional-pathological etiology is indubitable, the "loss of
personal identity" still remains an unsolved problem. We have seen that
it shades into retrograde amnesias as well as into the somnambulistic and
fugue states; with the latter it is frequently misidentified, as the dividing
line is by no means clear. The occurrence of conversion symptoms in the
course of recovery of these amnesias, and the fact that amnesias of definitely
organic origin may also occur as in the form of "loss of personal identity,"
show that even these amnesias—the most typically emotional-psychogenic
—present a psychosomatic problem. The present state of knowledge of
the memory disturbances summarized in this section is still far from satisfactory. Nevertheless, the material allowed for representing the disturbances belonging to this group as part of one continuum; they shade into
the retro- and anterograde amnesias already discussed, and the organic
amnesias to be discussed. It is hoped that we have prepared a continuous transition to the multiple personalities, to the discussion of which
we now turn.

C. MULTIPLE PERSONALITY

One of the most unusual memory disorders is that found in multiple
personalities. The phenomena of multiple personality are a realm,
covered by the fog of the uncanny, created in part by investigators who
linked these phenomena with parapsychology,[44] and in part by the fact
that the method most frequently applied in investigating them—namely
hypnosis—is a tool which itself is insufficiently known, and whose effect
on these personalities or whose role in originating them is entirely unclear.
The term "multiple personality" designates the manifestation by a single
person of two or more relatively distinct and different "personal identities,"
alternating or co-existing "co-consciously"; the activity in the period ruled
by one "personality" is not remembered in the period ruled by the other
"personalities." Yet this definition is neither accurate nor specific
enough. To make it accurate, more must be said about the function of

---

[44] See W. F. Prince (44) and T. W. Mitchel (45).

memory in the different personalities; to make it more specific, the nature of the differences between the personalities must be discussed. The statement that one personality does not remember the actions and thoughts of the other personalities, is inexact. There have been cases of multiple personalities for which this was reported to be absolutely true;[45] but in general, it is not the case. Thus, in the case of Mary Reynolds—reported by S. W. Mitchell (51)—for many years one personality did not possess the memories of the other; but when the "second" personality increasingly displaced the original and assumed some of its "favorable" characteristics, it also had vague memories of the life of the original personality.[46] The history of Hanna, described by Sidis and Goodhart (52), was similar, with the addition that in the dreams of the "second" personality memories of the original personality were present. Whether, on more careful investigation and follow-up, the cases in which total reciprocal amnesia[47] of the personalities was reported would have shown phenomena similar to the cases of Reynolds and Hanna, is mere speculation. Nevertheless, it can be concluded that the terms "reciprocal somnambulism"—suggested by Janet (37)—and "alternating personalities with reciprocal amnesia"—suggested by McDougall (54)—designate only extreme cases of a group of phenomena rather than a particular category. However, this group includes a great variety of phenomena. The cases of Reynolds and Hanna lead directly to the case of Felida X, described by Azam (55): in this case also the second personality gradually replaced the first; but although the first personality remembered nothing about the second, the second was always in possession of all the memories of the first. This and similar cases were called by Janet "dominating somnambulisms," and by McDougall "alternating personalities one of which is inclusive." This group shades imperceptibly into another, in which the memory interrelations are more complicated. The "CBA" case described by M. Prince (56) is an example. The original personality was C; A and B emerged later. B was nearly dominant; she possessed the memories of C and A, but not the memories of the hypnotic states of either personality. Similar complications were present in Prince's (57, 58) celebrated case of Miss Beauchamp. Whether without the influence of the investigator, and

---

[45] For instance the case of McNish (46), also discussed by Mitchill and Ellicot (53); the reports on the cases of Skae (47), Proust (48), Mesnet (49), which were summarized by Prince (50).

[46] Janet (37) wrote: "It seemed to her that she had, as it were, an obscure, dreamlike idea of a shadowy past which she could not quite grasp." (p. 77)

[47] The expression "amnesia" is generally used in this context. We shall use it so, although its accuracy is questionable: the "non-availability" of the memories of one personality to another is not identical with the "non-availability" to a person of the memories of a period of his life.

especially of his hypnotic manipulations, these complicated personalities could or would have come about is a question which cannot be answered.[48] The role that hypnosis may play in the development of multiple personalities, and the relation to them of hypnotic states, will become clearer after we have discussed those multiple personalities to which the described group leads. These are called by Prince and McDougall "coexisting or co-conscious personalities." Miss Beauchamp, the case reported by Cory (59), and many others may be ranked in this group. These cases are characterized by Prince (58) thus:

"The dissociated portion of consciousness may never have formed a part of the waking self, and consequently cannot properly be described as a split-off part of the mind. When it is not in evidence as an alternating personality it is not latent; it is co-conscious, and may have experiences and grow and develop in the subconscious. There is a doubling of consciousness without any true division of the normal self." (p. 98)

In other words, one of the personalities may exist, may observe the experiences of the manifest personality, may have access to its thoughts, feelings, and memories, and may have experiences of its own at the same time, without becoming manifest. This phenomenon is similar to those "alternating personalities one of which is inclusive"—that is, the memories of all the personalities are available to one personality. These co-conscious personalities may remain latent, may appear spontaneously, or may be discovered hypnotically.

Two extreme and clear-cut cases of such "co-conscious personalities" were reported by Erickson (60, 61, 62). As one of these—L and M—has never been hypnotized,[49] she is of special interest to us. M claims that she has always been in existence and remembers everything L ever did; but she never appeared as an acting personality until discovered by Erickson. The discovery happened through automatic writing and allied techniques, and it took a long time to teach M to talk. M appears only to Erickson, spontaneously or upon his request. L does not remember what happens when M "comes." M remembers what L does, although sometimes she says, "I was not there, but I can reach out into L's memory and get the information if you want it." Janet's case of Marceline (37, pp. 86,

---

[48] In this connection Janet (37) wrote:
"In these complex cases a new influence usually makes itself felt which complicates matters a great deal. I mean the influence of the observer himself, who, in the end, knows his subject too well and is too well known to him. Whatever precautions one may take, the ideas of the observer in the end influence the development of the somnambulisms of the subject, and give it an artificial complication." (p. 85)

[49] This fact and the account of the case are based on private communications from M. H. Erickson, and personal observations of the present author.

89) shows some similarities to this. Marceline suffered an incapacitating hysterical break. Janet induced a hypnotic state to make feeding possible, and found that in this state Marceline could cheerfully carry on normal life; whenever she relapsed, she was brought to Janet and he returned her to the desirable state. Peculiarly, the dominant state from the point of view of memory was the hypnotically-induced state. Both Erickson's case and Marceline show dormant co-conscious personalities invoked by the hypnotist or the investigator.

These cases argue for a continuous transition from the multiple personalities to the hypnotic states, fugues, and those somnambulistic states with which hysterical attacks, hypnotic states, and multiple personalities have generally been compared. The memory phenomena found in multiple personalities appear to shade into other phenomena of the pathology of memory which already have been discussed. McNish's extreme case with complete reciprocal amnesia is furthest from these similar memory phenomena; the other cases gradually come nearer. Let us summarize these common features:

a. The characteristic shared by hypnotic memory phenomena and those of multiple personality is the existence of an isolated memory system not available to the primary consciousness. The memory system of the hypnotic state, like that of the "dominant" type in multiple personality, is inclusive; the memories of waking experiences are available in the trance states. The hypnotic discovery[50] of many co-conscious personalities is a further link between these two memory phenomena. Finally, the fact that not all hypnotic states need have communicating memory systems shows a phenomenon of amnesia similar to that of multiple personalities. Janet (1) reported:

"Marguerite, put to sleep by M. Dutil, could not recover the recollections of the somnambulism which we had ourselves induced, and when put to sleep again by us, could not recover the remembrances of the somnambulism induced by M. Dutil. A patient . . . had been violated in a somnambulic state; put to sleep again she could, however, not recover the remembrance of this incident and then said: 'I cannot remember what has happened; it seems to me I was put to sleep differently' . . ." (pp. 420–421)

b. The relation of multiple personalities to fugues and somnambulistic states is indicated by Janet's designation of the multiple personalities as "somnambulisms." The facts corroborated the existence of an intimate relation. In fugues, the "personal identity" is lost and another "personality" seems to appear; a reciprocal amnesia exists between the normal and fugue states, but there is a communication between the memory sys-

---

[50] See M. Prince's (50) table, especially the column indicating the origin of the personalities.

tems of different fugue states[51] in the same individual. It is true that the fugue personality is usually incomplete—sometimes no more than a monoideic somnambulism—but so are many multiple personalities who are childish[52] or directed by one idea, and whose condition resembles a fugue-state.[53] The resemblance of certain multiple personalities to fugue-states has been emphasized by T. W. Mitchel (45):

"Thus we see that in the first fortnight of his secondary state, Ansel Bourne's conduct conformed to that of an ordinary fugue. He forgot his personal identity, assumed a new name, and wandered about from city to city. In the remaining six weeks he led a quiet respectable life as a small shopkeeper. In his second state he had no recollection of his former life, and when he came to himself he had no recollection of his life during the second state. The lost memories were, however, recovered during hypnosis, and the revelation so obtained of his frame of mind at the beginning of his fugue probably indicates the nature of the ideas that determined it. He said 'he wanted to get away somewhere—he didn't know where—and have rest.' When he opened his little shop the fugue proper came to an end. The idea which determined his flight was about to be realized, and while it was working itself out he lived the life of a secondary personality which was conditioned by the breach in the continuity of his memory, rather than by any great change in his character or conduct." (p. 112)

Not all multiple personalities resemble fugues. A fugue is never co-conscious; thus co-conscious multiple personalities resemble rather hypnotic states which are co-conscious. The more integrated, reality-adapted and mature a multiple personality is, the more it is distinct from a fugue-state. The more primitive and immature a multiple personality is, and the more it appears to be directed by a single striving, the more it resembles a fugue-state.

We have described the memory phenomena of multiple personality and have shown that they shade into memory phenomena whose emotional origin has already been discussed on these pages. We turn now to the material showing the role of emotions in these spectacular memory phenomena, and we will attempt to state more specifically the differences between the varying "behavior patterns" called here the "personalities" of a person. Although the genesis and the dynamics of the functioning of these multiple personalities may be unclear, the conviction that they are of emotional origin, and more specifically of hysterical origin, seems commonly accepted.[54] However, the literature contains frequent reports of multiple personalities whose origin was precipitated by organic traumata.[55] Whether

[51] See Bennet's case (33, p. 148).
[52] See W. F. Prince's (44) case or Goddard's (63) case.
[53] See Gaver's (64) case or Allen's (65) case.
[54] M. Prince (50) undertook an intensive discussion to prove this point.
[55] A discussion of these multiple personalities will be found on pp. 222-223.

multiple personalities in general are hysterical in origin is questionable. The description of some of the original personalities as "neurasthenic" sheds some doubt on their hysterical origin, although Prince (50) wrote:

". . . the neurasthenic state, one of the stigmata of hysteria, is pathologically a type of dissociation of personality." (p. 187)[56]

Erickson and Kubie (60), and Erickson and Rapaport (62) observed two dual personalities who were of the compulsive-obsessive type, and Oberndorf (66) described "co-conscious mentation" in general as an obsessive phenomenon. Finally, the hysterical origin of multiple personalities may be questioned if the psychoanalytic theory is taken into consideration.

There it is maintained that hysteria originates on the phallic level of psychosexual development, which immediately precedes the level of mature genitality; and the formation of the fundamentals of character occurs much earlier in the individual's development. The report on most cases clearly shows their emotional origin, even when one considers as of organic etiology the multiple personalities precipitated by epileptic attacks, "organic trauma," or "fever," and does not attempt to show that these can elicit only what is present in a latent form in the personality.

M. Prince (50) reviewed twenty cases of multiple personality. He did not include the cases of McNish, Ladame, Verriest, Bonamaison, Dufay and others mentioned by Janet (37). In the twenty cases, the number of multiples ranged from two to twelve personalities per person, and totalled sixty-five different personalities. The origins of these personalities, as tabulated by Prince on the basis of the original records, showed great variety: hypnosis, emotional shocks, hystero-epileptic attacks, fever, cataleptic and epileptic attacks, physical accidents, and so on. In a great number, no direct origin was recorded. Since Prince's tabulation a number of new cases of emotional origin—such as those of Gaver (64), Hart (68), Pech (69), Gordon (70, 71), Goddard (63), Wholey (72, 73), Allen (65), Erickson (60, 61, 62)—and a number of cases precipitated by organic traumata have been reported. They will be discussed later in this chapter.

The emotional origin of the multiple personalities is implied in the explanation of them by means of the dissociation concept, inasmuch as this concept is used also to explain hysterical and hypnotic phenomena. This concept has been already discussed on these pages in connection with Janet's explanation of monoideic somnambulisms and fugue states.[57] In multiple personalities the concept is called upon to explain a more intricate set of memory phenomena. Whatever the specific mechanism of the genesis of multiple personalities, they reveal the variety of memory

[56] See also Donley (67).
[57] See pp. 174, 196, 212–214.

phenomena which may be elicited by peculiarities of emotional organization. Psychoanalysis developed the concept of "repression"[58] to account for partial amnesias. In discussing the generalized amnesias in the first part of this chapter, we pointed out that the application of the "repression theory" to wholesale amnesias has not been satisfactory.[59] The concept dissociation has been frequently offered as an explanation of hypnotic amnesias[60] and generalized amnesias.[61] It now becomes necessary to turn our attention to the definition of the "dissociation" concept, and its relation to repression. McDougall (54) gave a direct discussion of these points which it will be worthwhile to quote:[62]

"If the case were one of repression only, we should expect to find that the patient avoids all reference to the incident the memory of which is repressed; we might even find, especially after the repression had been maintained for some time, that the patient could not easily remember it at will; and we might find evidences of the repressed affect in dreams and fantasies which she could not easily remember. Some degree of such repression takes place in many persons in connection with such painful incidents. We should also find evidence of repression and continuing conflict in a continuing distress of the patient, and perhaps in other signs that the conflict was consuming her energies internally.

"But, when dissociation has taken place, the state of the patient is different; she not only does not recur to the topic, or has difficulty in remembering it, but she seems to have lost all memory of it completely. So far as her waking life is concerned, the memory seems to have dropped away, to have ceased to exist. She shows no signs of continuing conflict, no distress; she shows rather an unnatural indifference, what the French have called 'une belle indifference' or 'une belle complaissance.' And, when the dissociated memory with its strong affect manifests itself, it does so, not by disturbing the judgment, producing dreams or fantasies, or otherwise affecting the conscious stream of the normal personality but rather by abolishing for the time being the normal personality and dominating the whole organism. This last feature of the dissociated activity does not always appear; rather in very many cases the dissociated system manifests itself by an 'automatic activity' that runs on beside or contemporaneously with the normal conscious activity." (p. 236)

"Another difference between the process of dissociation and the process of repression is that, whereas the latter is commonly a slow gradual process, attaining many different degrees that vary from moment to moment according to the reciprocal play of the repressed and the repressing forces, dissociation is apt to be a sudden process, instantaneously accomplished. It would, perhaps, not be strictly true to say that dissociation is an all-or-nothing process." (p. 237)

It appears that the differentiation which McDougall attempts is by no means as sharp as these statements would have it. First, the alternation

[58] See Chapter V, p. 166ff.
[59] See pp. 204–206.
[60] See Chapter VI, p. 174ff.
[61] See p. 196.
[62] See also B. Hart (74).

of personalities produces, like repression, much conflict and distress.[63] Secondly, the dissociated material, like the repressed, manifests itself in dreams and phantasies, McDougall's statement to the contrary notwithstanding. Thirdly, our discussion of the types of multiple personalities has shown that there is no absolute division between dissociated material and everyday material. Fourthly, the process of dissociation is frequently as gradual as that of repression, as anyone can ascertain by looking at M. Prince's (50) table in which the pace of onset is specifically tabulated. Thus, dissociation becomes a process different only in degree from repression. But this difference in degree, its origin, its mechanisms, are still entirely unexplained. Morton Prince (58), in developing the theory of multiple personality on the basis of the case of Miss Beauchamp, illuminated another aspect of dissociation which is of import in our present context. He attempted to show that underlying the dissociation of consciousness, and of memory and sensory systems, there is a dissociation of "instincts," "emotions," and "sentiments."[64] He showed for instance that hate, scorn, contempt, envy, jealousy, vengefulness, resentment, and joyfulness were present in Sally and absent in the original personality B I; but that self-abasement, disgust, fear, gratitude, self-reproach, anxiety, shame, bashfulness were absent in Sally and present in B I. The core of these differing behavior patterns appear to be differing "affects," "sentiments" and "attitudes." In other reports on multiple personalities similar, though perhaps less striking, differences may be found. For the theory of the "emotional influence on memory" this is of great significance, if M. Prince's interpretation of the case of Miss Beauchamp can be accepted at its face value. Then the following formulation could be advanced: multiple personalities are behavior- and memory-patterns organized around differing and dissociated sets of affects, sentiments, and attitudes. This dissociation may be conceived thus: not the memories pertaining to a single unacceptable striving are forgotten, as in repression proper, but a number of coherent strivings sufficient to yield the appearance of a "personal identity" become unacceptable to the personality proper; accordingly full sets of memories become unavailable. Multiple personalities become more clear-cut as the dissociation of sets of affects and strivings from each other becomes sharper; consequently, memories and reactions can no longer be elicited by different strivings, as is normally the case, but only by a specific set of strivings.

The transition would then be continuous between repression in which a memory connected with an unacceptable striving cannot emerge, and dis-

[63] See e.g. the cases of Felida X and Hanna, p. 207.
[64] See Prince (58, pp. 71–82).

sociation in which sets of strivings become unacceptable to the consciousness, sets of affects become alien to it, and memories of whole periods become unavailable.

This discussion has attempted to show how the phenomenon of multiple personality shades into other amnesias, such as the hypnotic, somnambulistic, fugue, and retrograde amnesias: like them, multiple personality also may be precipitated by psychic as well as physiological traumata; in both the core of the memory disturbance appears to be an emotional one.

5. AMNESIAS PRECIPITATED BY ORGANIC TRAUMATA

In this section we shall attempt to discuss the phenomena of memory pathology which are not of the group usually called Korsakow or amnesic syndrome, but which nevertheless are precipitated by organic brain damage. This delineation of our topic—a delineation made by exclusion—shows that we shall hardly deal with a unitary complex of problems. However, not only is it difficult to distinguish the Korsakow group from those disturbances to be considered here, but it is difficult to distinguish some disturbances subsumed usually in the organic group from functional disturbances. For instance, although amnesias following head injuries are on the whole reported to be retrograde,[65] careful recent studies[66] show that in these cases memory disturbances of the Korsakow type are also common. Amnesia for epileptic fugues, epileptic twilight states and epileptic major convulsions are usually considered in the organic group; but if the problem of "ideopathic epilepsies" and the fluid transition between "epileptic" and hysterical psychopathology are taken into consideration,[67] the justification for grouping the epileptic with the organic amnesias remains based only on the residual "pure" group in which the focal lesion accounting for the seizures is demonstrated beyond doubt. Other facts show even further the artificiality of the division: for example, the Korsakow syndrome is essentially an anterograde amnesia which has several varieties—senile, alcoholic, paretic—but the most spectacular anterograde amnesias in the organic group are not of the Korsakow type. The whole field of observation is too little explored and too much is entirely unknown to permit even the formation of hypotheses.[68] However, the division of the material into non-Korsakow and Korsakow organic amnesias provides an opportunity to discuss two different groups of problems.

[65] See Russel (22).
[66] See Schilder (75).
[67] In this connection see Maeder (76), Sidis (77), and Wittels (78).
[68] This situation is so immature that no discussion of the nature of different organic amnesias is found in such standard psychiatric textbooks as those of E. Bleuler (80) or Henderson and Gillespie (16).

A. FUNCTIONAL VS. ORGANIC FACTORS

For those interested in the role of emotions in the pathology of memory, the "organic" amnesias raise an important problem. If these amnesias are direct sequelae of the organic damage, we cannot hope by studying them to learn anything of the role of emotions. If, however, the amnesia is a psychological response to the organic damage and/or to the narcissistic blow it necessarily entails, then there is much to be learned concerning the role of emotions in the development of organic amnesias. Naturally, there is also a third possibility: that the amnesia implies both the direct sequelae of, and the psychological response to, the organic damage and that the differences in the relative weight of the participation of these two factors make for the great variety in the phenomenology of organic amnesias. That interaction of the organic and the functional was not taken into consideration until lately is revealed in the following discussion by Coriat (79), even though he was one of the pioneers of the functional point of view in this country:

"Amnesia is either a dissociation or a destruction of this reproductive activity, and according to the exact condition, it may be broadly divided into organic and functional. The factors in the production of the organic amnesias are the various poisons, of which alcohol is of prime importance, trauma, epilepsy, and diffuse or localised brain lesions, such as occurs in general paralysis, senile dementia, Korsakow's disease, tumors and hemorrhages. The functional amnesias stand in a causal relation to hysteria and the emotions, which factors are highly productive in causing dissociations of memory. So far as the synthesis of these dissociated memory disorders is concerned it is only in the functional and in a few of the organic types such as some alcoholic, epileptic or traumatic amnesias, that experimental procedure seems to be successful. Here there is no real oblivion or destruction of images, they are dissociated from the personal conscious perception. In the organic types the destruction is real, because the functioning tissue of the cortex itself suffers a physical deterioration." (pp. 109–110)

The present status of research is not advanced enough to settle the problems involved here. Evidence seems to indicate that a sharp dichotomy like that made by Coriat does not exist, and that there is a participation by both organic and emotional factors in the so-called "organic amnesias."

A portion of the material relevant to this problem is concerned with the recoverability of amnesias. It was long the belief that the irrecoverable loss of memories is to be ascribed to destruction of their traces in the brain. Thus, recoverability was considered the criterion of functional amnesias, and irrecoverability the criterion of organic amnesias. Such a dichotomy disregards the most frequent case—namely, that in which the loss is partly recoverable and partly irrecoverable. The increasing attention paid to functional disturbances in the course of this century has resulted in attempts to recover amnesias of apparently organic origin by employing techniques used in recovering functional amnesias, such as distraction, association, hypnosis, and drug hypnosis. For instance, Coriat (79) reported the successful recovery of the memories of the amnesic period of alcoholic amnesias, Naef (81) those of a traumatic amnesia, Muralt (82) and Schilder (83, 84) those of epileptic amnesias. J. Wagner (85) and Schilder (88) those of asphyxiation amnesias. Schultz (86), Stern (87), and Schneider (7) gave extensive reviews of similar pertinent material. A further step was made when Schilder (83) and others demonstrated, by the saving found in relearning of apparently lost and irrecoverable material, that some kind of trace must be left even in such cases. Oberholzer (89), Betlheim and Hartmann (90),[69] and Hartmann (91) were not satisfied with concluding from recoverability, or from demonstrability in saving, of amnesic material that the amnesia was of functional origin. They investigated the nature of retention in such amnesias, and were able to show that so-called Freudian mechanisms played a significant role in it. On the basis of this discovery they were satisfied that a functional factor was present in these organic amnesias.

These were the findings concerning the functional side of the picture; now let us turn to the organic side. Jones and Ghiselli (92) trained rats for certain sensory discrimination-habits; they found that after removing the parts of the brain above the mesencephalon and thus producing a loss of the habit, the habit was re-established by renewed training with a considerably smaller number of trials than was needed originally. They advanced the hypothesis that the retention of the engram is the function of the mesencephalic and even lower structures, and that the higher centers play only the role of a dynamic relay. According to these investigators, the higher centers send discharges to the lower centers in accordance with their own rhythms as well as with the sensory impulses reaching them, and thus elicit and relay—"translate"—memories. After destruction of this relay the habit is forgotten, and the re-learning process establishes a new "translation" of the engrams stored in the non-destroyed parts of the brain. Although the significance for human psychology of an animal experiment must always be evaluated with utmost caution, this experiment provides at least an analogy of what might happen in the organic sphere in the case of amnesias connected with organic traumata. It shows that retention, as indicated by saving in re-learning or the partial reversibility of the amnesia, is not necessarily a proof for the functional-emotional origin of the disturbance.

Having discussed material illuminating the problem of the functional-

[69] See for details Chapter VIII, p. 250ff.

emotional etiology of "organic amnesias," and the material illuminating the organic etiology of them, we shall discuss material which points to the interaction of both. This material pertains to the field of the organic psychoses, which apparently are related to the psychoses in general as are the organic amnesias to the amnesias in general. We shall use for the purpose of this discussion a typical representative of these organic psychoses: the psychosis of general paresis. In this disorder the brain damage is so obvious and impressive that until a few decades ago its purely organic origin was taken for granted. Only later did Naecke (93) begin to speak of an "axial"—organic-irreversible—and a "marginal"—functional-reversible—deterioration. Still later, Hollos and Ferenczi (94) showed that the psychosis of general paresis is a psychological response to the organic damage. Their conclusions, supported later by those of Schilder (95) and Katan (96),[70] were that in the psychosis of general paresis the debilitating organic damage is experienced by the patient as a narcissistic blow, and is responded to by a regression to a level of psychological development where the damage to the functions is not experienced as a loss. Kenyon, Rapaport, and Lozoff (97) attempted to analyze the psychosomatic relationship implicit in the development of a psychosis involving both organic loss and emotional-functional symptomatic response. Similar relationships may obtain between amnesia caused by organic damage—axial—and its functional extension—marginal—coming about as a psychological response to the damage itself, or to the narcissistic blow inflicted by the impotent fear and anxiety prevailing at the time of the injury. In support of such a theory would be the findings concerning the pre-morbid adjustment of the victims of organic amnesia which frequently show emotional lability. Such findings, although reported in the literature, are by no means general or unequivocal.

B. THE VARIETIES OF ORGANIC AMNESIA

In the organic amnesias, as in the functional amnesias, we have three groups: retrograde and anterograde amnesias, "loss of personal identity," and multiple personalities. We shall not discuss in detail the nature of the "organic involvement" or the "organic precipitating factor" in these amnesias in general, or in the cases to be discussed in particular. We shall consider as "organic" all those cases usually classed as "organic" in the literature, inasmuch as our aim is to show the presence of emotional factors in different cases rather than to establish their exact nature. What

---

[70] See the survey of the pertinent theories in Kenyon, Rapaport, and Lozoff (97), and corroborative observational and experimental test material in Kenyon and Rapaport (98), and Kenyon, Lozoff, and Rapaport (99).

is the organic involvement in the amnesias precipitated by asphyxiation? Is it ascribable to an anoxia similar to that which makes high flying and mountain-climbing dangerous? What is the organic involvement in carbon-monoxide poisoning, which so frequently results in spectacular irreversible amnesias without the presence of direct neurological indications of organic damage? The material surveyed does not answer these questions. It may be readily admitted that in a number of such cases the organic involvement may be questionable. It is beyond the scope of this discussion to investigate these problems; we shall limit ourselves to considering the emotional aspect of these cases.

a. Retrograde Amnesias

These amnesias usually cover a period previous to the organic trauma and are of rather short duration; long duration raises the suspicion of functional involvement (Russel, 22). In many cases the presence of strong emotional motives is apparent. Thus for instance Dunn (100) reported a case of amnesia following asphyxiation, and gave a description in which the role of the emotional factors can be readily seen. A young woman fell into a river and nearly drowned: subsequently she forgot her previous life and all the habits she had acquired; she recognized neither her surroundings nor her relatives, and lost the use of her senses except for sight and touch. Nevertheless, even in this primitivized state, she gave signs of terror upon seeing water or a picture of it, and responded affectionately to the young man who was interested in her before, and for a time after, her accident. These were the two ideas, obviously loaded with emotion, which she did not forget. The slow recovery was suddenly interrupted when the young man ceased to pay attention to her; a stuporous state ensued, and upon emergence from this she was again her own self. The emotional character of the retained ideas, and of the event restoring her memory, leave no doubt of the participation of the emotional factor, whatever its dynamics and its relation to any organic factors present. Such examples could be multiplied without limit; our aim is not to describe interesting and dramatic cases, but rather to show that ideas propelled by affects persist while all is forgotten, and that the forgotten re-emerges when strong emotional forces affect a psychic "shake-up."

b. Anterograde Amnesias

The anterograde amnesias reported in the literature have been, in most cases, precipitated by somatic traumata. Only a few functional cases, like those of Janet already discussed,[71] have been recorded and in these also retro- and anterograde amnesia were simultaneously present.

[71] See p. 194ff.

The most clear-cut case of pure and extreme anterograde amnesia was reported by Stoerring (23) in 1931, who called it "the first case of total and isolated loss of retention-ability." His patient suffered a carbon monoxide poisoning, after which he was unable to retain any impression or idea longer than two seconds and accordingly lived as though time had stopped for him at the date of the poisoning. The loss of retention (Merkfaehigkeit) was so impressive and so absolutely generalized that Stoerring was certain that he dealt here with a purely organic case, although *he was not able to report any neurological or other physical findings*. He compared the case with the Korsakow syndrome, concerning which he still held to the out-dated view—to be discussed in the next section—which considers the essence of this syndrome to be a loss of retention. Apparently Stoerring had only the possibility of an organic explanation in mind, and thus neglected to apply any constructive means by which the nature and finer structure of this spectacular amnesia could have been investigated or by which the patient's retention ability could have been restored. No hypnotic or drug-hypnotic attempts at investigating unconscious memories, or at restoring the lost memories, were reported. In spite of the limitations of Stoerring's approach, a few facts about the emotional make-up of the subject transpire in the report. We learn that the patient was a very meticulous, compulsive, and inhibited person before his accident; that he had an eight-year engagement and—although the author omits discussion of the patient's sexual life—apparently kept safe distance from his fiancée in this period; and that the patient's actions in his amnesic state were characterized by sudden impulses in which certain drives and feelings readily found expression.

Very similar to this case is that reported by Syz (24).[72] A 45-year old man suffered a fall, lost consciousness, vomited, and became confused and sleepless; his right side was paralyzed, his leg anesthetic. Five months later he lost retention for all occurrences subsequent to the accident, and continued to forget in an anterograde fashion all that he was experiencing. Three years later he commenced to improve physically, and was seen at that time by the author of the report. Although the amnesia was nearly as generalized as in Stoerring's case, the patient appeared to be greatly puzzled and felt that something must be wrong, and even expressed himself to this effect; in Stoerring's case this awareness could be elicited only by painstakingly confronting the patient with contradictions of the situation. The period of retention was somewhat longer than in Stoerring's case. Syz pointed out that the disturbance of gait, which was the most prominent symptom except for the memory disturbance, seemed to be of a functional nature. Additional striking features suggested that this amnesia

[72] See also Syz (101).

had strong emotional components. The patient had been known before the incapacitating accident as a "walking encyclopedia" because of his unusually good memory, and as a man of a somewhat exaggerated sense of justice and morality. He was a worker who read much, was socially active in organizing labor and making speeches, and was highly interested in politics and music. During the ᴄourse of his illness he was sensitive, moody, preoccupied, depressed, and moderately irritable. There was an "almost obsessive fear of falling, . . . suggestive of emotionally dynamic factors" (p. 368). Syz applied hypnosis in an endeavor to recover memories; he suggested to the patient that he would recall dreams in the morning, a time when otherwise he was unable to retain recent material. The material thus obtained showed that the patient's outstanding difficulty in emotional adjustment was a thorough dissatisfaction with his marital situation. He had married as a matter of moral self-protection when at 18 he felt himself "slipping," indulging in alcoholic and sexual "irregularities." His wife, a sentimental person, had withdrawn from him after the birth of their children; many years of sexual frustration followed, in which the patient had difficulty in controlling his wish for sexual attachments with more approachable women. After a week's work which yielded the material described, the patient brought a dream which proved to be a memory of an actual occurrence. The patient had overheard during his illness a conversation between his wife and another man which seemed to indicate that sexual relations existed between them. The recovery of this memory resulted in a gradual but steady general recovery from the amnesic state. The author concluded that this was a case of a post-traumatic disorder in which both organic and psychogenic factors were present, and wrote:

"As far as memory is concerned, one usually finds that the emotionally determined impairment of recall is limited to specific aspects of the personality and its life experiences. The case described here is unusual in that there was not merely a blotting out or repressing of specific memory material but the capacity of recall was quite generally impaired. We may say that a generalized functional change, probably first induced through an organic lesion, was employed in an unusual way in the process of neurotic equilibration." (p. 378)

Whether the view of Syz, according to which the process here encountered is different from that of repression, should be sustained, or whether it may be assumed that repression can be so general and rapid that the memory of new experiences immediately after occurrence is included in this process of repression, can not be yet decided; we lack sufficient systematic knowledge of this type of disturbance.

Another case of anterograde amnesia should be described, as it was reported of himself by a reputable psychologist and its short duration makes for its clarity.[73] Cason (102) describes a skating fall which resulted in a short anterograde amnesia, the progress of which was observed and recorded by his skating partner. Cason fell and struck his head, and apparently was amnesic for the following forty-eight minutes. The record of the friend shows that in this period Cason asked repeatedly, in spite of answers: "Will you tell me just exactly how I fell?" This case may be used to elucidate two aspects of anterograde amnesia. Anterograde amnesia may be described, in contrast to retrograde amnesia, as an amnesia in which the period forgotten is the period following that event which precipitated the onset of the amnesia. It may be described also as an amnesia in which experiences following the precipitating event are progressively forgotten as soon as they occur. Authors reporting cases of anterograde amnesia usually describe either one or the other aspect. For this reason, the literature does not make clear whether anterograde amnesia is always progressive, or whether it can set in at once after a period following the precipitating event has elapsed; it covers this period and may end with it or may thereafter become progressive. In Cason's case, the description of his repetition of his question seems to make it clear that the amnesia was progressive. His preoccupation with the idea of his fall has a monoideic character. The monoideic character of this case shows some similarity to that seen in the case observed by M. Gill and the present author.[74]

Cason resisted attempts to make him stop skating, and also attempts to help him to get home. The record of his partner concerning this period reads:

"Gradually X increased his speed while he practiced turning to the left and right with his arms held out in the opposite direction like I had shown him. I thought it rather funny that he should attempt to skate as fast as he did after he had suffered such a shock when he had struck head on the ice. In fact he skated faster and executed the curves with greater skill than he had done before his fall." (p. 109)

We learn further that Cason discussed his—apparently non-existent—skating superiority over his friend in a manner which may be called childish and aggressive. No neurological findings were present, and Cason was in good health at the time. An interpreter might maintain that the shock was not only a bodily but a narcissistic blow, to which the subject reacted in a childish, aggressive, and stubborn way; and apparently there was a need to amnesize this reaction. How the organic blow precipitates the amnesia and interlaces with the narcissistic blow is, of course, not solved by such speculation.

[73] For other cases see Ribot (6), p. 123 ff. and Koempfen (103), p. 489.
[74] See p. 201ff.

c. "Loss of Personal Identity"

The "loss of personal identity" has been considered as a typically "emotional" memory disturbance. Nevertheless, Abeles and Schilder (31) noted that cases of organic etiology also occur, and Gordon and Lawrence (36) discussed two such cases. These, it was described, showed organic lesions of traumatic and arteriosclerotic origin, respectively. Nevertheless, sodium amytal temporarily lifted the loss of personal identity; with the wearing off of the drug, the loss returned. Furthermore, gradual improvement of the memory, independent of drugs, was reported. Both cases, however, showed emotional features of the memory disturbance, and the authors concluded:

"With the demonstration of the organic background of the amnesic disturbance, however, we still are far from having proved the true nature of the amnesic disturbance. We have stated above that emotional factors may play a definite role in the fixation of memory imprints (engrams), and we know, too, that forgetting or inability to remember may have its special emotional implications. . . . However, the emotional reaction cannot be entirely held responsible for the character and extent of the amnesia. It would be unwise to conclude that because these patients do not remember the past, they do not want to remember the past, or because they do not know their names, they have the subconscious desire to cease continuity with their former existence. It seems more plausible to assume that for want of proper adaptive mechanisms which were put out of action, the bridges that connect past and present existence, cannot be immediately used. That under such abnormal situations factors of volitional repression may play an additional role cannot, however, be disregarded." (p. 110)

d. Multiple Personalities

The multiple personalities, and the alternating systems of memory and amnesia connected with them, which we have discussed in the chapter on functional amnesias, have also a counterpart in the organic group. The case precipitated by gas poisoning and described by Dana (104), the case precipitated by a heavy fall reported by Sidis and Goodhart (52), the case described by Gaver (64) precipitated by a blow on the head, the cases precipitated by shell-shock such as those described by Feiling (105) and Franz (106), the self-reported case of Ikin (107) precipitated by a delirium, are a few examples of this type.   Yet there is reason to doubt that many of these organically-precipitated multiple personalities are truly comparable with the multiple personalities of functional origin. In the case of T. Hanna the two personalities really alternated, and although the account was not specific with regard to this point, two sets of emotional attitudes were discernible. In the case reported by Franz (106), the alternation of personalities was present and was observed to depend on emotional factors:

" . . . it is worthy to note that every change which had been observed, or of which we have had reasonable information, was known to be preceded by a period in which he was under what is commonly called 'emotional strain.' He was worried financially, or he was irritated, or he was fearful, or he may have been too happy." (p. 188)

But in the remainder of the cases, what is described as "dual personality" could be equally well described as a total retrograde post-traumatic amnesia in the period of which much was re-learned; the person functioning with this partially re-learned knowledge was considered a second "personality," the more so as the recovery of the amnesia usually resulted in a forgetting of the period in which the total amnesia existed.[75]   This is a change parallel to that found in fugues, where simultaneously with the recovery of personal identity an amnesia for the period of "loss of personal identity" ensues; the usual explanation of this forgetting is the unacceptability of the central idea of the fugue.   Similar also is the amnesia of hypnosis; here Schilder[76] attributed the forgetting to the unacceptability to the waking consciousness of the "passive-masochistic" adjustment.   Whether such an explanation can be extended to the childishly helpless adjustment with which multiple personalities of the organic type—like Dana's case—start life anew, is yet to be answered.   Ikin's case of Vera was simply a history of a delirium with several distinct sets of intense, systematized delusions and hallucinations. This and many other organic cases should be regarded with caution, for the inclination is to designate as "multiple personality" anything which resembles it.[77]

The amnesias in the precipitation of which organic damage has played a significant role have in general shown some emotional involvement. That reversibility and irreversibility of an amnesia cannot be equated with functional and organic etiology has been suggested by the material surveyed.   These amnesias appeared to represent a psychosomatic problem, whose solution has hardly been attempted.   The problem of the role of pre-traumatic emotional make-up and personality structure in the genesis of such amnesias has been pointed out.

6. MEMORY-PATHOLOGY IN THE KORSAKOW SYNDROME

We have thus far avoided discussion of the memory phenomena found in the psychoses, such as memory-delusions, pseudo- and allomnesias, and

[75] The period *in which* a retrograde amnesia exists has to be carefully distinguished from the period *for which* the retrograde amnesia exists or, in other words, *over which* it extends.

[76] See pp. 175–176.

[77] Mitchel (45) wrote: "The terms double and multiple personality have been perhaps too freely applied to dissociations of consciousness whenever the accompanying amnesia is of any noticeable extent." (p. 139)

hallucinations. We have avoided even a discussion of the memory phenomena found in the neuroses, such as "obsessive ideas"; the only exception was our discussion of the gross amnesias. Our aim in this was to avoid entering into a discussion of the etiology of neuroses and psychoses; such a discussion would require an extended treatment for which neither the structure nor the scope of this monograph provided. Nevertheless, it seemed to us that the Korsakow syndrome must be included in our treatment, for it has been considered a memory-disturbance par excellence.

A. AUTISTIC THINKING

Before discussing the memory phenomena of this syndrome, we must dwell upon a point which has not been discussed explicitly in these pages. We refer to the concept of "autistic thinking."[78] It was in the psychoses that it was first discovered that, in addition to logical-realistic thinking, there exists another kind of thinking, called by Bleuler "autistic" (108) or "autistic-undisciplined" (109) thinking and by Jung (110) "introversive" thinking. Later it was realized that under many conditions, and to a certain extent in every person's normal thinking, autistic elements of this type appear to be present. The characterization of the dream and its mechanisms as autistic thinking was also suggested. Bleuler (108) wrote:

" . . . we find these mechanisms operating in the common dreams, in the daydreams of hysterics and normals, in the mythology and the related superstitions as well as in other deviations of thinking from reality. From the dream of the child, who on his stick, fancied to be a horse, plays 'general,' through the poet who abreacts his unhappy love or changes it into a happy one, to the hysterics and schizophrenics, who see their wishes fulfilled in hallucinations, there is a continuous transition showing only quantitative differences." (p. 2)

In the same work of Bleuler we find the following description of autistic thinking:

"Autistic thinking is directed thinking. It reflects fulfilment of wishes or strivings; it eliminates obstacles; in it, impossibilities are thought of as possibilities and realities. This is achieved by facilitation of those associations corresponding to, and inhibition of those conflicting with, these strivings; *that is to say, by the mechanism we know as the influence of affects.* To explain autistic thinking we do not need any new principles." (p. 4)

Here it is stated that the thinking of psychotics, and all thinking which is similar in principle and called autistic thinking, is affect-determined. Inasmuch as thought processes are built of emerging memories, the affective regulation of thinking pertains also to memory functioning.

[78] See also pp. 141ff., 156ff.

Influenced by Jung's, Bleuler's, and Freud's investigations of this mode of thinking, Varendonck (111) observed and analyzed a number of his own daydreams. Some of his conclusions will be of interest here:

"We conclude . . . that the *affects seem to constitute the active connection between memory and perception and conversely between perception and memory*. They preside at the transformation in the mind of memory elements into perceptions, and at the awakening of recollections . . ." (p. 197)

He writes further:

" . . . *in fore-conscious thinking the relation between memory and affect is causative; affects may stimulate recollection; conversely, remembrances may provoke dormant affects*." (p. 200)

Finally, in regard to daydreams he is most explicit:

" . . . *when we are daydreaming our phantasies owe their genesis to the influence of two inner factors: affect and memory, which often prove stronger than the power which consciousness has at its disposal*." (p. 204)

Though much was contributed to the problem of autistic thinking by ethnologists like Lévy-Bruehl (112), philosophers like Cassirer (113), and systematizing psychologists like Werner (114),[79] much remains to be learned about it. Its relation to unconscious and primary processes, as described by Freud,[80] has not yet been clarified. The formal characteristics of autistic thinking have been well summarized by Werner (114). The inner logic of this thinking has not yet, to our knowledge, been systematized; this "logic of affects" is still to be written.[81] It has been suggested that some of the laws ruling this logic are "the almightiness of thought," "the law of the 'talion,' " "the fulfilment of wishes," "suspension of the laws of logic such as 'identity' and 'the excluded third.' " In the annals of psychology the chapter on "autistic"—or, as it is frequently called, "primitive"—thinking has just begun to be written.

It is difficult to define the exact relation of autistic thinking to the Korsakow syndrome, which we shall now describe. We shall attempt to elucidate some aspects of this relationship. We may state here, however, that inasmuch as the Korsakow syndrome is the only psychosis whose phenomena we shall discuss, "autistic thinking," as characteristic of the thinking and memory functions of psychoses, constitutes a proper background.

[79] See also the review of his book by Rapaport (115).
[80] See p. 159ff.
[81] In this connection, see Alexander's attempt to discuss the logic of emotions (116).

B. THE KORSAKOW SYNDROME AND THE VIEWS CONCERNING IT

The textbook on psychiatry by Henderson and Gillespie (16) describes the Korsakow syndrome as follows:

"This psychosis first described by Korsakow consists in deficient power of retention for recent events, with a tendency to confabulate and disorientation for time, place, and person . . . Memory for remote events is usually good." (pp. 273–274)

This description shows that the memory disturbance is a central phenomenon of the Korsakow syndrome. The little that this quotation says about the Korsakow memory disturbance makes it appear to be an anterograde amnesia, with a tendency to replace by confabulation what cannot be remembered. Although the textbook quoted is a modern one, this view of the Korsakow disturbance is still Korsakow's view, and overlooks fifty years of clinical and experimental development.[82] We shall first outline here the historical development of knowledge concerning this memory disturbance, partly because, so far as we know, it has been scarcely summarized systematically in the literature in English, and partly because such a historical outline promises to show the relation of general psychological theory to the formation of clinical theories.

It is maintained by the French that Charcot, and by the Germans that Lilienfeld, reported the first case of this type. At any rate, Korsakow is credited with the first detailed description (118, 119). These three descriptions associated the disturbance with alcoholic polyneuritis; Jolly, according to the French, or Tilling, according to the Germans, was the first to show that this condition is neither necessarily alcoholic nor necessarily associated with polyneuritis, but is generally toxic. Since then, memory disturbance of the Korsakow type has been observed in cases of brain injury and in general paresis. Apparently, toxic, inflammatory, and even traumatic brain conditions may issue in the memory disturbance called the Korsakow syndrome.[83]

Korsakow, Kraepelin, and Bonhoeffer agreed in considering this memory disturbance a disturbance of registration. This view was precarious in more than one respect. First, it is difficult to establish a differentiation between the functions of perception (Wahrnehmung) and registration (Merkfaehigkeit). The assumption of a registration-disturbance implies a perception-disturbance, and for the latter there was generally no evidence in the amnesic syndrome. Secondly, although Korsakow and Bonhoeffer (120) upheld this view, they recorded cases in which apparently forgotten events were later remembered by Korsakow patients. Bonhoeffer for instance wrote:

[82] This formulation does not differ from that of J. M. Moll (117).
[83] See also on this point Henderson and Gillespie (116, pp. 273–274).

" . . . the influence of new experiences—though they are forgotten—is not lost, from the point of view of the personality. The whole character of intellectual maturity is retained in spite of the amnesia." (p. 78)

Gregor and Roemer (121), and Gregor (122), reported experiments which originally were designed to test *how long* Korsakow patients retain memories, and whether their memory can be improved by training. The results showed surprisingly good immediate memory functioning. In agreement with these authors, Kohnstamm (123) later emphasized that what is poor in the Korsakow patient is not his registration and recall in' learning, but his spontaneous registration and recall.[84]

Pick (124) and Gruenthal (125) continued this lead, and formulated the disturbance in terms of the Wuerzburg school of psychology. Thus they maintained that the Korsakow syndrome is a disturbance of thinking in which especially the orientation—"Einstellung"—towards the idea which is necessary to continue the chain of thought is disturbed. This "orientation" disturbance does not allow for finding the proper memory at the proper time, and thus gives the appearance of a mere memory disturbance.

Van der Horst (126) was not satisfied with this explanation, and attributed the "orientation" disturbance to a loss of the "temporal signs" of the memories. He maintained that memories usually have a temporal sign which plays a significant role in their proper and easy revival. The frequent reduplicating paramnesias[85] and the general laxity of temporal localization of events in the Korsakow patient served as objective evidence for the loss of temporal signs. Bouman and Gruenbaum's (127) interesting case in which a subject experienced 27 years of his life as three years, and the theory of time-experience which these authors built on it, seemed to support van der Horst's theory. These authors maintained that the

[84] Kohnstamm wrote: "From spontaneous registration to registration in learning there is a fluid transition with many intermediary stages. The first is the affect-toned registration, the second the interested and observing registration. In this manner do we read scientific literature which is retained to the degree to which we absorb it with interest. I retained much better the history which I witnessed through early reading of newspapers than the laboriously learned data of world history which I crammed in high school." (p. 378)

[85] Reduplicating paramnesia, like "déjà vue," is the phenomenon in which an event now encountered is experienced with the conviction, "I have already once experienced all this." Freud (128) and Poetzl (129) made it clear in their investigations that not two events were identical in these, but that the affective situation of the subject towards the recent event was identical with that experienced when having encountered another event in the past. Not an objective repetition of events but the subjective identity of affect is the basis of this memory phenomenon. Heymanns (130, 131), showing that "déjà vue" is more frequent in emotionally labile subjects, maintained that this finding vouches for an emotional origin of the phenomenon.

time-experiencing alone may be afflicted, and may account for other psychic disturbances.[86]

Burger (132) attempted to express the Korsakow memory disturbance, divested by this time of its apparent registration-disturbance and anterograde amnesia character, in terms of Gestalt psychology as it had been applied to psychopathology by K. Goldstein. Burger maintained that the patients are able to grasp and retain only simple relations and psychic whole-situations of simple structure. The remainder of the psychic contents remains a foggy "background" which cannot become a "figure" (Gestalt). This was, of course, only a restatement of what Pick and Gruenthal had formulated in other terms.

At this time Betlheim and Hartmann (90), Schilder (95), and Hartmann (91, 133) had conducted experiments investigating the memory functioning of the Korsakow patient; paretic-Korsakow cases were especially considered. These investigations showed that the memory-loss is only an apparent one, that what is present is a special memory organization resembling that seen in dreams, characterized by symbolization, distortion, condensation, and elimination of disagreeable parts and addition of other parts which transform the memory material in terms of "wishfulfilment."[87]

Krauss (134) attacked the problem with the methods of the pupils of Lewin.[88] He found that the tension systems which lend persistence to intentions, and which make for a resumption of interrupted activities and for their favoredness in retention over finished activities, are rapidly dissolved in the Korsakow patient.[89] He described clearly the emotional disturbance underlying the syndrome:

" . . . there is a lack of pregnance of feeling, imagination and thought-production; the stream of feeling is characterized by a dull flow and lack of differentiation and the 'emptiness' [experienced] is the lack of expressed events on this background." (p. 173)

The thinking of the Korsakow patient is characterized by his lack of "anticipations," which makes his conversation a monologue and prevents

[86] Bouman and Gruenbaum differentiate between chronognosy, chronology, and chronometry: (1) Chronognosy is the immanent time (Straus), the time of the inner life history (Binswanger), the leveling of time experiences, as they bring about the original time perspective. (2) Chronology is the inner life history made logical according to the pattern of the outside world history. (3) Chronometry is the scientific objectivation of chronology. The authors show that chronology and chronometry are retained by their patient; it is the chronognosy which is abnormal.

[87] See p. 161ff.

[88] See p. 94ff.

[89] A similar study was conducted on paretic patients in general by Golant-Rattner and Menteschaschwili (135); this study bears possible prognostic and diagnostic significance for the treatment of general paresis.

him from discoursive interaction with the thoughts of others. Action disintegrates, inasmuch as activities are not resumed and as saturation is extremely rapid. Self-correction is absent, as the thought content present monopolizes the field and opposite contents cannot be mobilized.

A synthetic picture of the disturbance was first given by Buerger-Prinz and Kaila (136), who investigated a number of cases intensively; they were aware of the earlier views, and discussed them in their report. They came to the conclusion that:

" . . . it is impossible to explain . . . [the Korsakow syndrome] by a pure 'memory-theory,' or even to maintain that the memory disturbances are its essential psycho-pathological symptoms. On the contrary: the whole emotionality and drive structure is changed. Nothing is lost, but the depth and width of action of the personality (Schilder) is absent. Situation follows situation; they exist momentarily and disappear without any after-effect . . . These disturbances start on the level on which memory functions are formed. The entire dynamics of the personality is changed. The strivings, drives, emotions are no longer driving forces . . . the patients lack spontaneity and await external impulses and can no longer do anything on their own." (pp. 554–555)

Their analysis of cases, showing how the memory and action disturbance originates in a central affective disturbance, deserves careful reading; it cannot be restated here. It will be proper, however, to discuss the problems of "orientation" and "temporal sign" in relation to the central affective or personality disturbance, for these lead back to the issue of autistic thinking.

c. "TIME-EXPERIENCING" AND "ORIENTATION" IN RELATION TO "AUTISTIC THINKING"

"Time-experiencing," the disturbance of which is considered by van der Horst to be the basis of the Korsakow memory-disturbance, appears to be itself a phenomenon dependent on affective life. We need only remind ourselves that certain individuals cannot delay communicating or putting into action ideas once conceived, while others can hardly be induced to do so; these "temperamental" differences are in themselves disturbances of time-experiencing. Hollos and Ferenczi (94) reported a long series of cases in which temporal relationships were changed in accordance with affective needs.[90] Hollos (137), Harnik (138), and Bonaparte (139) discussed time-experiencing from the psychoanalytic point of view, and showed its dependence on affective life. Spielrein's (140) paper, showing that the dream does not "know" time, leads to the investigations on the development of the time concept. H. Werner (114) has shown

[90] They reported that paretics frequently consider themselves of the age that immediately precedes their syphilitic infection, and so on.

that on developmental levels other than that of adults of the western civilization, the time concept as we know it is nonexistent; it lacks continuity, and is conceived in terms of space or recurring significant events. Thus what van der Horst observed was but one of the characteristics of autistic thinking as manifest in Korsakow patients. The problem of time-experiencing is in great need of a systematic exploration.[91]

"Orientation" or "anticipation," the disturbance of which was considered by Pick and Gruenthal to be the basis of the Korsakow memory disturbance, is an important but little known function. Thinking presupposes that the idea proper to continue the chain of thought will automatically emerge. This emergence is a memory function, for whatever emerges has been remembered in one form or another. The emerging memory is not a random one; it is one of many and is determined by selection, as even the simple free-association experiment shows. It is as though many strivings push ahead the ideas corresponding to them; the idea that finally emerges in consciousness is that one which is reality-adapted, for in it several strivings are expressed in a form of compromise. These compromises of strivings which are compatible with each other and with reality are usually rather stable, and their pushing into consciousness the idea which expresses them excludes from consciousness the incompatible strivings and the ideas corresponding to them. "Orientation" means that a given situation appeals to a certain set of strivings, which in response delivers the proper memories into consciousness. "Anticipation" is the expression of those who look at this process teleologically, and maintain that a thought process projects its continuation into the future as "anticipation" and that the memory fitting this anticipation is sought. In autistic thinking, in the dream, and in general in the "unconscious," all this does not hold true. The incompatible strivings and ideas coexist, merge, interchange. The lack of "orientation" and "anticipation" in the Korsakow patient is a type of thinking similar to "autistic thinking" proper. Incompatible ideas and strivings do not exclude each other; it is as though they were not in opposition but act side by side. The patient is a helpless object of the pushes of these strivings which neither form compromises nor prevent each other from entering consciousness. The same situation holds true for memory functioning in the Korsakow syndrome. Now a striving persists and a reduplicating paramnesia results; now they interchange and the continuity of experience is altogether broken. The strivings are no longer pitched to the environment or to each other, and stimulation does not necessarily arouse appropriate strivings and memories.

[91] In this connection see Israeli (141).

This appears to be the picture of the Korsakow syndrome, as fully as it can be derived from the literature. It is now beyond doubt that the Korsakow syndrome, which originally was considered to be a registration and retention loss due to organic lesions, has proved to imply important emotional components which effect the appearance of such losses. Further careful investigations may reveal much of the anatomy of thought and memory processes, which appear to be nowhere as amenable to investigation as in the Korsakow syndrome.

REFERENCES

(1) JANET, P. *The mental state of hystericals.* 535 pp. New York, Putnam's, 1901.

(2) BARNES, F. B. Some aspects of memory in the insane. *Amer. J. Psychol.* 19: 43–57, 1908.

(3) LILJENCRANTS, J. Memory defects in the organic psychoses. *Psychol. Monogr.* 32: 1–76, 1923.

(4) HUNT, J. McV. Psychological experiments with disordered persons. *Psychol. Bull.* 33: 1–58, 1936.

(5) JONES, E. Remarks on a case of complete autopsychic amnesia. *J. Abn. Psychol.* 4: 218–235, 1909.

(6) RIBOT, TH. *Diseases of memory.* 209 pp. London, Kegan, 5th ed., 1906.

(7) SCHNEIDER, K. Die Stoerungen des Gedaechtnisses. Pp. 508–526. In: *Handbuch der Geisteskrankheiten,* Vol. I. 732 pp. Ed. Bumke, O. Berlin, Springer, 1928.

(8) GILLESPIE, R. D. Amnesia. *Arch. Neurol. Psychiat.* 37: 748–764, 1937.

(9) BARTLETT, F. C. *Remembering: a study in experimental and social psychology.* 317 pp. Cambridge, Univ. Press, 1932.

(10) PICK, A. Zur Psychologie des Vergessens bei Geistes- und Nervenkranken. *Arch. Krim. Anthrop. Kriminal.* 18: 251–261, 1905.

(11) STRATTON, G. M. Retroactive hypermnesia and other emotional effects on memory. *Psychol. Rev.* 26: 474–486, 1919.

(12) LEAVITT, F. H. The etiology of temporary amnesia. *Amer. J. Psychiat.* 91: 1079–1088, 1935.

(13) MUNN, CH. Historical survey of the literature of stupor with the report of a case of twelve years' duration with complete amnesia for 10 years. *Amer. J. Psychiat.* 13: 1271–1283, 1934.

(14) FREUD, S., AND BREUER, J. On the psychical mechanism of hysterical phenomena. Pp. 24–41. In: *Collected Papers,* vol. 1. 359 pp. New Lond. Internat. Psychoanal. Press, 1924.

(15) FENICHEL, O. *Outline of clinical psychoanalysis.* 492 pp. New York, Psychoanal. Quart. Press, and Norton, 1934.

(16) HENDERSON, D. K., AND GILLESPIE, R. D. *A textbook of psychiatry.* 520 pp. Oxford Univ. Press, 1927.

(17) WECHSLER, I. S. *The neuroses.* 330 pp. Philadelphia, Saunders, 1929.

(18) RIVERS, W. H. R. *Instinct and the unconscious.* 277 pp. Cambridge Univ. Press, 1922.

(19) THOM, D. A., AND FENTON, N. Amnesias in war cases. *Amer. J. Insan.* 76: 437–448, 1920.

(20) KARDINER, A. *The traumatic neuroses of war.* 258 pp. Psychosom. Med. Monogr. New York, Nat. Res. Council 213, 1941.

(21) FREUD, S., FERENCZI, S., ABRAHAM, K., SIMMEL, E., AND JONES, E. *Psychoanalysis and the war neuroses.* 59 pp. London, Internat. Psychoanal. Press, 1921.

(22) RUSSEL, W. R. Amnesia following head injuries. *Lancet,* 229: 762–763, 1935.

(23) STOERRING, G. E. Ueber den ersten reinen Fall eines Menschen mit voelligem, isoliertem Verlust der Merkfaehigkeit. *Arch. Psychol.* 81: 257–284, 1931.

(24) SYZ, H. Recovery from loss of mnemic retention after head trauma. *J. gen. Psychol.* 17: 355–387, 1937.

(25) BONHOEFFER, K. *Die akuten Geisteskrankheiten der Gewohnheitstrinker.* 226 pp. Jena, Fischer, 1901.

(26) GILL, M., AND RAPAPORT, D. A case of loss of personal identity and its bearing on the theory of memory. To be published, 1942.

(27) SEARS, R. R. Functional abnormalities of memory with special reference to amnesia. *Psychol. Bull.* 33: 229–274, 1936.

(28) RAY, W. S. The relationship of retroactive inhibition, retrograde amnesia, and the loss of recent memory. *Psychol. Rev.* 44: 339–345, 1937.

(29) McGEOCH, J. A. Studies in retroactive inhibition. I. The temporal course of the inhibitory effects of interpolated learning. *J. gen. Psychol.* 9: 24–43, 1933.

(30) BRITT, S. H. Theories of retroactive inhibition. *Psychol. Rev.* 43: 207–216, 1936.

(31) ABELES, M., AND SCHILDER, P. Psychogenetic loss of personal identity: Amnesia. *Arch. Neurol. Psychiat.* 34: 587–604, 1935.

(32) GRIERSON, H. A. Memory and its disorders in relation to crime. *J. Ment. Sci.* 82: 360–370, 1936.

(33) BENNET, E. A. Fugue states. *Brit. J. Med. Psychol.* 8: 143–149, 1928.

(34) BRYAN, D. Note on cases of fugue. *Brit. J. Med. Psychol.* 8: 207–211, 1928.

(35) NAEF, M. Ein Fall von temporaerer, teilweise retrograder Amnesie, durch Suggestion geheilt. *Z. Hypnot.* 6: 321–354, 1897.

(36) GORDON, G. J., AND LAWRENCE, B. G. Loss of personal identity (amnesia) and its role in organic syndromes. *Delaware State Med. J.* 106–112, June, 1941.

(37) JANET, P. *The major symptoms of hysteria.* 345 pp. New York, Macmillan, 1907.

(38) MENNINGER, K. A. Cyclothymic fugues. Fugues associated with manic depressive psychosis: A case report. *J. Abn. Psychol.* 14: 54–63, 1919.

(39) FREUD, S. The interpretation of dreams. Pp. 181–549. In: *The basic writings of Sigmund Freud.* 1001 pp. Ed. Brill, A. A. New York, Modern Libr., 1938. First publ. *Die Traumdeutung,* Leipzig, Wien, Deuticke, 1900.

(40) DORCUS, R. M., AND SCHAFFER, G. W. *Textbook of abnormal psychology.* 389 pp. London, Allen, 1934.

(41) MENNINGER, K. A. *Man against himself.* 485 pp. New York, Harcourt, 1938.

(42) ERICKSON, M. H. The investigation of a specific amnesia. *Brit. J. Med. Psychol.* 13: 143–150, 1933.

(43) SCHILDER, P. The concept of hysteria. *J. Psychiat.* 95: 1389–1413, 1939.

(44) PRINCE, W. F. The Doris case of quintuple personality. *J. Abn. Psychol.* 11: 73–122, 1916.

(45) Mitchel, T. W.   Medical psychology and psychical research.   244 pp.   London, Methuen, 1922.

(46) McNish, R.   The philosophy of sleep.   336 pp.   Glasgow, M'Phun, 1838.

(47) Skae, D.   Case of intermittent mental disorder of the tertian type, with double consciousness.   Northern Med. J. (Edinburgh) 3: 10–13, 1845.

(48) Proust, N.   Automatisme ambulatoire chez un hystérique.   Revue de l'hypnotisme 4: 267–269, 1890.

(49) Mesnet, E.   De l'automatisme de la mémoire et du souvenir dans le somambulisme pathologique—considérations médico-légales.   Union médicale, 3 s., 18: 105–117, 1874.

(50) Prince, M.   Hysteria from the point of view of dissociated personality.   J. Abn. Psychol. 1: 170–187, 1906.

(51) Mitchell, S. W.   Mary Reynolds: a case of double consciousness.   Tr. Coll. Physicians, Philadelphia, 3 s., 10: 366–384, 1888.

(52) Sidis, B., and Goodhart, S. P.   Multiple personality.   453 pp.   New York, Appleton, 1919.

(53) Mitchill, S. L.   A double consciousness, or a duality of person in the same individual.   Med. Repository, n.s. 3: 185–186, 1816.

(54) McDougall, W.   Outline of abnormal psychology.   572 pp.   New York, Scribner, 1826.

(55) Azam, C. M. E.   Hypnotisme, double conscience and altérations de la personnalité.   283 pp.   Paris, Baillière, 1887.

(56) B.C.A.   My life as a dissociated personality.   J. Abn. Psychol. 3: 240–260, 311–334, 1908.

(57) Prince, M.   The dissociation of a personality.   569 pp.   New York, Longman's, 1920.

(58) Prince, M.   Miss Beauchamp: the theory of the psychogenesis of multiple personality.   J. Abn. Psychol. 15: 67–135, 1920.

(59) Cory, C. E.   A divided self.   J. Abn. Psychol. 14: 281–291, 1919.

(60) Erickson, M. H., and Kubie, L. S.   The permanent relief of an obsessional phobia by means of communications with an unsuspected dual personality.   Psychoanal. Quart. 8: 471–509, 1939.

(61) Erickson, M. H., and Kubie, L. S.   The translation of the cryptic automatic writing of one hypnotic subject by another in a trance-like dissociated state.   Psychoanal. Quart. 9: 51–63, 1940.

(62) Erickson, M. H., and Rapaport, D.   Findings on the nature of the personality structures in two different dual personalities by means of projective and psychometric tests.   Paper read at the 97th Annual Meeting Amer. Psychiat. Assn. Richmond, Va., 1941.

(63) Goddard, H. H.   A case of dual personality.   J. Abn. Soc. Psychol. 21: 170–191, 1926.

(64) Gaver, E. E.   A case of alternating personality characterized chiefly by ambulatory automatism and amnesia with results of hypnotic experiments.   J. A. M. A. 51: 9–13, 1908.

(65) Allen, I. M.   Somnambulism and dissociation of personality.   Brit. J. Med. Psychol. 11: 319–331, 1931.

(66) Oberndorf, C. P.   Co-conscious mentation.   Psychoanal. Quart. 10: 44–65, 1941.

(67) Donley, J. E.   On neurasthenia as a disintegration of personality.   J. Abn. Psychol. 1: 55–58, 1906.

(68) HART, B. A case of double personality. *J. Med. Sci.* 58: 236-243, 1912.

(69) PECH, M. W. A case of multiple personality, hysteria, or dementia praecox. *J. Abn. Psychol.* 17: 274-291, 1922-1923.

(70) GORDON, A. Dual personality apropos a case of amnesia with analysis. *Med. J. Rec.* 124: 12-14, 1926.

(71) GORDON, A. Dual personality apropos a case of amnesia with analysis. *Arch. Neurol. Psychiat.* 16: 379-382, 1926.

(72) WHOLEY, C. C. A case of multiple personality. *Psychoanal. Rev.* 13: 344-346, 1926.

(73) WHOLEY, C. C. A case of multiple personality. *Amer. J. Psychiat.* 12: 653-688, 1933.

(74) HART, B. The conception of dissociation. *Brit. J. Med. Psychol.* 6: 241-263, 1926.

(75) SCHILDER, P. Psychic disturbances after head injuries. *Amer. J. Psychiat.* 91: 155-187, 1934.

(76) MAEDER, A. Sexualitaet und Epilepsie. *Jhb. Psychoanal. Psychopath. Forsch.* 1: 119-154, 1909.

(77) SIDIS, B. *Psychopathological researches. Studies in mental dissociation.* 329 pp. New York, Steckert, 1902.

(78) WITTELS, F. Phantom formation in a case of epilepsy. *Psychoanal. Quart.* 9: 98-107, 1940.

(79) CORIAT, I. H. The experimental synthesis of the dissociated memories in alcoholic amnesia. *J. Abn. Psychol.* 1: 109-122, 1906.

(80) BLEULER, E. *Textbook of psychiatry.* 635 pp. Engl. ed. Brill, A. A. New York, Macmillan, 1924.

(81) NAEF, M. Ein Fall von temporaerer, totaler, teilweise retrograder Amnesie durch Suggestion geheilt. *Z. Hypnot.* 6: 321-354, 1897.

(82) MURALT, L. Zur Frage der epileptischen Amnesia. *Z. Hypnot.* 10: 75-90, 1902.

(83) SCHILDER, P. Zur Psychologie epileptischer Ausnahmszustaende (mit besonderer Beruecksichtigung des Gedaechtnisses). *Allg. Z. Psychiat.* 80: 33-79, 1924.

(84) SCHILDER, P. Zur Lehre von den Amnesien Epileptischer, von der Schlafmittelhypnose und vom Gedaechtnis. *Arch. Psychiat. Nervenkrankh.* 72: 326-340, 1924.

(85) WAGNER, J. Ueber einige Erscheinungen im Bereiche des Zentralnervensystems, welche nach Wiederbelebung Erhaengter beobachtet werden. *Jhb. Psychiat. Neurol.* 8: 313-332, 1889.

(86) SCHULTZ, J. H. Zur Psychopathologie und Psychotherapie amnestischer Zustaende. *Z. Neurol. Psychiat.* 29: 107-129, 1924.

(87) STERN, R. Ueber die Aufhellung von Amnesien bei pathol. Rauschzustaenden. *Z. Neurol. Psychiat.* 108: 601-624, 1927.

(88) SCHILDER, P. Aufhellung der retrograden Amnesie eines wiederbelebten Erhaengten durch Hypnose. *Med. Klin.* 19: 604-606, 1923.

(89) OBERHOLZER, E. Beteiligung des Unlustmotives an epileptischer Amnesie und deren Aufhellung. *Psychiat. Neurol. Wochenschr.* 16: 128-131, 1914.

(90) BETLHEIM, S., AND HARTMANN, H. Ueber Fehlreaktionen bei der Korsakowschen Psychose. *Arch. Psychiat. Nervenkrankh.* 72: 275-286, 1924.

(91) HARTMANN, H. Gedaechtnis und Lustprinzip. Untersuchungen an Korsakoff Kranken. *Z. Neurol. Psychiat.* 126: 496-519, 1930.

(92) JONES, F. N., AND GHISELLI, E. E. Organic amnesia and relearning. *Amer. J. Psychol.* 51: 169-170, 1938.

(93) NAECKE, P. Erblichkeit und Praedisposition, respektive Degeneration bei der progressiven Paralyse der Irren. *Arch. Psychiat.* 41: 278–299, 1906.

(94) HOLLOS, S., AND FERENCZI, S. *Psychoanalysis and the psychic disorder of general paresis.* 48 pp. New York, Nerv. Ment. Dis. Publ., 1925.

(95) SCHILDER, P. Studien zur Psychologie und Symptomatologie der progressiven Paralyse. *Abhandl. Neurol. Psychiat. Psychol. Grenzgeb.* 58: 1–176, 1930.

(96) KATAN, M. Abstract from Dutch Psychoanalytical Society. *Internat. J. Psychoanal.* 17: 301, 1931.

(97) KENYON, V. B., RAPAPORT, D., AND LOZOFF, M. Note on metrazol in general paresis: A psychosomatic study. *Psychiatry*, 4: 165–176, 1941.

(98) KENYON, V. B., AND RAPAPORT, D. The etiology of the psychosis of dementia paralytica with a preliminary report of the treatment of a case of this psychosis with metrazol. *J. Nerv. Ment. Dis.* 94: 147–159, 1941.

(99) KENYON, V. B., LOZOFF, M., AND RAPAPORT, D. Metrazol convulsions in the treatment of the psychosis of dementia paralytica. *Arch. Neurol. Psychiat.* 46: 884–896, 1941.

(100) DUNN, R. Case of suspension of the mental faculties, of the power of speech and special senses. *Lancet* 2: 536–538, 588–590, 1845.

(101) SYZ, H. Posttraumatic loss of reproductive memory and its restoration through hypnosis and analysis. *Med. Rec. N. Y.* 144: 313–317, 1936.

(102) CASON, H. A case of anterograde amnesia. *J. Abn. Psychol.* 30: 107–110, 1935.

(103) KOEMPFEN, M. Observation sur un cas de perte de mémoire, *Mémoires de l'Académie de Médecine*, 4: 489–494, 1835.

(104) DANA, C. L. The study of a case of amnesia or "double consciousness." *Psychol. Rev.* 1: 570–580, 1894.

(105) FEILING, A. Loss of personality from shell shock. *Lancet*, 189: 63–66, Part I, 1915.

(106) FRANZ, S, I. *Persons one and three.* 188 pp. New York, McGraw-Hill, 1933.

(107) IKIN, A. G. Vera; study in dissociation of personality. *Brit. J. Med. Psychol.* I. 4: 179–223, 1924; II. 4: 273–318, 1925.

(108) BLEULER, E. Das autistische Denken. *Jhb. Psychoanal. Psychopath. Forsch.* 4: 1–39, 1912.

(109) BLEULER, E. *Das autistisch-undisziplinierte Denken.* 188 pp. Berlin, Springer, 1922.

(110) JUNG, C. G. *Psychology of the unconscious.* 339 pp. New York, Moffat, 1921.

(111) VARENDONCK, J. *The psychology of day-dreams.* 367 pp. New York, Macmillan, 1921.

(112) LÉVY-BRUEHL, L. *Primitive mentality.* 458 pp. Trans. Clare, L. A. London, 1923.

(113) CASSIRER, E. *Philosophie der symbolischen Formen.* 320 pp. Berlin, Cassirer, 1925.

(114) WERNER, H. *Comparative psychology of mental development.* 510 pp. New York, Harper, 1940.

(115) RAPAPORT, D. Heinz Werner's: Comparative psychology of mental development. A critical review. *J. Genet. Psychol.* 59: 429–434, 1941.

(116) ALEXANDER, F. The logic of emotions and its dynamic background. *Internat. J. Psychoanal.* 16: 1–15, 1935.

(117) MOLL, J. M. The "amnestic" or "Korsakow's" syndrome, with alcoholic aetiology: An analysis of thirty cases. *J. Ment. Sci.* 61: 424–443, 1915.

(118) KORSAKOFF, S. S. Ueber eine besondere Form psychischer Stoerung. *Arch. Psychiat.* 21: 669–704, 1890.

(119) KORSAKOFF, S. S. Erinnerungstaeuschungen (Pseudoreminiszenzen) bei polyneuritischer Psychose. *Allg. Z. Psychiat. Neurol.* 47: 390–410, 1891.

(120) BONHOEFFER, K. Der Korsakowsche Symptomenkomplex in seinen Beziehungen zu den verschiedenen Krankheitsformen. *Allg. Z. Psychiat. Psychisch-Gerichtl. Med.* 61: 744–752, 1904.

(121) GREGOR, A., AND ROEMER, H. Beitraege zur Kenntnis der Gedaechtnisstoerung bei der Korsakowschen Psychose. *Monatschr. Psychiat. Neurol.* 21: 19–148, 1907.

(122) GREGOR, A. Beitraege zur Psychopathologie des Gedaechtnisses. *Monatschr. Psychiat. Neurol.* 25: 218; 339, 1909.

(123) KOHNSTAMM, O. Ueber das Krankheitsbild der retro-anterograden Amnesie und die Unterscheidung des spontanen und des lernenden Merkens. *Monatschr. Psychiat. Neurol.* 41: 373–382, 1917.

(124) PICK, A. Beitraege zur Pathologie des Denkenverlaufes beim Korsakoff. *Z. ges. Neurol. Psychiat.* 28: 344–383, 1915.

(125) GRUENTHAL, E. Zur Kenntnis der Psychopathologie des Korsakowschen Symptomenkomplexes. *Monatschr. Psychiat. Neurol.* 53: 89–132, 1923.

(126) HORST, VAN DER, N. Ueber die Psychologie des Korsakowsyndroms. *Monatschr. Psychiat. Neurol.* 83: 65–84, 1932.

(127) BOUMAN, L., AND GRUENBAUM, A. A. Eine Stoerung der Chronognosie und ihre Bedeutung im betreffenden Symptomenbild. *Monatschr. Psychiat. Neurol.* 73: 1–40, 1929.

(128) FREUD, S. Fausse reconnaissance (déjà raconté) in psychoanalytic treatment. Pp. 334–341. In: *Collected Papers*, vol. II. 404 pp. London, Hogarth, 1925.

(129) POETZL, O. Zur Metapsychologie des Déjà vue. *Imago* 12: 393–402, 1926.

(130) HEYMANNS, G. Eine Enquete ueber Depersonalisation und "Fausse reconnaissance." *Z. Psychol.* 36: 321–343, 1904.

(131) HEYMANNS, G. Weitere Daten ueber Depersonalisation und "Fausse reconnaissance." *Z. Psychol.* 43: 1–17, 1906.

(132) BURGER, H. Zur Psychologie des amnestischen Symptomenkomplexes. *Arch. Psychiat. Nervenkr.* 81: 348–352, 1927.

(133) HARTMANN, H. Zur Frage: Organischer Amnesie und Hypnose. Versuche an Korsakowkranken. *Wiener Klin. Wochenschr.* 40: 1507–1508, 1927.

(134) KRAUSS, S. Untersuchungen ueber Aufbau und Stoerung der menschlichen Handlung. *Arch. Psychol.* 77: 649–692, 1930.

(135) GOLANT-RATTNER, R. J., AND MENTESCHASCHWILI, T. Zur Frage der Stoerungen des Behaltens (Gedaechtnisstoerungen) bei progressiver Paralyse. *Monatschr. Psychiat. Neurol.* 85: 222–242, 1933.

(136) BUERGER-PRINZ, H., AND KAILA, M. Ueber die Struktur des amnestischen Symptomenkomplexes. *Z. Neurol. Psychiat.* 124: 553–595, 1930.

(137) HOLLOS, S. Ueber das Zeitgefuehl. *Internat. Z. Psychoanal.* 8: 421–439, 1922.

(138) HARNIK, F. Die triebhaft-affektiven Momente im Zeitgefuehl. *Internat. Z. Psychoanal.* 11: 32–58, 1925.

(139) BONAPARTE, M. Time and the Unconscious. *Internat. J. Psychoanal.* 21: 427–468, 1940.

(140) SPIELREIN, S. Die Zeit im unterschwelligen Seelenleben. *Imago*, 9: 300–317, 1923.

(141) ISRAELI, N. *Abnormal personality and time.* 123 pp. New York, The Science Press, 1936.

Chapter VIII

DIRECT EXPERIMENTAL EVIDENCE

In the preceding chapters we surveyed a variety of experiments and theories which claimed or could be interpreted to have shed light on the influence of emotions on the memory function. In this chapter we shall survey experiments which seem to promise to open a pathway to the "direct investigation" of this influence. Here we shall only describe and appraise the advantages of these experiments and their methods, without attempting to suggest new experimental set ups based on them

The expression "direct investigation" needs amplification. Let us again focus on the problem of investigating memory function in its three phases: registration, retention, recall. It must be clear that the facts of registration and retention are amenable to investigation only through recall. The investigation even of perception implies some kind of reporting, which in turn implies immediate recall. Perception is often viewed as an isolated process, probably because in everyday non-reflective experiencing it is not realized that the process which brings a percept into relation with the whole of psychic happening uses not the "percept" itself but some kind of "trace" of it. It is even clearer in the case of retention than in that of registration that our knowledge depends on recall, inasmuch as "recognition" and "saving in relearning" are but special—and may be considered incomplete—forms of recall. Thus the "direct investigation" of the influence of emotions on memory must include investigations of this influence on perception as well as on *any* type of reproduction. Accordingly, immediate report of visually perceived material, or reproduction of verbal material in visual imagery and dream images, will be dealt with as recall.

Our survey will be divided into four sections. The first will deal with experiments on the affective organization of visually perceived or reproduced material; the second with experiments on the affective organization of meaningful verbal material; the third with experiments demonstrating the affective organization of behavior; the fourth with experiments on the interrelation of physiological and memory changes, effected by emotional influence. This grouping of the material does not carry any theoretical implication, nor does it imply a sharp delineation between these groups. It is a grouping which seemed to make for a simple organization of our material, and may to a certain extent seem arbitrary. Thus, the second group is described as dealing with verbal material; but also in the first, third and fourth groups verbalization is involved. The justification for the descriptive designation of the groups lay in the major characteristic of each. Thus while in the first and fourth groups the verbalization is incidental, and conveys merely the visual perception or imagery, and while in the third group it is merely a part of the behavior investigated, in the second group it is the essential feature; all experiments of this group used verbal production or reproduction of stories.

In the previously surveyed material the presence of an "emotional influence" was inferred, either theoretically on the basis of clinical experience or statistically on the basis of experimentally-obtained data. These evidences were only inditial. Whenever only inditial evidence is brought forth, science turns to extreme cases where phenomena which usually are subtle and hidden are manifest in a striking, exaggerated form. This has been done in the experiments to be reported now. Those dealing with the affective organization of visually perceived material used either tachystoscopic—extremely short—presentation or psychotic subjects; those dealing with the affective organization of meaningful verbal material used psychotic and neurotic subjects or memory material originating in childhood; those dealing with the affective organization of behavior used posthypnotic suggestions. In the case of experiments investigating the interrelation of physiological and memory changes elicited by emotions, this principle of the "extreme case" is clearly stated by Luria (1).[1] The intricacy and multiple stratification of both memory and physiological functions of the human organism necessitated the isolation, through the "method of the extreme case," of that aspect of these functions in which we are interested. The influence of emotions on memory is one which is as hard to perceive as it is powerful, and is rendered palpable only by the "method of the extreme case."

For a better understanding of the first three groups of experiments, it seems necessary to discuss the concept of "projection." In current usage, this term carries two—at the first glance, widely divergent—connotations. First, the term denotes that mode of thinking in which one imputes his feelings and thoughts to others and looks upon them as external reality; this mode of thinking, though frequently encountered in normal people,[2] is the basis of paranoia and kindred psychoses. Secondly, the term de-

---

[1] "The observer, who investigates the intricate complexes of behavior has to approach the laws of normal behavior starting from those cases in which these *mechanisms are not hidden, i.e. from those of disturbed behavior.* . . . Of greatest value are for us thus the states of steady disturbances of the organism, the neuroses and psycho-neuroses as well as the passing disturbances of the equilibrium—the affects." (pp. 130–131)

[2] Wishful thinking is one example of this mode of thinking; the person takes his hopes as reality and interprets events accordingly.

notes the expression of one's personality in his behavior,[3] especially when confronted with a new unorganized situation; for example, an artist in his creation, or a subject taking a "projective personality test." On more thorough scrutiny, these two seemingly divergent conceptions of the term prove to shade imperceptibly into each other. Once it is realized that memory changes resulting from "emotional factors" are as revealing of emotions as a person's actions are of his personality, the concept "projection" becomes important for our problem.

The general and social psychological meaning of this concept was clearly outlined by L. Frank (3) who, in his discussion of the projective methods of investigating personality, wrote:

" . . . we may approach the personality and induce the individual to reveal his way of organizing experience by giving him a field (objects, materials, experiences) with relatively little structure and cultural patterning so that the personality can project upon that plastic field his way of seeing life, his meanings, significances, patterns, and especially his feelings. Thus we elicit a projection of the individual personality's *private world* because he has to organize the field, interpret the material and react affectively to it. More specifically, a projection method for study of personality involves the presentation of a stimulus-situation designed or chosen because it will mean to the subject, not what the experimenter has arbitrarily decided it should mean (as in most psychological experiments using standardized stimuli in order to be 'objective'), but rather whatever it must mean to the personality who gives it, or imposes upon it, his private, idiosyncratic meaning and organization. The subject then will respond to *his* meaning of the presented stimulus-situation by some form of action and feeling that is expressive of his personality." (pp. 402–403)

Here L. Frank expresses tendencies influential in modern ethno-psychology (Mead), field-psychology (Lewin), child psychology (L. Murphy), social psychology (G. Murphy), in addition to the tendencies and conclusions of modern projective testing methods used in clinical psychology, and of play techniques used in psychotherapy and psychiatric research. Of the origin of the mechanism of "projection" we read in Freud (4):

"In so far as it is auto-erotic, the ego has no need of the outside world, but, in consequence of experiences undergone by the instincts of self-preservation, it tends to find objects there and doubtless it cannot but for a time perceive inner instinctual stimuli as painful. Under the sway of the pleasure-principle there now takes place a further development. The objects presenting themselves, in so far as they are sources of pleasure, are absorbed by the ego into itself, 'introjected' (according to an expression coined by Ferenczi); while, on the other hand, the ego thrusts forth upon the external world whatever within itself gives rise to pain (the mechanism of projection)." (p. 78)

---

[3] This usage developed especially in relation to the "projective personality tests." For a detailed discussion of the function of projection, and the implied concept of behavior, see Rapaport (2).

In the discussion of psychoanalytic views[4] we saw that "pain" is equated with "tension"; thus we might expect that any tension may result in projection. This expectation is supported in Freud's (5) further discussion:

> "In an earlier passage we claimed that the still helpless organism had the capacity for making a first orientation in the world by means of its perceptions, distinguishing both 'outer' and 'inner' according to their relation to actions of the muscles. A perception which is made to disappear by motor activity is recognized as external, as reality; where such activity makes no difference, the perception originates within the subject's own body—it is not real. To be thus able not only to recognize, but at the same time to rid ,himself of, reality is of great value to the individual, and he would wish to be equipped with a similar weapon against the often merciless claims of his instincts. That is why he takes such pains to *project*, i. e. to transfer outwards, all that becomes troublesome to him from within." (p. 149)

The function of projection is shown to operate not only in perception, but also in dreams and in such pathological thought processes as phobias.

> "A dream indicates that something was going on which tended to disturb sleep, and it enables us to understand the way in which this disturbance can be warded off. The final outcome is that the sleeper has dreamed and is able to go on sleeping; the inner claim which wanted to absorb him has been replaced by an outer experience, the claim of which he has succeeded in discharging. A dream is, therefore, among other things, a *projection*: an externalization of an internal process. We remember that we have already met with projection elsewhere among the means adopted for defense. The mechanism of an hysterical phobia, too, culminated in the substitution of an outer danger, from which the person might strive to protect himself by flight, for an inner instinctual claim." (5, p. 139)

Finally, Freud shows that projection plays an important role in paranoid delusions (5, pp. 145–146).

It may be conjectured that the instinctual—affective—demands which tend to be projected in dreams, phobias, and delusions, are identical with those whose projection, when manifest in the organization of memories, is called "the influence of emotions on memory." There are differences between the paranoiac's projection, the projection in dreams, and the projective functions present in tests and in memory phenomena. The projection of the paranoiac totally disregards reality, and the dream projection disregards it in part; but in tests and in memory phenomena "reality testing" is unimpaired, and only in extreme cases—for instance, in interpretation of unorganized ink-blots and of photographs of ambiguous scenes—is the projective process demonstrable. The varied projection phenomena apparently form a continuous chain: hallucinations, delusions, phobias, dreams, day dreams, imagination, selective perception, memory errors and transformations, and organization of unorganized material.

[4] See pp. 30–31.

Projection was thus conceived by Freud as the extreme case of a subject's organizing his percepts, memories, and behavior according to the "pleasure principle," and attributing to the outside world that which is painful and tension-creating. The use of the word in the term "projective techniques" was a recognition that this process occurs to a degree in all perceiving, thinking, and behavior. Our perceiving is never photography, our memory never kinematographic projection, our thinking never pure logic, and our behavior never totally adapted to the "objective demands"—a non-existent quality—of reality. Projection, insofar as it uses that aspect of our thought processes which is called memory, is essentially a mechanism of emotional influence on memory. Thus, the projective personality tests should yield an additional contribution to our topic.

In the experiments to be discussed, the influence of emotional factors on memory will not be measured by the quantity of retained and forgotten material, which indicates only facilitation and inhibition of recall without revealing the underlying mechanisms. Such experiments demonstrate the influence of emotions on memory in a way which might well be expressed by a modified version of Lipmann's statement:[5] *they investigate the symptoms of affective influence exerted on the memory function.*

1. The Affective Organization of Visually Perceived or Reproduced Material

There is usually a high degree of agreement among subjects in the visual perception of everyday situations. Thus, it will not surprise us to find that the individual differences in reports of visually-perceived or visually-reproduced material—in other words, the affective organization of the pertinent memories—become perceptible only under extreme conditions. The extreme conditions to be dealt with will be states of tiredness or affective states conducive to a type of visual imagery called hypnagogic hallucination; tachystoscopic—extremely brief—presentation conducive to selective remembering; and presentation of accidental ink-blots requiring organization in terms of memories. We shall organize our material, in accordance with these three methods, and deal with (a) the problem of symbolism, already touched upon in Chapter V; (b) the organization of tachystoscopically-presented material; (c) the organization processes occurring at the visual presentation of the incidental ink-spots of the Rorschach test.

A. SYMBOLISM

A symbol is a thing which stands for and represents something else. In our culture it is a common procedure to symbolize abstract ideas by visual analogues. In folklore and mythology, gods and spirits are represented by symbols; the affective reason for the substitution is only too transparent.[6] Generally, the visual representation of ideas appears to be the essence of symbolization. This is similar to what happens in dreams,[7] where the dream thought is represented for the most part in visual images, and in hallucinations, where the delusional idea of the patient emerges in visual—and sometimes auditory—images.[8] According to Freud, what happens in these cases is that the wish or striving, which usually is regulated and steered by external stimulation through perceptions, now being unacceptable finds its way blocked and takes a reverse course. This reverse course is characterized by the fact that instead of striving to obtain its aim in reality, it achieves it by reviving memories by lending extreme vividness to the memory traces representing the goal symbolically. Symbolization is a representation, or in other words reproduction, of an idea in visual images using the available memory-traces for this purpose.

Symbols thus may be conceived of as the reproduction of ideas and of relations once perceived; but their relation to the memory aspect of the organization of our thought processes is complicated. Silberer (8, 9, 10) discovered a method to investigate symbolism, a discussion of which may augment understanding of our problem. He observed that while concentrating in a tired state, his problem frequently presented itself to him in symbolic visual images.[9] This phenomenon, called by Silberer "autosymbolic phenomenon" or "hypnagogic hallucination," may be interpreted as an immediate recall. This recall is symbolically transformed,

[6] See Cassirer (6).

[7] Freud, S. (7, pp. 292–295).

[8] See p. 158.

[9] E.g. ". . . thinking about the essence of trans-subjectively valid judgments, the author has a hallucination of a sphere which includes the heads of people, while the bodies are outside the sphere." (8, p. 517)

Further examples of Silberer are quoted by Freud (7):

"Example 1.—I remember that I have to correct a halting passage in an essay.
Symbol.—I see myself planing a piece of wood.

Example 5.—I endeavor to call to my mind the aim of certain metaphysical studies which I am proposing to undertake.

This aim, I reflect, consists in working one's way through, while seeking for the basis of existence, to ever higher forms of consciousness or levels of being.
Symbol.—I run a long knife under a cake as though to take a slice out of it.
. . .

Example 9.—I lost the thread of a train of thoughts. I make an effort to find it again, but have to recognize that the point of departure has completely escaped me.

Symbol.—Part of a form of type—the last lines of which have fallen out." (p. 365)

and is a symptom rather than a direct revival of the memory traces in question.[10] Symbolism in this formulation appears as a memory phenomenon. The conditions of occurrence of this specific memory function are described by Silberer (9) as follows:

"The apperceptive ability to support an idea in consciousness may suffer . . .disturbance or limitation from two sources: the insufficiency might be caused first by insufficiency of development (such as is found in children, pathological individuals, and primitives), or by a passing weakness of apperceptive abilities due to a general decrease of mental energy, as in sleep; secondly, it might come about as the result of interference by affects, which interfere with the emergence of the idea either by means of pleasure-pain mechanism or by depriving the attention function of a part of its energy, using it for autonomous complexes[11] . . .
"The affects may be limited to disturbing apperception . . . or may do active work too inasmuch as they . . . bring to consciousness the complexes to which they belong." (p. 608)

There is sufficient reason to assume that the symbolization which Silberer attributes to the interference of affects, and the symbolization which he attributes to "insufficiency," may be brought to a common denominator. When affects become all too strong, or when transient or developmental "insufficiencies" facilitate their operation, they manifest themselves by making for a symbolic reproduction of ideas. Thus, according to Silberer's theory, in states of tiredness or primitive development, and under the pressure of affects inhibited in their free manifestation, the revival of memory traces may occur in symbolic form.[12] Jones (11), although taking exception to many of Silberer's ideas, agreed with him on essentials:

"All symbolism betokens a relative incapacity for either apprehension or presentation, primarily the former; this may be either affective or intellectual in origin, the first of these two factors being far more important." (pp. 179–180)

T. W. Moore (12) followed Silberer's experimental method and corroborated his results. Schroetter (13) demonstrated the phenomenon of symbolism by a different experimental method: he instructed deeply hypnotized persons to dream of sexual activities, and found that the sug-

[10] The symbolic transformation is an example of how affects, attitudes, and dynamic schemes of ideas may choose different visual or verbal forms of appearance. The identity of idea and symbol lies apparently only in the identity of the affects, attitudes, and dynamic schemes.
[11] "Autonomous complexes" is Silberer's expression for complexes in Jung's sense (see p. 45ff.).
[12] A similar theory in reference to dreams was expressed by Stekel: "The dream is essentially a play of presentations in a parade of affects." (Silberer 9, p. 612).

gested sexual material appeared in the dreams in the form of well known symbols. Similar results were obtained by Roffenstein (14).[13] These summarized experiments indicate that one of the influences of affects on memory is the symbolic transformation of memories in reproduction.

B. TACHYSTOSCOPIC EXPERIMENTS

Observations on normal subjects after tachystoscopic presentation (Schuman, 15), on patients with a total lesion of the central direct field of vision (Poppelreuter, 16), and on latent hemianoptic, alcohol-hallucinosis, and agnosia patients (Poetzl, 17), showed a delayed, piecemeal emergence of the visual impressions. For example, a patient with a destroyed central field of vision was shown a man with a green neck-tie and a gold tie-pin. At first he reported that he saw nothing; after several minutes he reported that he saw a yellow flower on a green background. It was assumed that these originate in the peripheral vision, and that in normal vision they are suppressed by a central abstractive process. When this process is inactive—as in agnosia and hallucinosis—or when time conditions —as in brief exposure—inhibit its efficiency, the emergence of the impression obtained in central vision is followed by a delayed emergence of the fractional impressions obtained in peripheral vision. Poetzl (17) assumed that the "central abstractive process" which suppresses the partial impressions obtained in peripheral vision is inactive in dream-work also. This assumption led him to the investigation of the effect of tachystoscopically-presented pictures on dreams. He exposed pictures of landscapes and street scenes to normal subjects for ten sigmas;[14] their impressions were immediately recorded, and they were instructed to observe and record their dreams and daydreams for the subsequent twenty-four hours. Sketch-drawings by the subjects of their original impressions and of their subsequent dreams and daydreams were obtained, and associations to them were recorded. With nine of the twelve subjects the experiments' results were striking:

(1) The impressions reported immediately after presentation occurred neither in the dreams nor in the daydreams; these three kinds of impressions were mutually exclusive, but complementary (p. 348).

(2) The sketch-drawings showed good agreement, in that their geometry was congruous; the later ones filled in the gaps of the original sketch, but while they retained their geometrical configuration, their contents were symbolically transformed (p. 315).

[13] See Freud (18, p. 36), and Freud (7, pp. 364–365).
[14] 1 sigma = $\frac{1}{1000}$ second.

(3) The part of the picture which had remained "unobserved" in the tachystoscopic presentation was found to be connected with an affective conflict of the subject. The omitted parts, symbolically transformed, appeared in either the dreams, the daydreams, or the associations (p. 314).

This experiment appears to imply the influence of a selective affective factor which makes a part of the tachystoscopically-perceived impressions unavailable for immediate reproduction. It is as though the impression were organized into a foreground and a background. The suppressed parts are not lost, but emerge in symbolical form in dreams and associations when the pressure of the suppressing force is weakened.

Allers and Teller (19), in an attempt to disprove Poetzl's psychoanalytic interpretations, repeated the experiment and found a delayed emergence of partial impressions in "picture-like processes interpolated between the stimulus and reaction word of the association experiment."

Malamud and Linder (20), and Malamud (21) repeated Poetzl's experiment on psychiatric patients. They used an exposure time of thirty seconds, apparently assuming that the apperceptive difficulty is present in these cases and need not be introduced by tachystoscopic presentation. Art reproductions, chosen to correspond to the central emotional problem of the subject, were used. The results corroborated Poetzl's findings. Malamud and Linder formulated their problem as follows:

"In our experiments, therefore, we are to deal with the following problems: 1. Is it true that contents in our recent experiences that are forgotten are actually merely repressed and can be shown to recur in our dreams? 2. Do these contents bear a definite relationship to earlier incidents that have been repressed because of their conflicting tendencies? 3. Do both these experiences as uncovered in the analysis of dreams bear definite relationship to the life problems of the person and, in disease, to the conflict that is instrumental in causing the disease process?" (p. 1084)

These were their conclusions:

" . . . (1) the factors regarded by the psychoanalytic theory as uniformly occurring in dreams were demonstrated in the dreams of a number of our patients, and (2) they could be experimentally induced.

"In reference to the questions, that in our introduction, were taken as the basis of the present experiment, these results permit the following answers: 1. Some contents in the recent experiences of our subjects that were left out of their descriptions were subsequently shown to recur in their dreams. 2. These contents seemed to have a definite relationship to experiences in the earlier life of the person. 3. Both of these experiences were found to be definitely related to those problems in the subjects' lives that, as far as could be judged, formed the central feature of the disease process." (p. 1098)

Schilder (22) reported a series of tachystoscopic experiments which corroborated Poetzl's findings,[15] and concluded:

"Tachystoscopic experiences show, therefore, a tendency to illusional changes according to the emotional need of the individual." (p. 599)

The tachyscoscopic experiments thus appear to show that affective factors, when their operation is facilitated by brief presentation or by their exaggerated strength as in psychiatric cases, organize a visual impression into an acceptable foreground and an unacceptable, and therefore suppressed, background. This organization prevents the immediate recall of the part of the impression so selected, and allows only its symbolic reproduction in dreams and daydreams.

C. THE RORSCHACH TEST

This test consists of ten ink blots, partly in different shades of gray and partly in colors, which are presented to the subject with the question: "What might this be?" In terms of memory experimentation, this is a test of directed associations and has some similarity to the "experience associations";[16] in both the subject is asked to give a specific kind of association, and not simply the first idea coming to mind. But in the "experience association" the reaction to be given is an experience; in the Rorschach Test the reaction must fit the ink blot. Rorschach (23) maintained that the processes underlying the test are association-processes, and explained that the test-protocol of every individual reflects his unique association-mechanism. Binswanger (24) objected to considering the processes underlying the Rorschach Test to be an association-process; he considered them as complex as thought-processes. Binswanger's argument does not take cognizance of the fact that the association-process investigated in an association-experiment is an artifact, an arbitrary simplification of the process occurring in everyday life; but that in the Rorschach Test the association-process is more thoroughly embedded in the "organization of thought processes," and thus resembles the phenomenon occurring in everyday life. The Rorschach test, being thus a directed

---

[15] He wrote: "In tachystoscopic experiments which were made with Dr. Ross we exposed to subjects among others, pictures of a boy in which ohe arm or one leg was missing. A great number of the subjects saw the complete figure. They did not want to accept the fact of mutilation. In some cases the subject declared that the boy was running—representing a compromise between what they saw and what they wanted to see. The tachystoscopic experience is therefore more plastic to the wishes of the subject. That came especially clearly into the foreground in children to whom a naked figure was shown. Depending on their modesty, they saw the figure dressed (the time of exposition varied between $\frac{1}{10}$ and $\frac{1}{100}$ of a second)." (p. 599)

[16] See p. 51ff.

association test, reflects the memory function in its individual differences and cannot but show the influence of affective factors on the organization of memories. The process is the following: the ink-blot mobilizes memories having features similar to those of the ink-blot, and the memory which fits best is given as the response. When emotions are aroused, the process of selecting the best-fitting response is influenced, interfered with, or completely blocked; it is rarely facilitated.

We cannot go into further details of the Rorschach procedure;[17] we have attempted to demonstrate only that it has a bearing on the memory problem. We shall now sum up the role of the "affective factor" in the memory processes involved in this test procedure.

1. The *reaction-time* is the period elapsing between the presentation of a Rorschach card and the first response. This reaction-time appears to be a subtle indicator of emotional reaction. Rorschach found that an unusually long reaction-time to the first card containing bright colors is a characteristically neurotic manifestation. In general, long reaction-time to any card appears to indicate that the card arouses a reaction of special emotional significance. The affective factor which lengthens the reaction-time usually impairs the quality of the responses—the degree to which they "fit" the cards—and disturbs their sequence.[18] Depressive, inhibited, and pedantic subjects usually have long reaction-times.

2. The *reaction to colors and to shadings* of gray and black were found to reflect the pattern of the subjects' emotional reactions. Experience with the test showed that impulsive subjects give either inadequate or no form-reactions to bright colors, and that anxious subjects show a similar impediment of reaction to dark shadings: thus, the former will call a red blot blood, a green one grass; the latter will see in the dark blot clouds, smoke, or impending disaster. The inhibited, rigid, or pedantic subject will not react at all to color and shading, and will regard only the form of the blots. Between these extremes we find subjects who attempt more or less successfully to reconcile form with color and shading. The influence of affects and anxieties—reflected by the reactions to color and shading, respectively—consists here in making difficult a free and rich mobilization of memories fitting the ink blots.

3. The *contents* of the responses may reflect the preponderant affective problems and attitudes of the patient. Symbolic or straight-forward sex-responses reflect sex-preoccupation; an abundance of anatomical

---

[17] See Rorschach (23), Rorschach and Oberholzer (25), Rickers-Ovsiankina (26), and Beck (27).

[18] See Rapaport, D. Reaction Time and Succession in the Rorschach Ink-Blot Test. Paper read before the March, 1939 meeting of the New York Branch of the Rorschach Institute.

responses reflects under certain conditions bodily preoccupation; the character of reactions describing movements of human beings express the general attitude of the patient toward life. For example, such attitudes are reflected in responses which describe a bent or erect figure.[19] The contents, inasmuch as they reveal the subject's attitudes and preoccupations, are that aspect of the test in which the projective mechanism underlying the test becomes directly obvious.

We might sum up the relevance of the Rorschach Test to our problem thus: the test invokes a complicated memory mechanism similar to that at work in everyday life; reaction time, effect of color and shading on the responses, and content of responses reveal the influence of affects on this memory mechanism. The subject's task is to organize an ink blot in terms of his memory images; this organization process reveals the main organizing factors of his personality—primarily those of an affective nature—and their influence on his intellectual makeup.

2. The Affective Organization of Verbal Material

In Chapters V and VI we encountered phenomena of forgetting due to repression, and processes of recovering forgotten material. In most of these instances the fact of forgetting was the primary observation, and the forgotten material became known to the observer only after it had been recovered with his assistance. How the original amnesized experience and its recovered memory compare is a moot question; in general, the problem of how *any* experience and its recall compare has remained uninvestigated. General psychological experiments have dealt only with the recall of single words and similar material, and association experiments raised the question without attacking it experimentally. Criminological experiments on the psychology of testimony show that the attitudes and strivings of a person distort his memory of experiences, but the mechanism of these distortions has not been clarified. It has long been known that "quod volumus facile credimus" (what we wish we easily believe). Similarly, the principles governing the creation of stories have remained unexplained, although it is known that a writer reflects himself in his work. There are few reports of cases—except for genuine amnesias—where an important relevant life-experience covering a relatively long period of time was reported and afterwards forgotten by the subject. Such a forgetting differs from genuine retrograde amnesias in that not all the experiences of the period in question are forgotten, but only a specific chain of continuous experiences within that period.[20] An interesting

[19] See Furrer (28).
[20] This type of forgetting has been called by Erickson "specific amnesia."

case in which original experiences and their recall were both investigated is reported by Erickson (29). Two female children, who had been sold by their parents for purposes of sexual misuse and who had suffered severe lacerations and infections, described their experiences in detail to the examining psychiatrist called in by the police. The psychiatrist interviewed the children six months later, and wrote:

"Even close questioning about the injuries sustained and the venereal infection elicited either resentful denials or trivial explanations, and they seemed to have no real recognition of the whole experience as an actual happening in their own lives. At no time could their sincerity or their full belief in their statements be denied." (p. 3)

The aim of the following survey is to evaluate clinical observations of this sort, and to facilitate general scientific agreement on the fact and nature of affectively-motivated forgetting by systematizing the reports of experiments in which these phenomena were elicited under controlled conditions.

The experiments to be reported in this section deal with the reproduction of stories presented to the subject, and the production by the subject of stories on a given theme. The nature of the influence of affective factors on memory is inferred from the changes found in the reproduced story, and from the principles governing the production of original stories. Three kinds of experiment will be considered: (a) immediate-recall experiments, in which the subject reproduces a story read to him in the experimental situation; (b) delayed-recall experiments, in which the subject reproduces well-known children's stories remembered from childhood; (c) production experiments, in which the subject produces a story around a verbally- or photographically-presented theme.

These three types of experiment constitute a continuum ranging from the reproduction of learned material to free fantasy creations; the common denominator of this continuum is the organizing affective-factor which influences memory and thought production. That memory distortions of learned material are attributable to emotional influence was demonstrated by Freud (30) in his "Psychopathology of Everyday Life." He reported several examples of faulty reproduction of poems, and traced the errors to emotional factors which suppressed the original and substituted other material.[21] This is a familiar experience to those who make it a habit to memorize and reproduce selections from poetry. Stalnaker, and White and his collaborators were impressed in their hypnotic experiments by the freedom with which subjects supplanted portions of poetry

[21] See pp. 46 and 73 of the "Psychopathology of Everyday Life" (30).

by their own constructions. Hull assumed that these constructions are evidence of an unreliability of hypnotic memory.[22] Yet if these hypnotic memory phenomena are viewed in the light of the evidence offered by Freud, they allow for another interpretation. In the normal state repression results in the forgetting of certain portions of a selection; in the hypnotic state the repression is weakened and a compromise ensues, in which the repressed material is partly recovered in a distorted manner giving the impression of a free construction. Affective influences, as we have already seen in the chapter on psychoanalysis, may make for forgetting as well as for "transformation" or distortion of memory material in the normal state also.

A. IMMEDIATE RECALL OF STORIES

The peculiarity of memory distortions found in the reproduction of meaningful material early attracted the attention of a few investigators, but the problem was not pursued with the vigor it warranted. Koeppen and Kutzinsky (31) reported a series of experiments on the reproduction of simple stories by varying clinical groups of psychotics. This material was analyzed in terms similar to those used in early association experiments.[23] These investigations were concerned with formal, logical, grammatical relations; nevertheless, we occasionally find in them observations directly pertinent to our topic:

" . . . it was shown how strongly the expansive power of pathological feeling complexes, and the attitudes arising from these, influence recall. The attitude towards the task changed, another feeling reaction towards the story took the place of the normal one, and the story as a unity became falsified and distorted. All this could occur with perfectly intact intellection, good memory, good attention, and a retained ability of differentiation and combination, just as a result of the power asserted by the pathological complexes and attitudes . . . furthermore, we saw distortions in the attitude towards the task to recall the story resulting in changes in its content. The attitude had to be considered sometimes as disturbed, sometimes as normal, according to whether the affect was normal or pathological." (pp. 218–219)

These experiments led to several further attempts. Levy-Suhl (32) published similar experiments. Betlheim and Hartmann (33) presented stories of crude sexual content to patients with Korsakow syndrome, and found that in reproduction[24] the crude sexual content appeared in symbolic translation. Schilder (34) conducted a thorough experiment on paretic patients, using the method and the story material of Koeppen and Kutzinsky; his findings described exhaustively the organization of the

---

[22] See p. 177ff.
[23] See pp. 41–42.
[24] See also Schilder (35, pp. 161–162), and Freud (18, p. 36).

memory and thought processes of paretics.[25] The nucleus of his findings was that the paretic's memory and thought disturbance, as revealed in the reproduction of stories, is characterized by a ready penetration into consciousness of the subject's preconscious wishes and affective attitudes, which distort the reproduction of the story in a manner found only in dreams. Schilder not only showed the logical-grammatical form of the distortions, but also the affective factors underlying them. His conclusions concerning the formal, logical characteristics of the distortions were the following:

"1) concrete concepts were replaced by generalities; 2) concepts were replaced by coordinated and apparently more familiar concepts; 3) affectively significant and unacceptable situations were weakened and generalized to diminish their significance; 4) the repetition of a motif was present; 5) the grasp of both whole and detail was insufficient." (p. 26)

The affective determination of the characteristics of these distortions was summed up as follows:

"1) the substitution of a concept by a coordinate concept takes place to satisfy an affective need; 2) the patient puts himself in the place of the main figure; 3) a motif once touched upon is woven further into the story; 4) disagreeable facts are substituted by diametrically opposite facts; 5) in the reproduction, primitive wishes of the subjects appear as fulfilled, without regard to the meaning of the story; 6) the reproduction is characteristically infantile." (p. 26)

"1) the original misapprehension is retained in the free reproduction; 2) on the side of the misapprehension traces of the correct apprehension may emerge; 3) details which did not occur in the immediate reproduction may after several days emerge in free reproductions; 4) contradictory and senseless portions of the reproduction are left uncorrected with striking carelessness." (p. 27)

Similar investigations on patients in other psychotic groups were reported by Curran and Schilder (37). In a similar investigation with catatonic schizophrenic patients, the present author found a pronounced tendency to eliminate aggressive contents in the recall of a story.[26]

B. THE RECALL OF STORIES HEARD IN CHILDHOOD

Despert (38) conducted a series of experiments using other methods in addition to Koeppen and Kutzinsky's. She asked problem children to reproduce well-known children's stories, and demonstrated that in the reproduction the children distorted the stories to fit their "emotional" needs. This method of reproduction of stories was used with a therapeutic, cathartic aim. In different phases of the therapeutic process,

[25] For a general discussion of memory and thought organization see Schilder (36).
[26] See Rapaport, D., "Selective Remembering, a Study of the Recall of Stories by Catatonic Patients," Unpublished.

different types of distortion occurred. In the initial phase of the treatment a child may distort a story into a tragedy; in a phase of release, a happy ending may be given. The characters and problems in the story are adapted by the child to represent members and problems of his family. Despert demonstrated the affective character of the distortions in reproduction by comparing the original story, its reproduction, and the case history.

A similar study was conducted by M. Brenman[27] who asked her subjects to recall fairy tales—such as Little Red Riding Hood, The Three Bears, and so on—which they had heard during their childhood and had not re-read since. The reproductions thus obtained were compared with the available versons of the original and showed impressive omissions and distortions. In order to gain insight into the nature of these distortions, the experimenter hypnotized the subjects and again asked them to reproduce the story. Control experiments in which the hypnotic reproduction preceded the normal reproduction were also conducted. Thematic Apperception Tests[28] were administered in order to obtain information concerning the main strivings and problems of the subjects. The comparison of normal and hypnotic reproductions with each other and with the results of the Thematic Apperception Test indicated that the omissions and distortions in the normal reproduction correspond to "emotional needs" of the subjects.

C. AFFECTIVE ORGANIZATION IN SPONTANEOUS STORY PRODUCTION

Another method adopted by Despert, that of asking for stories around a given topic—"Tell me a story about a little boy and the father and the mother"—leads us to the third type of experiment which in this group plays the same role as the Rorschach Test plays in the group surveyed in the previous section; both are "projective techniques." Morgan and Murray (39) published a report on "A Method for Investigating Fantasies" (Thematic Apperception Test). They presented a series of photographs of indefinite scenes, and gave the following instructions:

"This is a test of your creative imagination. I shall show you a picture and I want you to make up a plot or story for which it might be used as an illustration. What is the relation of the individuals in the picture? What has happened to them? What are their present thoughts and feelings? What will be the outcome? Do your very best. Since I am asking you to indulge your literary imagination you may make your story as long and as detailed as you wish." (40, p. 532)

---

[27] Brenman, M. "Studies of Normal and Hypnotic Recall of Fairy Tales Heard in Childhood." Unpublished study from the Psychological Laboratory of the Menninger Clinic.

[28] This test will be discussed in the next section of this chapter.

Murray later (41) elaborated on this, and on other methods of investigating fantasy which, though relevant to our topic, cannot be discussed here. A further discussion of this method was given by Murray in his "Explorations in Personality" (40). He found that the main strivings of the figures in the stories represent the subject's main strivings, which were designated by him as "needs." The main obstacles and difficulties included in the stories were found to represent what the subject experiences as the main pressures exerted on him by his environment; these were called by Murray "presses." These fantasy productions are essentially memory-productions around a given topic, and are similar to wishful memory- and fantasy-productions of everyday life. They were recognized by Murray to be essentially projections of memory products upon the figures presented in the test pictures, and their organizing factors—the "needs" and "presses"—were considered affective attitudes Murray's findings were corroborated by J. B. Rotter (42), R. Harrison (43) and Slutz (49), and were further developed by Massermann and Balken (44, 45, 46). Similar experiments with different picture material were conducted by Symonds (50) on adolescents, by Schwartz (47) on school children, and by Amen (48) on pre-school children.

Our summary of the experiments with verbal material has included immediate recall of stories, reproductions of stories heard in childhood, and production of stories around a visually presented scene, and has indicated the operation of affective forces in reproductive and productive memory. The specific mechanisms of this affective influence on memory are implicit in these experiments and procedures, and explicit statement of them must await further exploration.

3. The Affective Organization of Behavior

In discussing the "affective organization of behavior," we remain within the field of memory, for all behavior is to a degree symptomatic of memory organization. The behavior symptoms of the affective influence on memory organization are the subject matter of this section. The phenomenon of parapraxis, in general, belongs to the group of these phenomena, since parapraxes may be considered symptomatic of memory disturbances of affective origin.[29] The parapraxes to be discussed here were elicited experimentally by hypnosis; the instructions of the hypnotist which elicited the parapraxes were not remembered by the subject in the post-hypnotic state in which the parapraxes occurred, just as the influences underlying parapraxes in everyday life are not known to the individual.

Erickson (51) published a report on the "Experimental Demonstration

[29] See Chapter V, pp. 142ff, 148ff.

of the Psychopathology of Everyday Life." In the experiment here reported and in others,[30] Erickson suggested to subjects in a deep trance that in the normal state they recall as their own an experience which had been suggested by the hypnotist. The "experience" was one of which the subject was to be ashamed; and the suggestion was given that he make an effort to conceal it. The subjects when brought out of the trance were painfully aware of the memory of the suggested experience, but were unaware that it was only a suggestion; they behaved as though it were an actual experience of their past. Although they displayed unusual skill in hiding it, they made slips of the tongue and erroneously carried out actions indicative of the presence of the "memory." In another instance, Erickson describes how a subject was given the post-hypnotic suggestion to be bored by the current conversation, but to attempt to conceal his boredom; the subject effected interruptions in the conversation, and then made the slip described here:

"Finally he interrupted Dr. D., saying, 'Excuse me, I feel an awful draft,' and got up to close the door. As he did so he was asked what he was doing. He replied, 'The air seems to be awful hot ('hot air!'); I thought I would shut off the draft.' When the hypnotist pretended not to understand and asked him what he was doing the subject replied, 'Why, I just shut the bore.' His remark was then repeated by the hypnotist for the benefit of those in the audience who had not heard it. When the subject heard his statement given as 'shutting the bore,' he started visibly, seemed tremendously embarrassed, and with much urgency turned to Dr. D. saying, 'Did I say that? I didn't mean that. I just meant I closed the door.' He was apologetic in his whole manner and bearing." (p. 341)

Similar parapraxes have been demonstrated by Brenman:[31]

"In one instance, a somnambulistic subject was instructed in hypnosis that upon returning to her normal state she would falsely recall having had a dream the night before in which a specific green pencil had played such a role as to frighten her deeply. In the posthypnotic state, she had occasion to write her name and address for which purpose the experimenter proffered the green pencil. She demurred, saying she had a pencil. When it appeared that she did not, the experimenter again extended the green pencil. The subject put out her hand and grasped the pencil so awkwardly that it immediately fell to the floor. The experimenter picked it up and once more gave it to the subject. She took it and began to write her name; however, she pressed so hard that the point broke, rendering the pencil unfit for further use. The subject left the room and borrowed a new pencil although she might easily have sharpened the old one."

In these experiments, an affect was implanted experimentally in the subjects by the use of hypnosis, and its effect on memory organization was witnessed. It produced parapraxes and slips of the tongue in the same

[30] See TPR, the internal bulletin of the Menninger Clinic, Dec. 1940.
[31] Brenman, M., unpublished paper.

way that unacceptable affects and strivings produce them in everyday life. The fact that parapraxes can be produced experimentally should prove useful in future experimentation directed towards clarifying specific mechanisms of the emotional influence on memory.

Projective play-techniques used recently, as well as the techniques of clay modeling, finger paint, and drawing, belong to the realm of "affective organization of behavior." In these techniques children and psychotics enact their problems and even their early memories. Although these techniques may also contribute to an understanding of our problem, a discussion of them would lead to many problems distant from our central topic.[32]

4. The Interrelation of Physiological and Memory Changes Concomitant with Emotions

In Chapter III we discussed[33] some association and recall experiments in which physiological measurements, such as PGR and heart rate, were used to establish the presence and quantity of emotions. The difficulty inherent in these experiments was that they assumed, first, that what the applied physiological methods measured was emotion, and secondly, that the influence of emotion on memory bears a proportional relation to these physiological measures. The type of experiment to be surveyed here was based on somewhat different assumptions, and looked for qualitative rather than quantitative interrelations between physiological and mental phenomena. The method most used was the association-method. The relevance of the association-method lay in the fact that underlying every memory phenomena there is an association process; it is this process which the association experiment probes. This association process is not based on contiguity and similarity, but rather on strivings which find expression through relevant chains of memories.

Outstanding among these experiments is that originated by Luria (53). Luria's theory (1) may be outlined as follows: human behavior can be investigated either by immediate observation—in which, however, the dynamics of underlying behavior remain intangible—or by investigating experimentally a representation of these dynamics in a relatively independent motor system. In an association experiment Luria instructed the subject to react to a stimulus-word with a reaction-word, and simultaneously to press a lever with his dominant hand. At the same time the involuntary movements of the other hand, considered by Luria to belong to an independent motor system, were registered by an automatic recorder. The pressure-curve thus obtained was investigated under systematically-

[32] See L. Bender's (52) survey of this material.
[33] See pp. 47, 51, 80.

varied psychological conditions. This procedure may seem not to differ from those just criticized; but if we consider Luria's theory, his experiment appears in a new light. He maintained that while the *voluntary* motor process hides rather than expresses the dynamic processes underlying behavior, the *involuntary* motor process reveals the underlying dynamics. Accordingly, with his association-pressure technique (Die Methode der abbildenden Motorik) Luria investigated various disturbances of the pressure-curve. Investigations were made in four different types of affective situations:

"We used the following cases in which a situation known to us left marked trace in the subject:

"(a) *Natural affects*. *Mass-affect*, which is in many people concentrated on a certain situation; e.g. states preceding an operation or following a massive shock.

"(b) *Natural affects* of a shock: e.g. in *criminals* after committing a crime.

"(c) *Artificial affects*. Suggestion of affective complexes in hypnosis.

"(d) *Artificial conflicts*, which are induced in the laboratory by the method of conflicting individual tendencies." (p. 139)

What Luria measured here may justifiably be called symptoms of affect-toned memories, measured by the disturbances of the associations and of the pressure-curves. The relation of the pressure-curve to the affects was not assumed a priori; the affects were introduced into the experiment by a systematic selection of affective life-situations, or by experimental induction. Luria was aware of the presence of other factors disturbing the pressure curve, as for example the difficulty of such a task as to give subordinate reaction words to stimulus words which hardly allow for such. He maintained, however, that their effect on the pressure-curve differed discernibly from that of the affective factors. He also reported having found a means of differentiating conscious and unconscious factors disturbing the pressure-curve. He maintained that his hypnotic experiments proved the existence of a close relationship between the symptoms of the memory disturbances shown in the associative-reactions and the disturbances of the pressure-curve.[34] These hypnotic experiments were repeated by Huston, Shakow, and Erickson (56),[35] who investigated the effects of a hypnotically-induced complex and related the associative

[34] ". . . there is an evident appearance of the affective situation in the consciousness of the subject followed by a motor storm, which for a time breaks up any normal reaction process." (53, p. 156)

"The affective complex constructed by us, though not yet being conscious, creates an affective state and determines the flow of the free associative series." (53, p. 157)

[35] See also Luria (54) on fact diagnosis, and Lebedinsky and Luria (55) on clinical diagnosis.

reactions to the pressure-curves; they corroborated Luria's findings, and reported further:

"Our results indicate that the more discharge at a verbal level, the less at a nonverbal level, and vice versa." (p. 93)

They concluded:

"The hypothesis is suggested that there may be 'levels of discharge' so that if excitation created by the conflict is not discharged verbally there is a spread to voluntary and involuntary motor levels. An implication of this hypothesis is that the motor aspects of the Luria technique sometimes may not reveal the presence of the conflict." (p. 95)

The theory of "levels of discharge" advanced here is in harmony with the theories of emotion, discussed in Chapters II[36] and V,[37] according to which the central process underlying emotions may find discharge in very different physiological and psychological phenomena. Reymart and Speer (57) found that the Luria Technique indicates tensions rather than emotions, and that "any disturbance in the total organism might register itself in terms of muscular tension" (p. 200). The fact remains that Luria's experiments, as well as that of Huston, Shakow, and Erickson, provide evidence that the affects and the "complex indicators" in the association-experiment are connected with definite changes of the pressure-curve. Furthermore, Luria maintains that disturbances of the pressure-curve resulting from affects are distinguishable from effects on the curve of "any disturbance in the total organism."

These experiments have three advantages: they investigate a well established affect; they investigate its influence on the memory function as well as on the physiological—motor—function; and they advance a theory of "levels of discharge," according to which the emotional tension may find discharge on various levels of the functioning of the organism. This theory seems to be in accord with the Freudian concept of affects, according to which the "affect charge" either gains a peripheral discharge, or is mastered psychologically and exerts its effect on mental functioning.

Although we have here avoided experiments using the method of conditioning, one such experiment by Diven (58) will be discussed because of its unusually careful construction and conclusions. First, it will be worthwhile to make clear our reasons for avoiding discussion of conditioning experiments. Those conducted on animals, which have been so

[36] See pp. 36–37.
[37] See p. 165ff.

frequently quoted by authors dealing with memory and specifically with the influence of emotions on memory, have been avoided because our aim was to shed light on the role in memory function of the delicate entity called the "emotional factor." It has been repeatedly stressed that we have only introspective evidence of the presence of this factor, and that the gap is still unbridged between emotional experience and its observable physiological and behavioral manifestations. In animal experimentation, only behavior and physiology are observable; thus we have not sought contributions to our topic in the field of animal experimentation. Another reason for avoiding the method of conditioning was mentioned previously:[38] conditioning limits the freedom of reaction, and thus is not comparable to life situations in which the effect of emotional factors on memory is palpable. A further reason has been pointed out by Finch and Culler (59): in the learning-process repetition supports remembering; but in the process of conditioning, repetition of the conditioned response without the unconditioned stimulus results in extinction. To our knowledge, the exact relation between learning and conditioning is still unsolved; thus no reliable inferences from one to the other are possible.[39]

Diven's experiment will be discussed in spite of these reservations, because in human beings in a conditioning situation he observed phenomena similar to the Freudian mechanisms of displacement, repression, and so on. Diven investigated the conditioning effect of electric shock on motor, autonomic, and memory processes. The value of simultaneous investigation of these three levels of functioning of the organism lay in the fact that the emotional effect of the electric shock was assumed to manifest itself not only in memory phenomena, but on the other two levels as well. Thus Diven's experiment, like Luria's, indicates that emotional expression, emotional behavior, and emotional influence on thought- and memory-processes are discharge phenomena of one common factor; and that this factor—"the emotional factor"—may find its discharge through autonomic channels in physiological phenomena, or through involuntary innervations in motility, or through thought and memory processes by means of neural mechanisms still unknown.

In an association experiment Diven used a series of stimulus words, one pair of which recurred frequently. In one phase of the experiment—called the "conditioning sessions"—an electric shock was administered simultaneously with the second word of the recurring pair, the "critical word"; the reaction time was measured. The subject was then asked to recall the stimulus words. This was followed by a "deconditioning session"

[38] See p. 78.
[39] For an excellent survey of the experiments and theories concerning the relation between learning and conditioning, see Hilgard and Marquis (60).

in which no electric shocks were given, and again the subject was asked to recall the stimulus words. Simultaneously with the associative-reactions representing the psychological level, a modified Luria Technique was applied to measure the reaction on the "cerebro-spinal" level, and a PGR measurement of the reaction on the autonomic level was taken. Varying intervals between conditioning, deconditioning, and recall, as well as parallel experiments without the electric shock, were used as controls. In the analysis of his results, Diven differentiated between subjects who became aware and subjects who did not become aware of the significance of the critical and pre-critical stimuli.[40] We shall quote here only that section which deals with the recall tests, and shall not discuss the other interesting findings which also show a striking parallel to Freudian mechanisms:

"1. The average number of words recalled after deconditioning is much larger than in the recall before deconditioning and the difference is completely reliable. 2. This increase or 'release' is not a practice effect from the word list having been repeated, because it does not occur where the word list is likewise repeated but no 'trauma' is imposed. 3. This may be interpreted as a dynamic process resulting from 'Primary and Secondary Displacement,'[41] further corroborated by all the evidence following in this section. 4. Traumatic terms constitute a significant majority of the words actually recalled before deconditioning. 5. This traumatic preponderance or 'vividness' of conscious content at first recall does not occur in the control experiments where no trauma was imposed, neutral terms being favored. 6. *With 24–48 hour incubation the preponderance in first recall is Neutral (chance distribution), in the 48 hour experiment the average number of words in the first recall increases significantly over other experiments,*[42] *and this is reflected in the increased Neutral character of the associations.* This may be tentatively accepted as a demonstration of dynamic repression, further corroborated by conclusions 7 and 8 following. 7. The G.S.R. data, taken immediately after this 'Neutral recall,' show marked auto-

[40] The pre-critical stimulus was the first word of the recurring pair, and always immediately preceded an electric shock.
[41] Diven defines "primary and secondary displacement" as follows:
"*Displacement.* (a) Direct or '*Primary Displacement* of affect' from natural emotional objects, ideas or situations to neutral ones can take place unconsciously when experience brings them into functional relation, thereby endowing a formerly neutral term with power to form affective symbolic 'complexes' and produce neurotic symptoms both mental and physical, chronic and acute. (b) '*Secondary Displacement* of affect' may accrue unconsciously from the Primary to other formerly neutral terms which are in some way *meaningfully related to the Primary*, even when the secondary term has never been connected with the 'trauma' (natural stimulus) which began the displacement sequence or complex formation. The Secondary Displacements can, in their turn, amalgamate complexes with resulting neurotic symptoms. (c) A Primary Displacement can lose its dynamic strength without affecting the strength of complexes built up by Secondary Displacement from that Primary." (p. 291)
[42] Italics mine.—D. R.

nomic displacement to the traumatic categories. 8. The recall AFTER deconditioning shows a REVERSAL from a Neutral to a traumatic majority; which may be tentatively cited as demonstrating what is known to the clinician as 'reactivation of a repressed complex.' 9. The dynamic system, which we suggest to be operative, conforms to hypothesis regarding consciousness-unconscious functional similarity since the KIND of behavior is parallel throughout. 10. The experimental data further conform to hypothesis regarding the relatively greater strength of unconsciously integrated complexes; as shown by (a) the increase in the average number of words recalled after incubation is greater for unconscious than for conscious S's;[43] (b) the proportion of traumatic terms in this increase is greater in the unconsciously integrated system, and (c) the unconsciously developed system is more fixed in its reactivity since (i) in the second recall conscious S's produce fewer and unconscious S's more words, (ii) the unconscious system contains more traumatic words, (iii) in the release of words AFTER deconditioning (2nd recall increase over the 1st) the conscious S's release toward the Neutral terms whereas unconscious S's release toward the traumatic words, (iv) repression effects are more marked for unconscious S's, i.e., the increase for Neutral terms in first recall after incubation was 32.9% for the unconscious S's, 22.8% for the conscious; at the same time, conscious S's lost 1.0% of traumatic terms while unconscious S's showed an increase of 8.0 in traumatic terms in addition to their greater increase in Neutral words, (v) what was pointed out as a phenomenon analogous to 'reactivation of a repressed complex' in the second recall after incubation is more marked in unconscious than in conscious S's." (pp. 307–308)

The great number—fifty-two—of subjects used, the factual treatment of the data, the careful definition of the terms, their pertinence to the Freudian theory, and the unpretentiousness of the conclusions make it probable that Diven's findings will be corroborated. Their significance lies in the fact that they are in striking contrast to any expectation based on the general psychological theory of memory, specifically on the laws of frequency and time-decrement; they are further significant in that the effect of the electric shock on memory is dealt with not only quantitatively but qualitatively.

5. SUMMARY

1. The experiments surveyed in this chapter offer direct evidence concerning the influence of emotions on memory.
2. The material consisted of experiments on
   (a) the affective organization of visually perceived or reproduced material,
   (b) the affective organization of verbal material,
   (c) the affective organization of behavior,
   (d) the interrelation of the effect of emotions on physiological and memory phenomena.

[43] The terms "conscious" and "unconscious" are used here loosely by Diven to designate those subjects who were aware or were unaware of the significance of the critical and pre-critical stimuli.

3. The phenomena investigated in these experiments have been recognized to be "projective" products. The problem of projection has been discussed and experience with modern projective technique adduced as supporting material.

4. It was stressed that these experiments attacked an unexplored field. Further investigation of this field may be expected to clarify much of the unknown mechanisms of the influence of emotions on memory.

REFERENCES

(1) LURIA, A. R. Die Methode der abbildenden Motorik bei Kommunikation der Systeme und ihre Anwendung auf die Affektpsychologie. *Psychol. Forsch.* 12: 127–179, 1929.

(2) RAPAPORT, D. Principles underlying projective techniques. To be publ. in *Character and Personality*, 1942.

(3) FRANK, L. K. Projective methods for the study of personality. *J. Psychol.* 8: 389–413, 1939.

(4) FREUD, S. Instincts and their vicissitudes. Pp. 60–83, In: *Collected Papers*, vol. IV. 588 pp. London, Hogarth, 1925. First publ. in *Internat. Z. Psychoanal.* 3: 84–100, 1915.

(5) FREUD, S. *Metapsychological supplement to the theory of dreams.* Pp. 137–151. In: *Collected Papers*, vol. IV. 508 pp. London, Hogarth, 1925. First publ. in *Internat. Z. Psychoanal.* 4: 277–287, 1916–1918.

(6) CASSIRER, E. *Philosophie der symbolischen Formen*, 32 pp. Berlin, Cassirer, 1925.

(7) FREUD, S. The interpretation of dreams. Pp. 179–549. In: *The basic writings of Sigmund Freud.* 1001 pp. Ed. Brill, A. A. New York, Modern Libr., 1938. First publ. *Die Traumdeutung*, Leipzig, Wien, Deuticke, 1900.

(8) SILBERER, H. Bericht ueber eine Methode gewisse symbolische Halluzinationserscheinungen hervorzurufen und zu beobachten. *Jhb. Psychoanal. Psychopath. Forsch.* 1: 513–525, 1909.

(9) SILBERER, H. Zur Symbolbildung. *Jhb. Psychoanal. Psychopath. Forsch.* 4: 607–683, 1912.

(10) SILBERER, H. Ueber die Symbolbildung. *Jhb. Psychoanal. Psychopath. Forsch.* 3: 661–723, 1912.

(11) JONES, E. *Papers on psycho-analysis*, 643 pp. Baltimore, Wood, 1938.

(12) MOORE, Th. W. Hypnotic analogies. *Psychol. Monogr.* 27: 387–400, 1919.

(13) SCHROTTER, K. Experimentelle Traeume. *Zentralbl. Psychoanal.* 2: 638–646, 1912.

(14) ROFFENSTEIN, S. Experimentelle Symboltraeume. Ein Beitrag zur Diskussion ueber Psychoanalyse. *Z. ges. Neurol. Psychiat.* 87: 362–372, 1924.

(15) SCHUMAN, F. Psychologie des Lesens. Pp. 152–183. In: *Bericht ueber den II. Kongr. Exp. Psychol. Wuerzburg.* 266 pp. Leipzig, Barth, 1907.

(16) POPPELREUTER, W. *Die psychischen Schaedigungen durch Kopfschuss im Kriege.* Pp. 54–57. Bd. 1. Leipzig, Voss, 1917.

(17) POETZL, O. Experimentell erregte Traumbilder in ihren Beziehungen zum indirekten Sehen. *Z. ges. Neurol. Psychiat.* 37: 278–349, 1917.

(18) FREUD, S. *New introductory lectures on psychoanalysis.* 257 pp. New York, Norton, 1933.

(19) ALLERS, R., AND TELLER, I. Ueber die Verwertung unbemerkter Eindruecke bei Assoziationen. *Z. ges. Neurol. Psychiat.* 89: 492–513, 1924.

(20) MALAMUD, W., AND LINDER, F. E. Dreams and their relationship to recent impressions. *Arch. Neurol. Psychiat.* 25: 1081–1099, 1931.

(21) MALAMUD, W. Dream analysis. Its application in therapy and research in mental diseases. *Arch. Neurol. Psychiat.* 31: 356–372, 1934.

(22) SCHILDER, P. Experiments on after images, imagination, and hallucinations. *Amer. J. Psychiat.* 13: 597–611, 1933–1934.

(23) RORSCHACH, H. *Psychodiagnostik.* 255 pp. 2 vol., Bern, Huber, 3rd ed., 1937.

(24) BINSWANGER, L. Bemerkungen zu Hermann Rorschachs Psychodiagnostik. *Internat. Z. Psychoanal.* 9: 512–523, 1923.

(25) RORSCHACH, H., AND OBERHOLZER, E. The application of the interpretation of form to psychoanalysis. *J. Nerv. Ment. Dis.* 60: 225–248, 359–379, 1924.

(26) RICKERS-OVSIANKINA, M. The Rorschach test as applied to normal and schizophrenic subjects. *Brit. J. Med. Psychol.* 17: 227–257, 1938.

(27) BECK, S. J. *Introduction to the Rorschach method.* 278 pp. New York, Amer. Orthopsychiat. Ass'n., 1937.

(28) FURRER, A. Ueber die Bedeutung der "B" im Rorschachschen Versuch. *Imago,* 11: 58–85, 1925.

(29) ERICKSON, M. H. Negation or reversal of legal testimony. *Arch. Neurol. Psychiat.* 40: 548–553, 1938.

(30) FREUD, S. *Psychopathology of everyday life.* Pp. 35–178. In: *The basic writings of Sigmund Freud.* 1001 pp. Ed. Brill, A. A. New York Modern Libr., 1938. First publ. in *Monatschr. Psychiat.* X.

(31) KOEPPEN, M., AND KUTZINSKI, A. *Systematische Beobachtungen ueber die Wiedergabe kleiner Erzaehlungen durch Geisteskranke.* 233 pp. Berlin, Karger, 1910.

(32) LEVY-SUHL, M. Ueber experimentelle Beeinflussung des Vorstellungsverlaufs bei Geisteskranken. *Z. Psychol.* 42: 128–161, 1906; 45: 221–340, 1907; 59: 1–90, 1911.

(33) BETLHEIM, S., AND HARTMANN, H. Ueber Fehlreaktionen bei der Korsakowschen Psychose. *Arch. Psychiat. Nervenkrankh.* 72: 275–286, 1924.

(34) SCHILDER, P. Studien zur Psychologie und Symptomaṭologie der progressiven Paralyse. *Abhandl. Neurol. Psychiat. Psychol. Grenzgeb.* 58: 1–176, 1930.

(35) SCHILDER, P. *Introduction to psychoanalytic psychiatry.* Trans. Glueck, B. 180 pp. New York, Nerv. Ment. Dis. Publ., 1928.

(36) SCHILDER, P. Ueber Gedankenentwicklung. *Z. ges. Neurol. Psychiat.* 59: 250–263, 1920.

(37) CURRAN, F. J., AND SCHILDER, P. Experiments in repetition and recall. *J. Genet. Psychol.* 51: 163–187, 1937.

(38) DESPERT, J. L. *Emotional problems in children.* 128 pp. Utica, N. Y., State Hosp., Press, 1938.

(39) MORGAN, C. D., AND MURRAY, H. A. A method for investigating fantasies. The thematic apperception test. *Arch. Neurol. Psychiat.* 34: 289–306, 1935.

(40) MURRAY, H. A. *Explorations in personality.* 761 pp. New York, Oxford Univ. Press, 1938.

(41) MURRAY, H. A. Techniques for a systematic investigation of fantasv. *J. Psychol.* 3: 115–143, 1937.

(42) ROTTER, J. B. Studies in the use and validity of the Thematic Apperception Test with mentally disordered patients. I. Method of analysis and clinical problems. *Character and Personality* 9: 18–34, 1940.

(43) HARRISON, R.   Studies in the use and validity of the Thematic Apperception Test with mentally disordered patients. II. A quantitative validity study. III. Validation by the method of "blind analysis." *Character and Personality* 9: 122–138, 1940.

(44) MASSERMANN, J. H., AND BALKEN, E. R.   The clinical application of phantasy studies. *J. Psychol.* 6: 81–88, 1938.

(45) MASSERMANN, J. H., AND BALKEN, E. R.   The psychoanalytic and psychiatric significance of phantasy. *Psychoanal. Rev.* 26: 343–379, 535–549, 1939.

(46) BALKEN, E. R., AND MASSERMANN, J. H.   The language of phantasy: III. The language of the phantasies of patients with conversion hysteria, anxiety state, and obsessive-compulsive neuroses. *J. Psychol.* 10: 75–86, 1940.

(47) SCHWARTZ, L. A.   Social situation pictures in the psychiatric interviews. *Amer. J. Orthopsychiat.* 2: 124–133, 1932.

(48) AMEN, E. W.,   Individual differences in appreceptive reaction: a study of the response of pre-school children to pictures. *Genet. Psychol. Monogr.* 23: 319–385, 1941.

(49) SLUTZ, M.   The contributions of the thematic apperception tests to a developmental study.   Paper read at the Midw. Psychol. Meeting Athens, Ohio, 1941.

(50) SYMONDS, P.   Criteria for the selection of pictures for the investigation of adolescent fantasies. *J. Abn. Soc. Psychol.* 34: 271–274, 1939.

(51) ERICKSON, M. H.   Experimental demonstrations of the psychopathology of everyday life. *Psychoanal. Quart.* 8: 338–353, 1939.

(52) BENDER, L.   A visual motor Gestalt test and its clinical use.   176 pp.   New York, Amer. Orthopsychiat. Ass'n., 1938.

(53) LURIA, A. R.   The nature of human conflicts or emotion, conflict and will.   431 pp.   Trans. Gantt, W. H.   New York, Liveright, 1932.

(54) LURIA, A. R.   Die Methode der abbildenden Motorik in der Tatbestandsdiagnostik. *Z. angew. Psychol.* 35: 139–183, 1930.

(55) LEBEDINSKY, M. S., AND LURIA, A. R.   Die Methode der abbildenden Motorik in der Untersuchung der Nervenkrankheiten. *Arch. Psychiat.* 87: 471–497, 1929.

56) HUSTON, P. E., SHAKOW, D., AND ERICKSON, M. H.   A study of hypnotically induced complexes by means of the Luria technique. *J. gen. Psychol.* 11: 65–97, 1934.

(57) REYMART, M. L., AND SPEER, G. S.   Does the Luria technique measure emotion or merely bodily tension? *Character and Personality.* 7: 190–200, 1939.

(58) DIVEN, K.   Certain determinants in the conditioning of anxiety reactions. *J. Psychol.* 3: 219–308, 1937.

(59) FINCH, G., AND CULLER, E.   Relation of forgetting to experimental extinction. *Amer. J. Psychol.* 47: 656–662, 1935.

(60) HILGARD, E. AND MARQUIS, D. G.   *Conditioning and learning.*   429 pp.   New York, Appleton, 1940.

CHAPTER IX

CONCLUSIONS AND IMPLICATIONS

It is related of the great physicist and stern examiner, Count Eoetvoes, that at an examination he asked a student to give the analytic definition of kinetic energy. The student's answer was unsatisfactory. Eoetvoes then asked him to give the analytic definition of potential energy. Again, the student failed. Upon being dismissed, he implored the professor for a last chance. Eoetvoes then yielded, and gave a final question: "What is the difference between the analytic definitions of kinetic and of potential energy?"

Upon setting out to survey the literature of the relation of emotions to memory, we felt much like the pupil of Eoetvoes: we aimed at determining the relation of two entities which, in the present state of our knowledge, are indistinct. Have we failed? and if so, have we at least found out what must be clarified before the solution to our problem may be achieved? In this chapter we shall summarize and discuss such aspects of our survey as will help the reader to find his own answer.

1. The Nature of a Critical Survey in General and of Our Survey in Particular

We have surveyed a variety of contributions found in psychological, psychiatric, and psychoanalytic literature, which appeared relevant to the problem of the role of emotions in memory functioning. Our survey could not be an "objective" one independent of our views, for it necessitated selection as well as organization of the material. Selecting the pertinent material involved a selective principle; and the conception of "emotional influence on memory" is by no means so distinct and crystallized as to yield a selective principle independent of the views of the surveyor. The material thus selected necessitated interpretation; partly because we had to demonstrate the pertinence of material collected in fields remote from what is usually considered the realm of memory investigation, and partly because we had to discuss the pertinence of material of authors who claimed to deal with "emotional influence on memory." Thus, in organizing, coordinating and subordinating observations, results, and theories, we were led by our views of the meaning of the material.

The concept "critical survey" warrants a short discussion. It may be interpreted in several ways: as scrutiny of a certain field of knowledge in the light of a well-established larger field, of which it is but a part; or, scrutiny of a field in the light of its own aims and results; or, scrutiny of a field with regard to its inner consistency. The sense in which these pages may be called a "critical survey," though nearest to the latter, differs from each of these. We have attempted to infer what in each field was considered to be the effect of "emotions" on the memory function, and what was the nature in each field of the phenomenon called "emotion" or "affect" or other equivalents. Whenever it seemed obvious to us, we pointed out the relation between the conclusions of different fields. We have refrained, however, from suggesting any general theory to link the findings of the different fields. This method we considered to be in keeping with the present state of knowledge in our field. Our survey has shown that although abundant facts have been accumulated relevant to our problem, the interrelations of those facts will have to be subjected to crucial experiments before an attempt at a unitary theory can be made.

2. The Problems Which Initiated This Survey

It seems to us that our survey will not be complete without a description of the main problems in the field, both as we saw them prior to this survey and as we see them now.

Originally our problem was posed by the fact that in the taking of case-histories, clinical psychologists and psychiatrists and other medical men frequently find that the patient "forgets" to give what is obviously the most pertinent information, or unwittingly gives false replies to crucial questions. These peculiar phenomena of "forgetting," as well as the generalized amnesias to which it was considered intimately related, were conceived and designated as being of an "emotional origin." Our task was to investigate whether and in what sense this is generally maintained, and what the basis of the assertion is. We turned to the literature to see what is known from experiments and observations concerning the process of this "influence of emotions on memory." The pursuit of our aim led us to several problems. We encountered a wealth of experimental reports, of which the more cautious claimed to investigate "differences in retention of pleasant, unpleasant and indifferent words"; others claimed to investigate "the influence of emotions on memory"; the boldest claimed to be "experimental investigations of repression." The task was to evaluate the bearing of these experiments on our problem. At the outset we attributed small significance to these experiments, and expected to gain little by studying them.

Scrutiny of them, however, led us to problems which proved to be of paramount importance for our survey. The problem presented itself thus: how can we formulate the influence of emotions on memory if we conceive of emotions—as is usually done—in such physiological terms as "peripheral changes" and "hypothalamic localization," while conceiving of memory processes—as is usually done—in such psychological terms as "recognition" and "reproduction"? Our initial view was that as the interrelation of psychological and physiological phenomena is an enigma, and as psychological and physiological terminologies are far from being integrated into one unequivocal terminology, our survey would be of value only if we were able to discuss both memory and emotions in one or the other terminology. The problem was to find out which terminology was more suitable to the present state of research in the fields of "memory," "emotions," and "emotional influence on memory."

This investigation led us to the problem of how to define emotions; for in the literature we found that such expressions as "emotion," "emotional," "affect," "affective," were used in so many diversified contexts that it was difficult to see what—if any—meaning is common to these concepts. Initially we believed that the use of these terms was careless and rendered the concept "emotion" a scientifically useless generality.

Another problem was that of dealing with the relevant psychoanalytic material. A great part of the experimental work on the influence of emotions on memory has been done in an effort to investigate the psychoanalytic theory of forgetting. Psychoanalytic literature contains a wealth of observations and theoretical considerations pertinent to the role of "emotional factors" in remembering; furthermore, the search for a positive and purely psychological theory of emotions and of their role in psychic life leads inevitably to the psychoanalytic theory. Thus we decided to devote extended discussions to it.

The difficulties of this theory for non-psychoanalytically trained psychologists and other experimental scientists are several. The theory is based on clinical procedures, the methodology of which is not yet explored; consequently it is difficult to distinguish between psychoanalytic observation and psychoanalytic theory—that is, between fact and interpretation. Furthermore, in the rapidity with which this theory developed, an expression used first to designate a certain phenomenon or function would be later assigned a second meaning, although the first meaning would survive and be used simultaneously with the second; as a consequence, outsiders frequently quote divergent definitions of identical expressions.

This theory commanded our special attention in spite of these difficulties: no other purely psychological theory of emotions existed; and the dynamic theory of memory explaining the work of memory in everyday life—to which psychoanalytic theory contributed a great deal—is still young. It was difficult to integrate this theory into our material, for we had to avoid certain errors frequently committed by psychologists whose attention has been attracted by the psychoanalytic theory. First, it has usually been taken for granted, on the basis of identical or similar wordings, that concepts of the psychoanalytic theory are identical with those of general psychology. This assumption is unwarranted; in psychoanalytic concepts, words which are commonly used terms in psychology—as, "pain," "pleasure," "inhibition," "unconscious"—carry a specific technical meaning. Secondly, the difficult task of analyzing the psychoanalytic literature to the end of obtaining the full implication of any one of, its concepts, statements, or theories has been rarely undertaken by experimenters. It cannot be denied that this literature, with its new terminology and its fusion of case material and theoretical conclusions, demands much of the reader. Thirdly, psychoanalytic observations, being life observations, are difficult to approach experimentally; a similar situation obtains in biology, a much older science, where there is still a great difference between experimenting on preparations and on living substance.

It was our view that the difficulties warrant an intensive rather than perfunctory treatment of the psychoanalytic theory by experimental and general psychologists; and we decided to attempt to systematize *what is maintained* by this theory pertinent to our problem, in order to make clear precisely what an intricacy of interrelations must be regarded by the experimentalist when attempting to test its tenets.

Such were the most general problems we encountered, and such the initial views we held, when we commenced to organize this survey.

3. The Views Arrived at by This Survey

Let us now outline to what extent our initial view has changed, and to what views we have been led by the material organized in this survey.

Has our survey elucidated the problem of the forgettings occurring in medical anamnesis, and of the wholesale amnesias? Neither a flat affirmative nor negative would be the correct answer. Rather, this survey embedded these phenomena into a great continuity of other phenomena, showing that what happens in "forgetting" and "amnesia" are specific cases of what happens in "remembering" in general. If it is maintained that "forgetting" and "amnesia" are of "emotional origin," our survey has shown that so is a wealth of other memory phenomena; so are other psychological phenomena—for instance, perception—which shade into those of memory. Memory theory has already experienced one revolution wrought by Gestalt theory. This replaced the laws of "frequency of repetition" and "time decrement" by explaining strength of retention and loss of retention in terms of "meaningfulness" and "organization," and by explaining the dependence of remembering on the logical relevance and structural properties of the memorized material. If we have read well the bearing of the material surveyed, it is safe to assert that a new revolution of the theory of memory is in the offing.

It has been said that Gestalt psychology has shown that the laws of memory of the Ebbinghaus type refer only to special cases of memories of *minimal* organization, and that the more general theory of memory is the theory built by Gestalt psychology on "meaning" and "organization." If this formulation is correct, the thesis of the new memory theory may be formulated thus: the memory laws based on logical "meaning" and "organization" of the memory material refer only to special cases of memory organization; the more general theory of memory is the theory based on "emotional organization" of memories—in other words, on the organization of memories by strivings. Bartlett's formulation of this theory was that "reproduction is the justification of an attitude." Mueller-Freienfels' formulation was that "it is the 'feeling and attitudes' that use memories and let them be more than flatus vocis." The memory investigations of the Ebbinghaus type dealt with nonsense or logically non-relevant material; the memory investigations of the Gestalt psychologists dealt with logically "meaningful" material; but the subject matter of the new memory investigations is the emotionally relevant experiential material of everyday life. This new theory does not disregard the fact that the meaningless, and the merely logically-meaningful, also frequently become the subject matter of memory-functioning; but it maintains that these are extreme cases and frequently artifacts in a great continuum, the fundamental organizing factors of which are "emotional." The picture of this "new revolution of the theory of memory" should not be drawn too glibly. It is more a promise than a reality. In different fields relevant to memory function we have found indications for such a theory in experimental facts, in observations, in theoretical remarks of authors, and even in some attempts at theoretical formulations. But this new theory has not yet been born; the findings, observations, and theoretical attempts have remained abrupt and uncontinued beginnings. Conceptual confusion, unfinished experiments with indications of a trend, insignificant experiments with pretentious claims, many important contributions which have not been considered pertinent to the problem, many pertinent experiments with important results which attracted little attention because of an unpretentious presentation—this is the real situation in the field.

However, although the theory of "emotional organization of memory" has not yet crystallized, it seems safe to assert that this "organization" may manifest itself in many different forms.

The variety of effects which the emotional influence may have on memory organization will become clear to us when we describe the view we have gained of the significance of the experiments of general psychologists on the "influence of emotions on memory." As we have already stated, many of these experiments claimed to prove or disprove the psychoanalytic theory of forgetting. The origin of these claims was perhaps that, except for the questionable "law of effect," no other theory could have served as a background to these experiments; for no other has discussed directly an "influence of emotions on memory." When commencing our survey of these experiments, we doubted their significance for our problem. On the basis of the material collected, however, we have had to modify this view.

On the one hand, it became clear that with few exceptions these experiments are *not* pertinent to the psychoanalytic theory of forgetting and repression. It has been shown in our survey that they were based on the false assumption that this theory taught the "forgetting of the unpleasant." This thesis was understood in general psychological terms, and the possibility that in its original context it had a different meaning was rarely investigated. Thus, the real theory—"*the avoidance of arousal of pain through memory*," a formulation which allows for manifold mechanisms of executing the "avoidance"—was usually missed.

On the other hand, the consistency of the more recent and methodologically more adequate experiments could not be dismissed. The more personally relevant the material was, and the more individually its affective tone was determined in the experiment, the more consistent the results became. These experiments tended to show that the more intensely the material was liked or disliked—or, as the experimenters put it, the greater the affective intensity—the better it was retained. There appeared to be a tendency also towards favored retention of the pleasant over the unpleasant; this, however, appeared to be less significant, and increased with the meaningfulness and relevance of the material. Our initial view of the insignificant and the *necessarily* contradictory results of these experiments had to yield to the consistency of the results. The material obtained revealed a "lawfulness," which may be stated as follows: (a) "emotional factors" whose presence was indicated by the subject, either when rating the memory material in question or when reporting in retrospect the experiences of the course of the memory experiment, had some influence on memory; (b) this influence depends both on the intensity and quality of the "emotional factor"; (c) the more intellectualized and conventionalized the nature of the "emotional factor," and the more purely quantitative the method of experimentation employed, the more the *intensity* of the "emotional factor" was correlated with the influence exerted on memory; the more qualitative the methods and the more genuine the emotional experiences employed, the more obvious was the influence of the *quality* of the "emotional factor"; (d) in the experiments employing more genuine emotional factors, the qualitative influence of the emotions on the memory process, such as their influence on the sequence of emergence of memories and their resulting spotlike forgetting, and slips of tongue as well as distortion of the material, was reported.

Thus, a hierarchy of emotional factors and of their influence on memory unfolded before us in these experiments. Even within the narrow range of emotional factors employed—which with few exceptions were more or less conventionalized—we found a wide variety of the degree of conventionalization and a correspondingly wide variety of emotional influences on memory. Following this hierarchy beyond the realm of these experiments, we found that "emotional factors" may not only quantitatively facilitate or inhibit remembering, or result in forgetting. They were found to organize the emerging memories, condensing, distorting, and symbolically replacing them. They were found to lend persistence to certain ideas, impelling them steadily into consciousness in an obsessive fashion. They appeared to be the basis of the blotting out of memories of certain periods of life which were organized around specific strivings, when later these strivings were superseded by others or became unacceptable. They were seen as the basis of organization of those impressively segregated systems of memory which characterize alternating multiple personalities. They were shown to be the basis of the hypnotic hypermnesias in which the removal of inhibitions made strivings more free and allowed for richer, though less exact, reproduction. For the most part it was not clear what was the difference between these "emotional factors" that made possible this wide variety of memory phenomena. Our impression, however, was that here too there exists a hierarchy of emotional factors and of their influence on memory. The structure of this hierarchy is in need of exploration. Our task seemed to be finished when we had organized the material so as to show these hierarchic variations of the influence of emotions on memory and the shading of these variations into each other in a continuum.

To understand the mechanisms of the "influence of emotions on memory," we attempted to understand their interrelationship. The survey of the literature seemed to bear out our initial views. The viewing of emotions in physiological terms prevented many investigators from seeing the possible interrelationship of emotions and memory; it prevented psychological analysis of this relationship. This approach resulted in vague speculations or in a fact-bound experimentation which, as it was not guided by theoretical considerations, did not yield theoretical results; thus, despite the increase of the volume of experimentation, the field remained in an undeveloped, unsystematized state. The main difficulty

of this approach was that Cannon's theory of the physiological concomitants of emotions had no counterpart in a physiological theory of
memory; for in spite of Lashley's, Jacobson's, and others' experimentation, nothing is known about the physiological concomitants of the psychological processes of learning and remembering. The clarification of the
interrelationship of emotions and memory in psychological terms appeared
possible, however. Having investigated this interrelationship, we concluded that it is not necessary to assume that emotions have an influence
on memory; it is possible that the basic psychological factors or dynamics
underlying the experiencing of emotions are identical with those which
come to expression in the form of memory organization attributed to
emotional influence. Thus, memory organization and emotional experience would be two among many possible expressions of these basic factors,
which may be called psychic energies, strivings, or drives. The hierarchy
of the emotional factors discussed would be a hierarchy of these basic
factors of personality organization; the hierarchy of "emotional influences
on memory" would be a hierarchy of the manifestation of these basic
organizing factors in memory-functioning.

This leads to the view of emotions which we have drawn from this
survey. The material surveyed appeared to indicate that it is possible
and perhaps useful to build a psychological theory of emotions, which
later can be amalgamated with corresponding physiological theory and
knowledge. Such a theory would be based on these recognitions: (a)
that the emotions are expressions or discharge processes of energies, but
not energies in themselves; (b) that the underlying field dynamics, of
which emotions are discharge processes, are unconscious; (c) that inherent
to the conditions characteristic of the genesis of emotions are conflicting
instinctual strivings; (d) that the discharge process may be of one of many
processes. These discharge processes may be of the following kinds:
(1) peripheral physiological changes, either transient, as in the case of
emotional expression and related physiological changes, or chronic, as in
the case of psychosomatic disturbances; (2) changes in the usual routine
habitual behavior, either transient, as in the case of rage, or chronic, as
in the case of behavior disorders of children; (3) organization of the thought
and memory processes of the person either in a transient fashion, as in the
case of slips of the tongue, or in a chronic fashion, as in the case of normal
and pathological thinking.

This formulation of the concept "emotion," as a discharge process of
the central organizing dynamics of the personality, may explain the widespread and apparently loose usage of the term. This loose usage appears
thus to be not merely terminological carelessness, but rather an indication of

a vague recognition that all the phenomena designated as "emotional" are comparable manifestations or discharge processes of the basic dynamics of psychic life.

Our survey indicated that corresponding to the different discharge processes, and even within each of them, there appears to be a whole hierarchy of emotional factors, ranging from those which are genuine and deep-seated to those which are intellectualized and conventionalized. The need to investigate and clarify the problems of such a hierarchy was indicated, and the need to clarify its terminology appeared urgent. A similar terminological problem was present in regard to the physiological manifestations and the psychological experience of emotions. It appeared reasonable that these should be terminologically distinguished, and MacCurdy's suggestion to refer to the experience as *affect* and to the physiological manifestations as *emotion* appeared tentatively plausible.

Finally, the close study of psychoanalytic theory appeared to us to have proved useful. It seemed that we succeeded in deriving a rich contribution to our problem from the psychoanalytic literature. But it also became apparent that many fields—especially that dealt with in the chapter on "memory pathology"—though closely bordering on the domain of psychoanalytic investigations proper, have not been penetrated sufficiently by this theory. It also was obvious that the psychoanalytic findings will become "common treasure" only after psychoanalysts and psychologists have applied themselves to translate into a common language the tenets of psychoanalytic theory. Otherwise the confusion concerning psychoanalytic theories, and the misunderstandings and misinterpretations of it, can only grow worse—if that is possible. Inasmuch as the investigations on "emotional influence" lead to unconscious determining factors and to the dynamics of personality organization—problems which have not been more intensively investigated by any other group or school of psychologists—the need to clarify psychoanalytic tenets, and so make them amenable to scrutiny, appears to be one of the immediate needs revealed by this survey.

INDEX OF AUTHORS

INDEX OF SUBJECTS